MARKED

STEVE ROSS

SEABURY BOOKS

an imprint of

CHURCH PUBLISHING, NEW YORK

Writer and Artist: Steve Ross

Lettering and Production: Dave Sharpe

www.MarkedGraphicNovel.com

A catalog record for this book is available from the Library of Congress.

ISBN: 1-59627-002-0

Seabury Books
Church Publishing Inc.
445 Fifth Avenue
New York, NY 10016
www.seaburybooks.com

5 4 3 2 1

Introduction

After introducing television in England years ago, the BBC surveyed the nation to see whether patrons preferred it to radio. A little boy crossed out the questions and carefully scrawled on his card, "I prefer radio. The pictures are better."

So it is with the Bible. From Cecil B. DeMille to Sunday School illustrated scriptures, many of us prefer to let the powerful texts form pictures in our mind's eye. The problem, or course, is we've seen too many bad Bible movies, and there are still some of us who may never recover from well-meaning but often saccharine Sunday School pictures.

What Steve Ross has done is to take us to an entirely new visual place. He uses the style of the graphic novel and lets the vividness of the Gospel according to Mark inhabit it. It's not likely you will have seen his pictures before.

He has also brought to this work his own deep faith, his Christian practice, his own very real urban sensibility, and his own faithful reflection on the gospel—as it is read, taught, preached and reflected upon his own parish.

There is power in his art, through his faith. Steve will likely redefine the pictures in your head. In the end, as in the Gospel itself, his retelling offers love, joy, and hope. But to get there requires going through the Story and its stories. We might want label it up front the way we should label the New Testament itself: Let the reader beware.

The Rev. William McD. Tully
Rector, St. Bartholomew's Church, New York City

Acknowledgements

I am not a theologian, nor do I play one on TV. Instead, I rely on some enormously gifted people whose insight, eloquence and passion found it's way into much of this book; Rev. William McD. Tully, Rector of St. Bartholomew's in New York City, Rev. Mary E. Haddad and my dear friend, Rev. Jay Sidebotham.

Writers often talk about projects and characters taking on a life of their own. As this book started to head off into unknown territory I came to depend heavily on my editors, Ken Arnold, Lucas Smith and Johnny Ross, who never ceased to surprise me with their willingness to go further and take more chances.

Finally, much thanks to Dave Sharpe, Stefan Killen and Amy Davis for their production expertise.

Steve Ross

To Julie, Emilie and Daniel

The best audience I could ever wish for

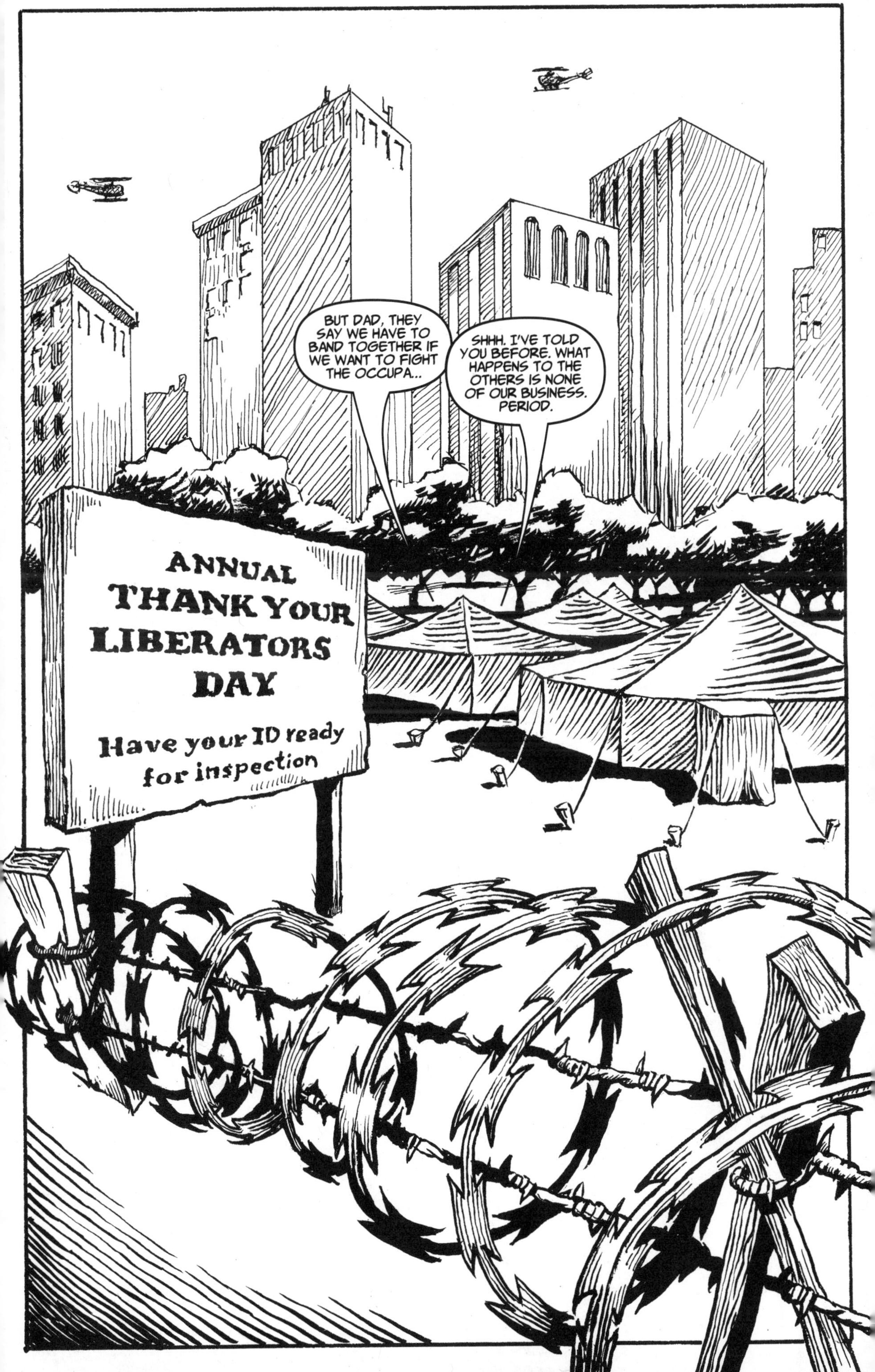
BUT DAD, THEY SAY WE HAVE TO BAND TOGETHER IF WE WANT TO FIGHT THE OCCUPA...
SHHH. I'VE TOLD YOU BEFORE. WHAT HAPPENS TO THE OTHERS IS NONE OF OUR BUSINESS. PERIOD.
ANNUAL THANK YOUR LIBERATORS DAY
Have your ID ready for inspection

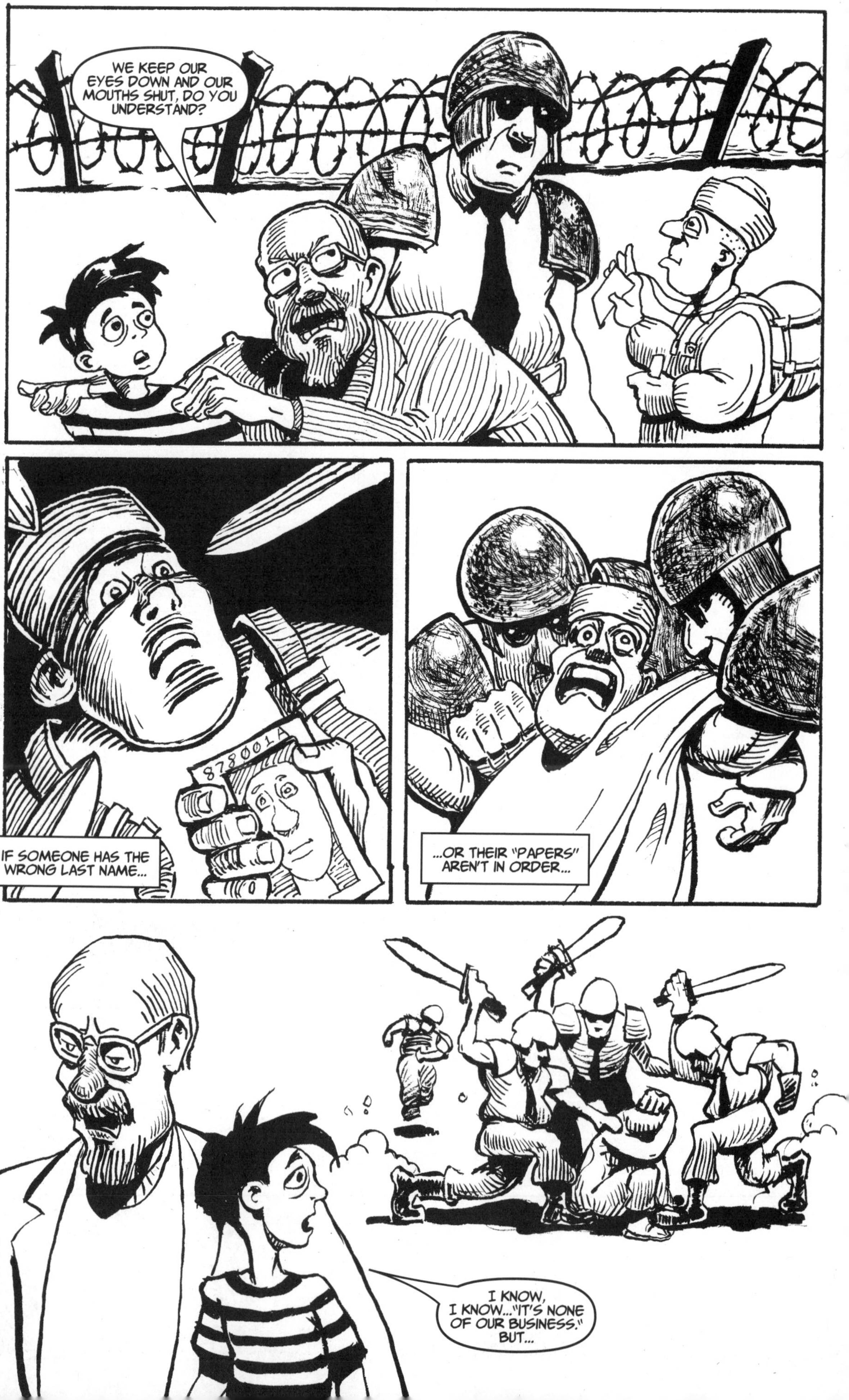

WE KEEP OUR EYES DOWN AND OUR MOUTHS SHUT, DO YOU UNDERSTAND?
878001A
IF SOMEONE HAS THE WRONG LAST NAME...
...OR THEIR "PAPERS" AREN'T IN ORDER...
I KNOW, I KNOW..."IT'S NONE OF OUR BUSINESS." BUT...

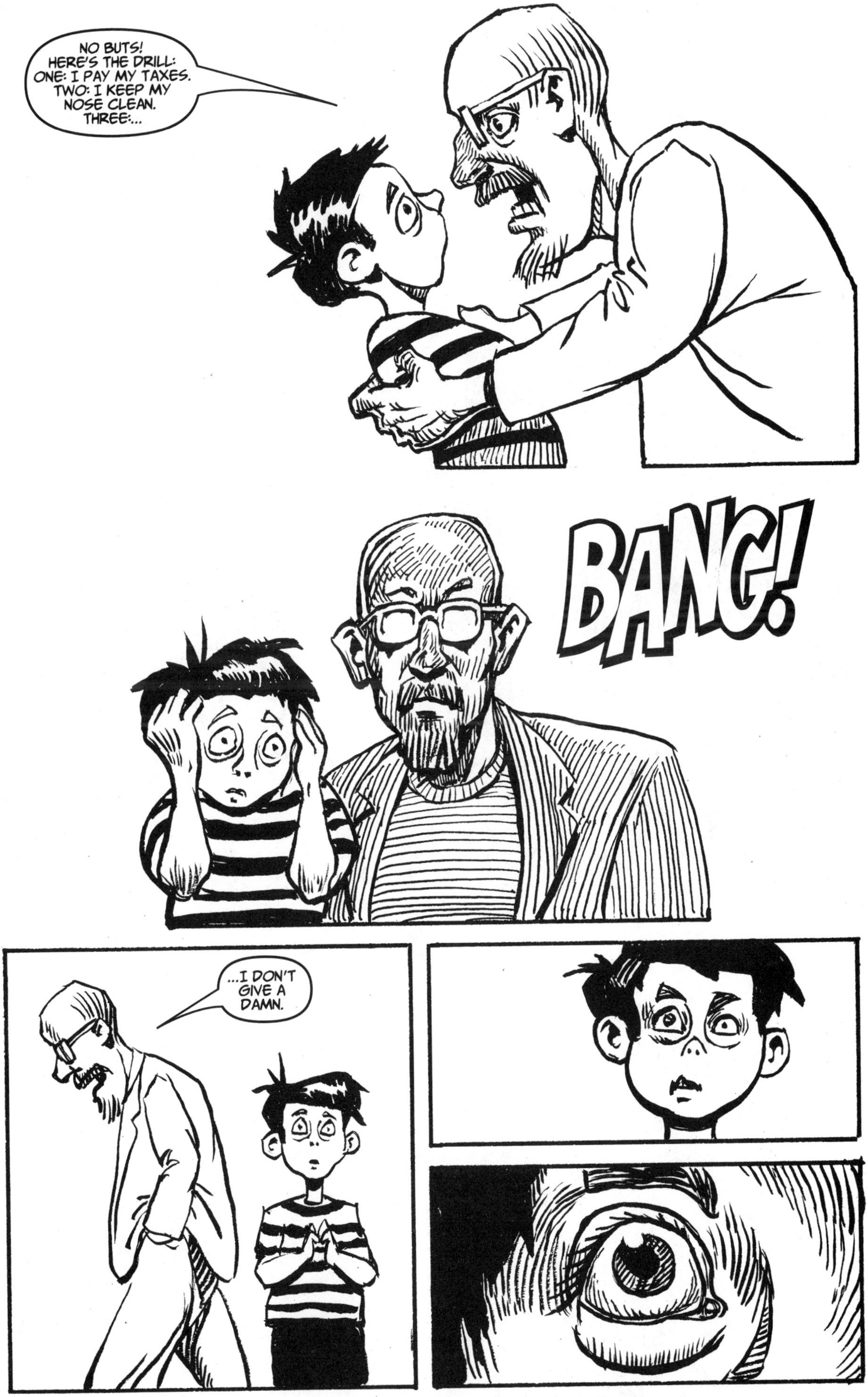
NO BUTS! HERE'S THE DRILL: ONE: I PAY MY TAXES. TWO: I KEEP MY NOSE CLEAN. THREE:...
BANG!
...I DON'T GIVE A DAMN.

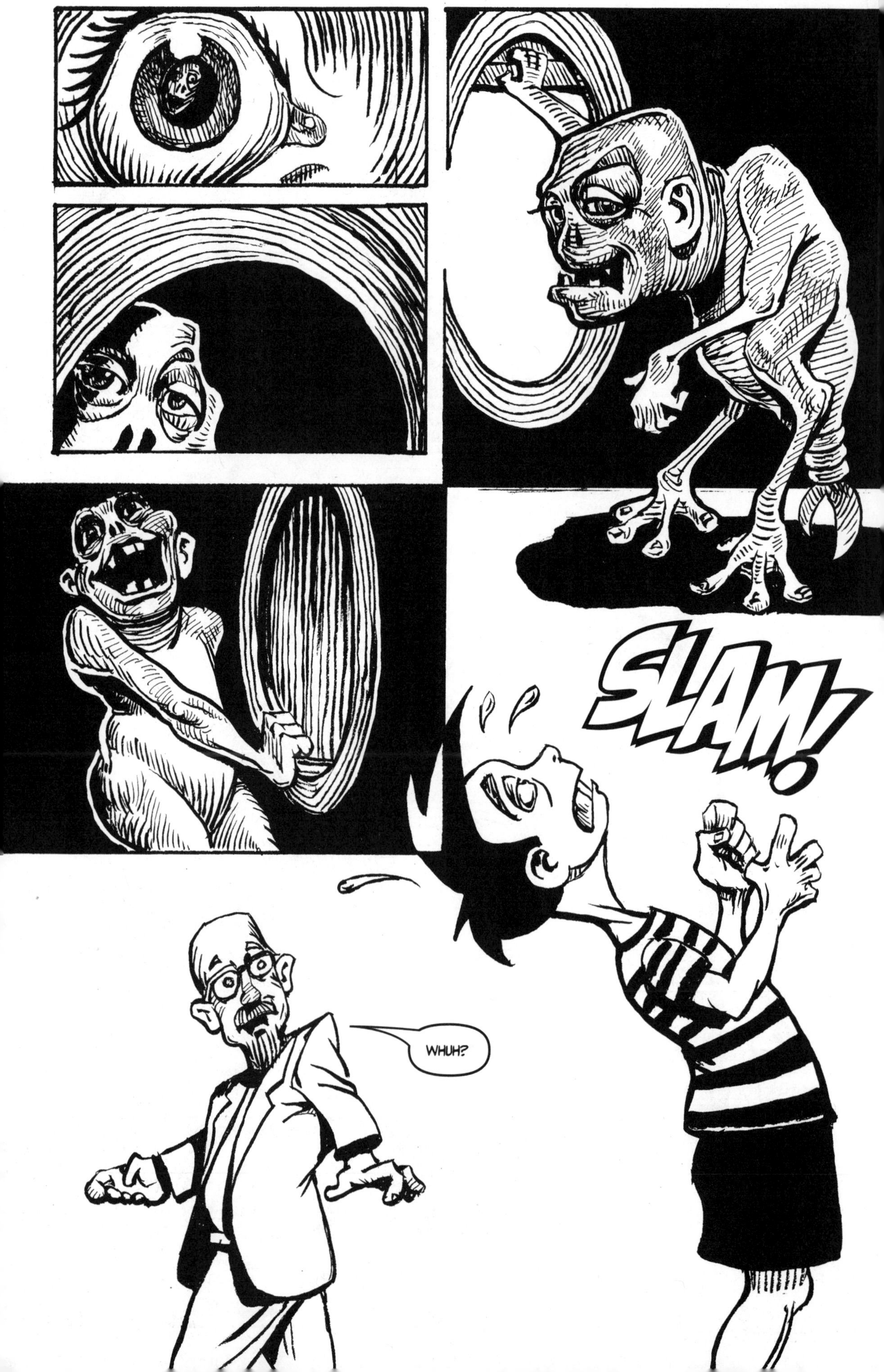
SLAM!
WHUH?

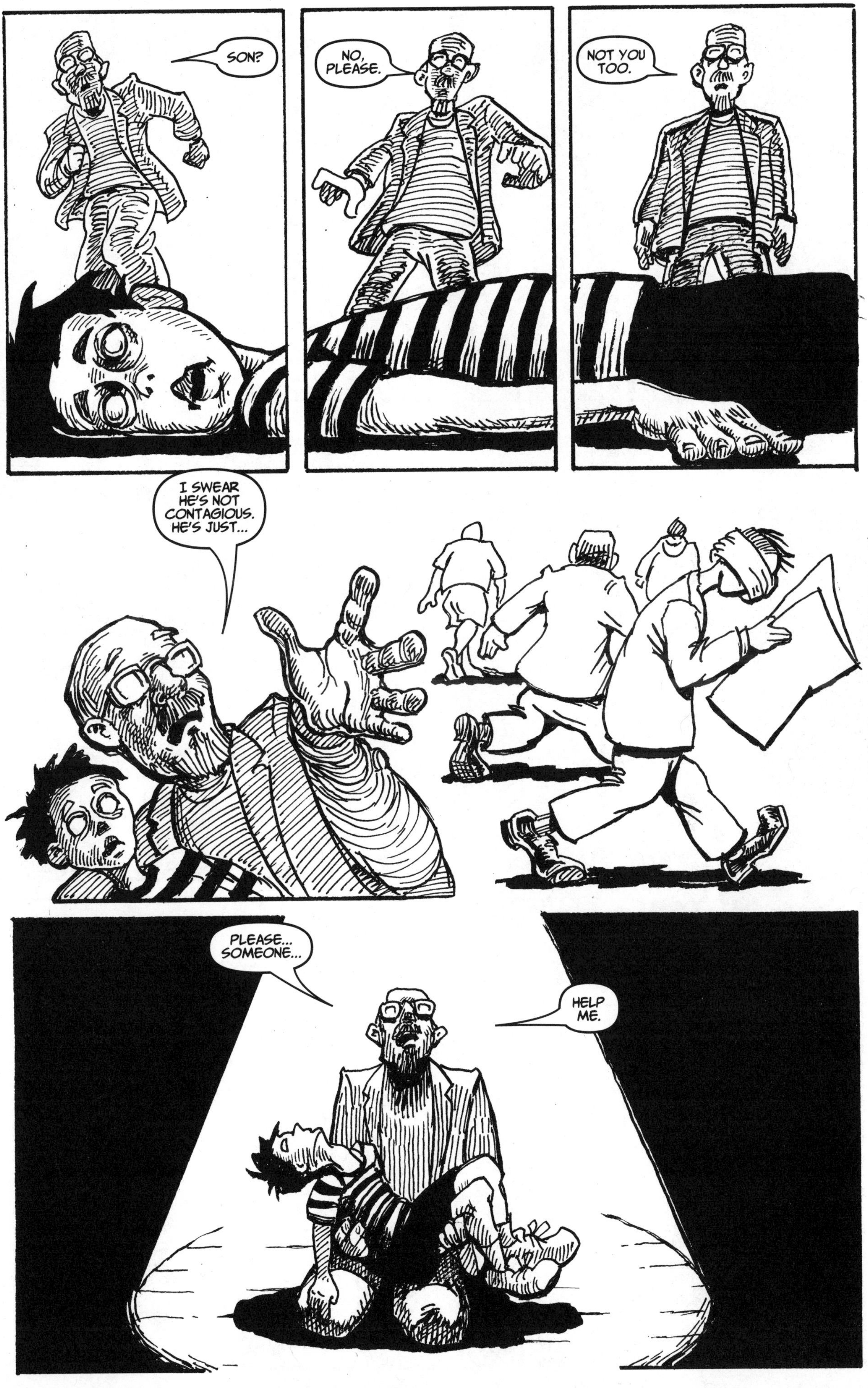
SON?
NO, PLEASE.
NOT YOU TOO.
I SWEAR HE'S NOT CONTAGIOUS. HE'S JUST...
PLEASE... SOMEONE...
HELP ME.

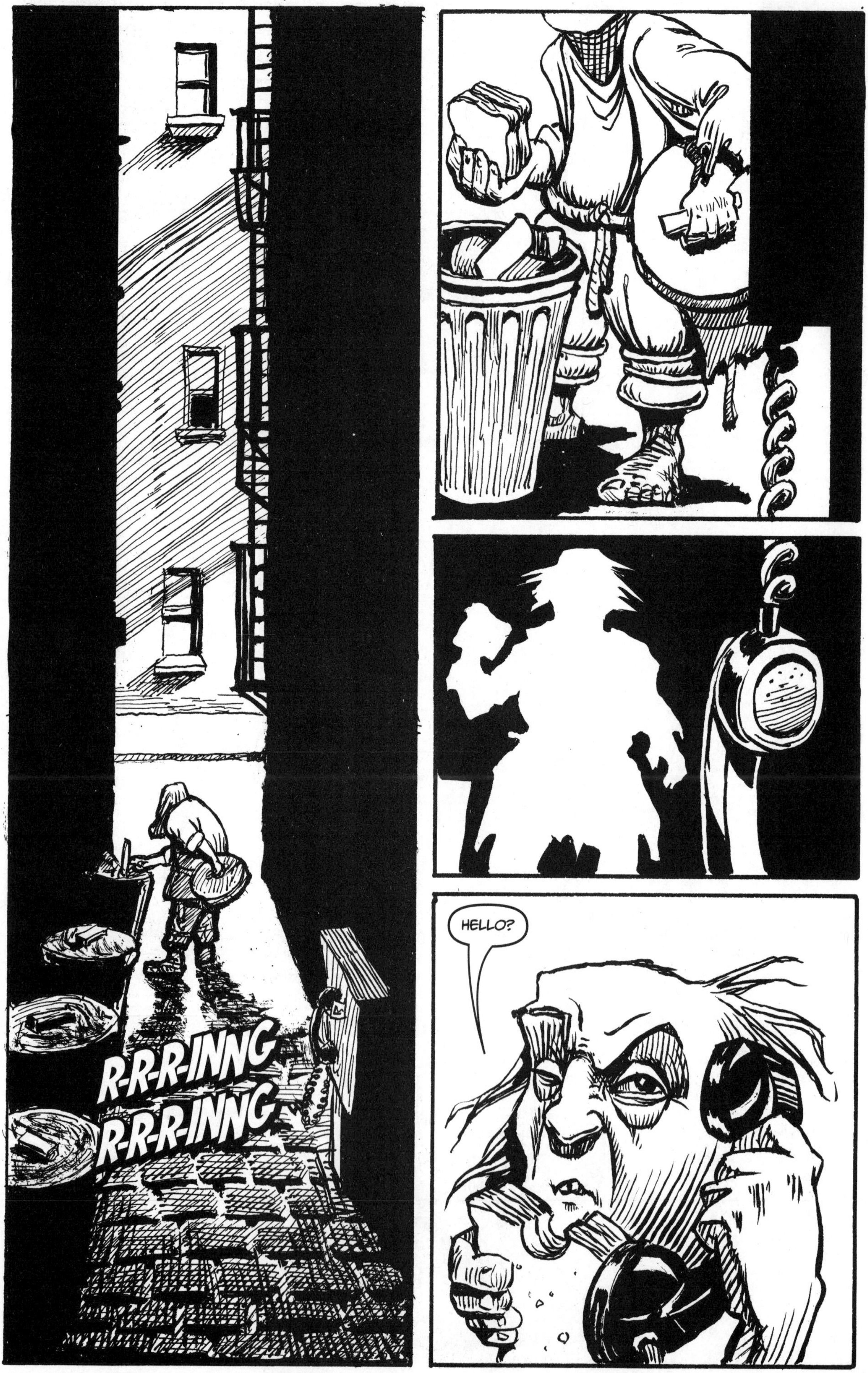
R-R-R-INNG
R-R-R-INNG
HELLO?

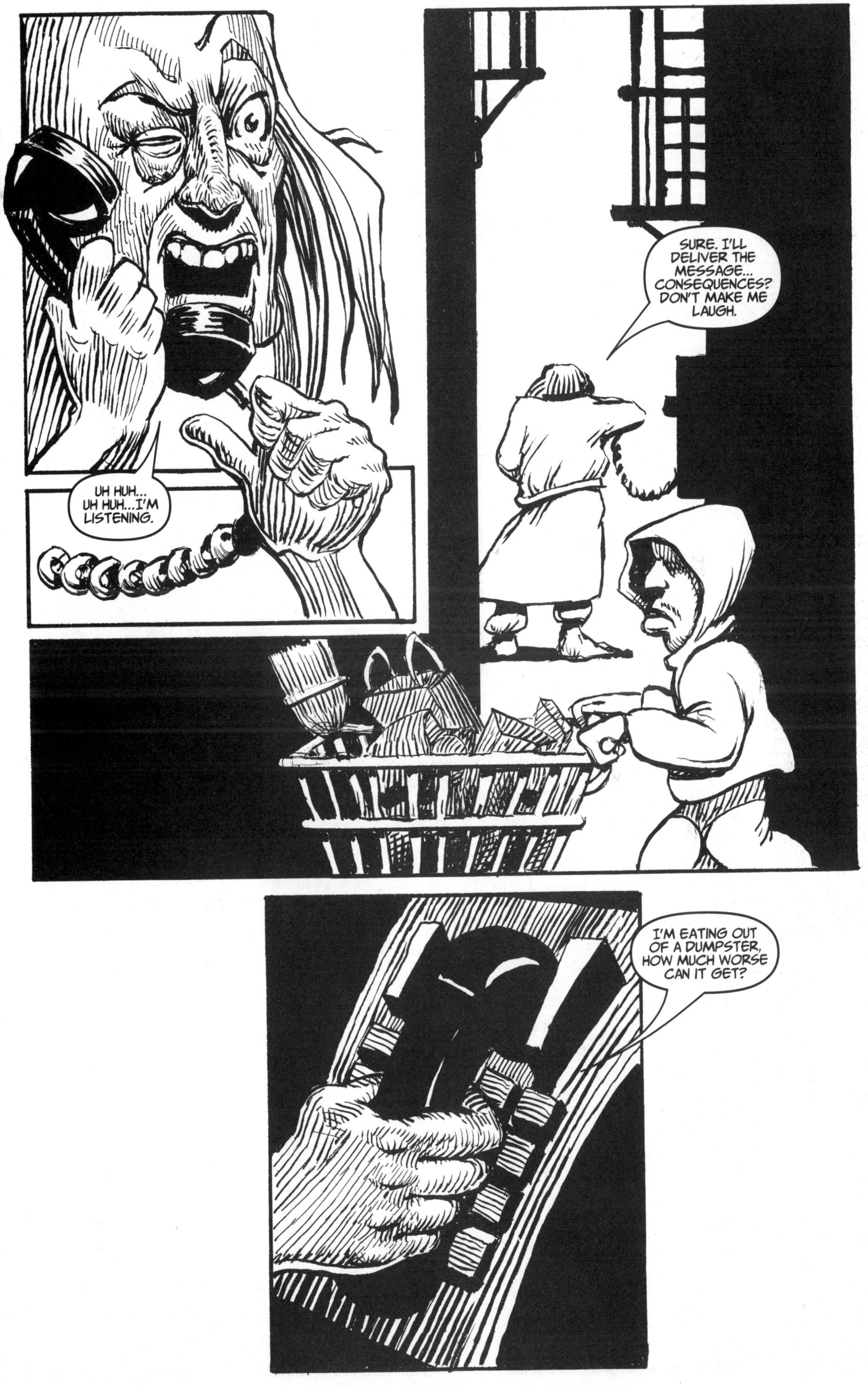
UH HUH...
UH HUH...I'M
LISTENING.
SURE. I'LL
DELIVER THE
MESSAGE...
CONSEQUENCES?
DON'T MAKE ME
LAUGH.
I'M EATING OUT
OF A DUMPSTER,
HOW MUCH WORSE
CAN IT GET?

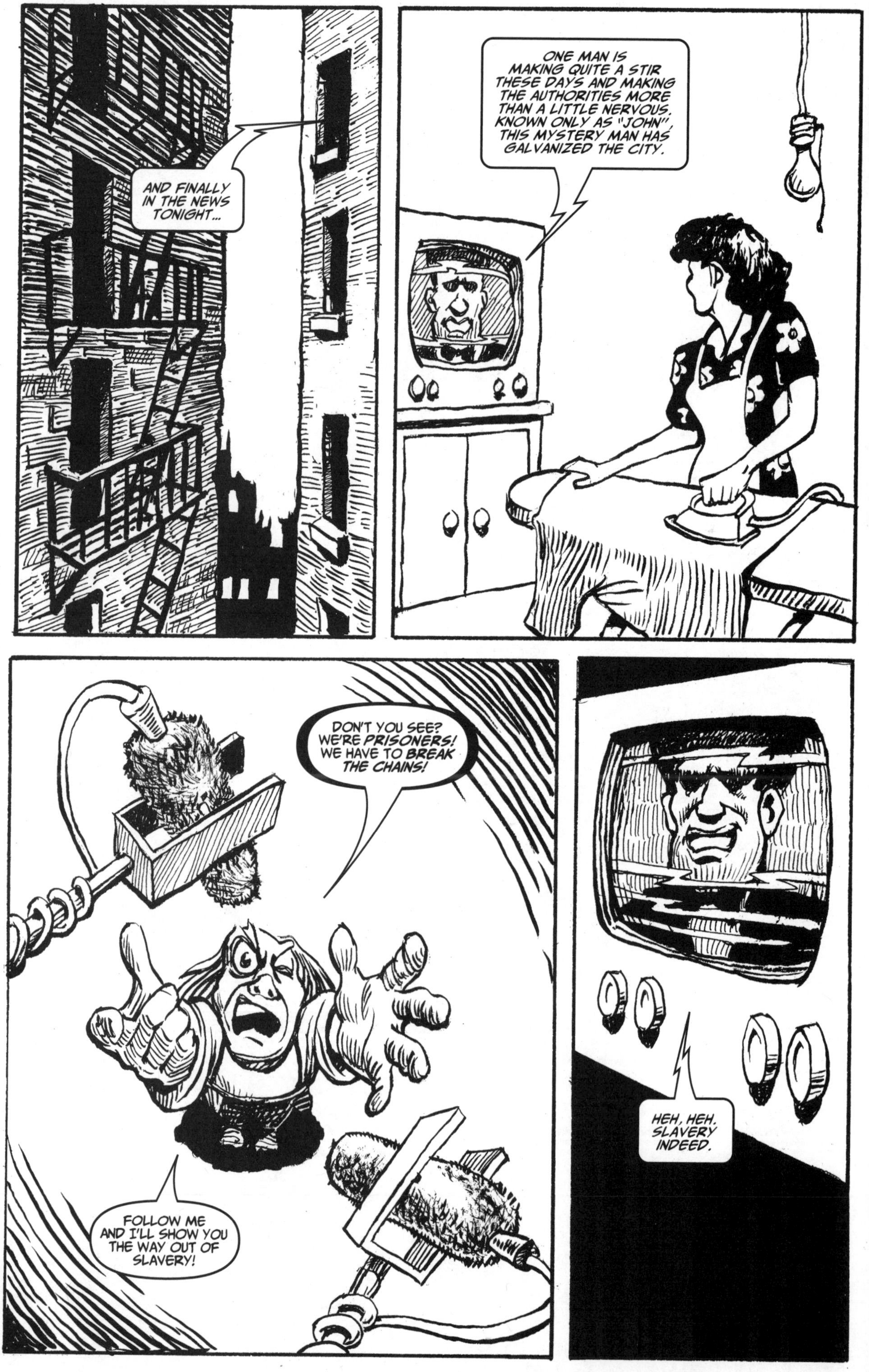
AND FINALLY IN THE NEWS TONIGHT...
ONE MAN IS MAKING QUITE A STIR THESE DAYS AND MAKING THE AUTHORITIES MORE THAN A LITTLE NERVOUS. KNOWN ONLY AS "JOHN", THIS MYSTERY MAN HAS GALVANIZED THE CITY.
DON'T YOU SEE? WE'RE PRISONERS! WE HAVE TO BREAK THE CHAINS!
FOLLOW ME AND I'LL SHOW YOU THE WAY OUT OF SLAVERY!
HEH, HEH. SLAVERY INDEED.

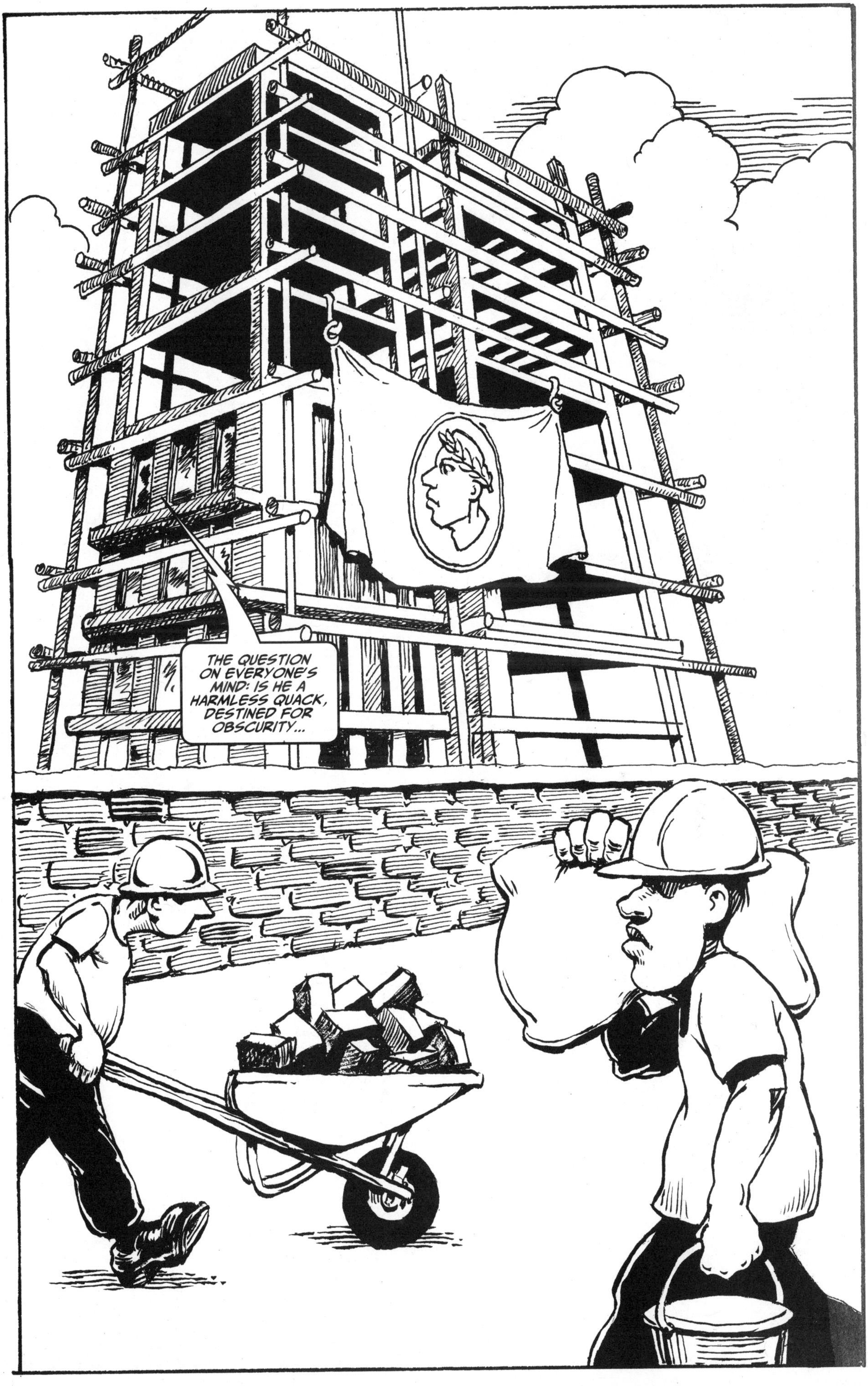
THE QUESTION ON EVERYONE'S MIND: IS HE A HARMLESS QUACK, DESTINED FOR OBSCURITY...

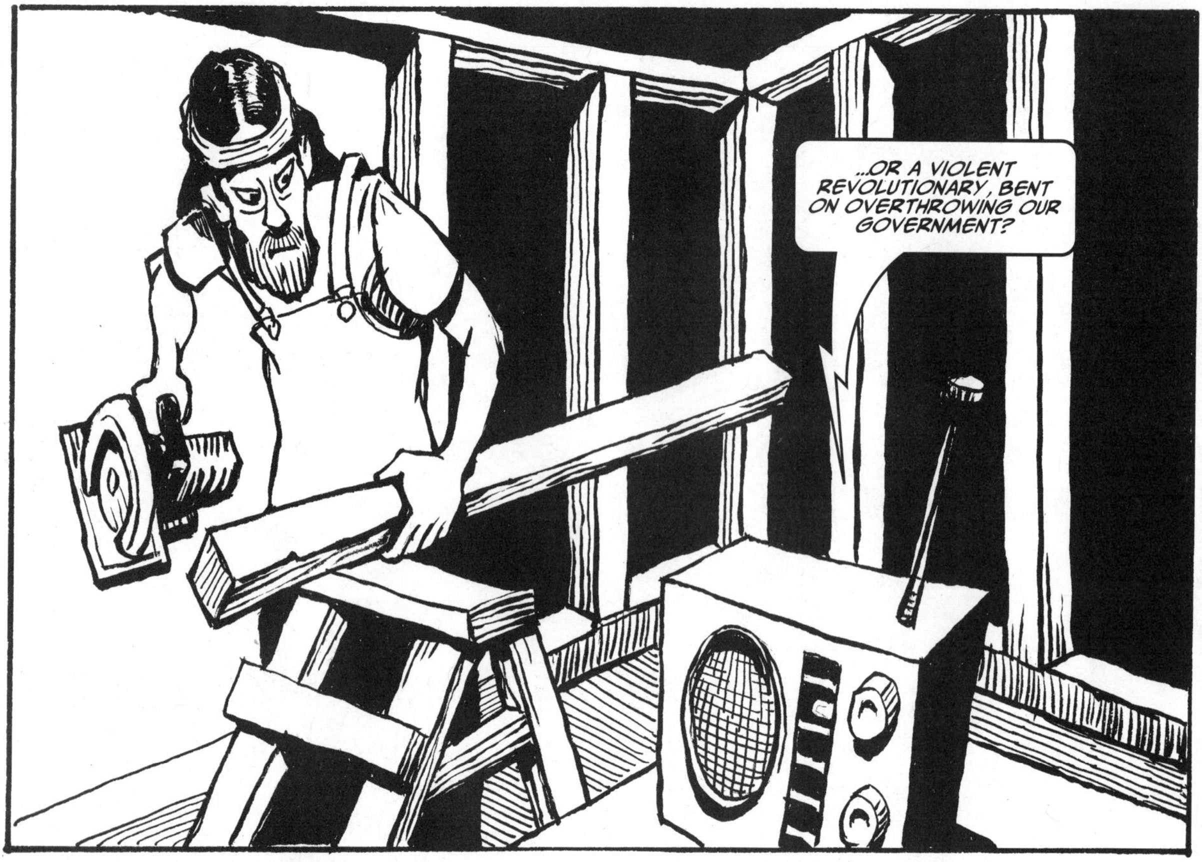
...OR A VIOLENT REVOLUTIONARY, BENT ON OVERTHROWING OUR GOVERNMENT?

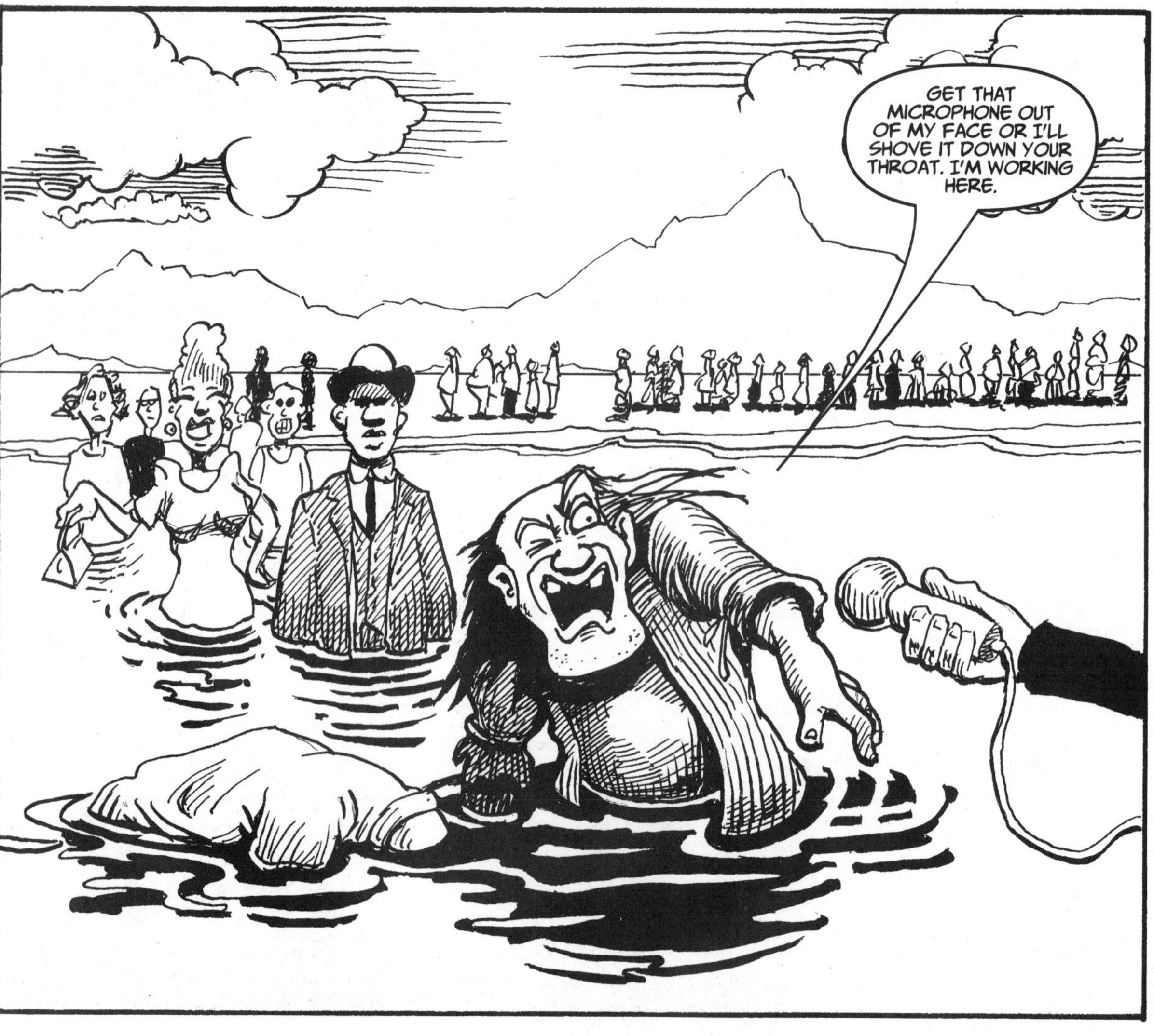
GET THAT MICROPHONE OUT OF MY FACE OR I'LL SHOVE IT DOWN YOUR THROAT. I'M WORKING HERE.

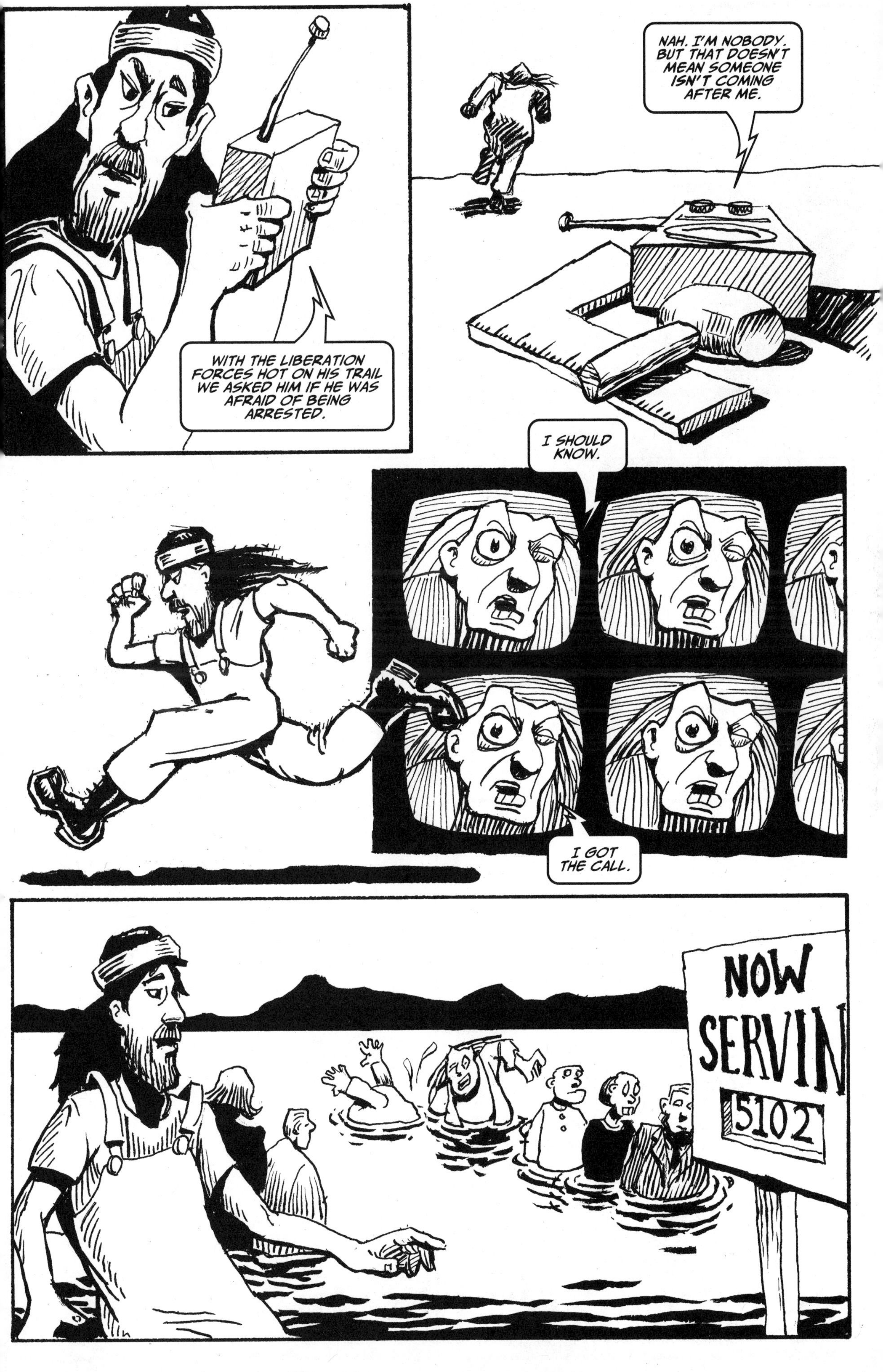
WITH THE LIBERATION FORCES HOT ON HIS TRAIL WE ASKED HIM IF HE WAS AFRAID OF BEING ARRESTED.
NAH. I'M NOBODY. BUT THAT DOESN'T MEAN SOMEONE ISN'T COMING AFTER ME.
I SHOULD KNOW.
I GOT THE CALL.
NOW SERVIN
5102

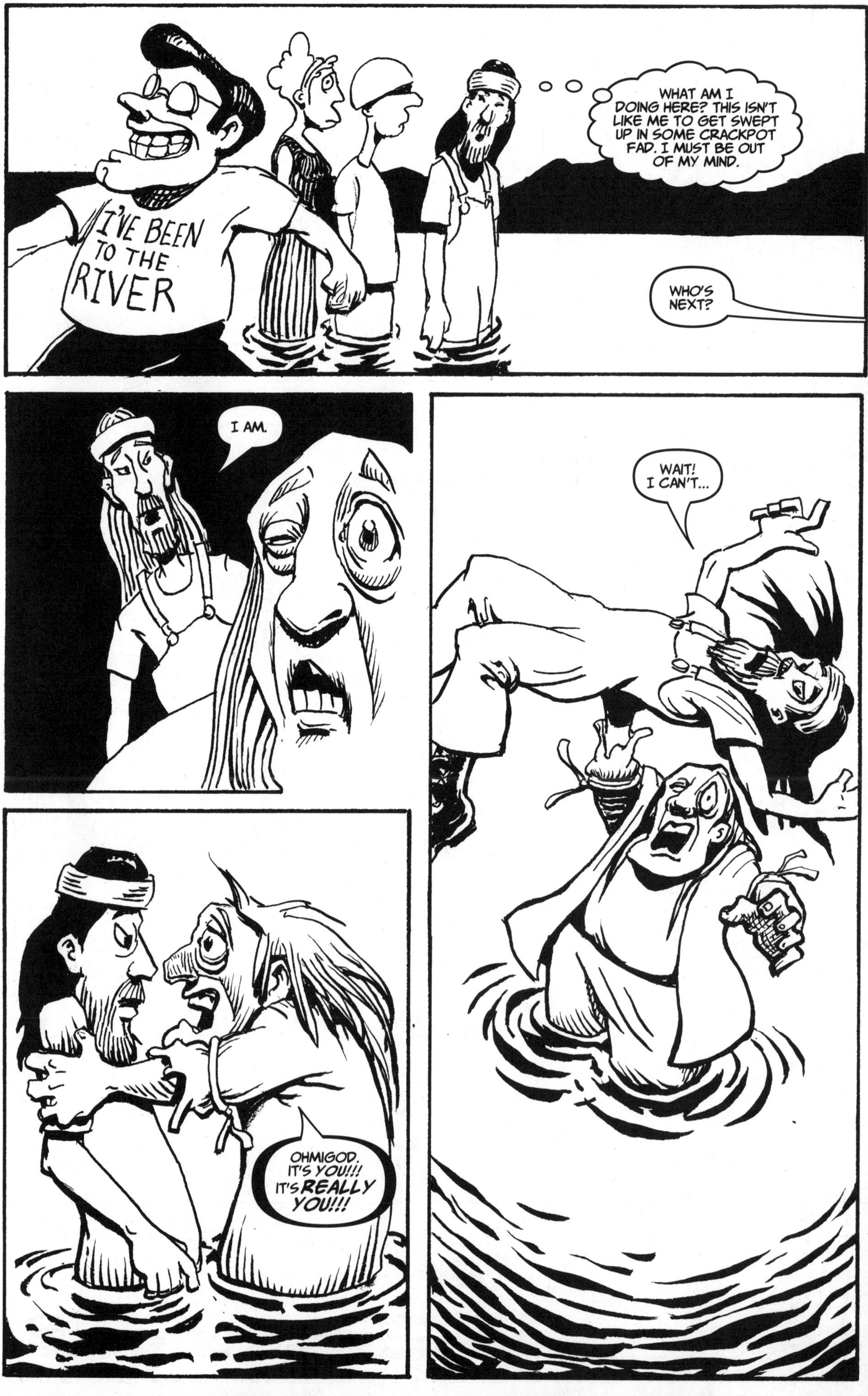

I'VE BEEN TO THE RIVER
WHAT AM I DOING HERE? THIS ISN'T LIKE ME TO GET SWEPT UP IN SOME CRACKPOT FAD. I MUST BE OUT OF MY MIND.
WHO'S NEXT?
I AM.
WAIT! I CAN'T...
OHMIGOD. IT'S YOU!!! IT'S REALLY YOU!!!

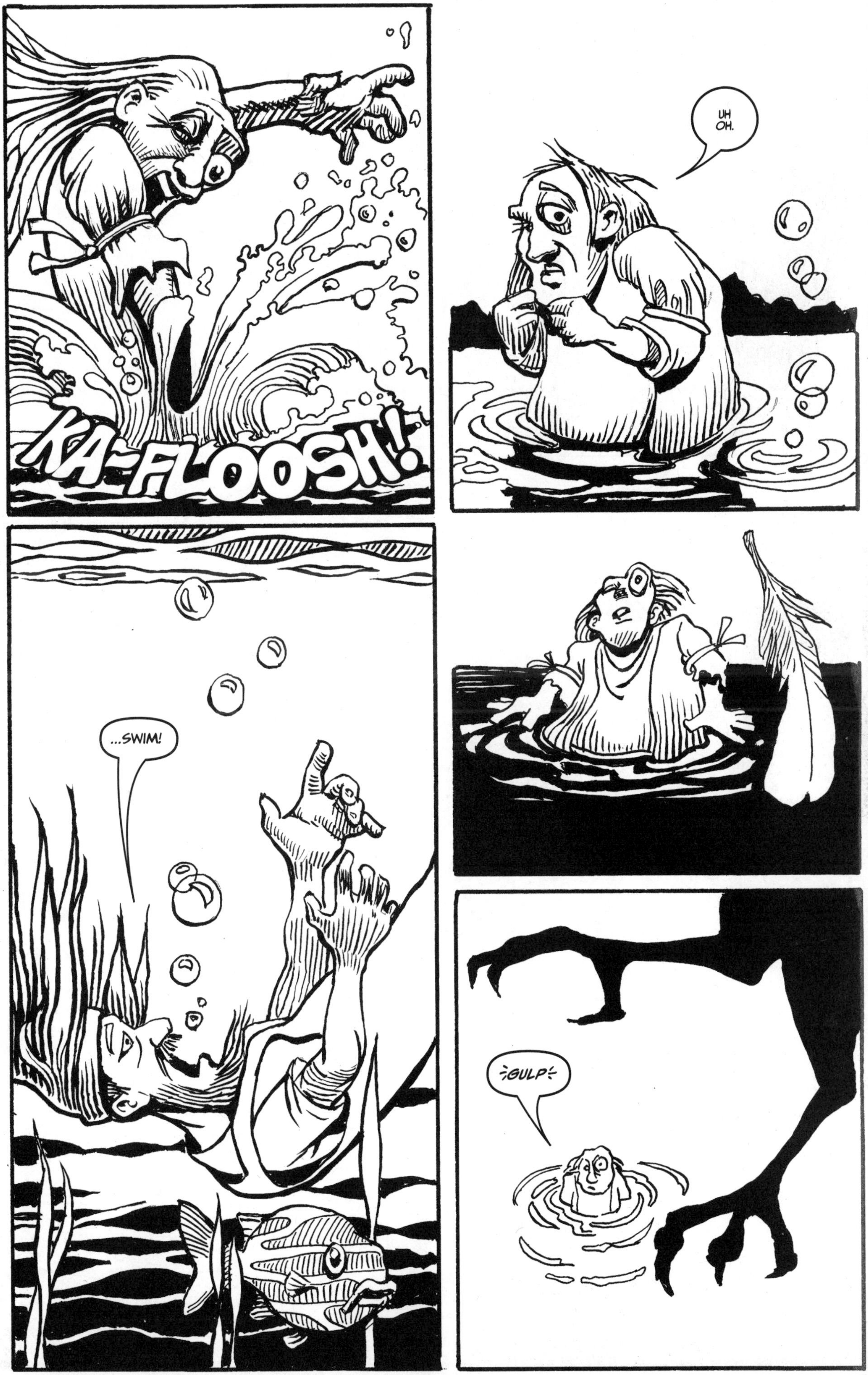
KA-FLOOSH!
UH OH.
...SWIM!
GULP

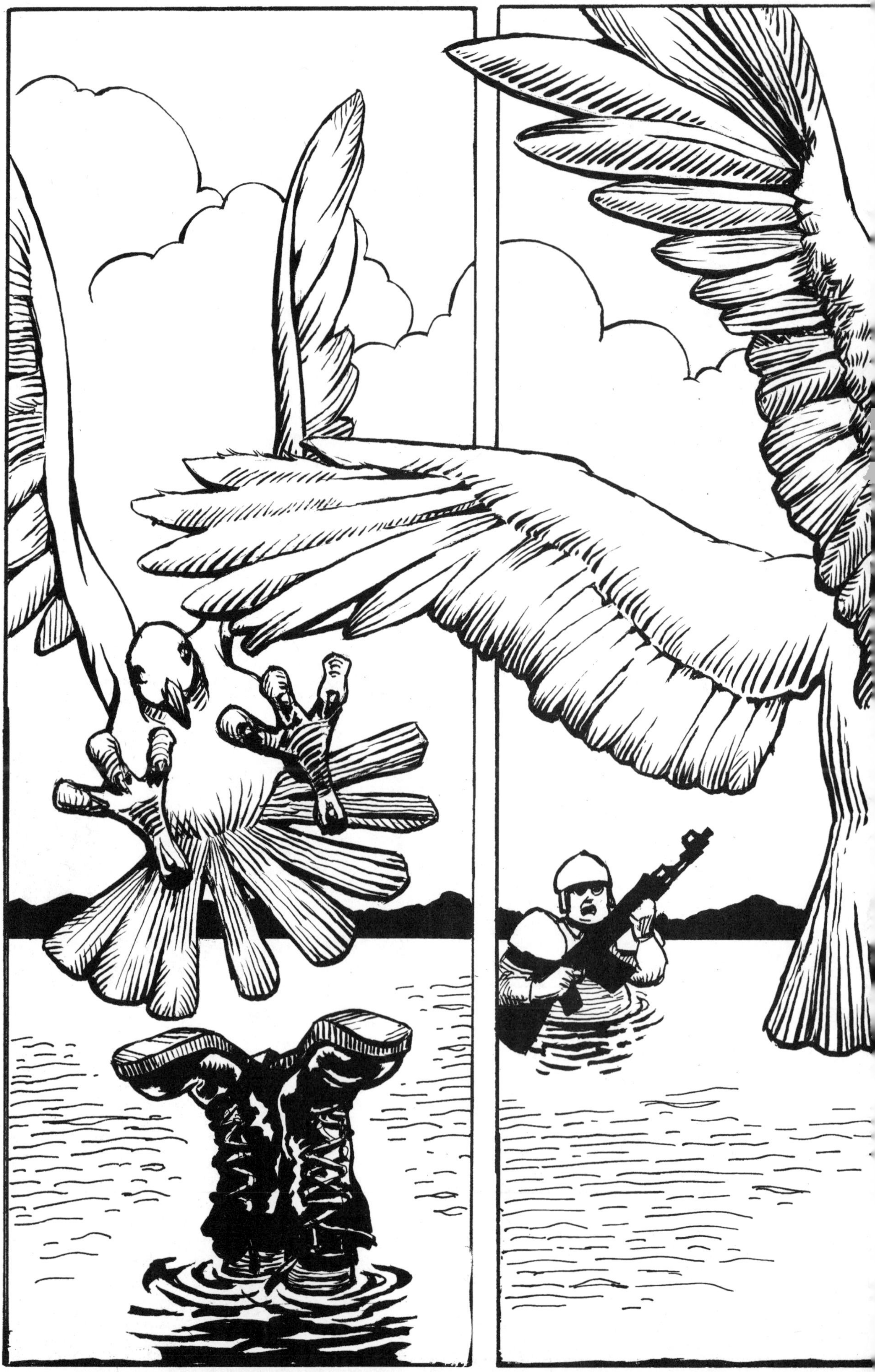

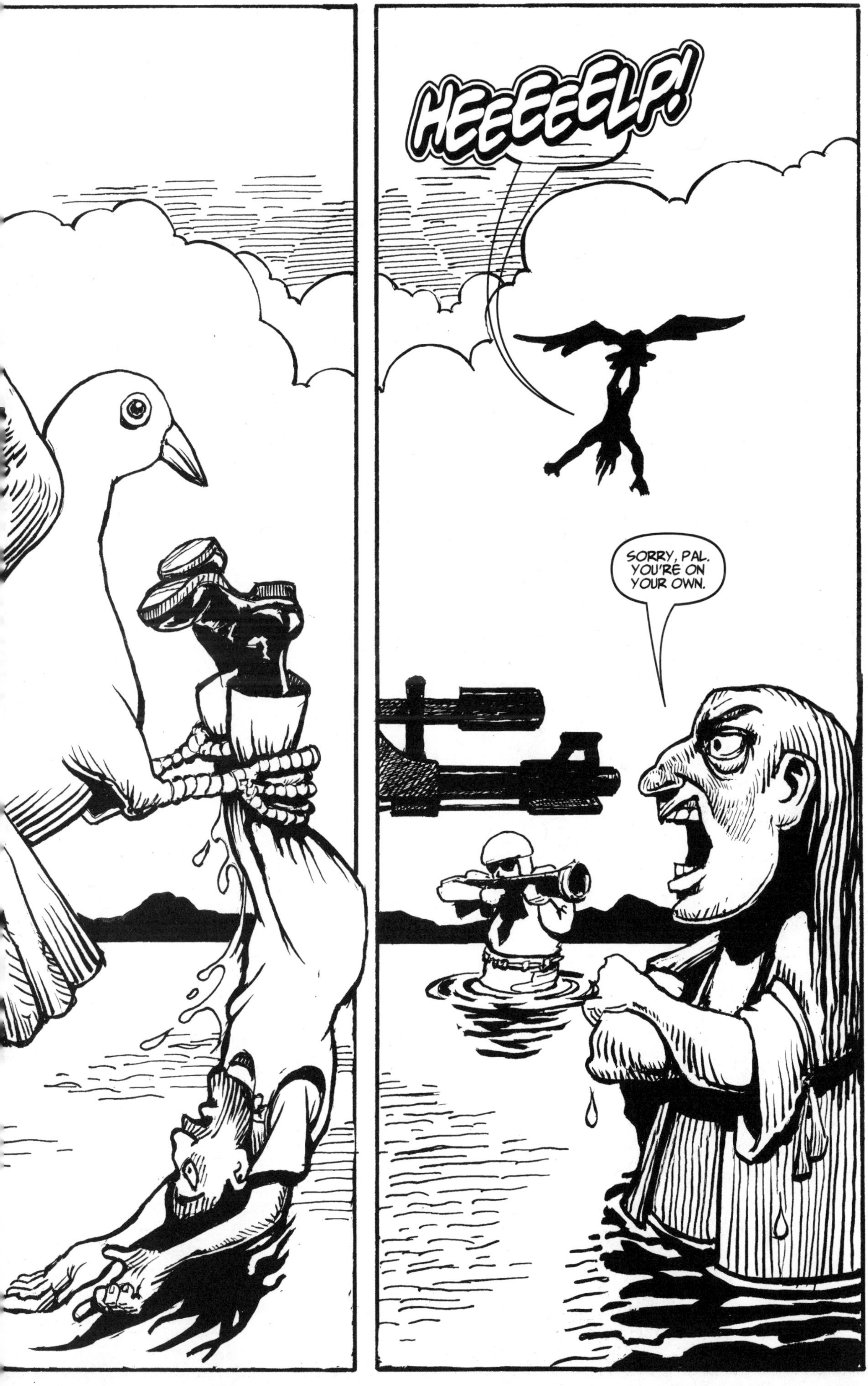
HEEEEELP!
SORRY, PAL. YOU'RE ON YOUR OWN.

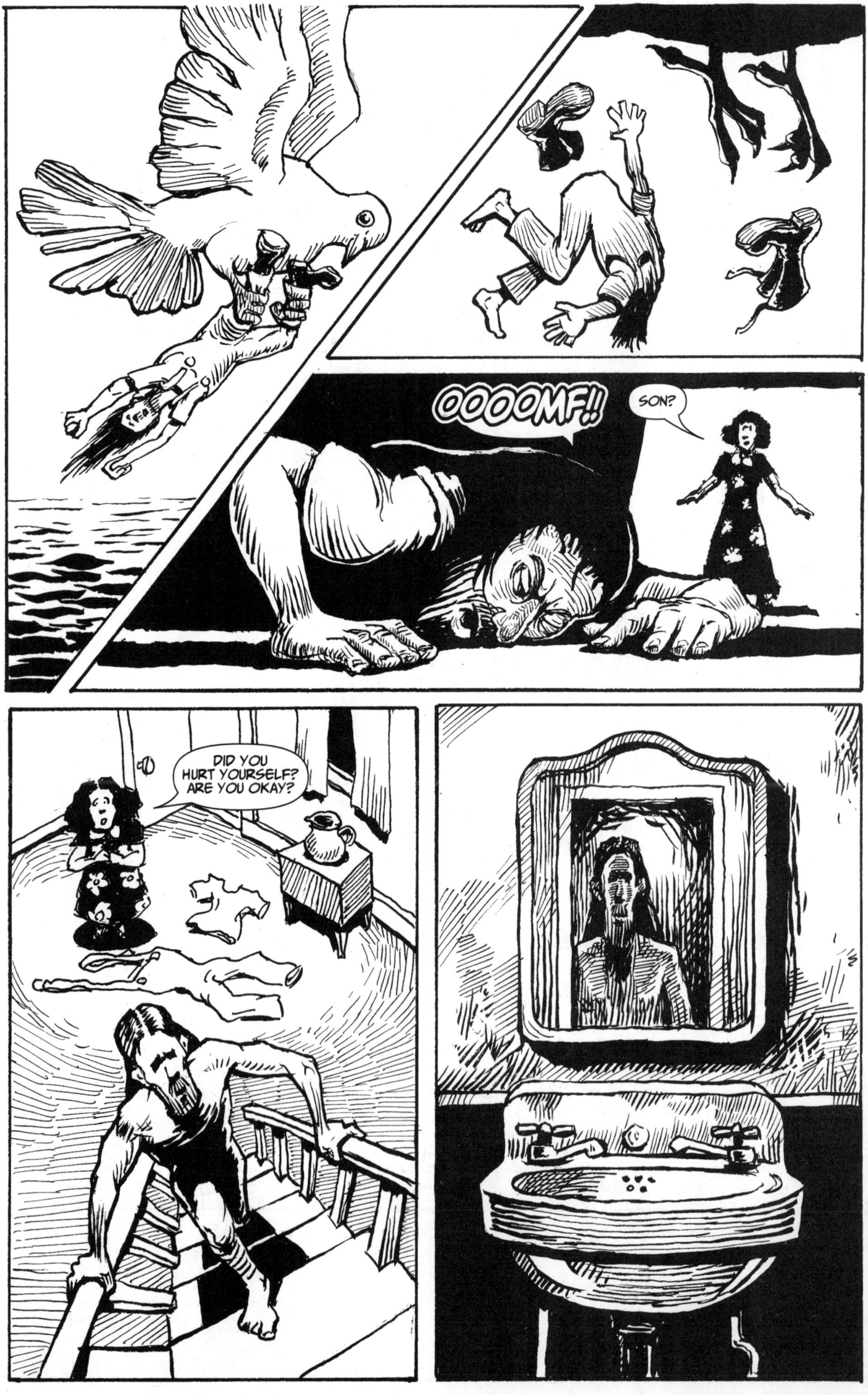
OOOOMF!!
SON?
DID YOU HURT YOURSELF? ARE YOU OKAY?

SON, PLEASE ANSWER ME.

I JUST... I JUST WANT TO HELP.

DID SOMETHING HAPPEN AT WORK? CAN I GET YOU A BITE TO EAT?

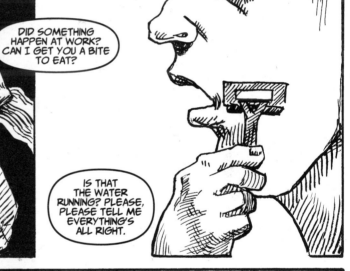

IS THAT THE WATER RUNNING? PLEASE, PLEASE TELL ME EVERYTHING'S ALL RIGHT.

SCR EEEEEEE EEE--

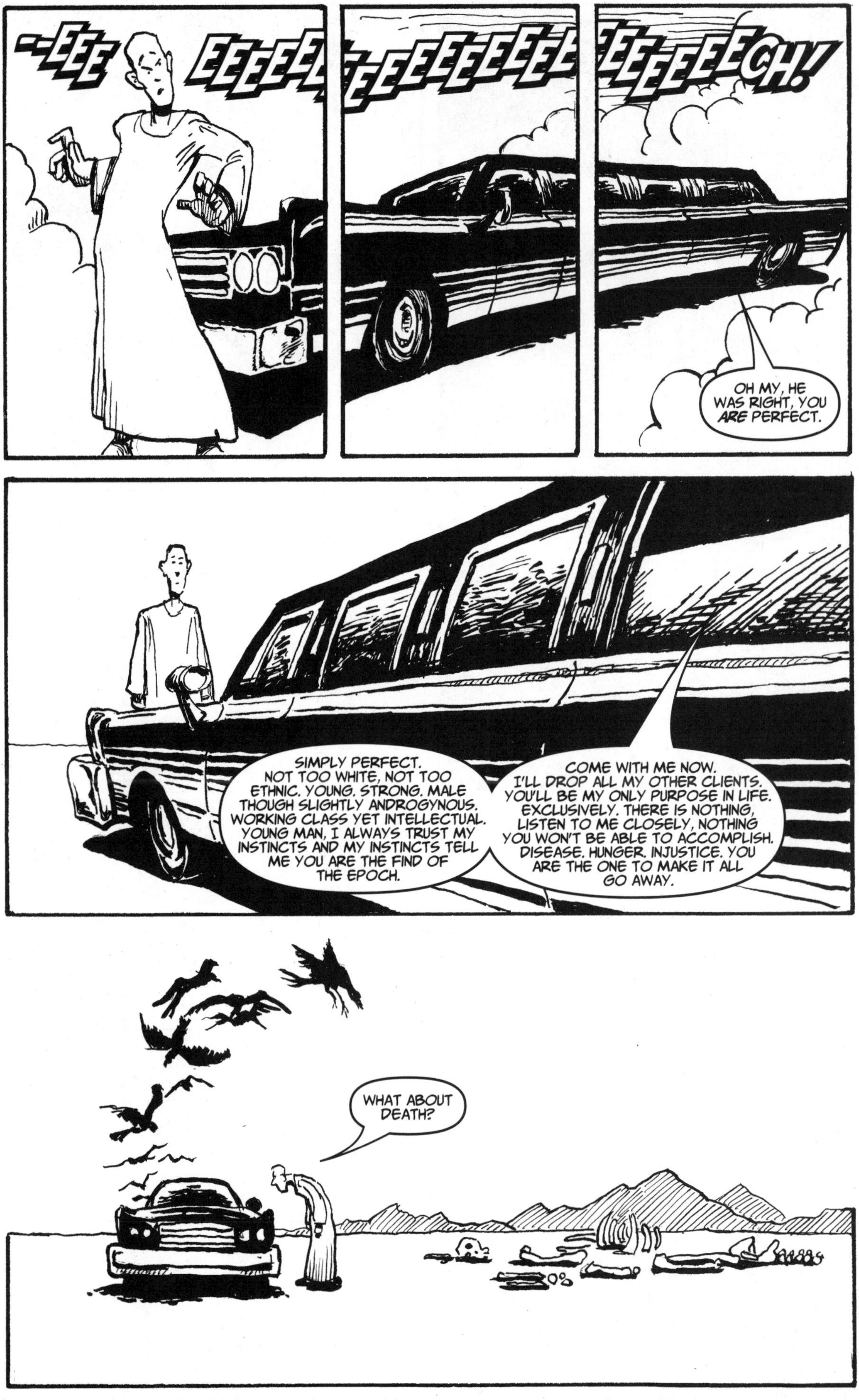
--EEE EEEEEEEEEEEEEEEEEEEEEEEEEEEEECH!
OH MY, HE WAS RIGHT, YOU *ARE* PERFECT.
SIMPLY PERFECT. NOT TOO WHITE, NOT TOO ETHNIC. YOUNG. STRONG. MALE THOUGH SLIGHTLY ANDROGYNOUS. WORKING CLASS YET INTELLECTUAL. YOUNG MAN, I ALWAYS TRUST MY INSTINCTS AND MY INSTINCTS TELL ME YOU ARE THE FIND OF THE EPOCH.
COME WITH ME NOW. I'LL DROP ALL MY OTHER CLIENTS. YOU'LL BE MY ONLY PURPOSE IN LIFE. EXCLUSIVELY. THERE IS NOTHING, LISTEN TO ME CLOSELY, NOTHING YOU WON'T BE ABLE TO ACCOMPLISH. DISEASE. HUNGER. INJUSTICE. YOU ARE THE ONE TO MAKE IT ALL GO AWAY.
WHAT ABOUT DEATH?

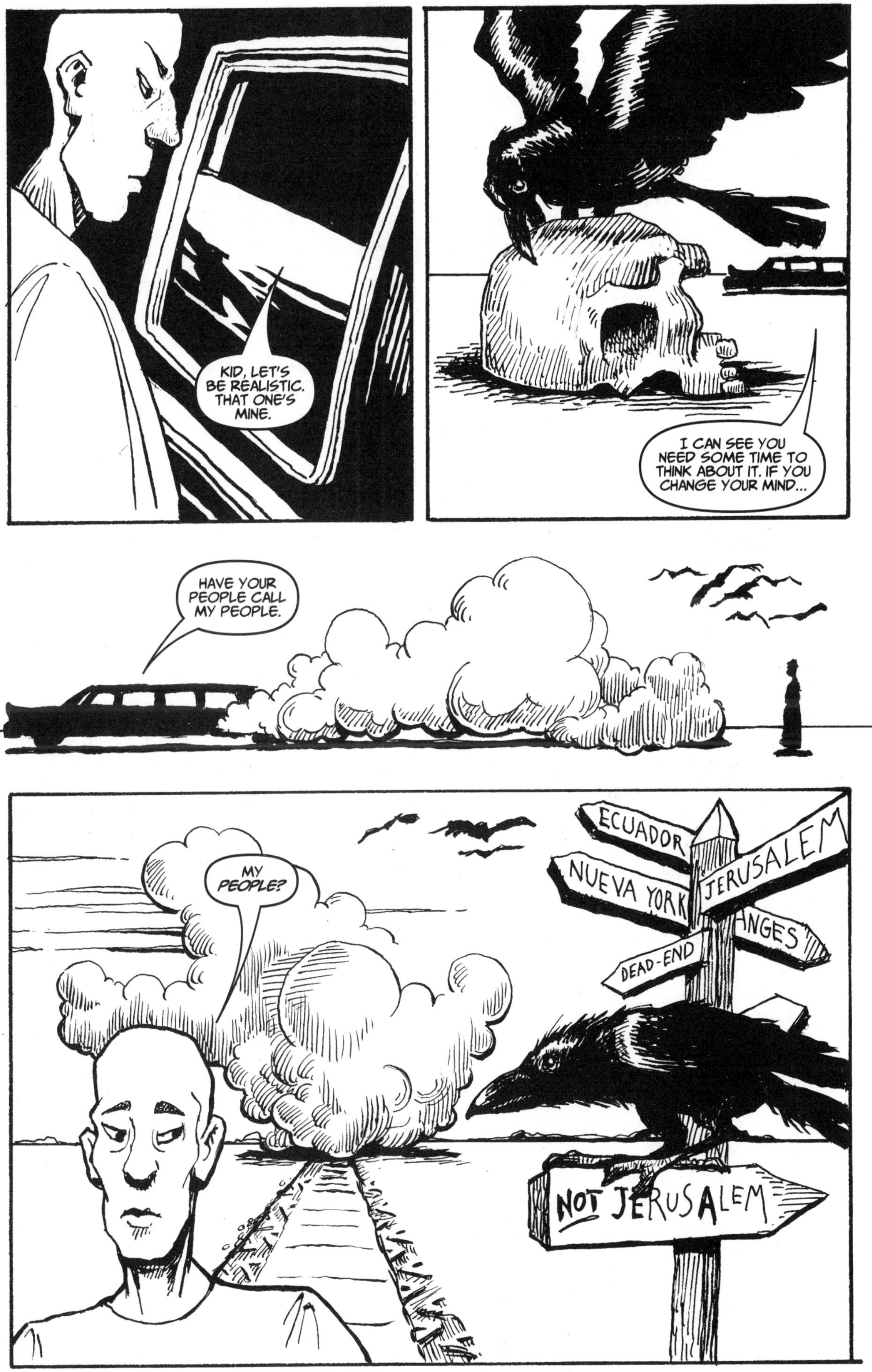
KID, LET'S BE REALISTIC. THAT ONE'S MINE.
I CAN SEE YOU NEED SOME TIME TO THINK ABOUT IT. IF YOU CHANGE YOUR MIND...
HAVE YOUR PEOPLE CALL MY PEOPLE.
MY *PEOPLE?*
ECUADOR
JERUSALEM
NUEVA YORK
ANGES
DEAD-END
NOT JERUSALEM

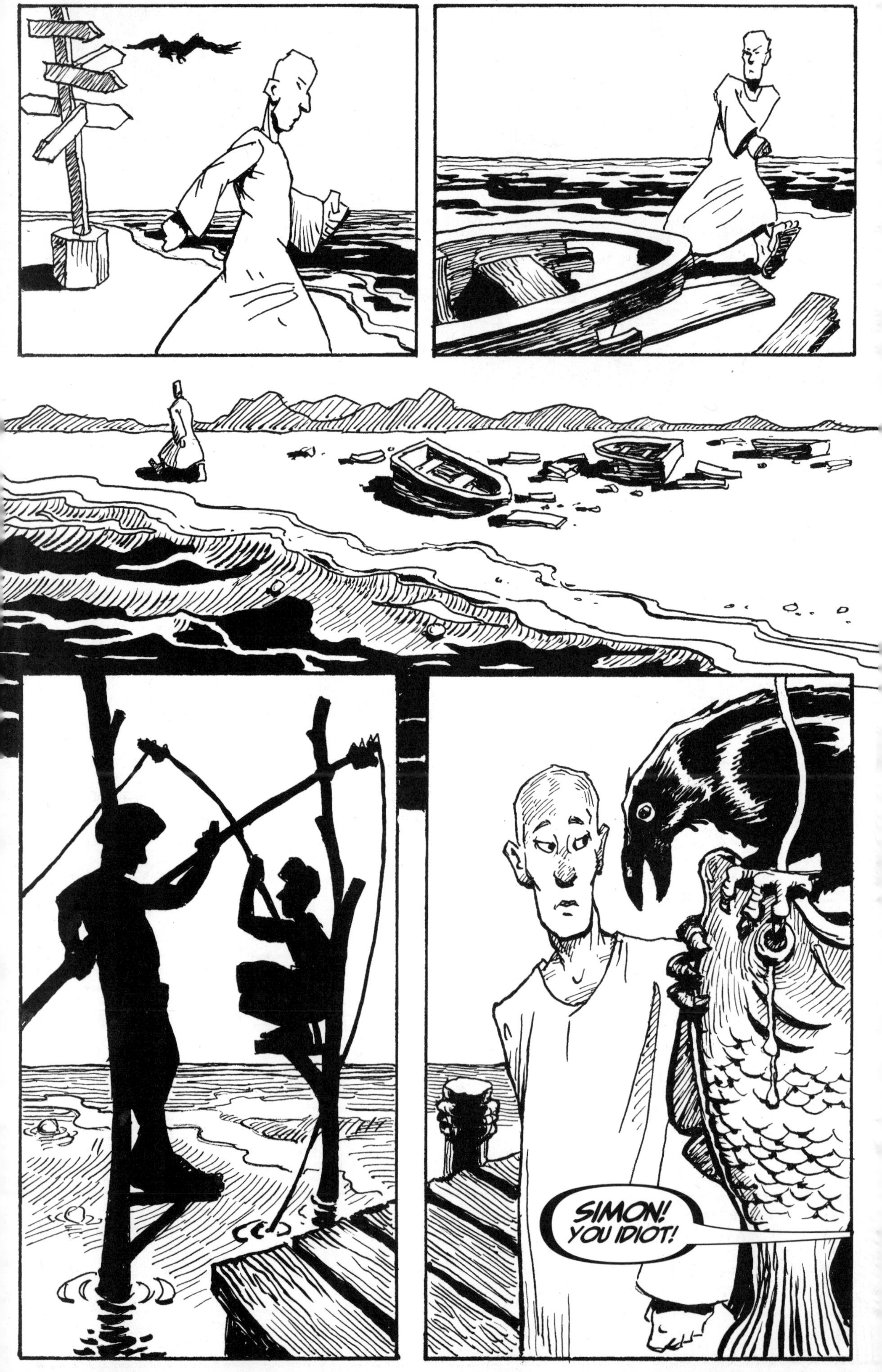
SIMON!
YOU IDIOT!

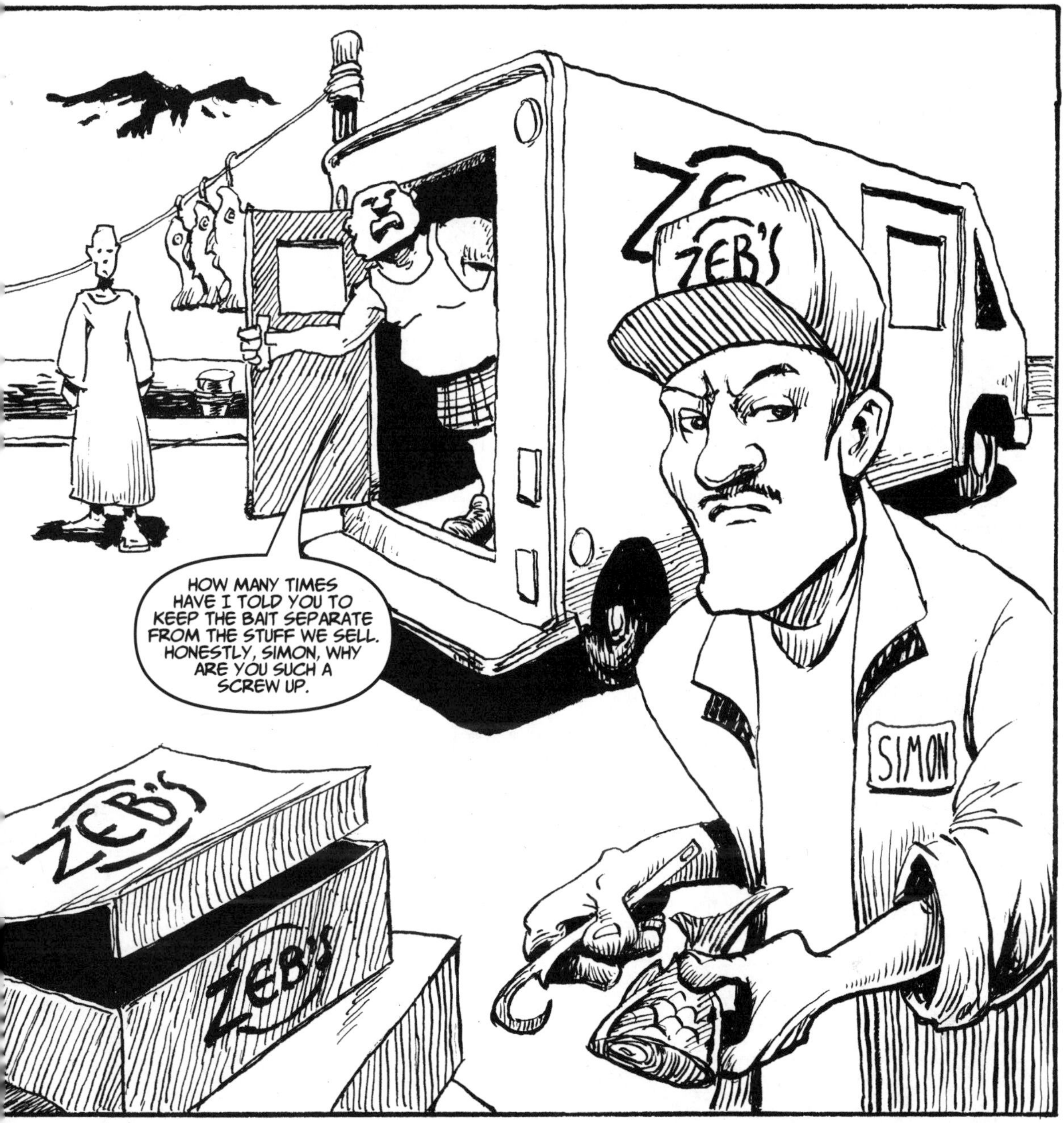
ZEB'S
HOW MANY TIMES HAVE I TOLD YOU TO KEEP THE BAIT SEPARATE FROM THE STUFF WE SELL. HONESTLY, SIMON, WHY ARE YOU SUCH A SCREW UP.
SIMON
ZEB'S
ZEB'S

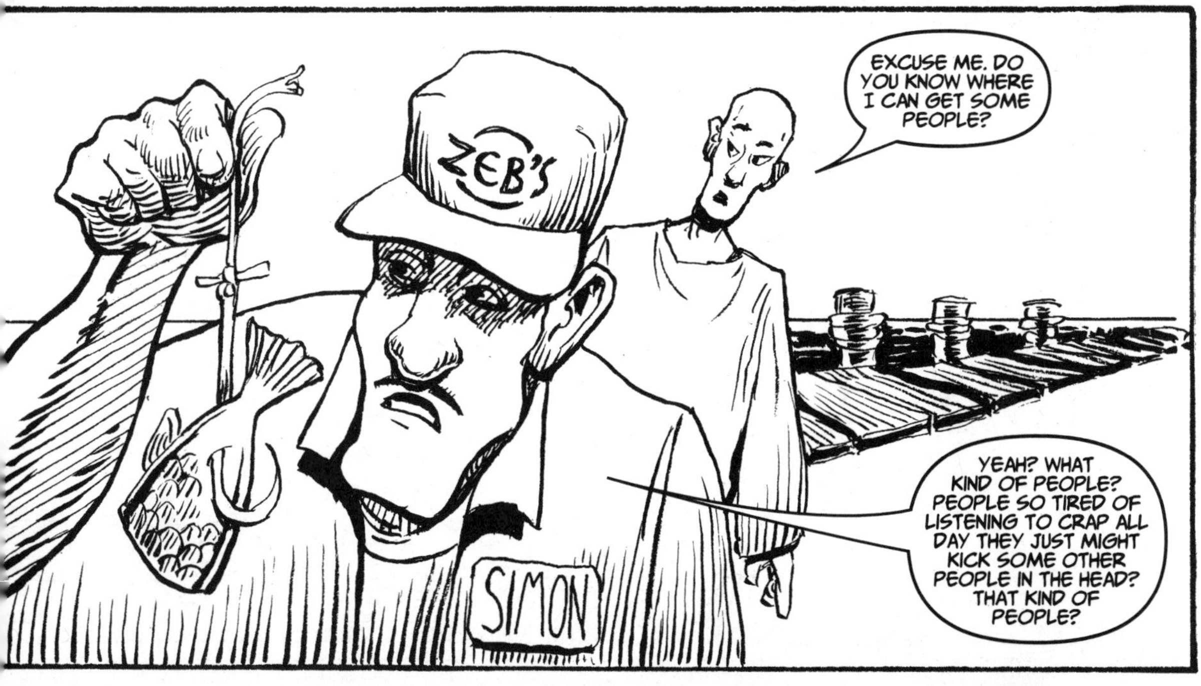
EXCUSE ME. DO YOU KNOW WHERE I CAN GET SOME PEOPLE?
ZEB'S
YEAH? WHAT KIND OF PEOPLE? PEOPLE SO TIRED OF LISTENING TO CRAP ALL DAY THEY JUST MIGHT KICK SOME OTHER PEOPLE IN THE HEAD? THAT KIND OF PEOPLE?
SIMON

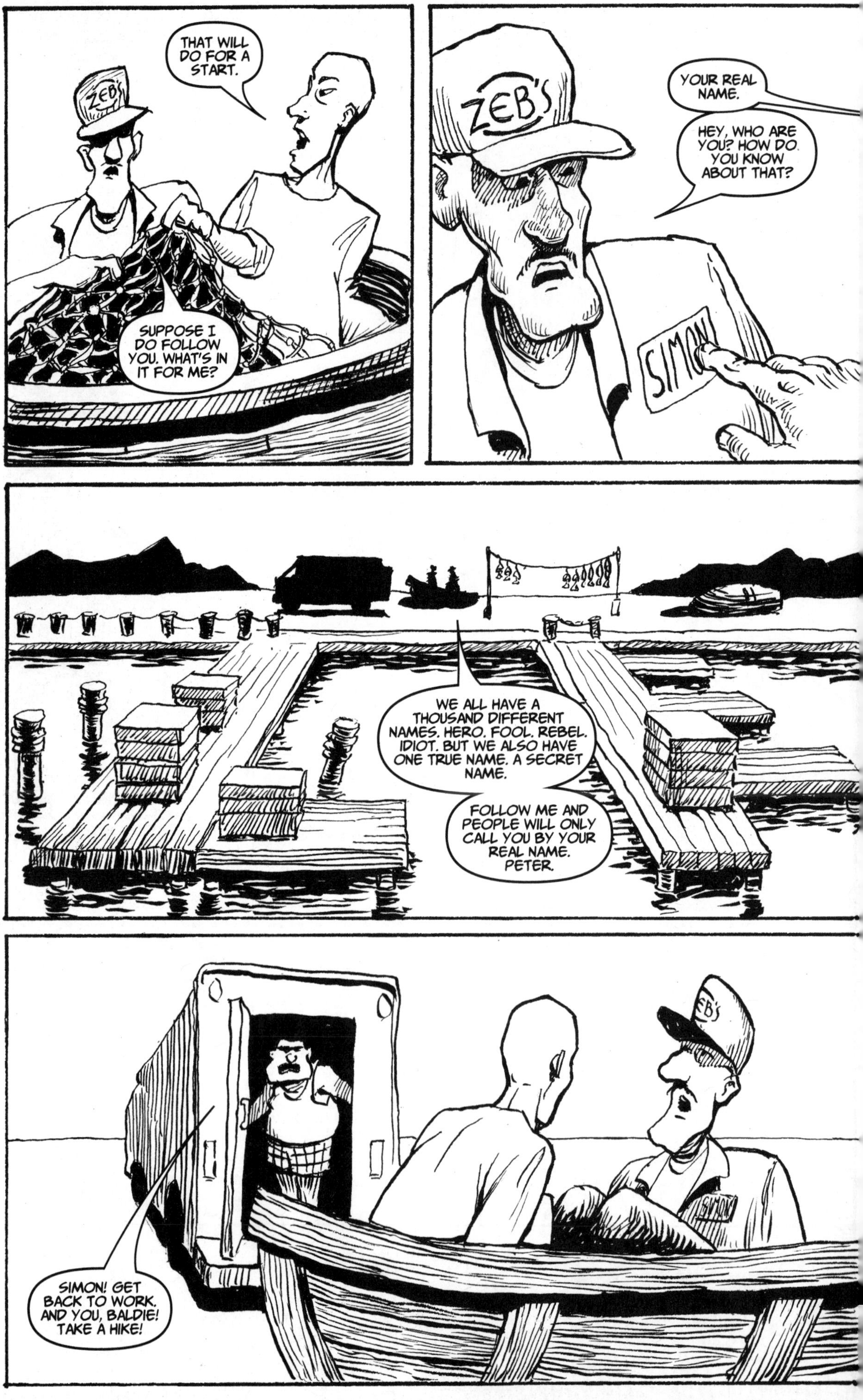
THAT WILL DO FOR A START.
SUPPOSE I DO FOLLOW YOU. WHAT'S IN IT FOR ME?
ZEB'S
YOUR REAL NAME.
HEY, WHO ARE YOU? HOW DO YOU KNOW ABOUT THAT?
SIMON
WE ALL HAVE A THOUSAND DIFFERENT NAMES. HERO. FOOL. REBEL. IDIOT. BUT WE ALSO HAVE ONE TRUE NAME. A SECRET NAME.
FOLLOW ME AND PEOPLE WILL ONLY CALL YOU BY YOUR REAL NAME. PETER.
SIMON! GET BACK TO WORK. AND YOU, BALDIE! TAKE A HIKE!

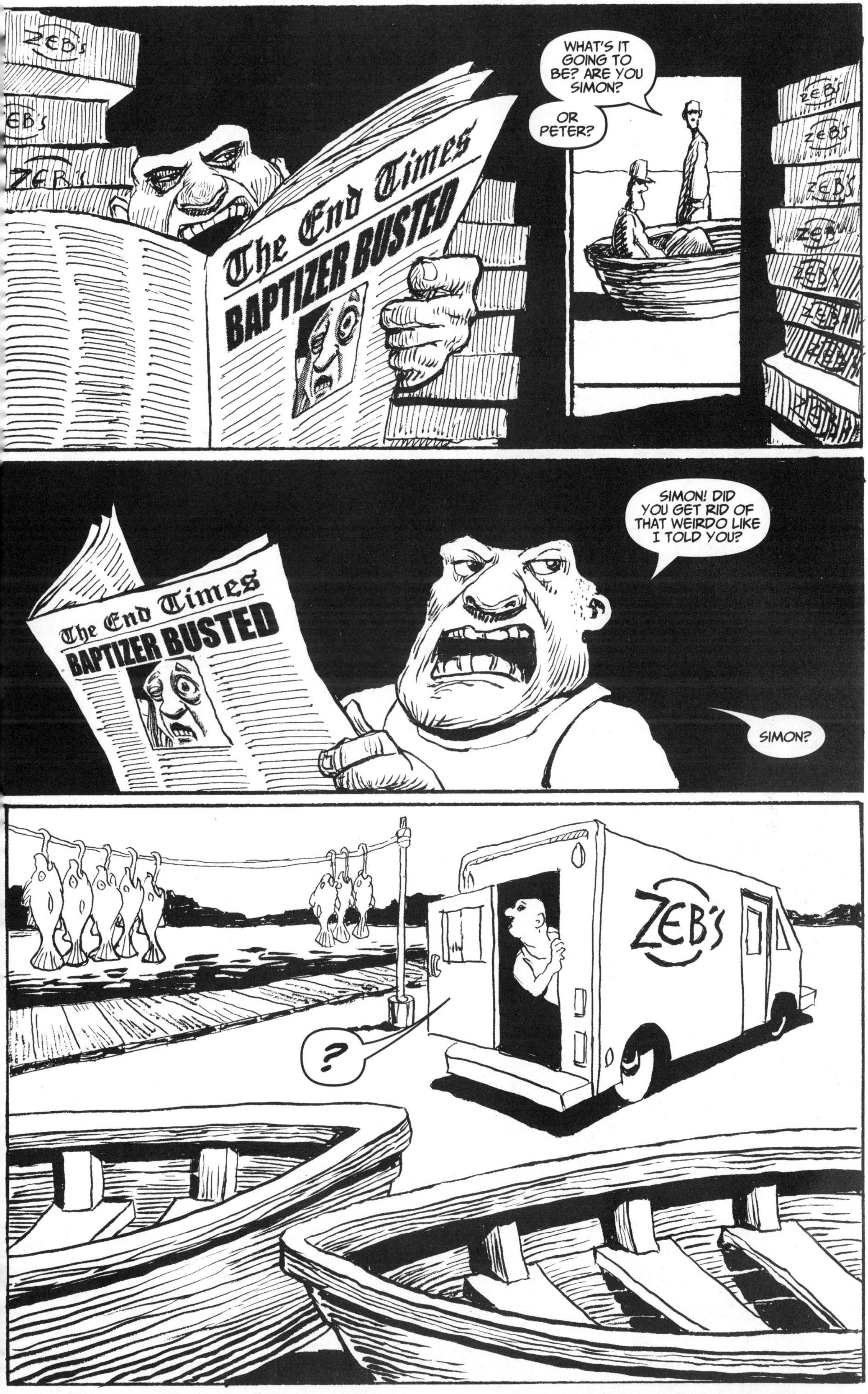
ZEB'S
The End Times
BAPTIZER BUSTED
WHAT'S IT GOING TO BE? ARE YOU SIMON?
OR PETER?
The End Times
BAPTIZER BUSTED
SIMON! DID YOU GET RID OF THAT WEIRDO LIKE I TOLD YOU?
SIMON?
ZEB'S
?

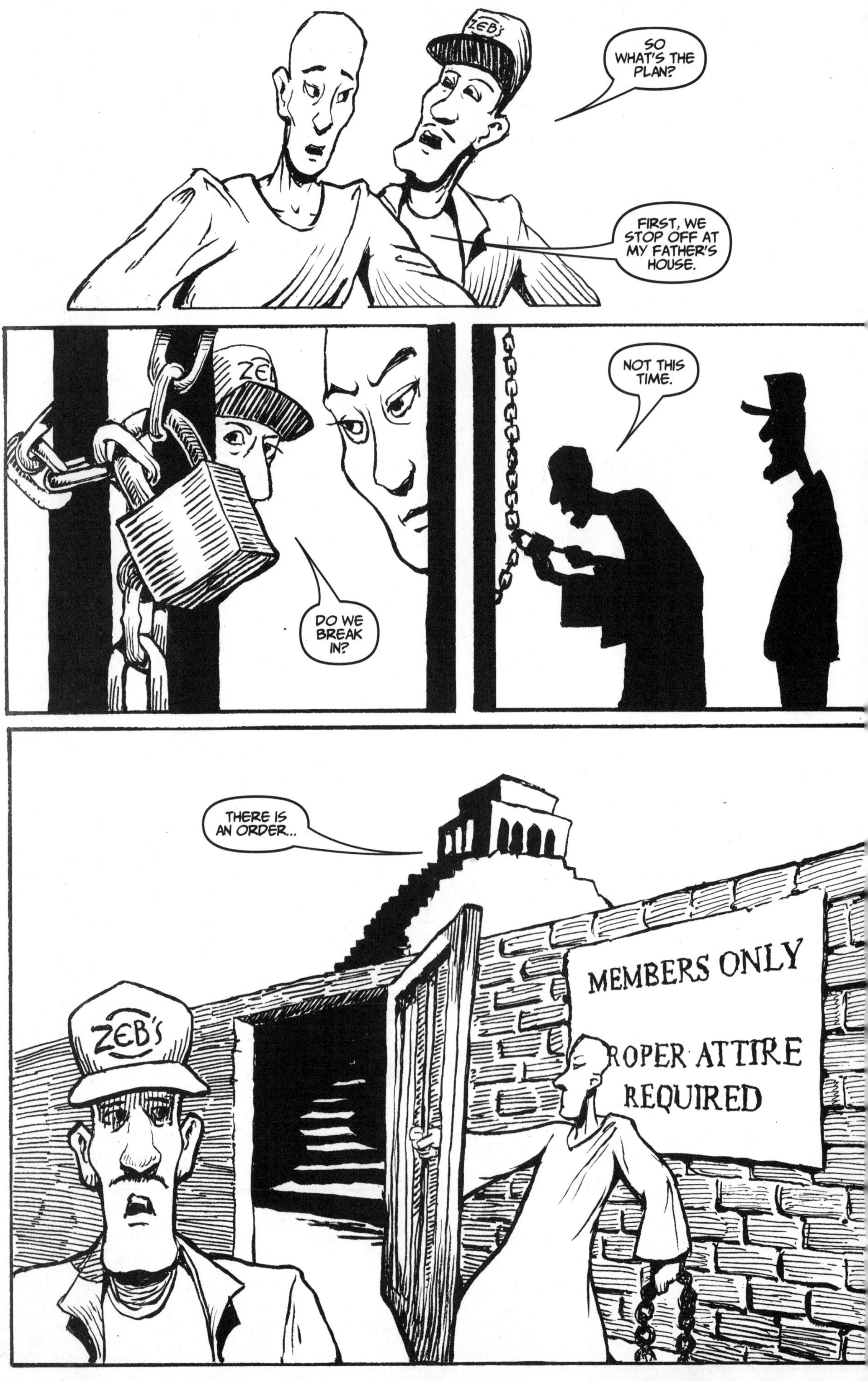
SO WHAT'S THE PLAN?
FIRST, WE STOP OFF AT MY FATHER'S HOUSE.
DO WE BREAK IN?
NOT THIS TIME.
THERE IS AN ORDER...
MEMBERS ONLY
ROPER ATTIRE REQUIRED
ZEB's

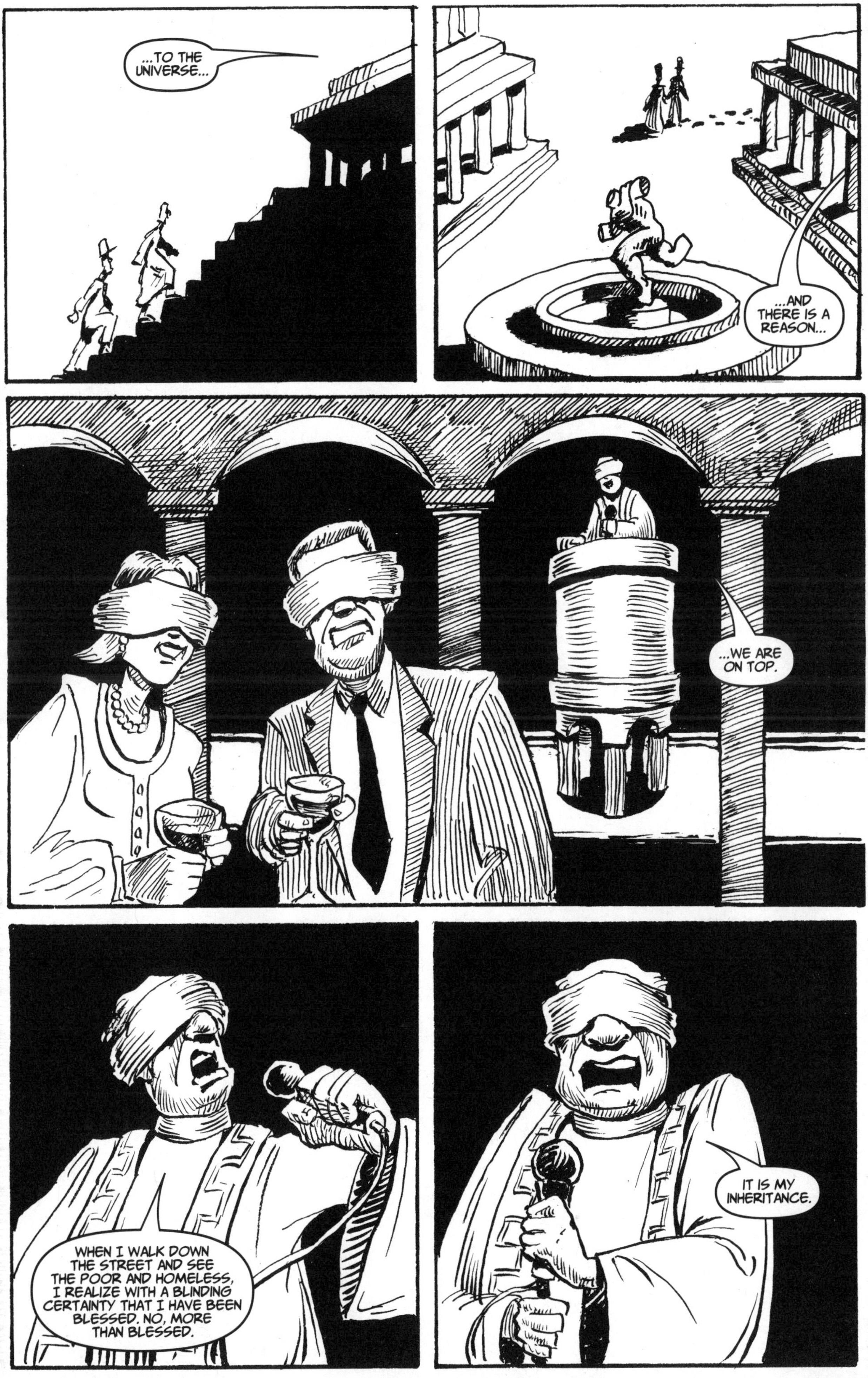
...TO THE UNIVERSE...
...AND THERE IS A REASON...
...WE ARE ON TOP.
WHEN I WALK DOWN THE STREET AND SEE THE POOR AND HOMELESS, I REALIZE WITH A BLINDING CERTAINTY THAT I HAVE BEEN BLESSED. NO, MORE THAN BLESSED.
IT IS MY INHERITANCE.

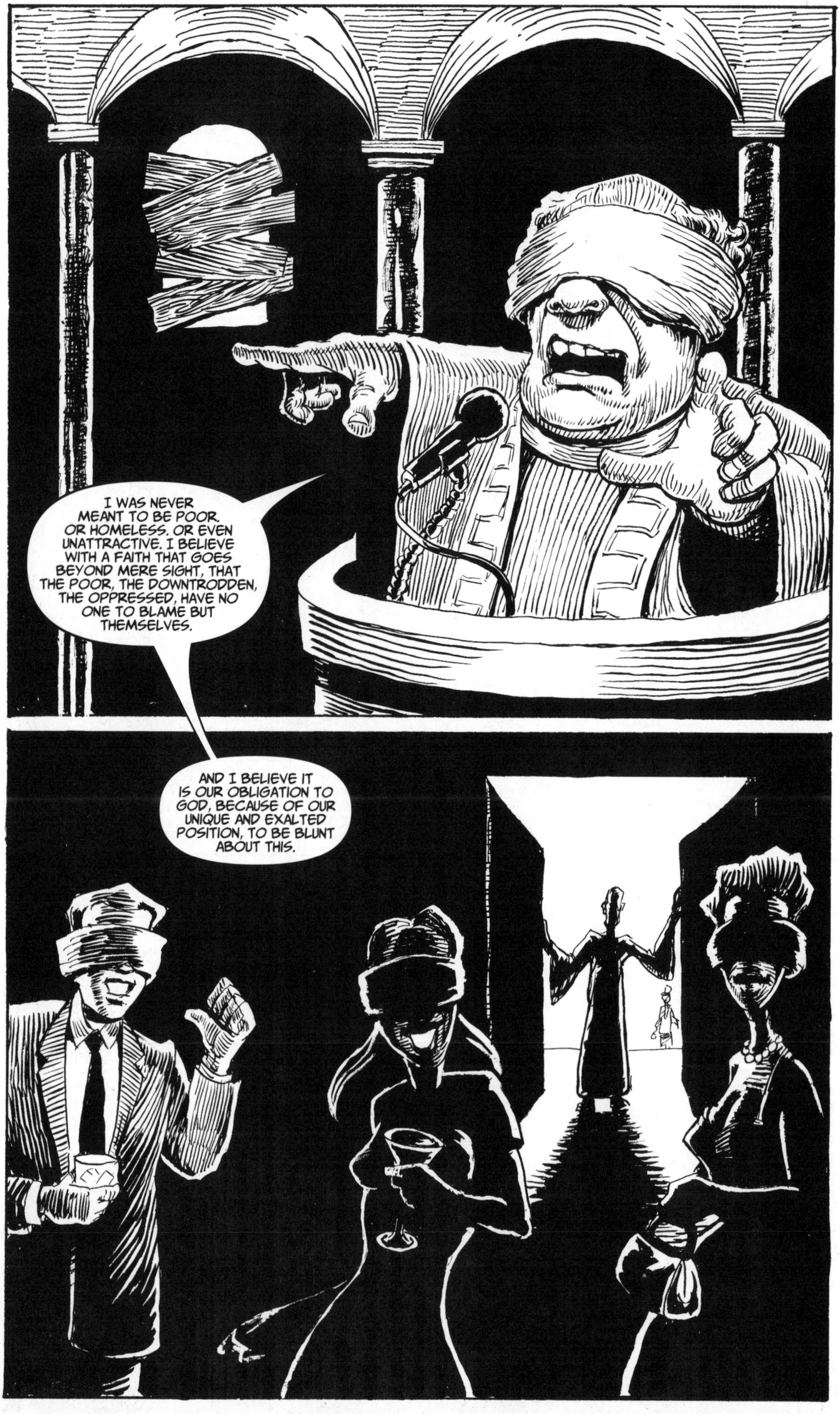
I WAS NEVER MEANT TO BE POOR. OR HOMELESS. OR EVEN UNATTRACTIVE. I BELIEVE WITH A FAITH THAT GOES BEYOND MERE SIGHT, THAT THE POOR, THE DOWNTRODDEN, THE OPPRESSED, HAVE NO ONE TO BLAME BUT THEMSELVES.
AND I BELIEVE IT IS OUR OBLIGATION TO GOD, BECAUSE OF OUR UNIQUE AND EXALTED POSITION, TO BE BLUNT ABOUT THIS.

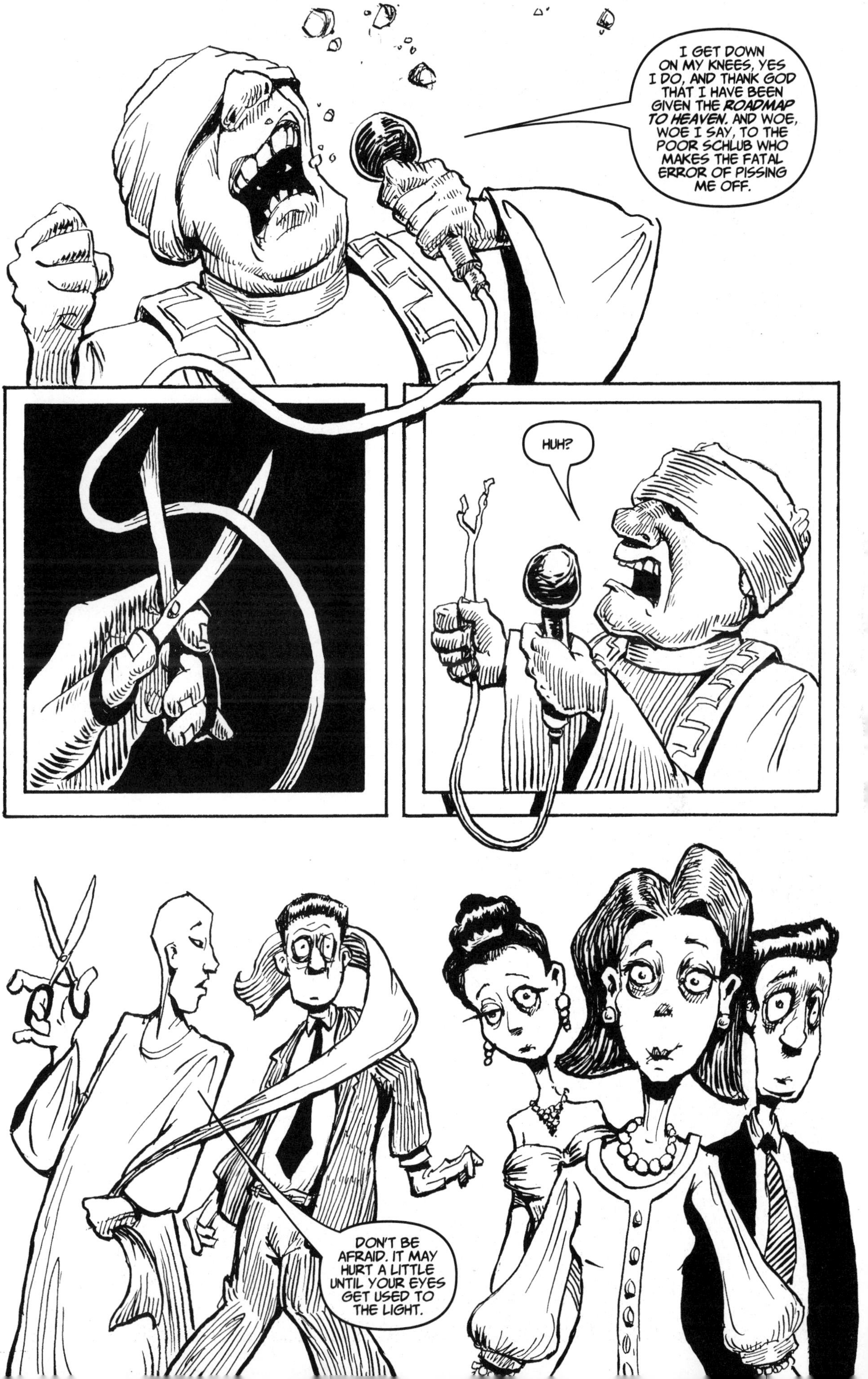
I GET DOWN ON MY KNEES, YES I DO, AND THANK GOD THAT I HAVE BEEN GIVEN THE *ROADMAP TO HEAVEN.* AND WOE, WOE I SAY, TO THE POOR SCHLUB WHO MAKES THE FATAL ERROR OF PISSING ME OFF.
HUH?
DON'T BE AFRAID. IT MAY HURT A LITTLE UNTIL YOUR EYES GET USED TO THE LIGHT.

YOU FOOL!

YOU ARE NOT WELCOME HERE! GET OUT!

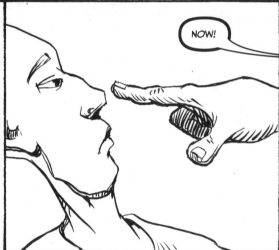

NOW!

THESE POOR STUPID PEOPLE DON'T NEED TO KNOW THEY'RE WANDERING AROUND IN THE DARK. THEY'RE USED TO IT BY NOW!

BUT YOU DON'T FOOL ME. I KNOW WHO YOU ARE. I KNOW WHAT YOU ARE.

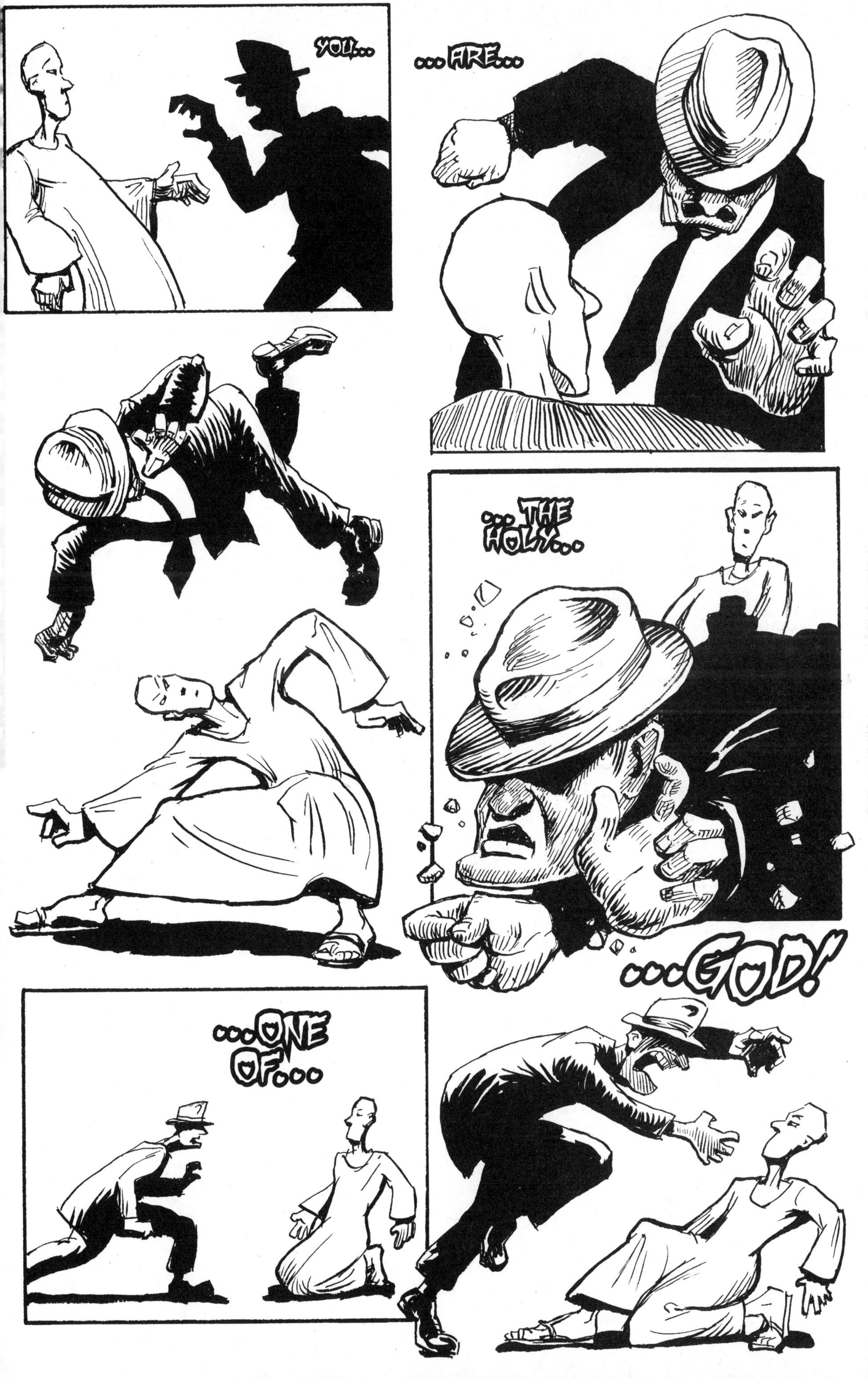
YOU...
...ARE...
...THE HOLY...
...GOD!
...ONE OF...

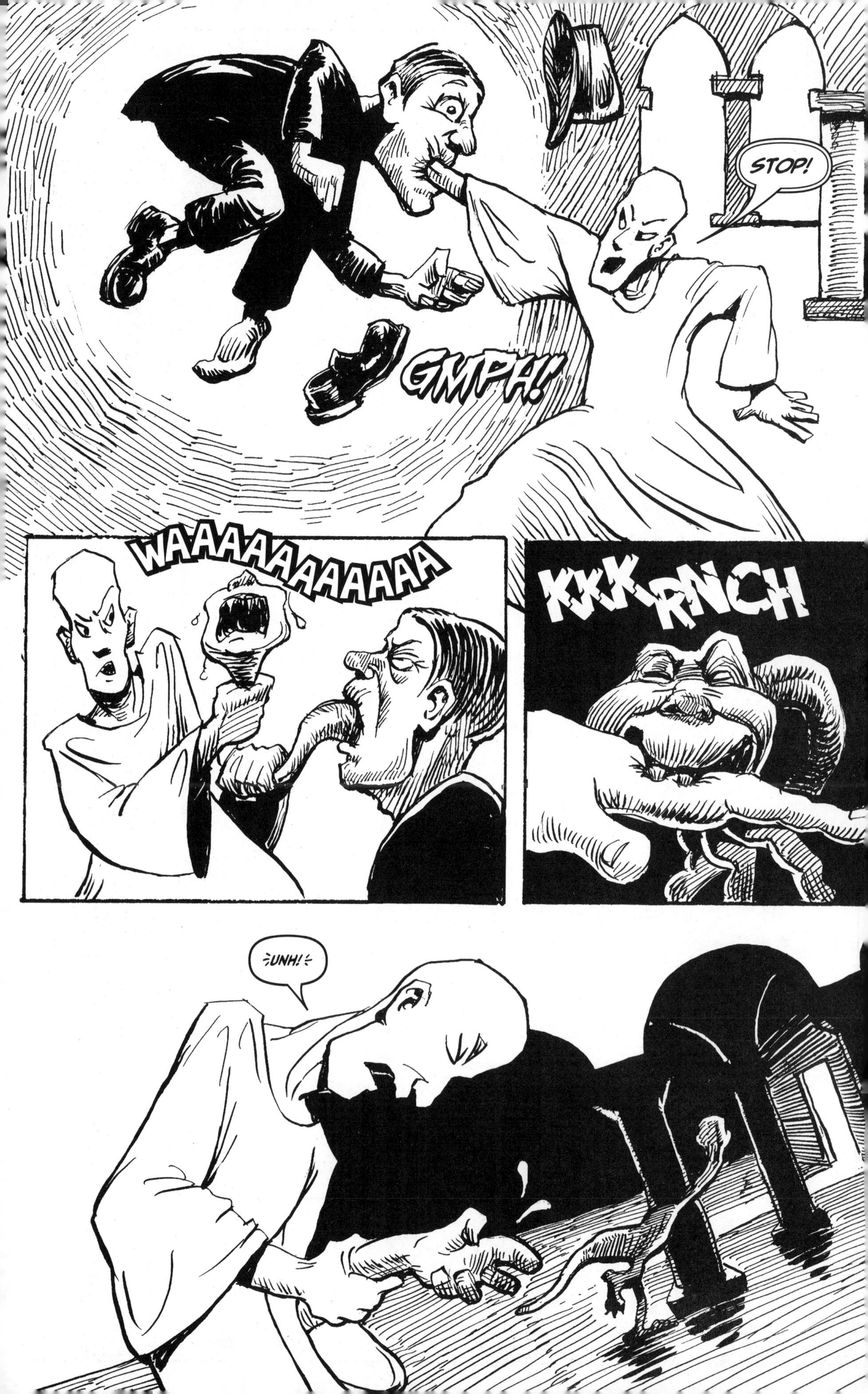
STOP!
GMPH!
WAAAAAAAAAAAA
KKKRNCH
UNH!

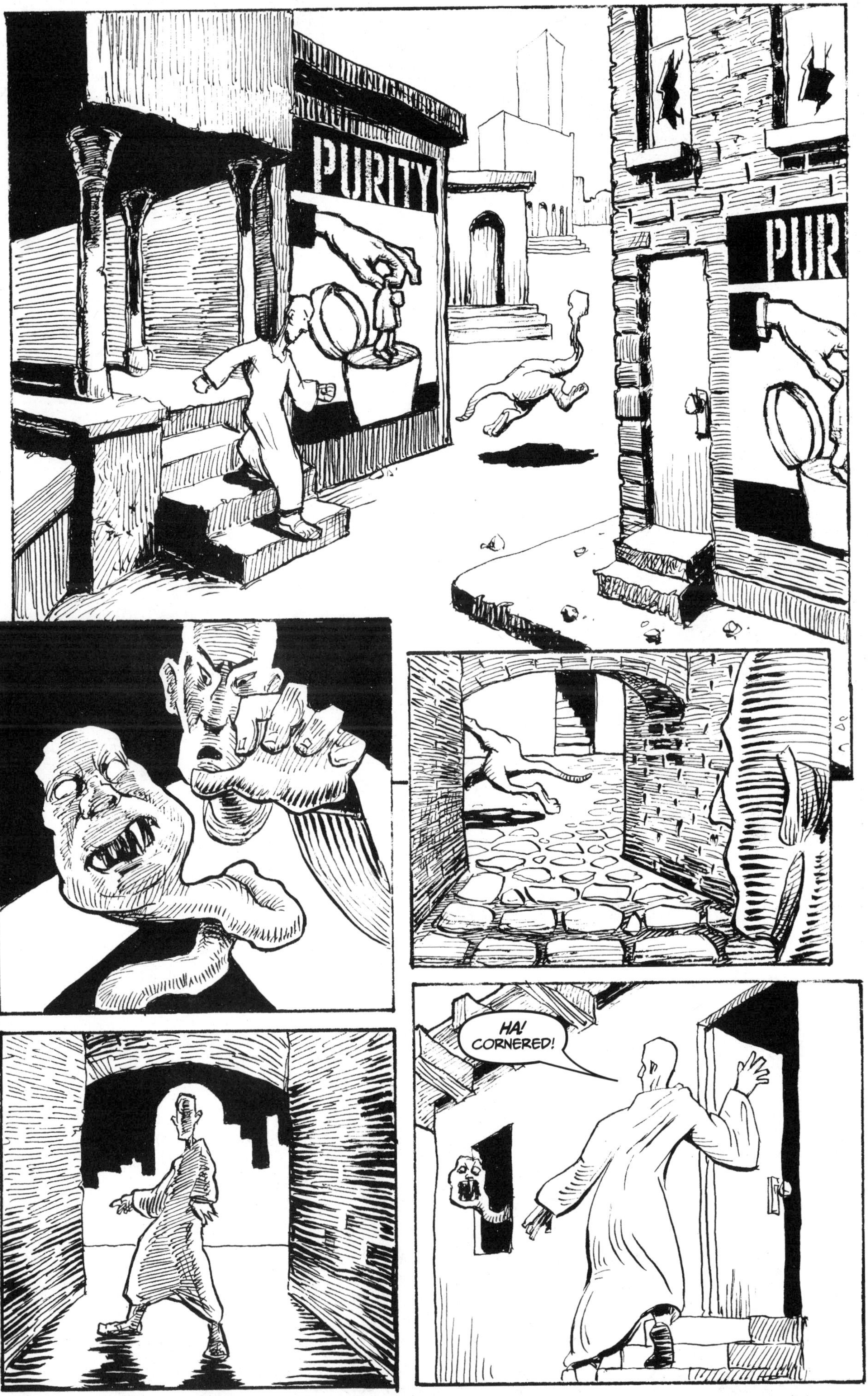
PURITY
PUR
HA! CORNERED!

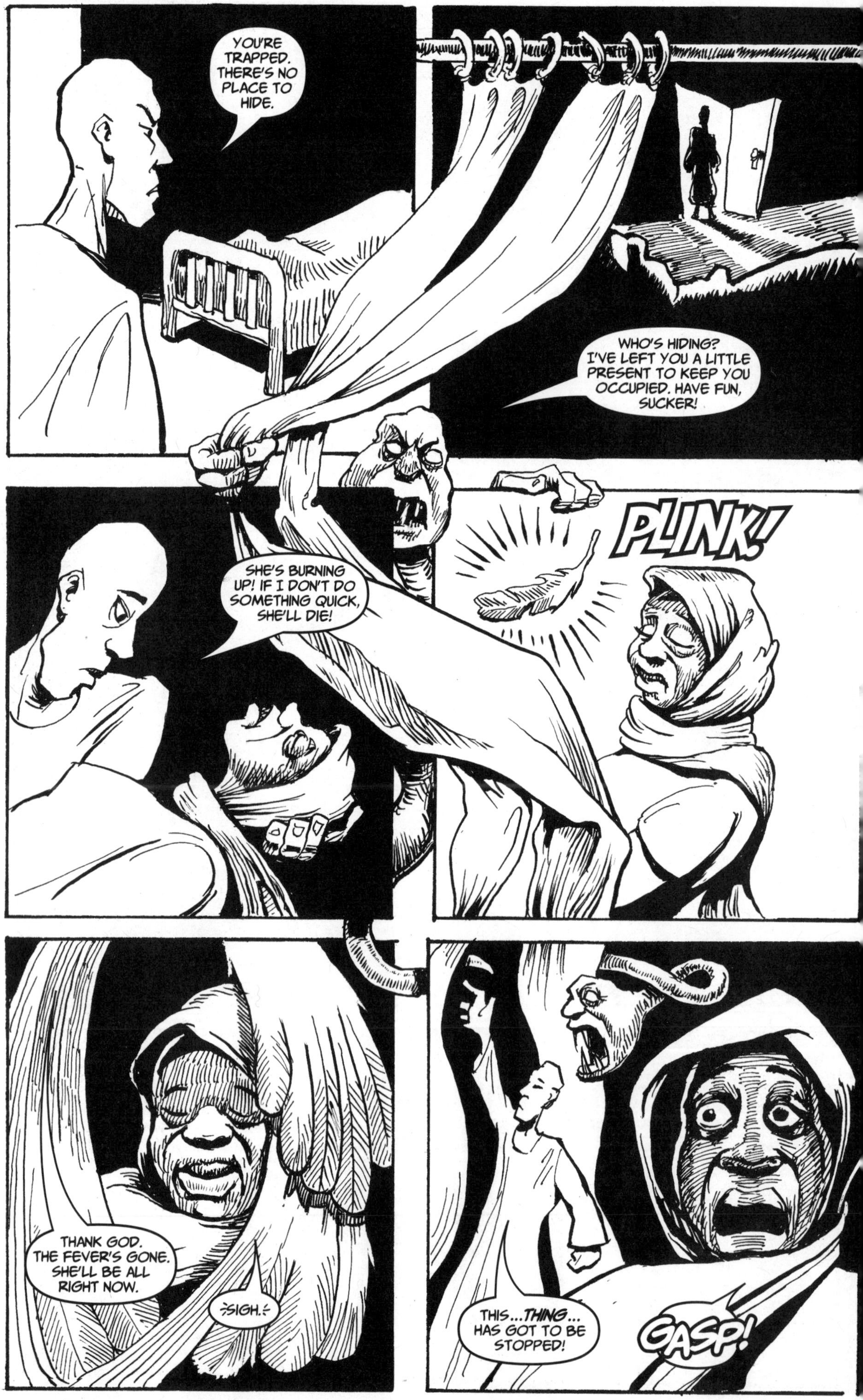
YOU'RE TRAPPED. THERE'S NO PLACE TO HIDE.
WHO'S HIDING? I'VE LEFT YOU A LITTLE PRESENT TO KEEP YOU OCCUPIED. HAVE FUN, SUCKER!
SHE'S BURNING UP! IF I DON'T DO SOMETHING QUICK, SHE'LL DIE!
PLINK!
THANK GOD. THE FEVER'S GONE. SHE'LL BE ALL RIGHT NOW.
SIGH.
THIS...THING... HAS GOT TO BE STOPPED!
GASP!

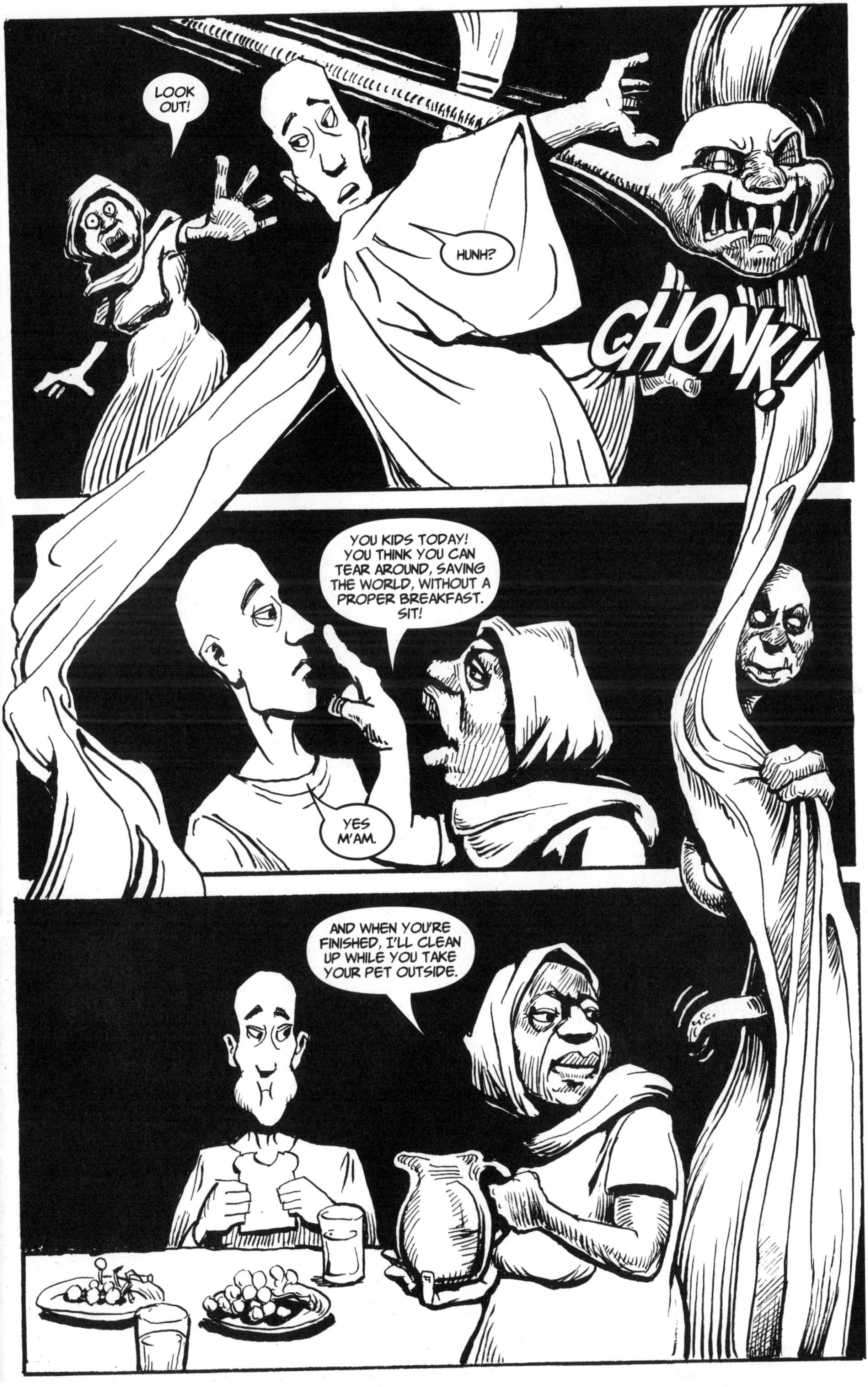
LOOK OUT!
HUNH?
CHONK!
YOU KIDS TODAY! YOU THINK YOU CAN TEAR AROUND, SAVING THE WORLD, WITHOUT A PROPER BREAKFAST. SIT!
YES M'AM.
AND WHEN YOU'RE FINISHED, I'LL CLEAN UP WHILE YOU TAKE YOUR PET OUTSIDE.

OH I'LL TAKE HIM OUTSIDE ALRIGHT--

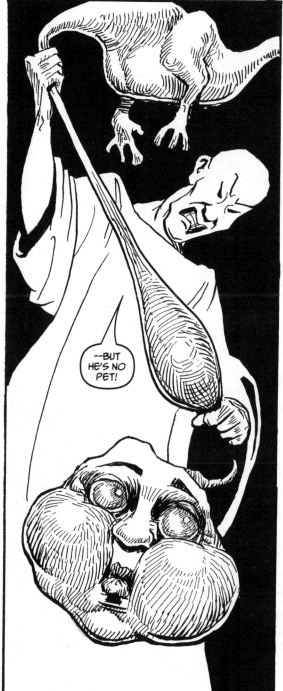

--BUT HE'S NO PET!

WOOOSH!

?

KHUNK!

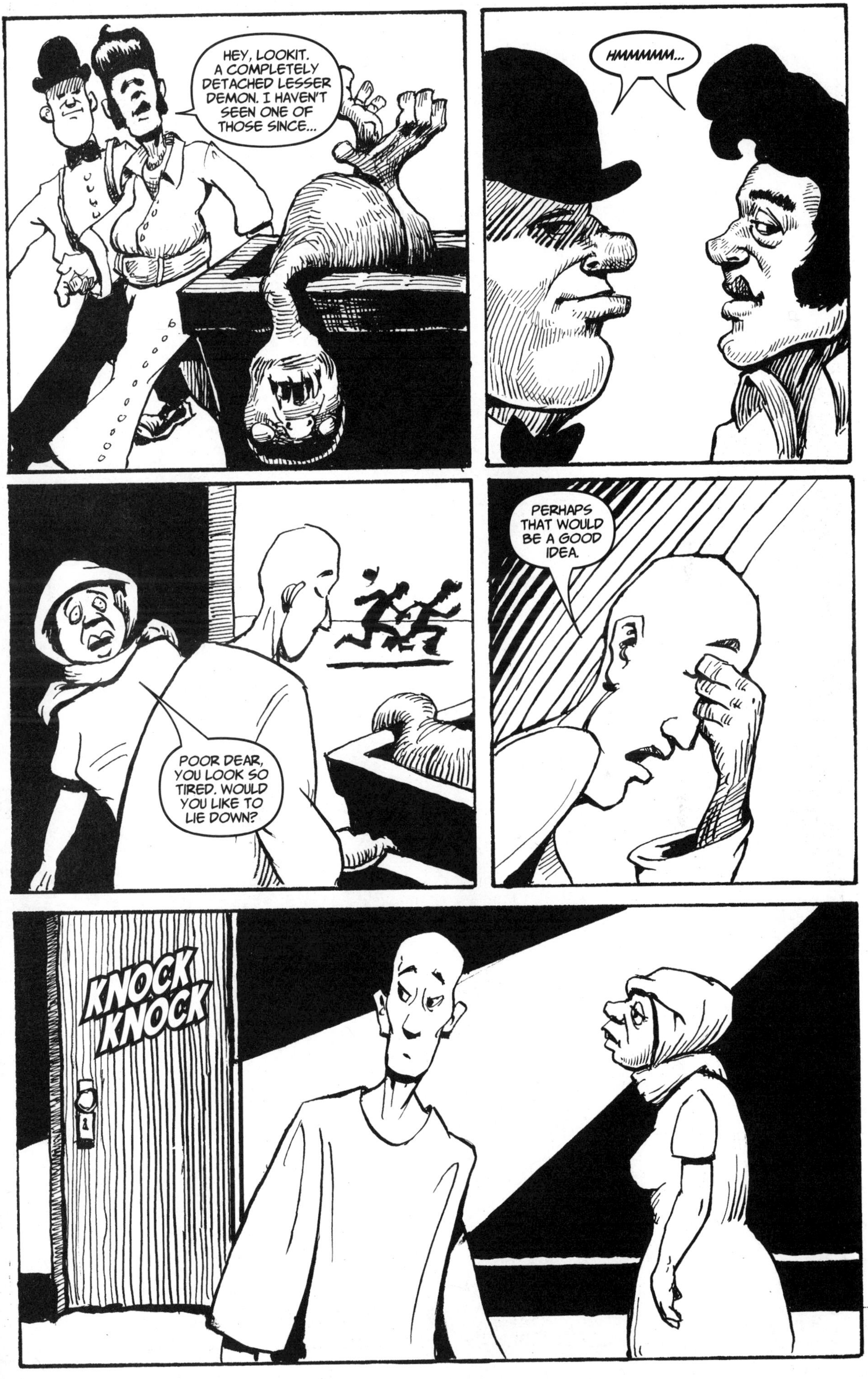
HEY, LOOKIT. A COMPLETELY DETACHED LESSER DEMON. I HAVEN'T SEEN ONE OF THOSE SINCE...
HMMMMM...
POOR DEAR, YOU LOOK SO TIRED. WOULD YOU LIKE TO LIE DOWN?
PERHAPS THAT WOULD BE A GOOD IDEA.
KNOCK KNOCK

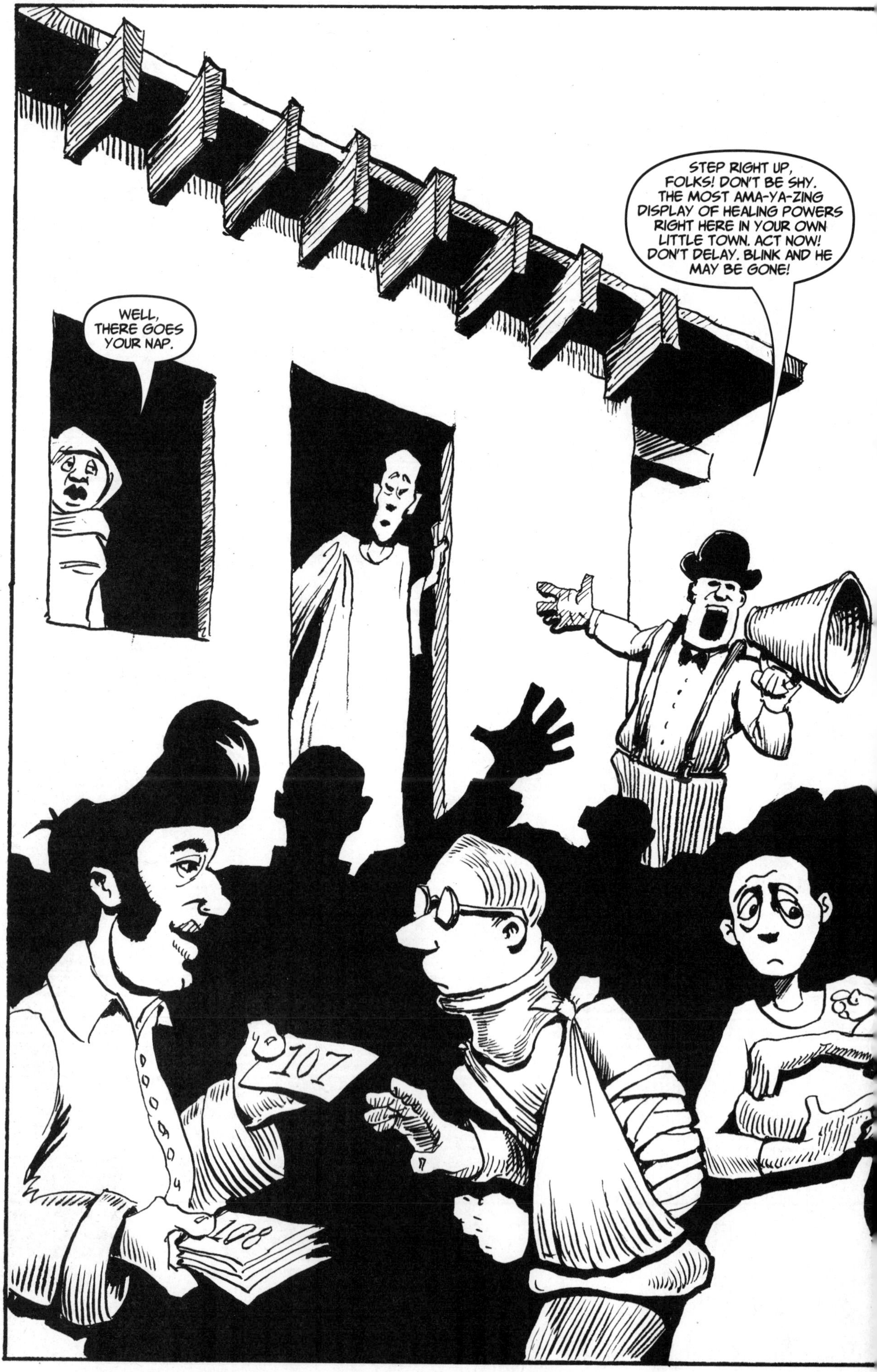
WELL, THERE GOES YOUR NAP.
STEP RIGHT UP, FOLKS! DON'T BE SHY. THE MOST AMA-YA-ZING DISPLAY OF HEALING POWERS RIGHT HERE IN YOUR OWN LITTLE TOWN. ACT NOW! DON'T DELAY. BLINK AND HE MAY BE GONE!
107
108

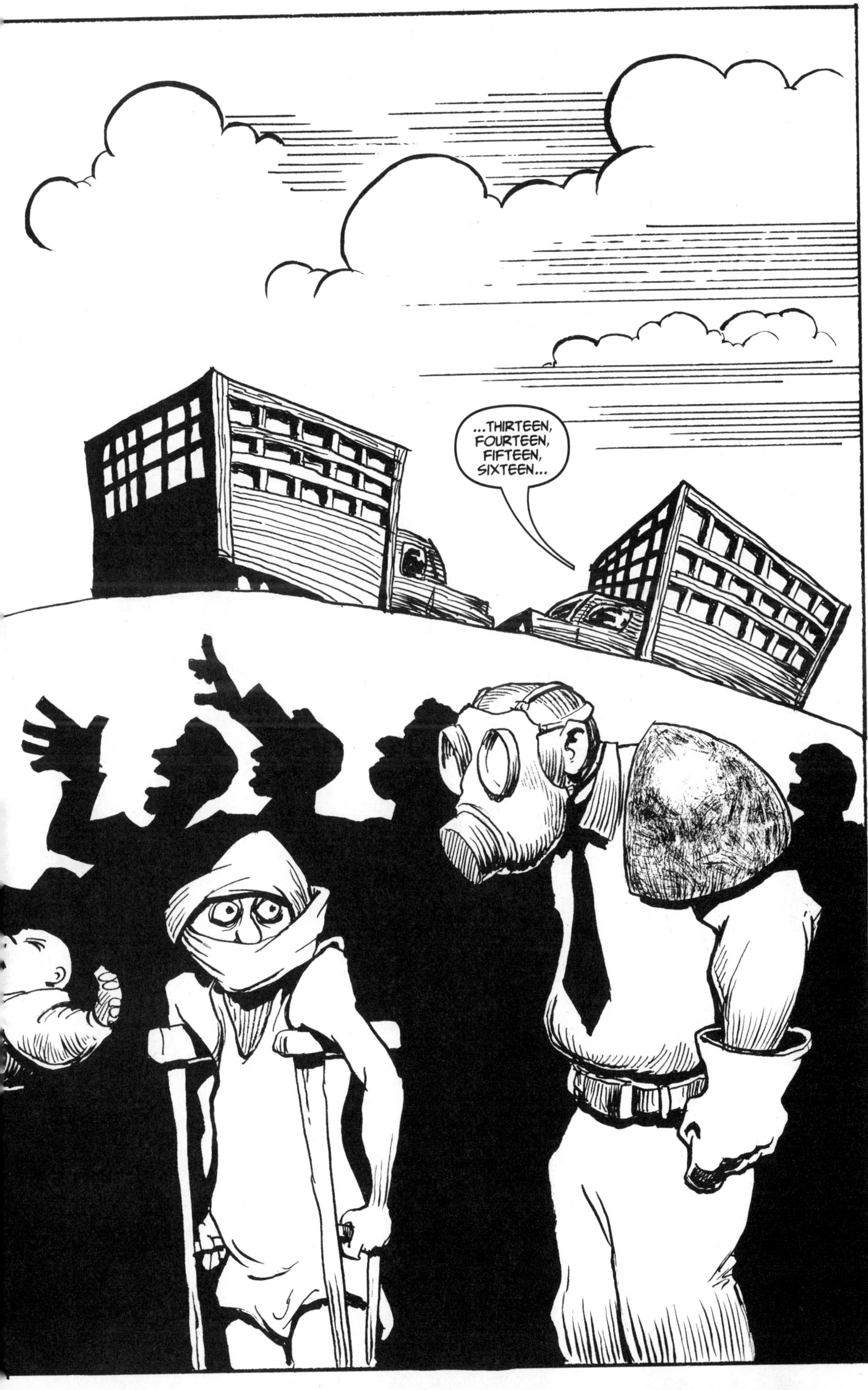
...THIRTEEN, FOURTEEN, FIFTEEN, SIXTEEN...

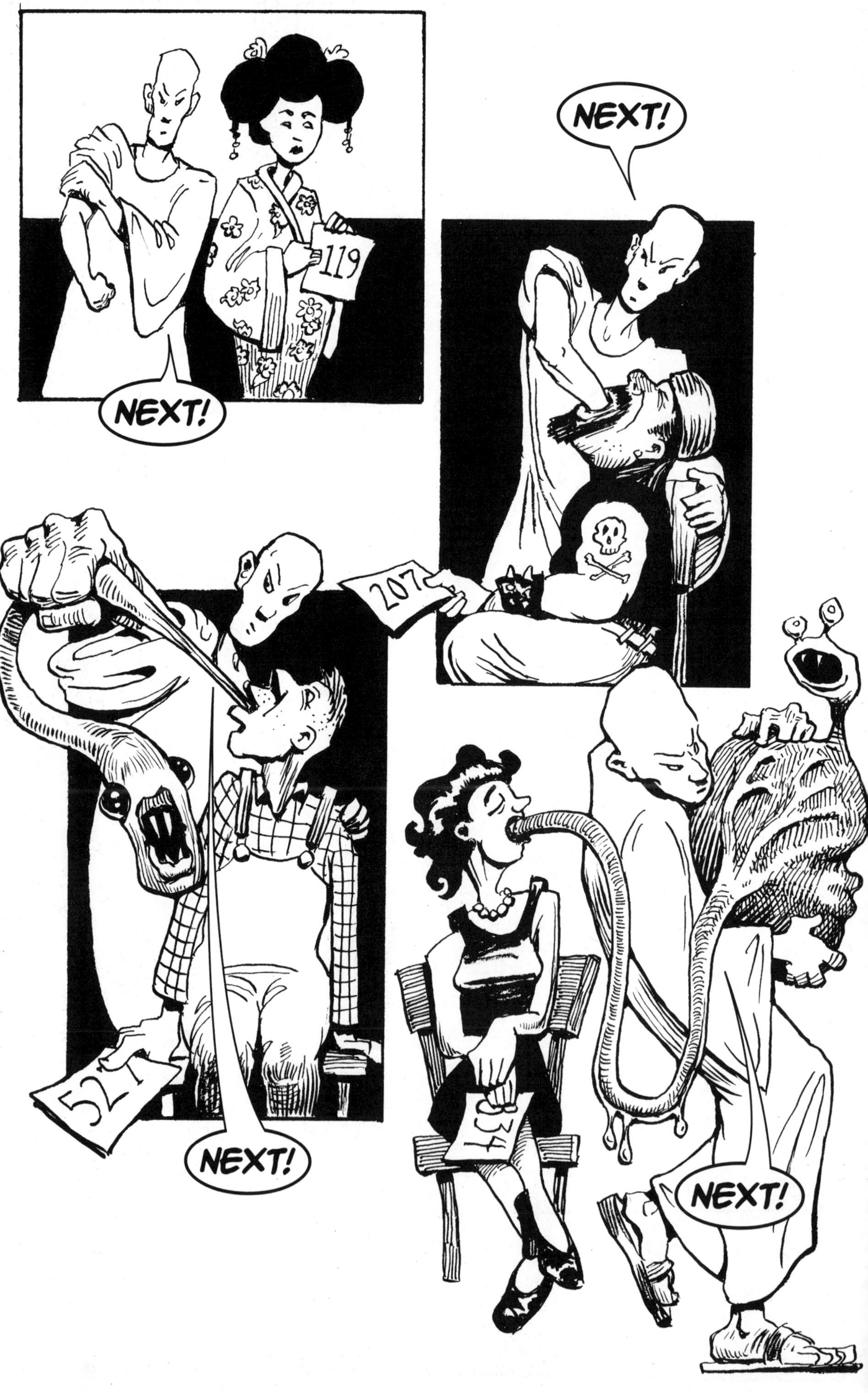

NEXT!
119
NEXT!
207
NEXT!
521
NEXT!
834

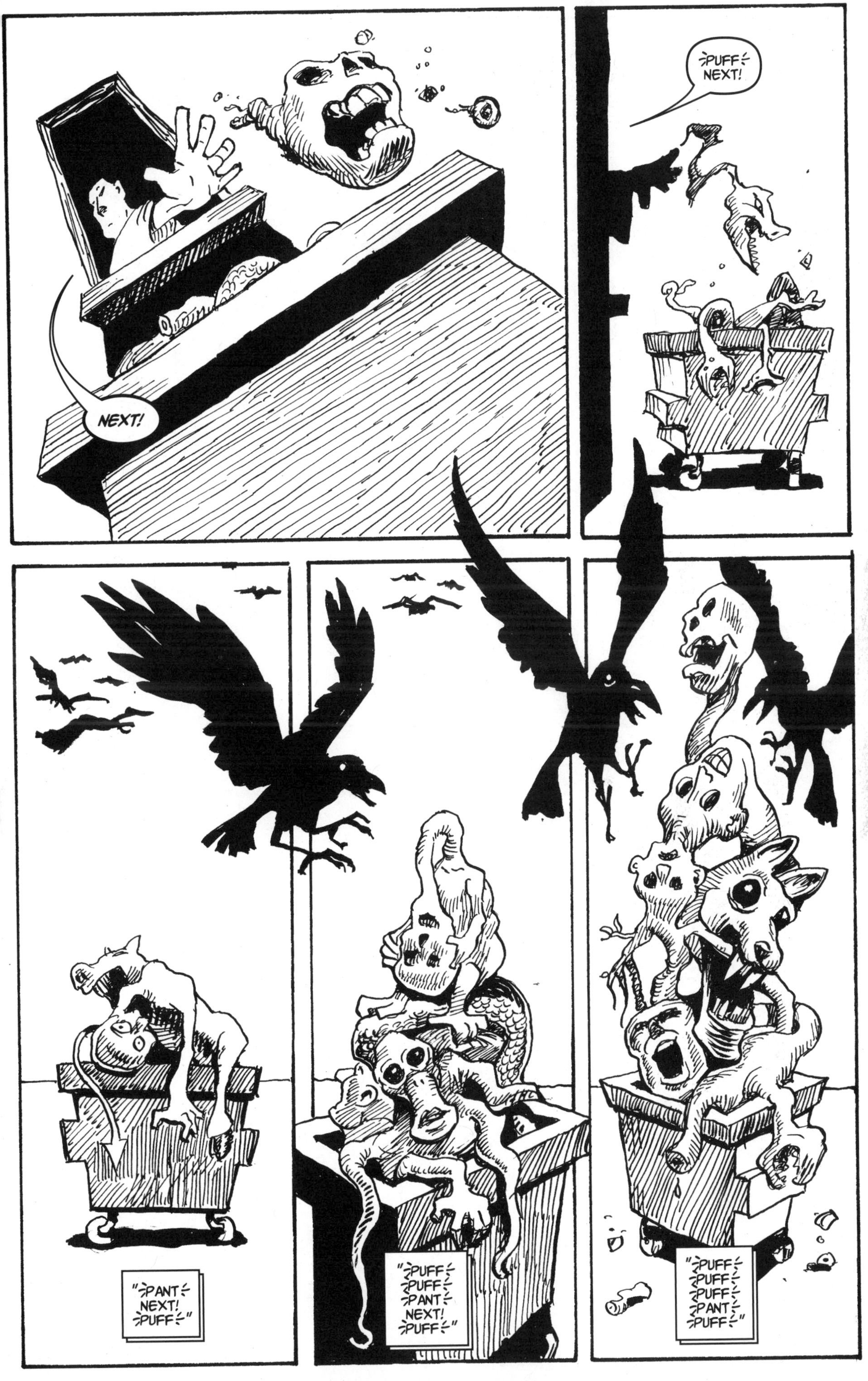
NEXT!
PUFF NEXT!
"PANT NEXT! PUFF"
"PUFF PUFF PANT NEXT! PUFF"
"PUFF PUFF PUFF PANT PUFF"

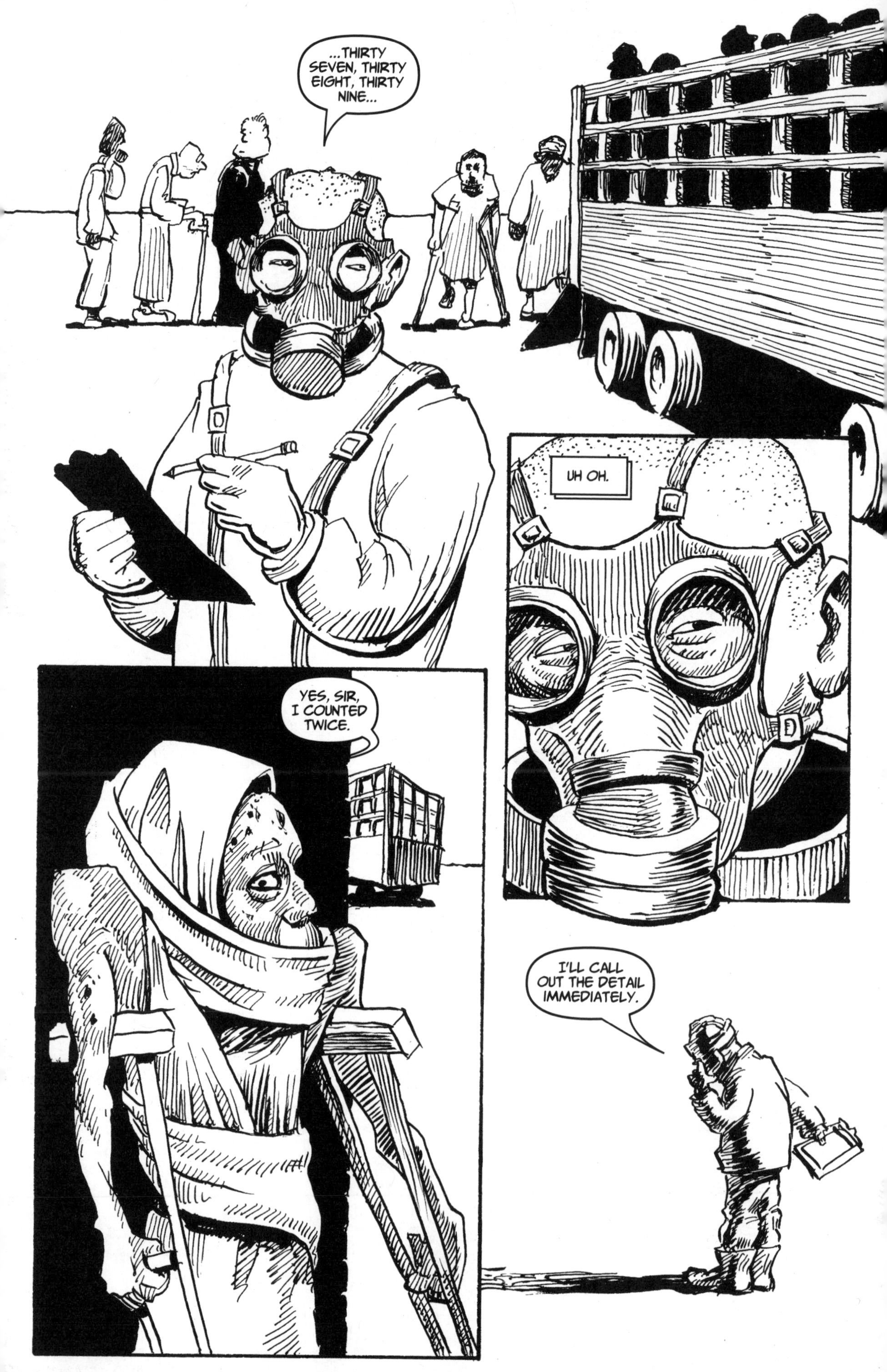
...THIRTY SEVEN, THIRTY EIGHT, THIRTY NINE...
UH OH.
YES, SIR, I COUNTED TWICE.
I'LL CALL OUT THE DETAIL IMMEDIATELY.

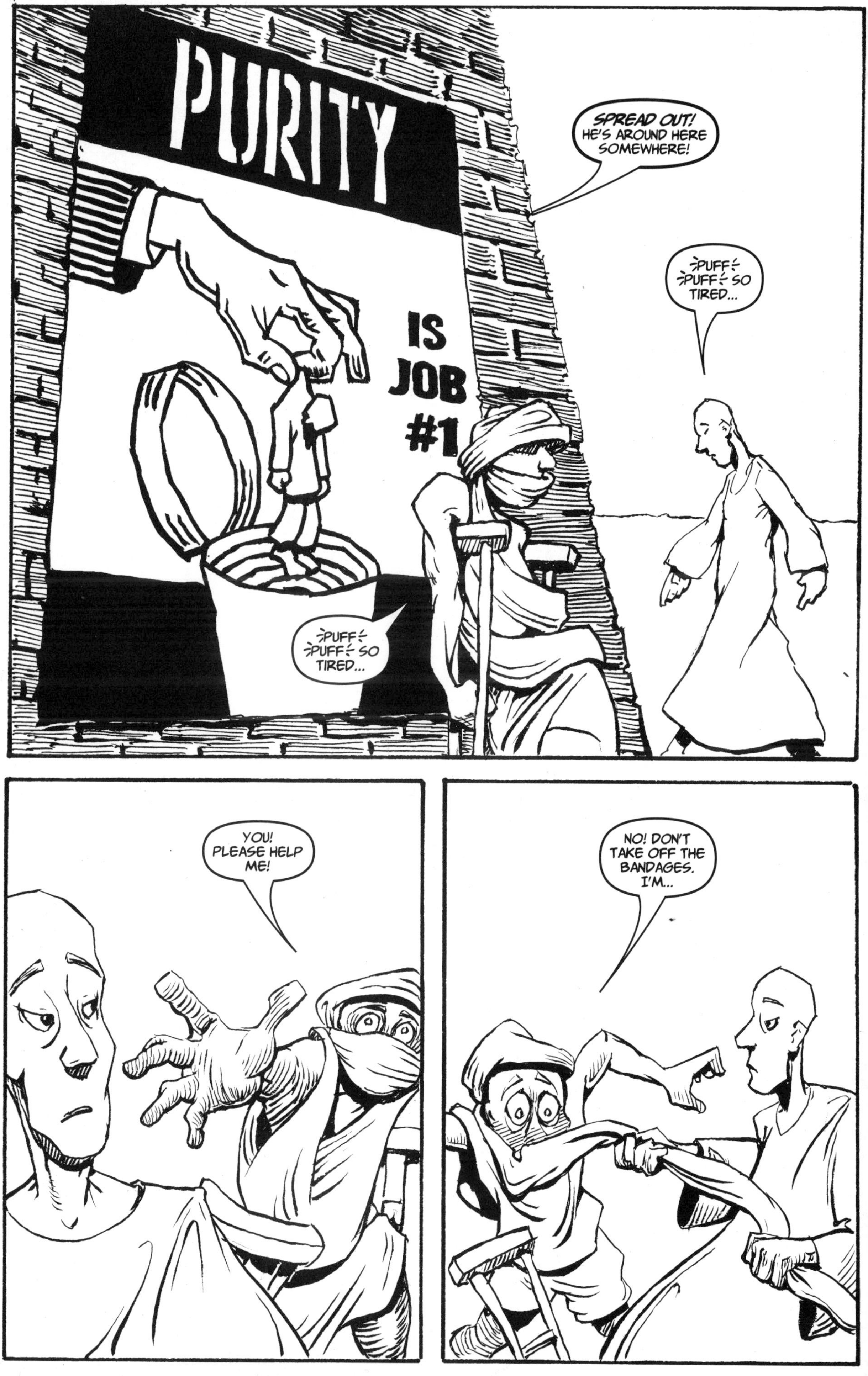
PURITY
IS JOB #1
SPREAD OUT! HE'S AROUND HERE SOMEWHERE!
PUFF PUFF SO TIRED...
PUFF PUFF SO TIRED...
YOU! PLEASE HELP ME!
NO! DON'T TAKE OFF THE BANDAGES. I'M...

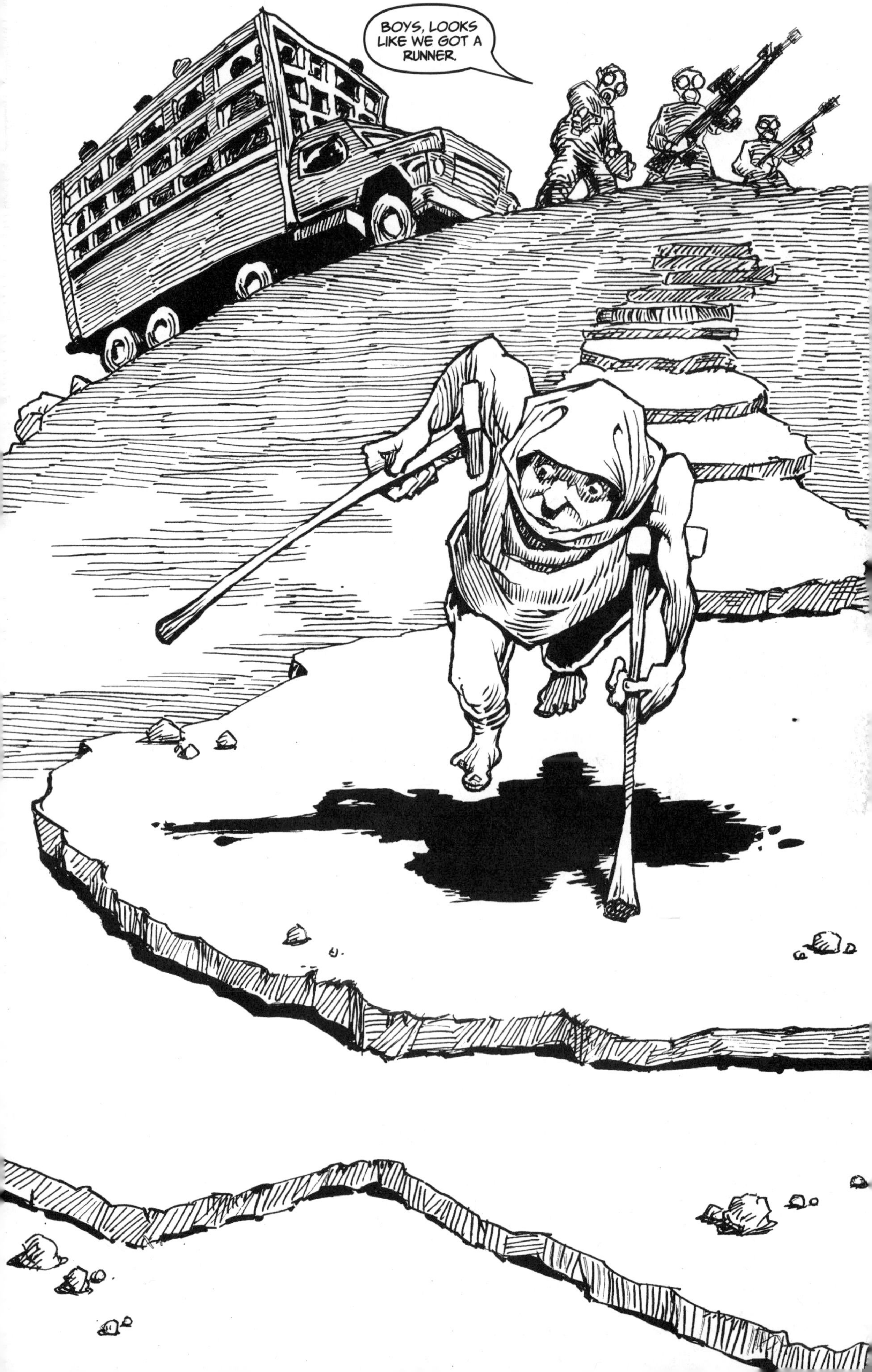
BOYS, LOOKS LIKE WE GOT A RUNNER.

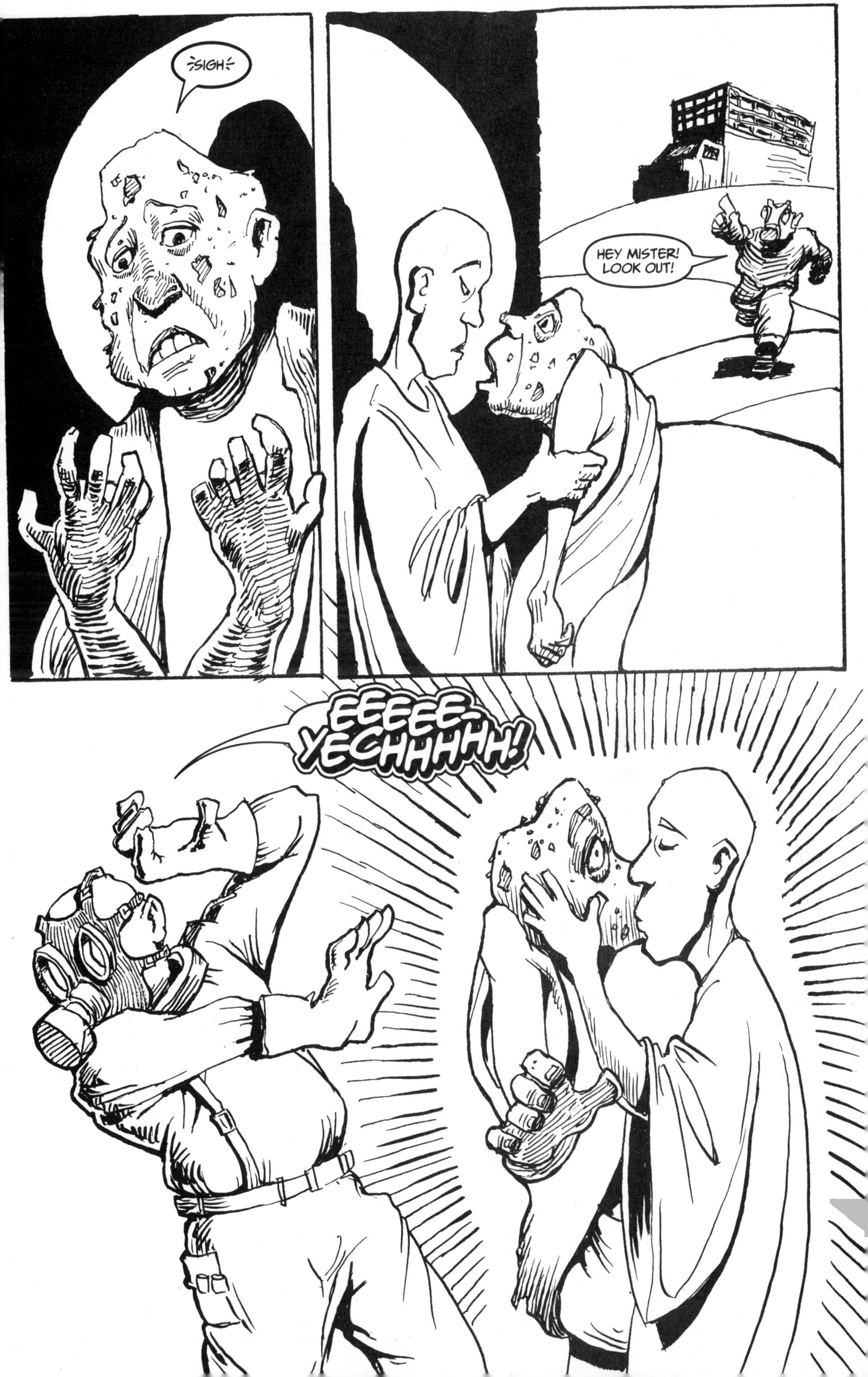
SIGH
HEY MISTER! LOOK OUT!
EEEEEE-YECHHHHH!

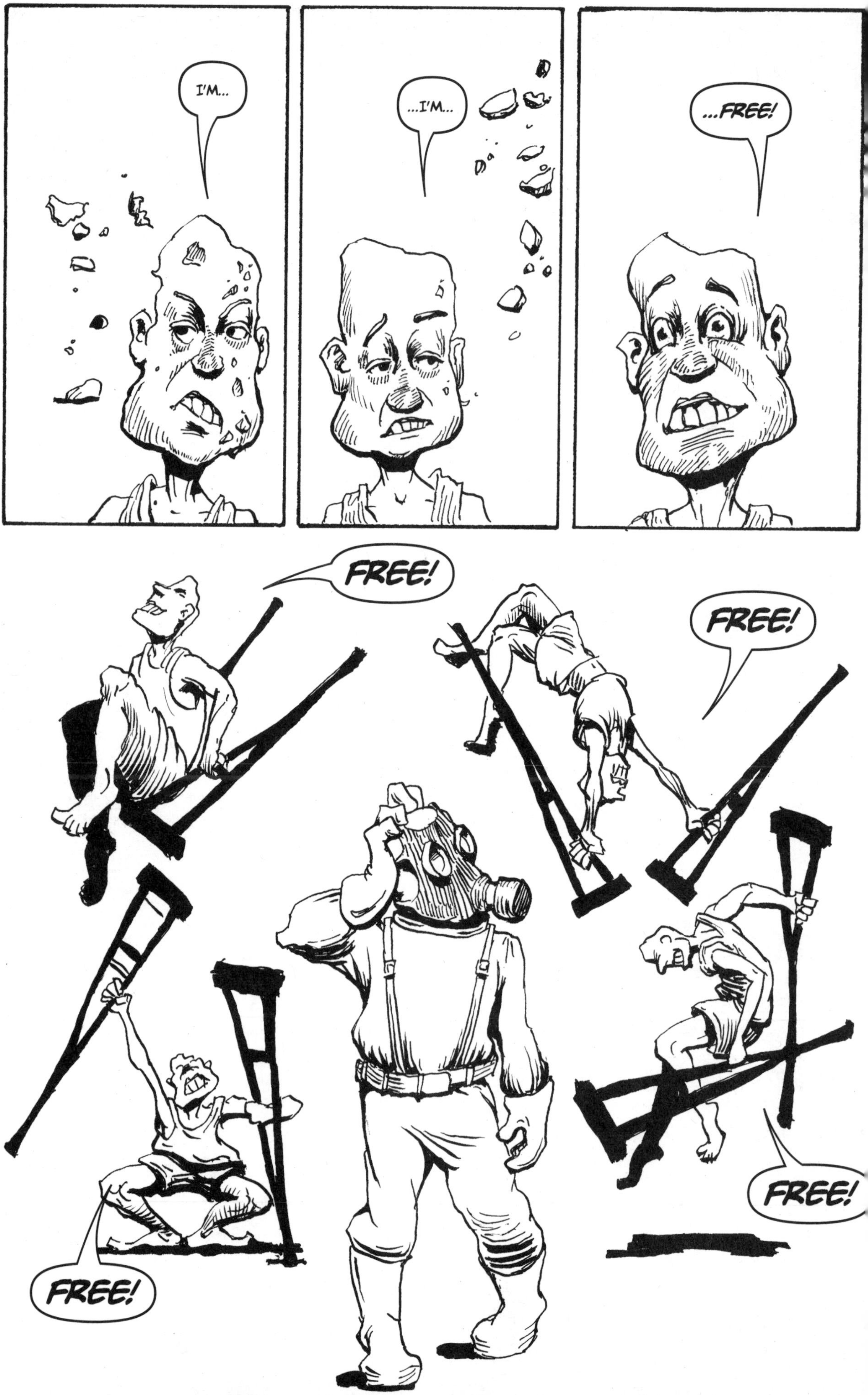
I'M...
...I'M...
...FREE!
FREE!
FREE!
FREE!
FREE!

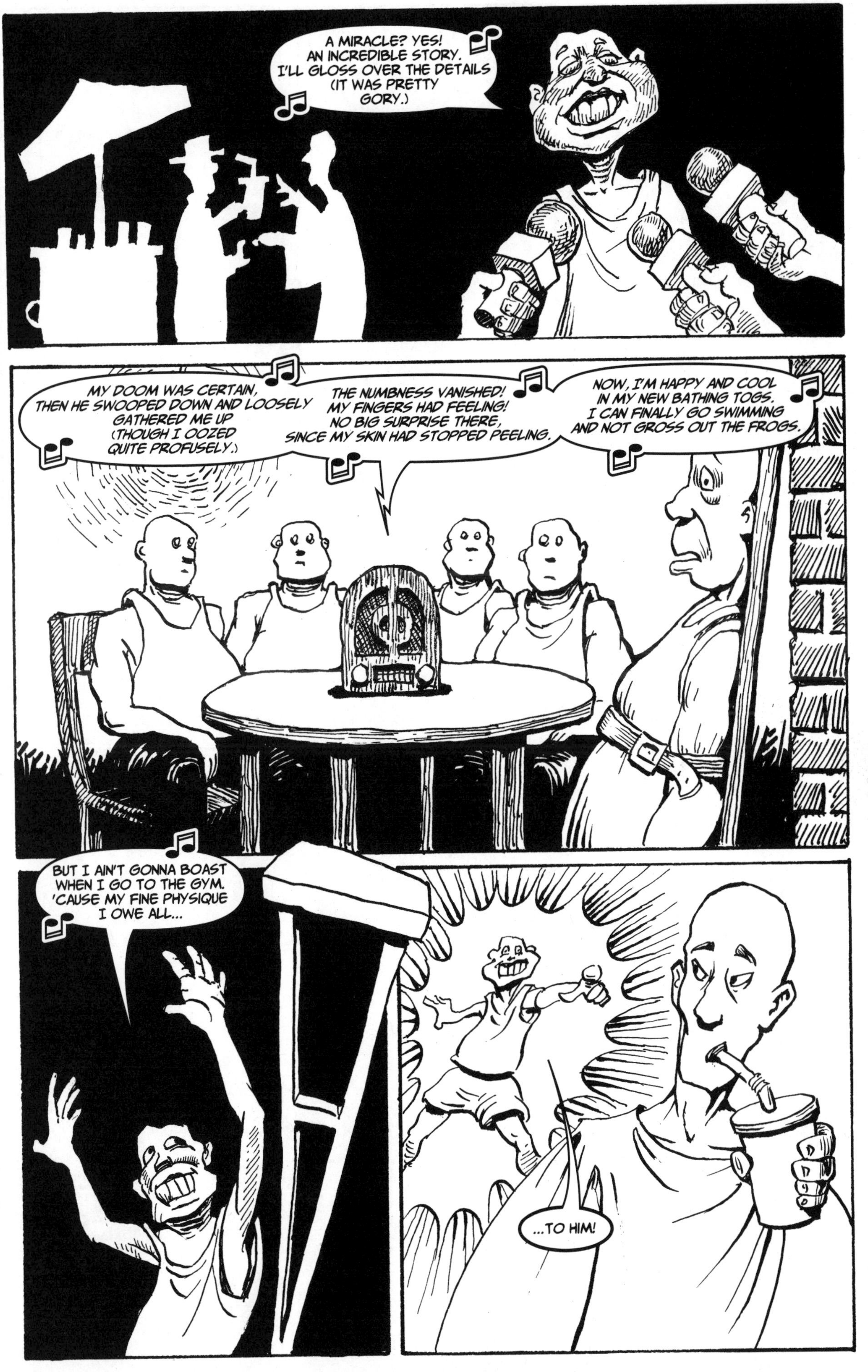
A MIRACLE? YES! AN INCREDIBLE STORY. I'LL GLOSS OVER THE DETAILS (IT WAS PRETTY GORY.)
MY DOOM WAS CERTAIN, THEN HE SWOOPED DOWN AND LOOSELY GATHERED ME UP (THOUGH I OOZED QUITE PROFUSELY.)
THE NUMBNESS VANISHED! MY FINGERS HAD FEELING! NO BIG SURPRISE THERE, SINCE MY SKIN HAD STOPPED PEELING.
NOW, I'M HAPPY AND COOL IN MY NEW BATHING TOGS. I CAN FINALLY GO SWIMMING AND NOT GROSS OUT THE FROGS.
BUT I AIN'T GONNA BOAST WHEN I GO TO THE GYM. 'CAUSE MY FINE PHYSIQUE I OWE ALL...
...TO HIM!

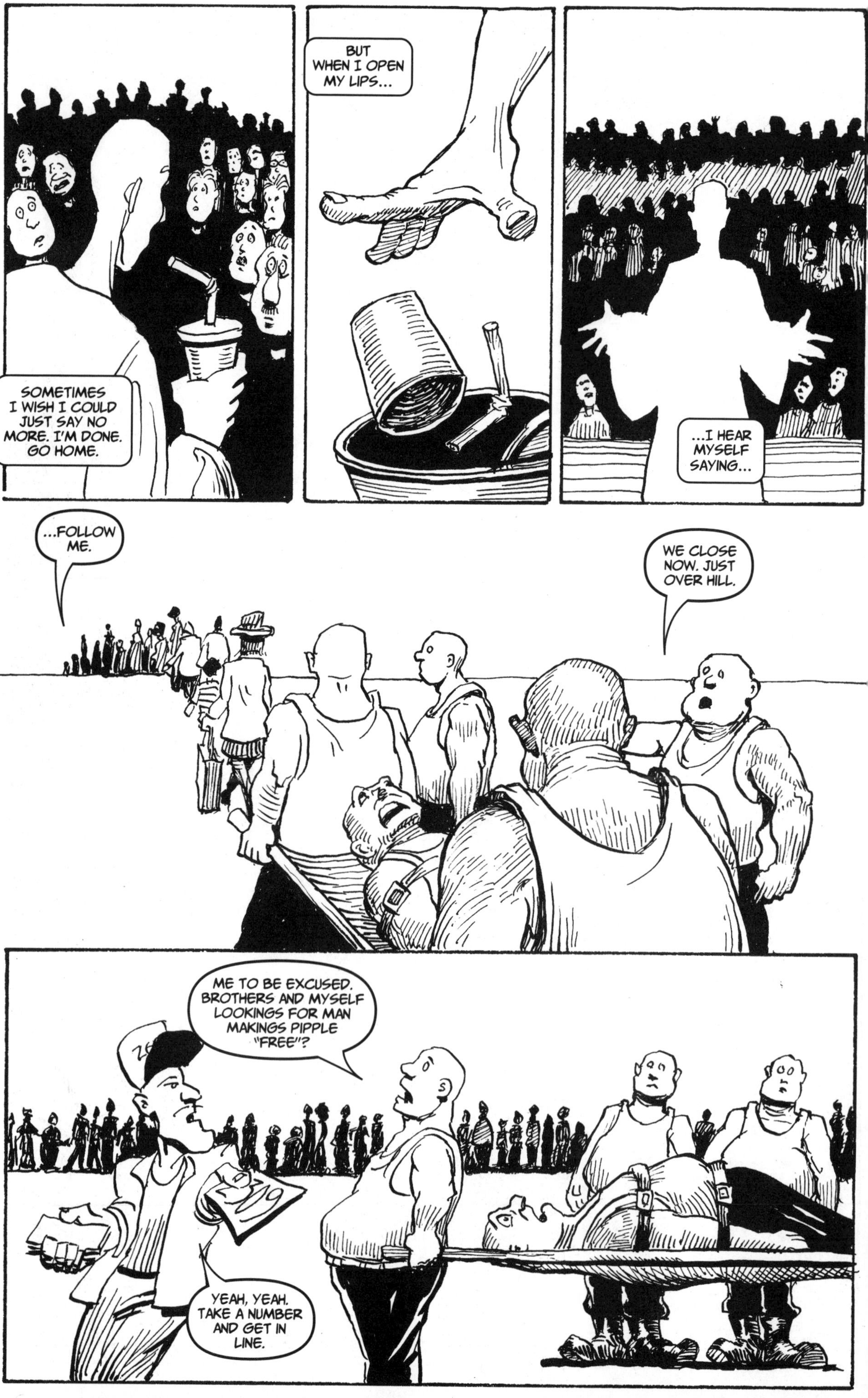
SOMETIMES I WISH I COULD JUST SAY NO MORE. I'M DONE. GO HOME.
BUT WHEN I OPEN MY LIPS...
...I HEAR MYSELF SAYING...
...FOLLOW ME.
WE CLOSE NOW. JUST OVER HILL.
ME TO BE EXCUSED. BROTHERS AND MYSELF LOOKINGS FOR MAN MAKINGS PIPPLE "FREE"?
YEAH, YEAH. TAKE A NUMBER AND GET IN LINE.

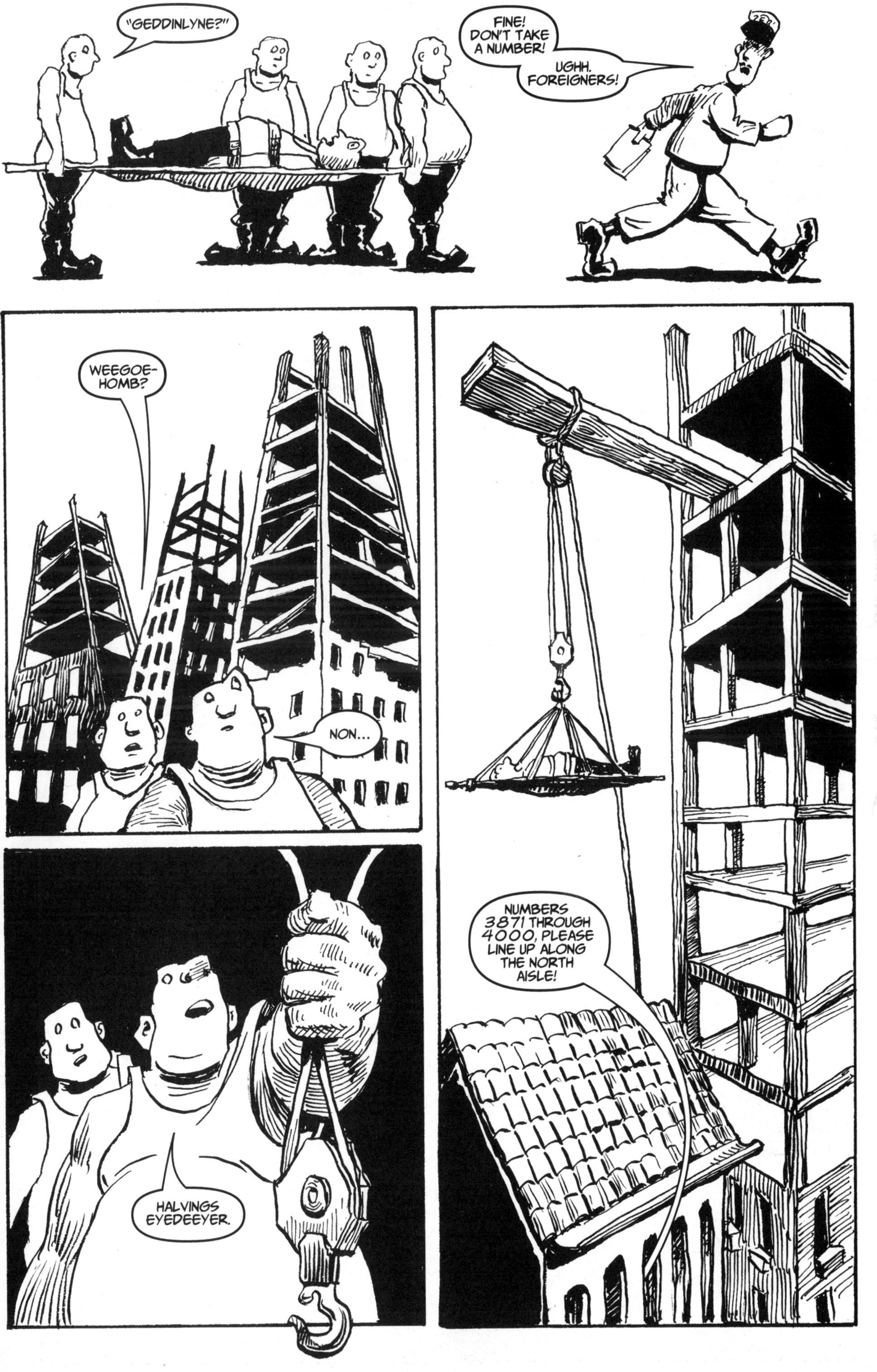
"GEDDINLYNE?"
FINE! DON'T TAKE A NUMBER!
UGHH. FOREIGNERS!
WEEGOE-HOMB?
NON...
HALVINGS EYEDEEYER.
NUMBERS 3871 THROUGH 4000, PLEASE LINE UP ALONG THE NORTH AISLE!

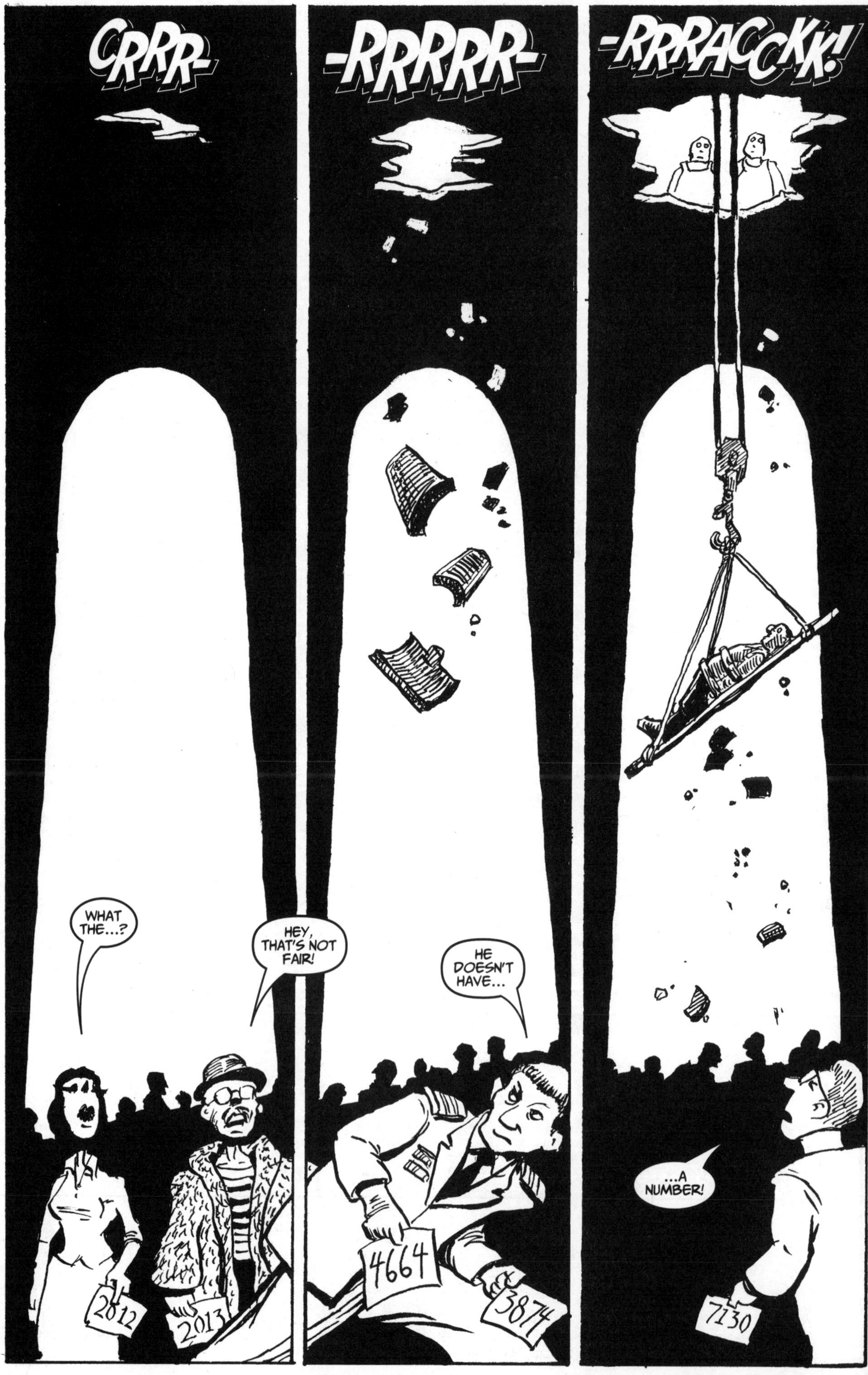
CRRR-
WHAT THE...?
HEY, THAT'S NOT FAIR!
2012
2013
-RRRRR-
HE DOESN'T HAVE...
4664
3874
-RRRACCKK!
...A NUMBER!
7130

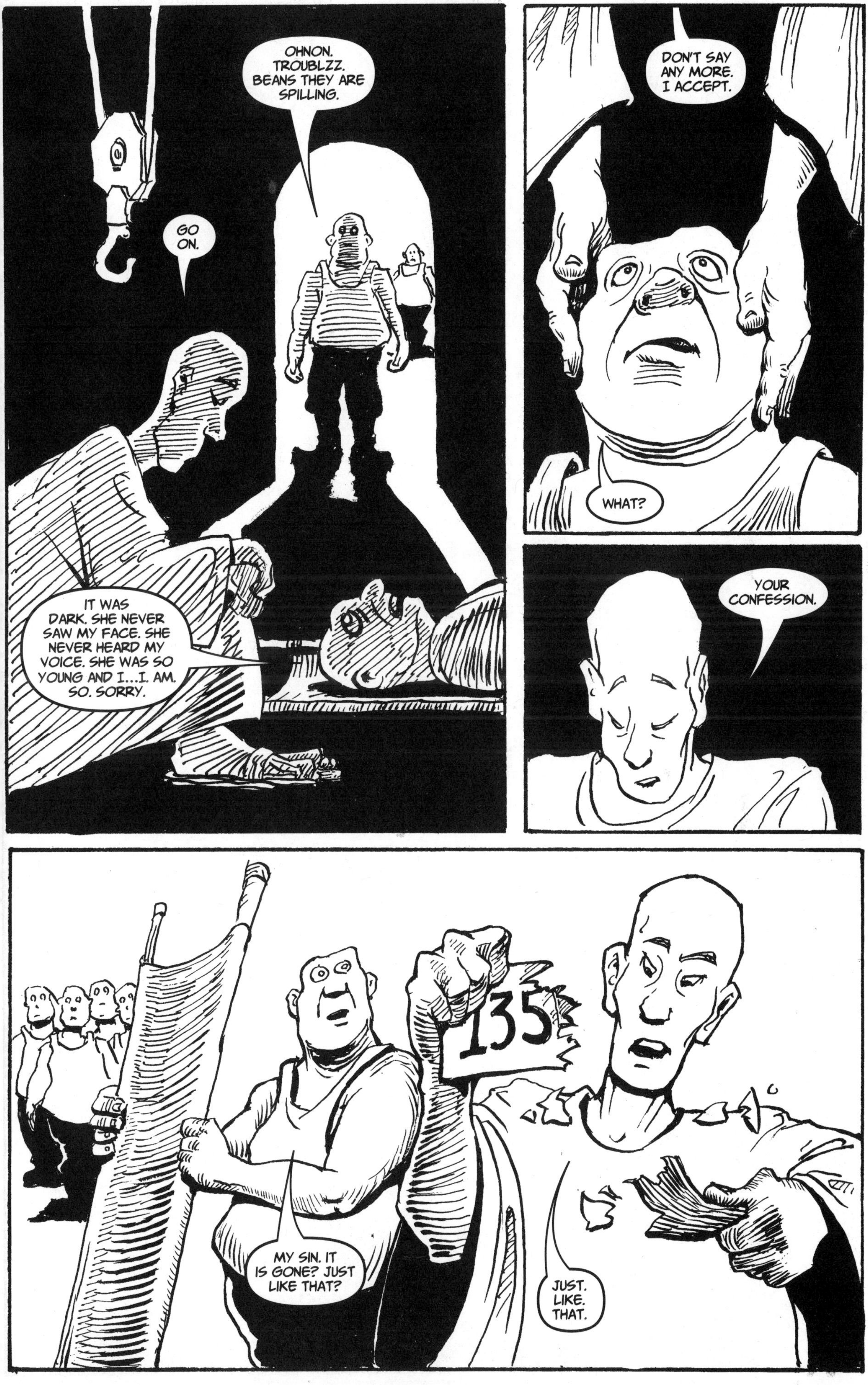
OHNON. TROUBLZZ. BEANS THEY ARE SPILLING.
GO ON.
IT WAS DARK. SHE NEVER SAW MY FACE. SHE NEVER HEARD MY VOICE. SHE WAS SO YOUNG AND I...I. AM. SO. SORRY.
DON'T SAY ANY MORE. I ACCEPT.
WHAT?
YOUR CONFESSION.
135
MY SIN. IT IS GONE? JUST LIKE THAT?
JUST. LIKE. THAT.

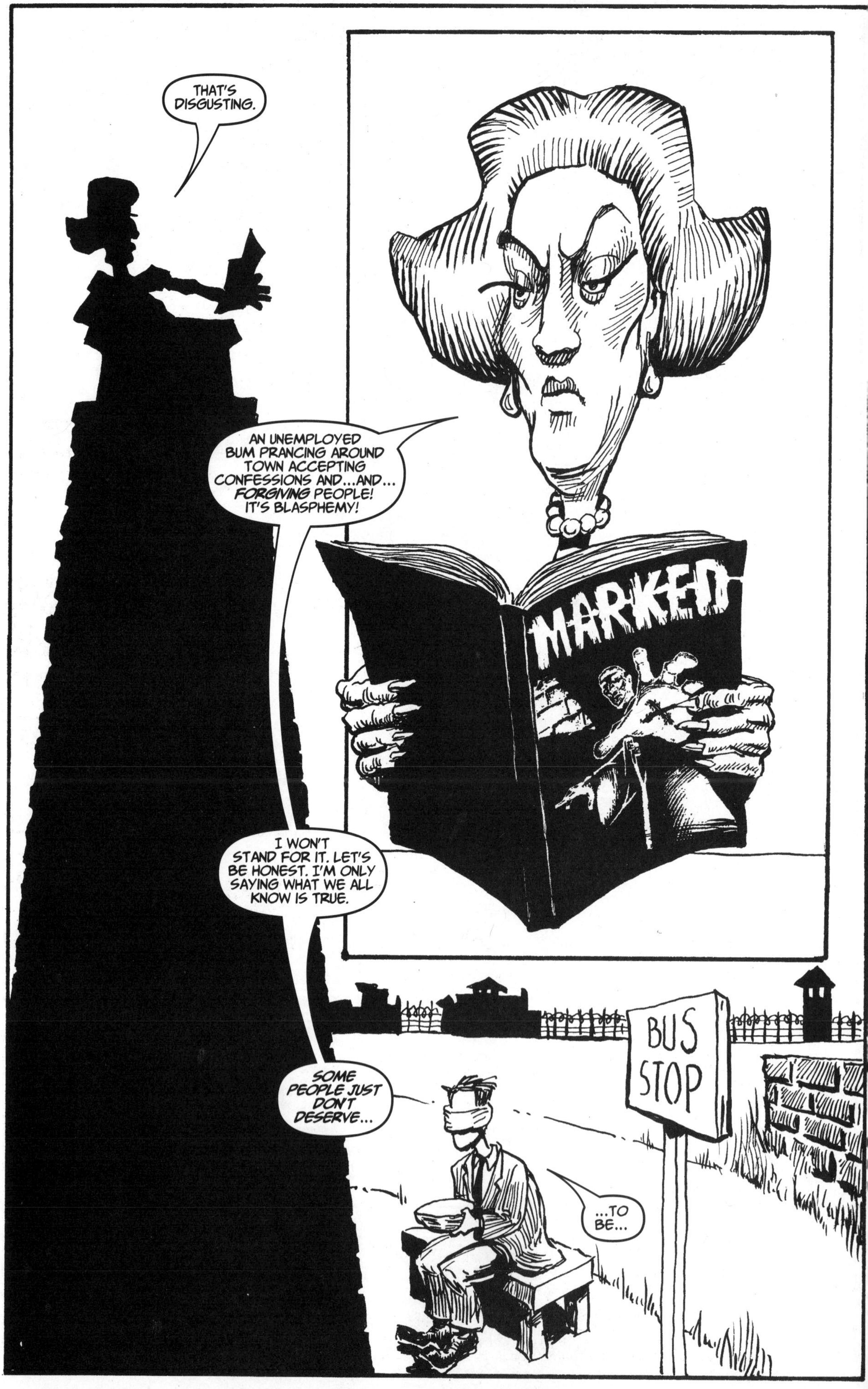
THAT'S DISGUSTING.
AN UNEMPLOYED BUM PRANCING AROUND TOWN ACCEPTING CONFESSIONS AND...AND... FORGIVING PEOPLE! IT'S BLASPHEMY!
MARKED
I WON'T STAND FOR IT. LET'S BE HONEST. I'M ONLY SAYING WHAT WE ALL KNOW IS TRUE.
BUS STOP
SOME PEOPLE JUST DON'T DESERVE...
...TO BE...

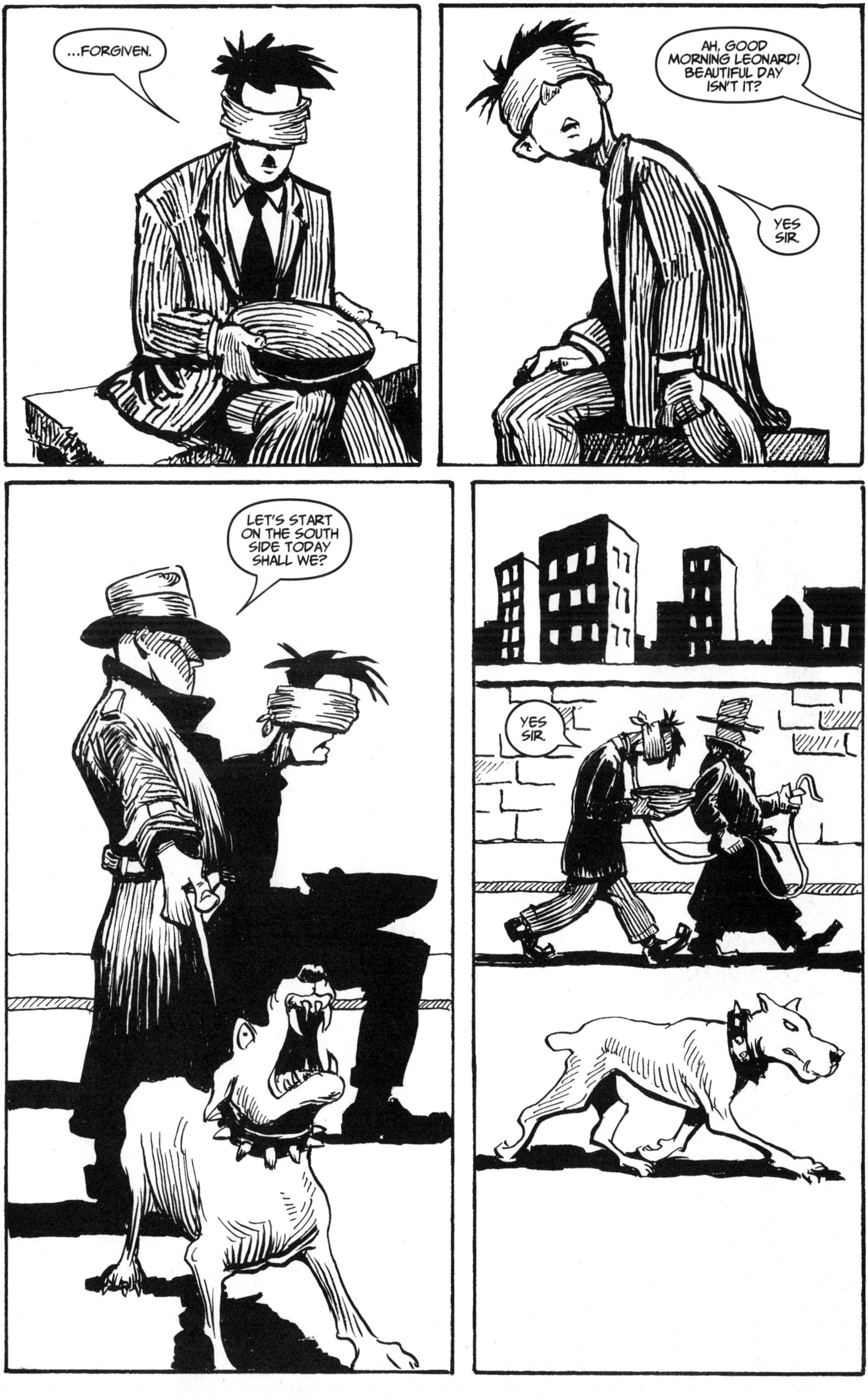
...FORGIVEN.
AH, GOOD MORNING LEONARD! BEAUTIFUL DAY ISN'T IT?
YES SIR.
LET'S START ON THE SOUTH SIDE TODAY SHALL WE?
YES SIR.

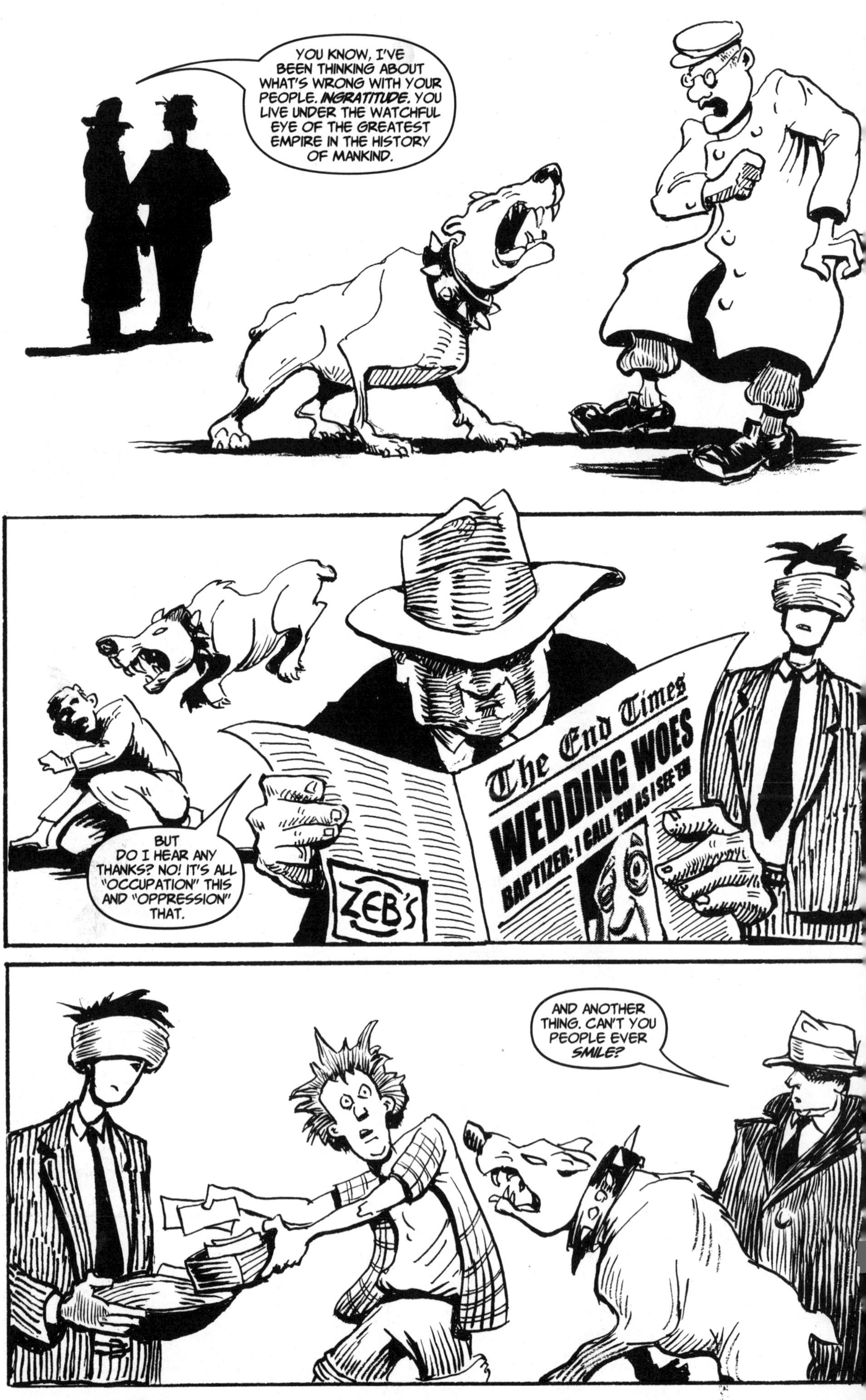
YOU KNOW, I'VE BEEN THINKING ABOUT WHAT'S WRONG WITH YOUR PEOPLE. *INGRATITUDE.* YOU LIVE UNDER THE WATCHFUL EYE OF THE GREATEST EMPIRE IN THE HISTORY OF MANKIND.
The End Times
WEDDING WOES
BAPTIZER: I CALL 'EM AS I SEE 'EM
ZEB'S
BUT DO I HEAR ANY THANKS? NO! IT'S ALL "OCCUPATION" THIS AND "OPPRESSION" THAT.
AND ANOTHER THING. CAN'T YOU PEOPLE EVER *SMILE?*

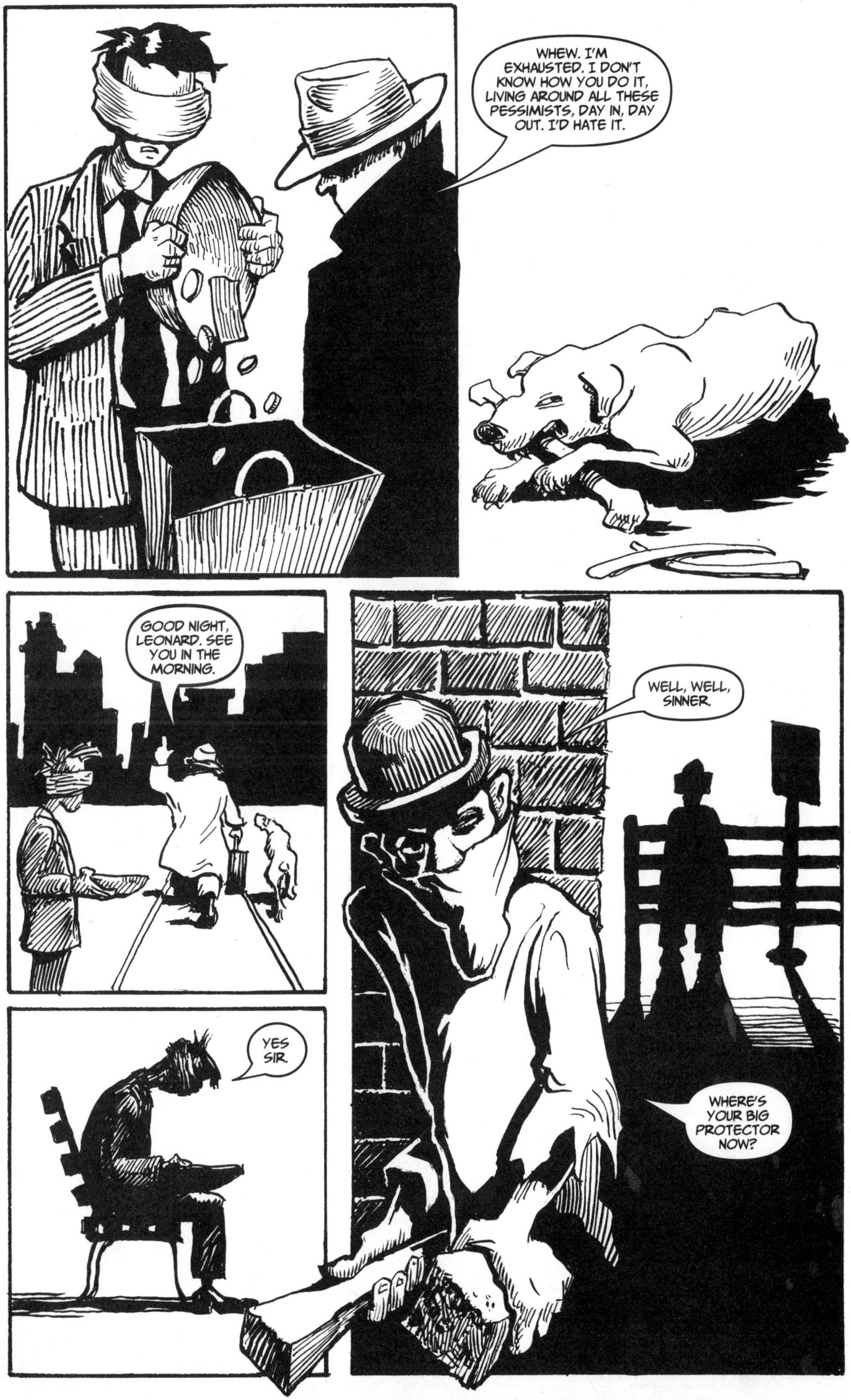
WHEW. I'M EXHAUSTED. I DON'T KNOW HOW YOU DO IT, LIVING AROUND ALL THESE PESSIMISTS, DAY IN, DAY OUT. I'D HATE IT.
GOOD NIGHT, LEONARD. SEE YOU IN THE MORNING.
YES SIR.
WELL, WELL, SINNER.
WHERE'S YOUR BIG PROTECTOR NOW?

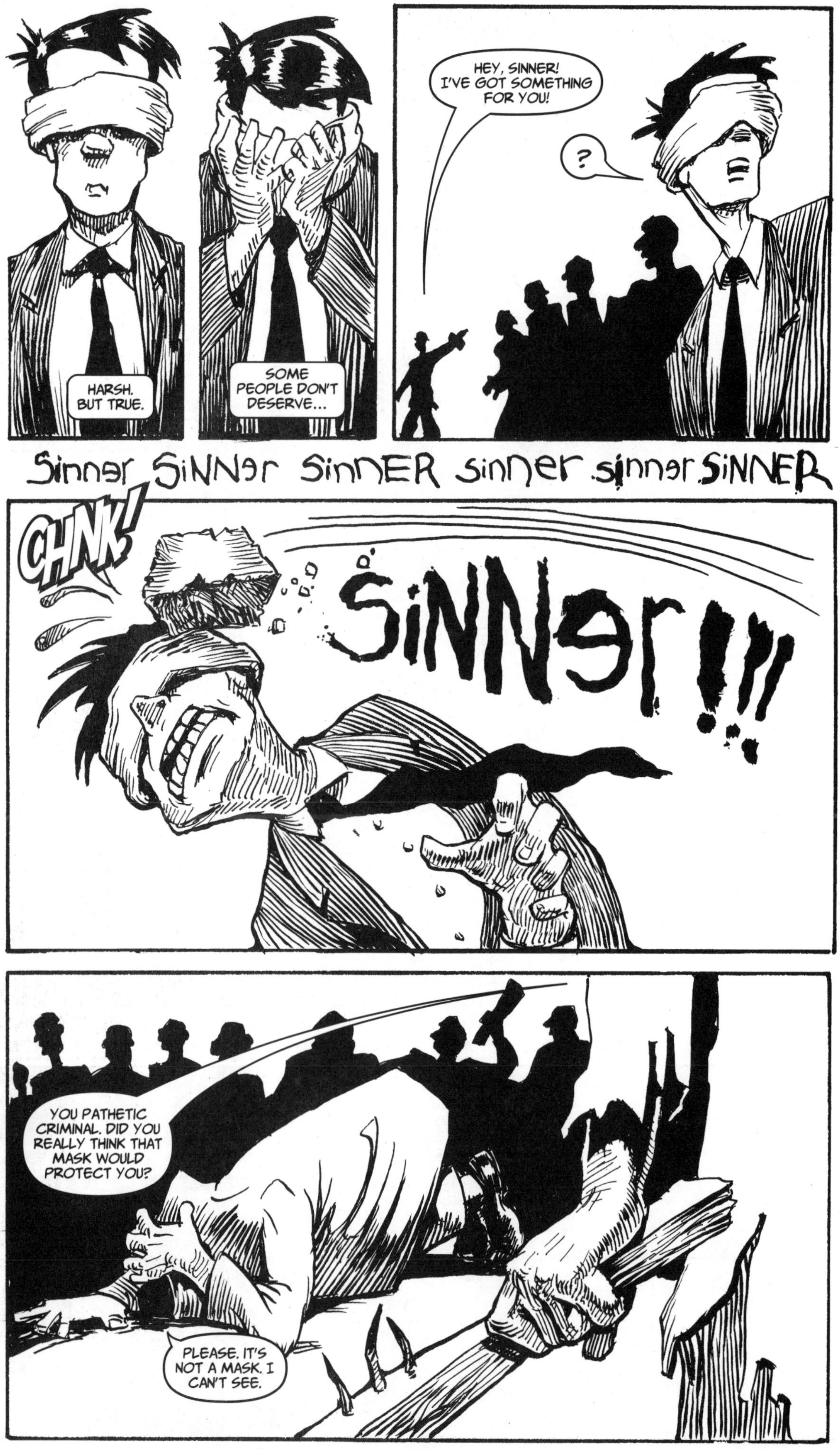
HARSH. BUT TRUE.
SOME PEOPLE DON'T DESERVE...
HEY, SINNER! I'VE GOT SOMETHING FOR YOU!
?
Sinner SiNNer SinnER sinner sinner SiNNER
CHNK!
SiNNer!!!
YOU PATHETIC CRIMINAL. DID YOU REALLY THINK THAT MASK WOULD PROTECT YOU?
PLEASE. IT'S NOT A MASK. I CAN'T SEE.

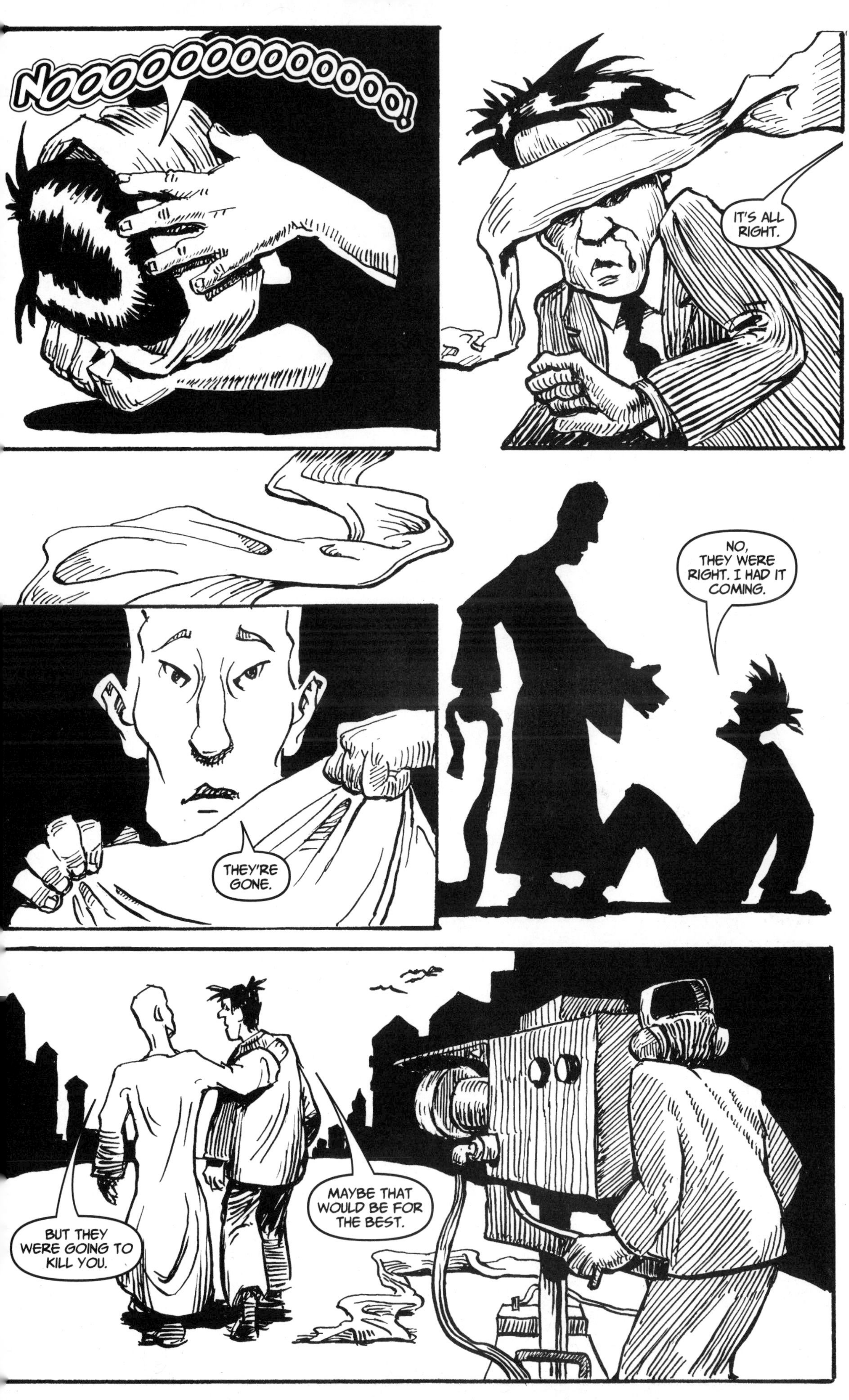
Noooooooooooooo!
IT'S ALL RIGHT.
THEY'RE GONE.
NO, THEY WERE RIGHT. I HAD IT COMING.
BUT THEY WERE GOING TO KILL YOU.
MAYBE THAT WOULD BE FOR THE BEST.

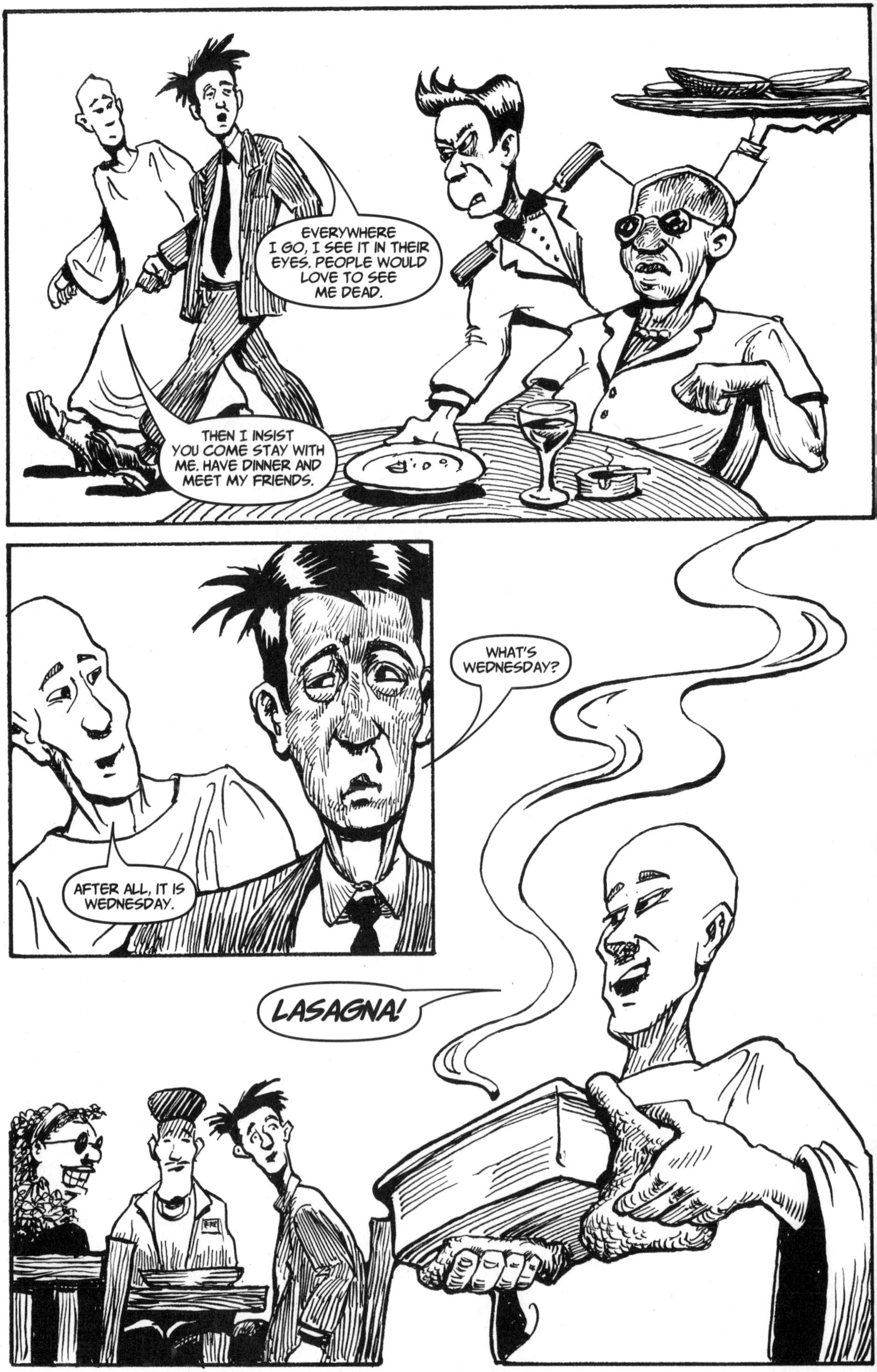
EVERYWHERE I GO, I SEE IT IN THEIR EYES. PEOPLE WOULD LOVE TO SEE ME DEAD.
THEN I INSIST YOU COME STAY WITH ME. HAVE DINNER AND MEET MY FRIENDS.
AFTER ALL, IT IS WEDNESDAY.
WHAT'S WEDNESDAY?
LASAGNA!

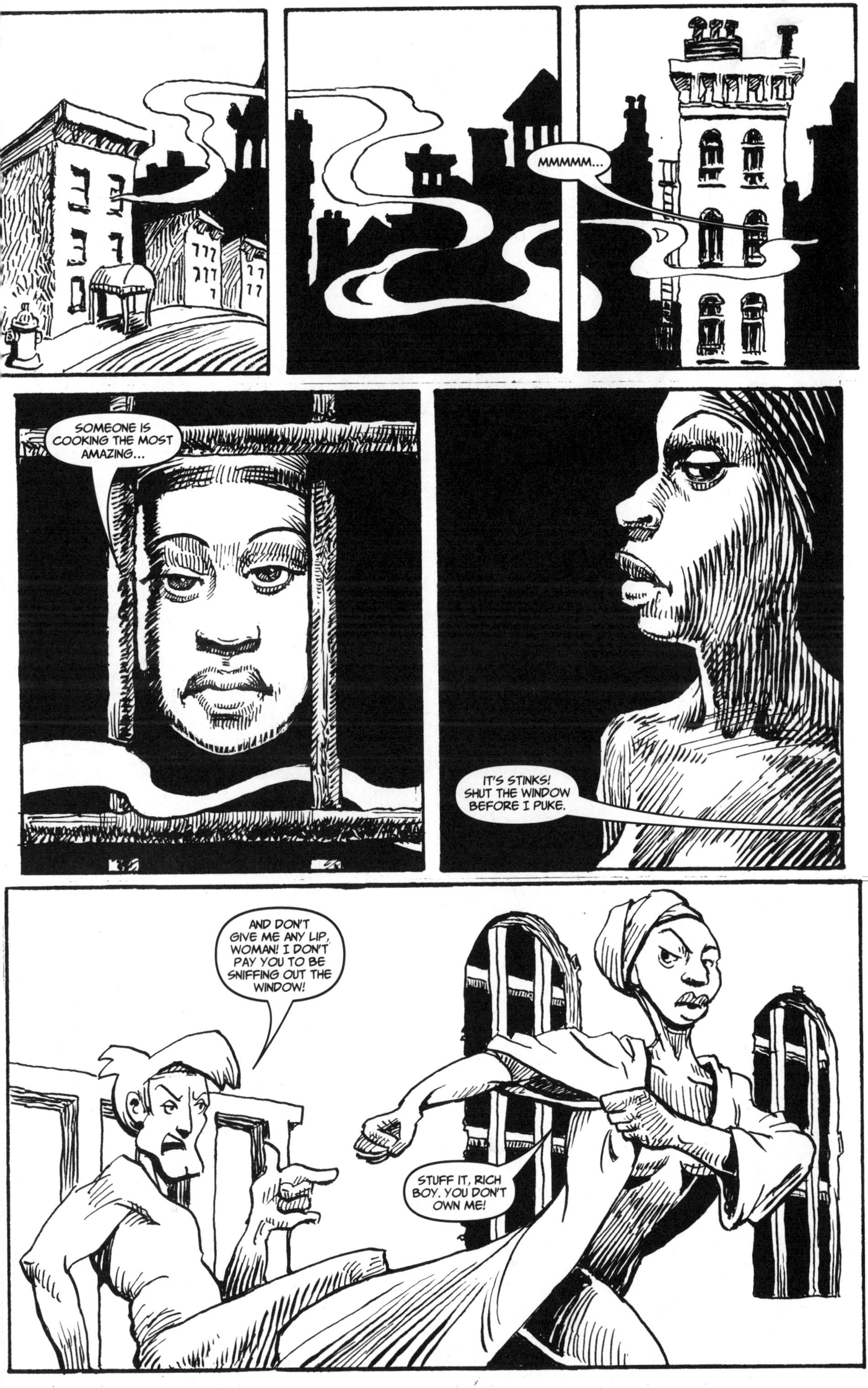
MMMMM...
SOMEONE IS COOKING THE MOST AMAZING...
IT'S STINKS! SHUT THE WINDOW BEFORE I PUKE.
AND DON'T GIVE ME ANY LIP, WOMAN! I DON'T PAY YOU TO BE SNIFFING OUT THE WINDOW!
STUFF IT, RICH BOY. YOU DON'T OWN ME!

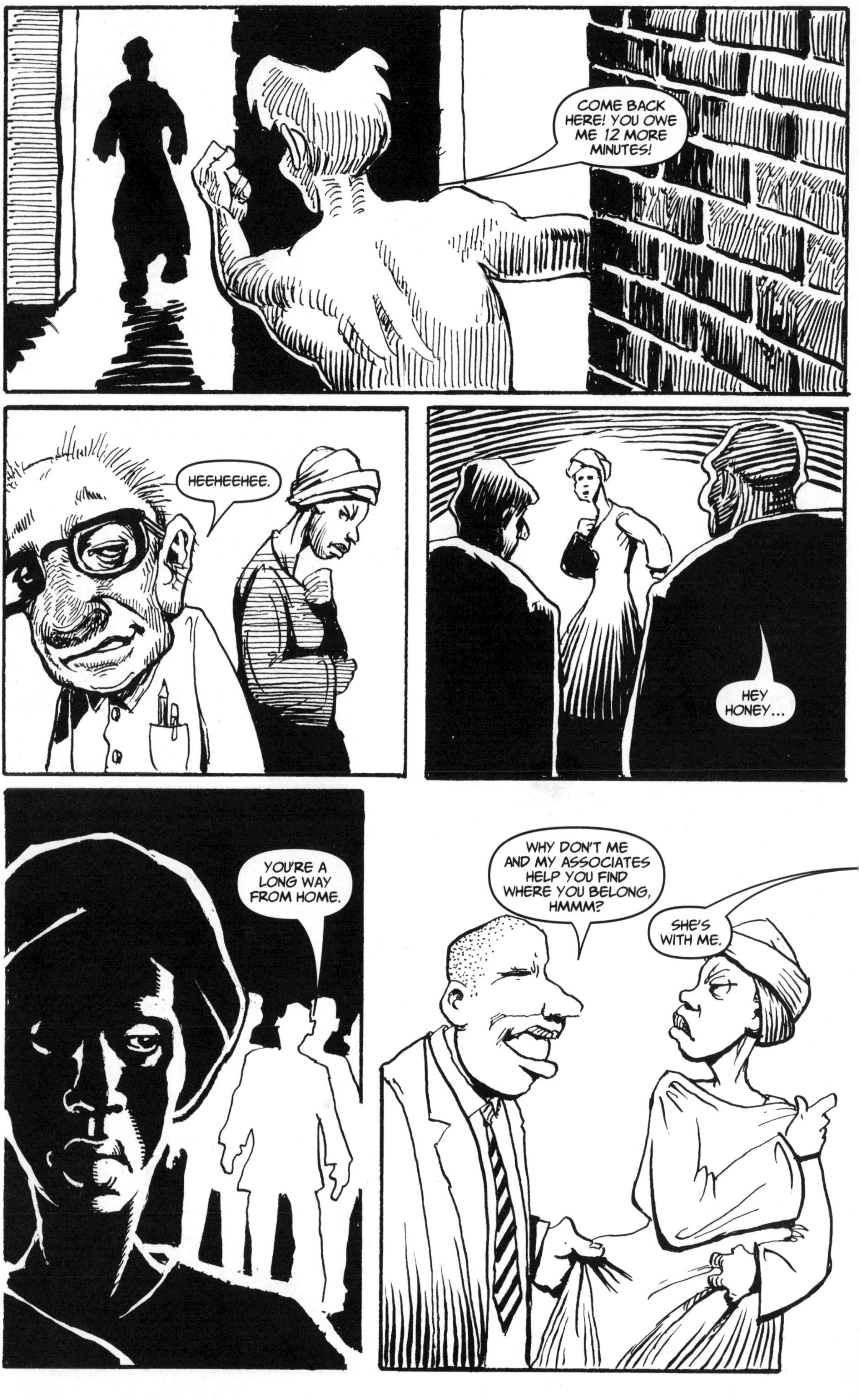
COME BACK HERE! YOU OWE ME 12 MORE MINUTES!
HEEHEEHEE.
HEY HONEY...
YOU'RE A LONG WAY FROM HOME.
WHY DON'T ME AND MY ASSOCIATES HELP YOU FIND WHERE YOU BELONG, HMMM?
SHE'S WITH ME.

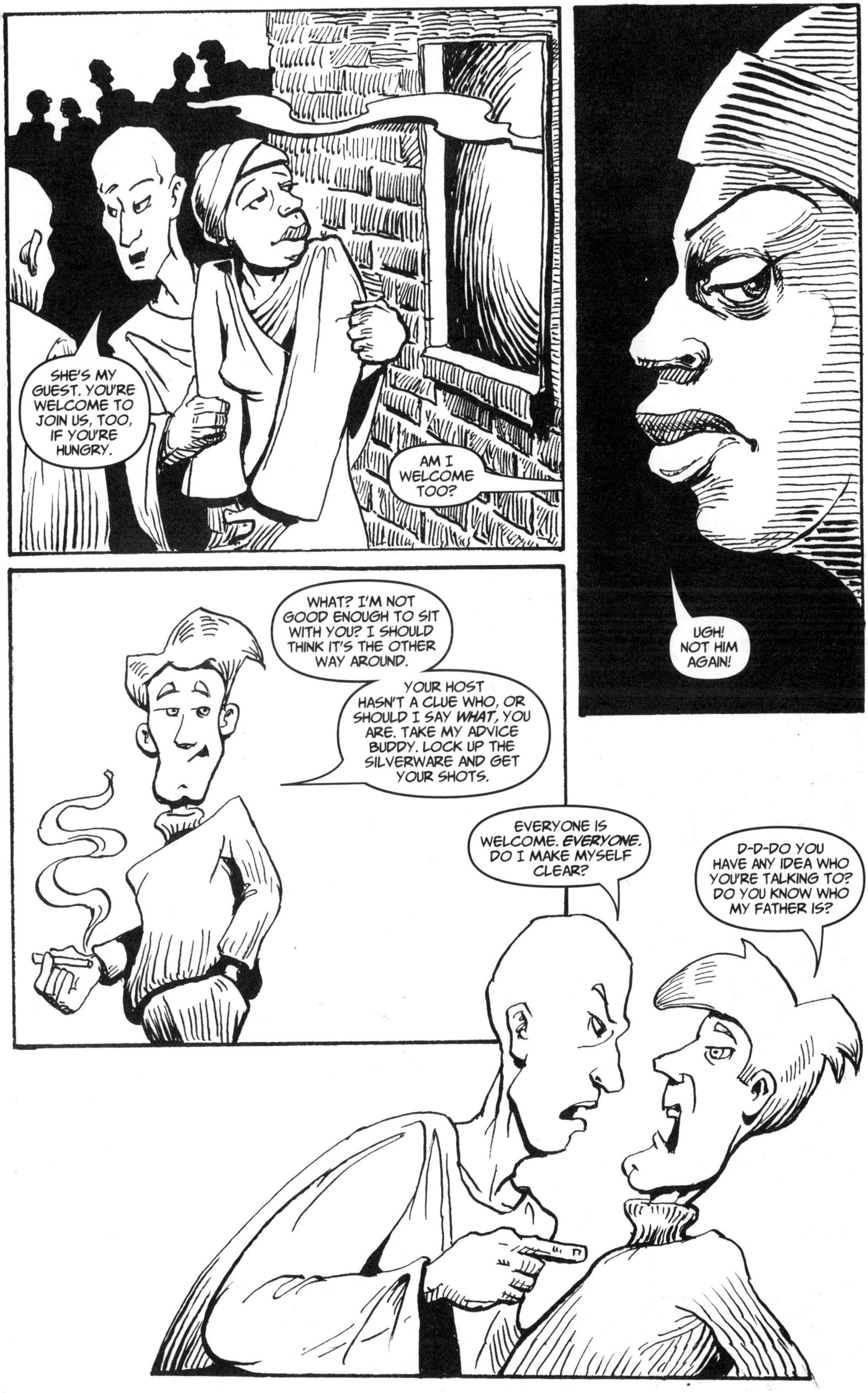
SHE'S MY GUEST. YOU'RE WELCOME TO JOIN US, TOO, IF YOU'RE HUNGRY.
AM I WELCOME TOO?
UGH! NOT HIM AGAIN!
WHAT? I'M NOT GOOD ENOUGH TO SIT WITH YOU? I SHOULD THINK IT'S THE OTHER WAY AROUND.
YOUR HOST HASN'T A CLUE WHO, OR SHOULD I SAY *WHAT*, YOU ARE. TAKE MY ADVICE BUDDY. LOCK UP THE SILVERWARE AND GET YOUR SHOTS.
EVERYONE IS WELCOME. *EVERYONE.* DO I MAKE MYSELF CLEAR?
D-D-DO YOU HAVE ANY IDEA WHO YOU'RE TALKING TO? DO YOU KNOW WHO MY FATHER IS?

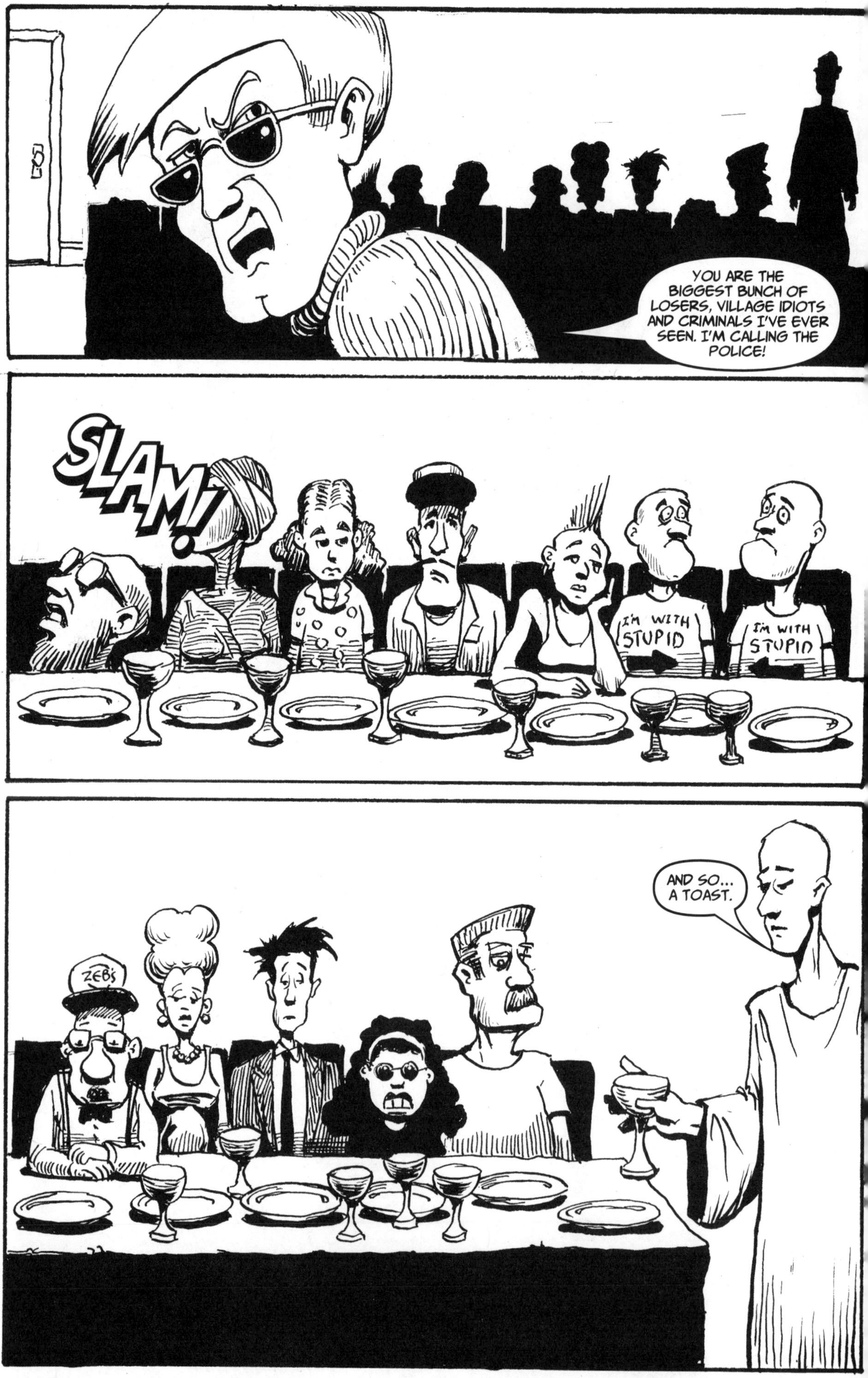
YOU ARE THE BIGGEST BUNCH OF LOSERS, VILLAGE IDIOTS AND CRIMINALS I'VE EVER SEEN. I'M CALLING THE POLICE!
SLAM!
I'M WITH STUPID
I'M WITH STUPID
AND SO... A TOAST.
ZEB'S

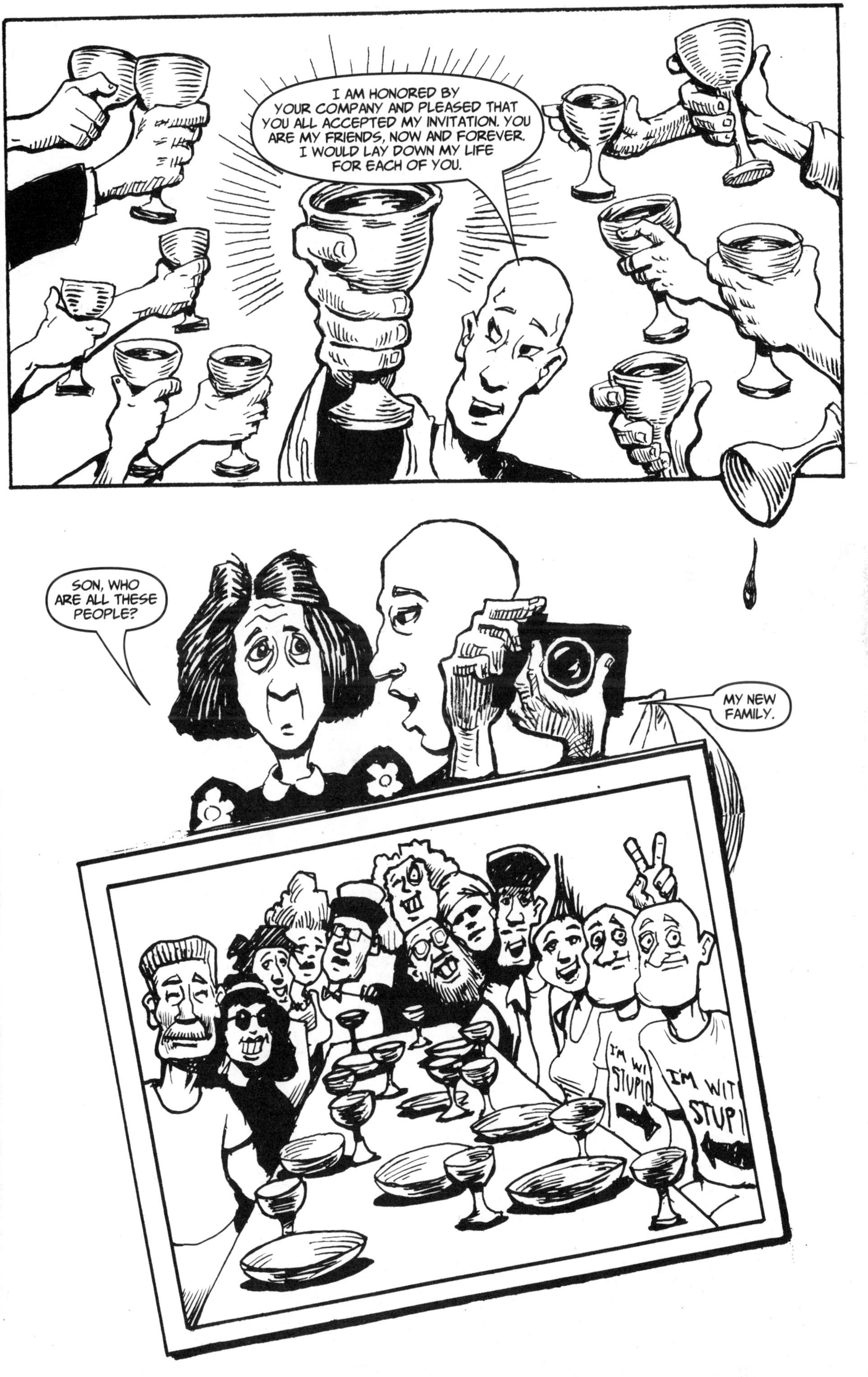
I AM HONORED BY YOUR COMPANY AND PLEASED THAT YOU ALL ACCEPTED MY INVITATION. YOU ARE MY FRIENDS, NOW AND FOREVER. I WOULD LAY DOWN MY LIFE FOR EACH OF YOU.
SON, WHO ARE ALL THESE PEOPLE?
MY NEW FAMILY.
I'M WIT STUPI
I'M WIT STUP

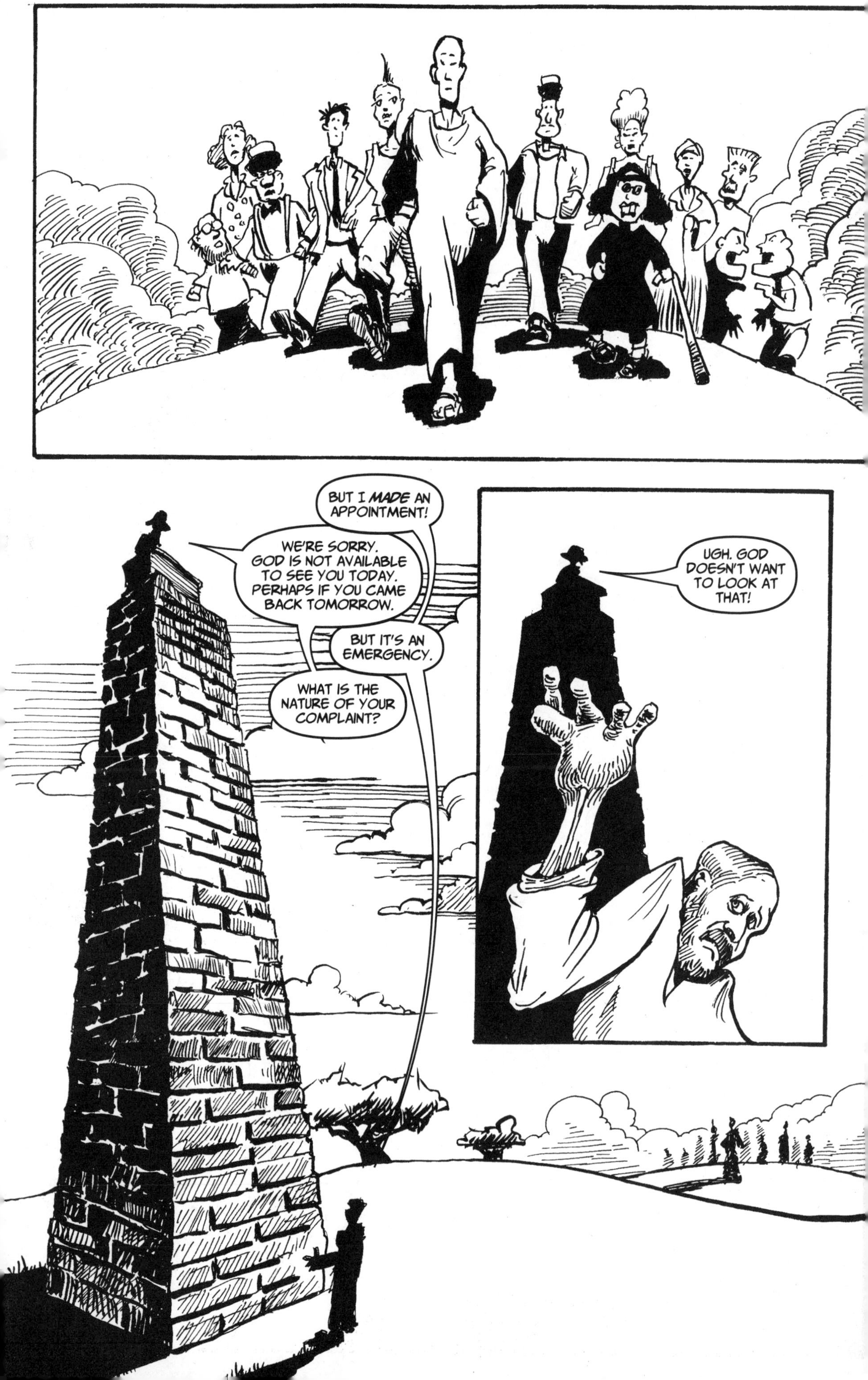
WE'RE SORRY. GOD IS NOT AVAILABLE TO SEE YOU TODAY. PERHAPS IF YOU CAME BACK TOMORROW.
BUT I *MADE* AN APPOINTMENT!
BUT IT'S AN EMERGENCY.
WHAT IS THE NATURE OF YOUR COMPLAINT?
UGH. GOD DOESN'T WANT TO LOOK AT THAT!

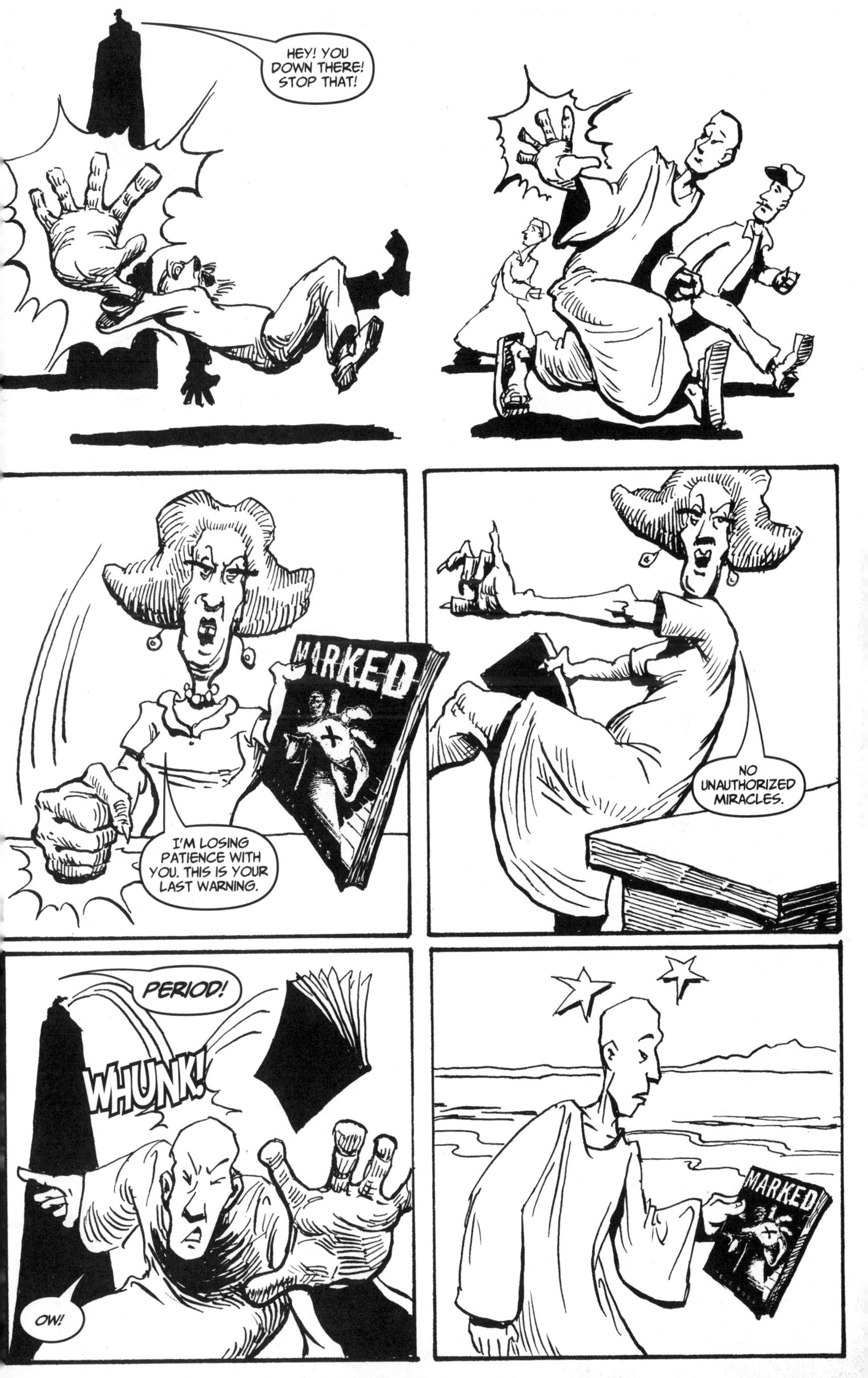
HEY! YOU DOWN THERE! STOP THAT!
MARKED
I'M LOSING PATIENCE WITH YOU. THIS IS YOUR LAST WARNING.
NO UNAUTHORIZED MIRACLES.
PERIOD!
WHUNK!
OW!
MARKED

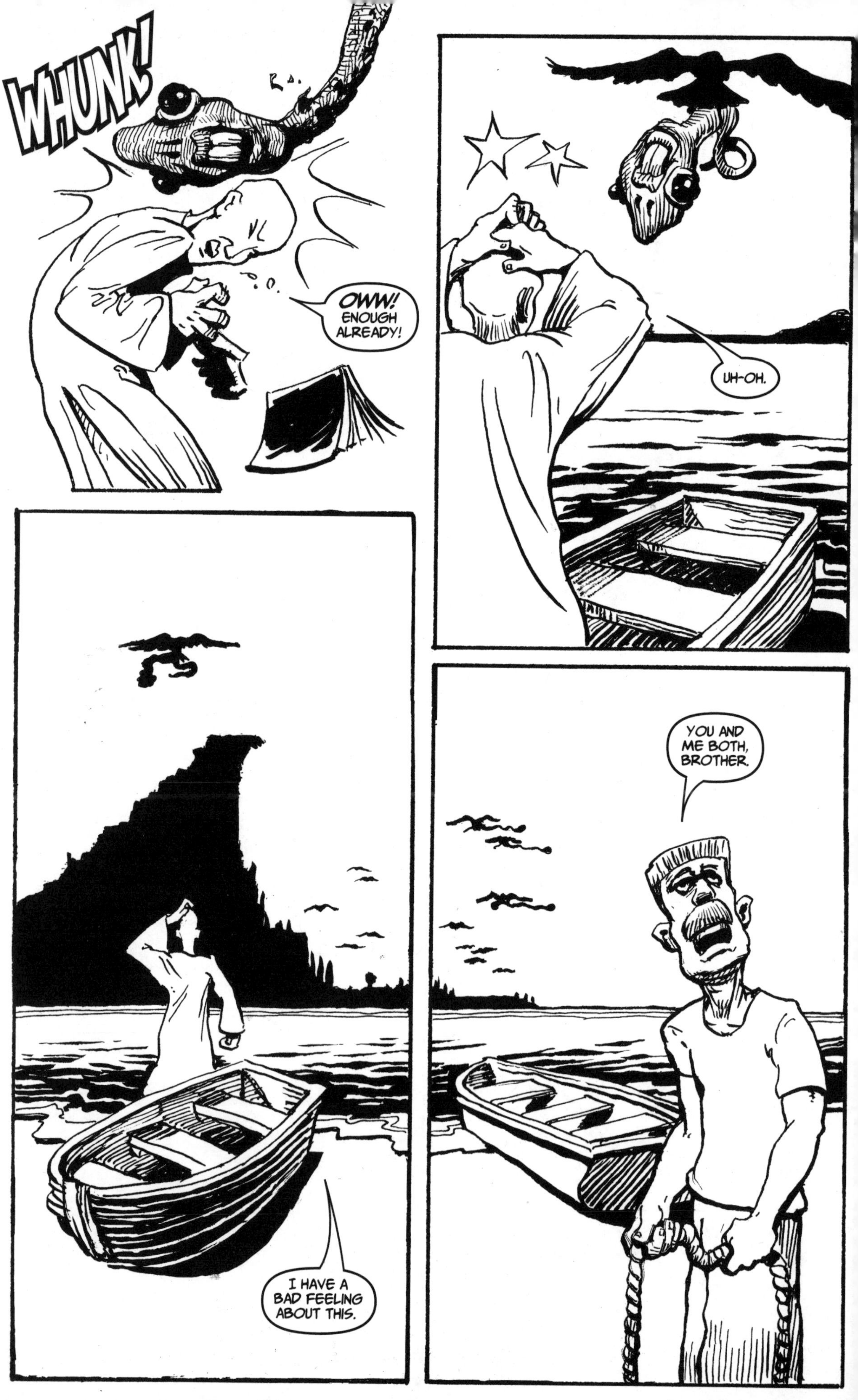
WHUNK!
OWW! ENOUGH ALREADY!
UH-OH.
I HAVE A BAD FEELING ABOUT THIS.
YOU AND ME BOTH, BROTHER.

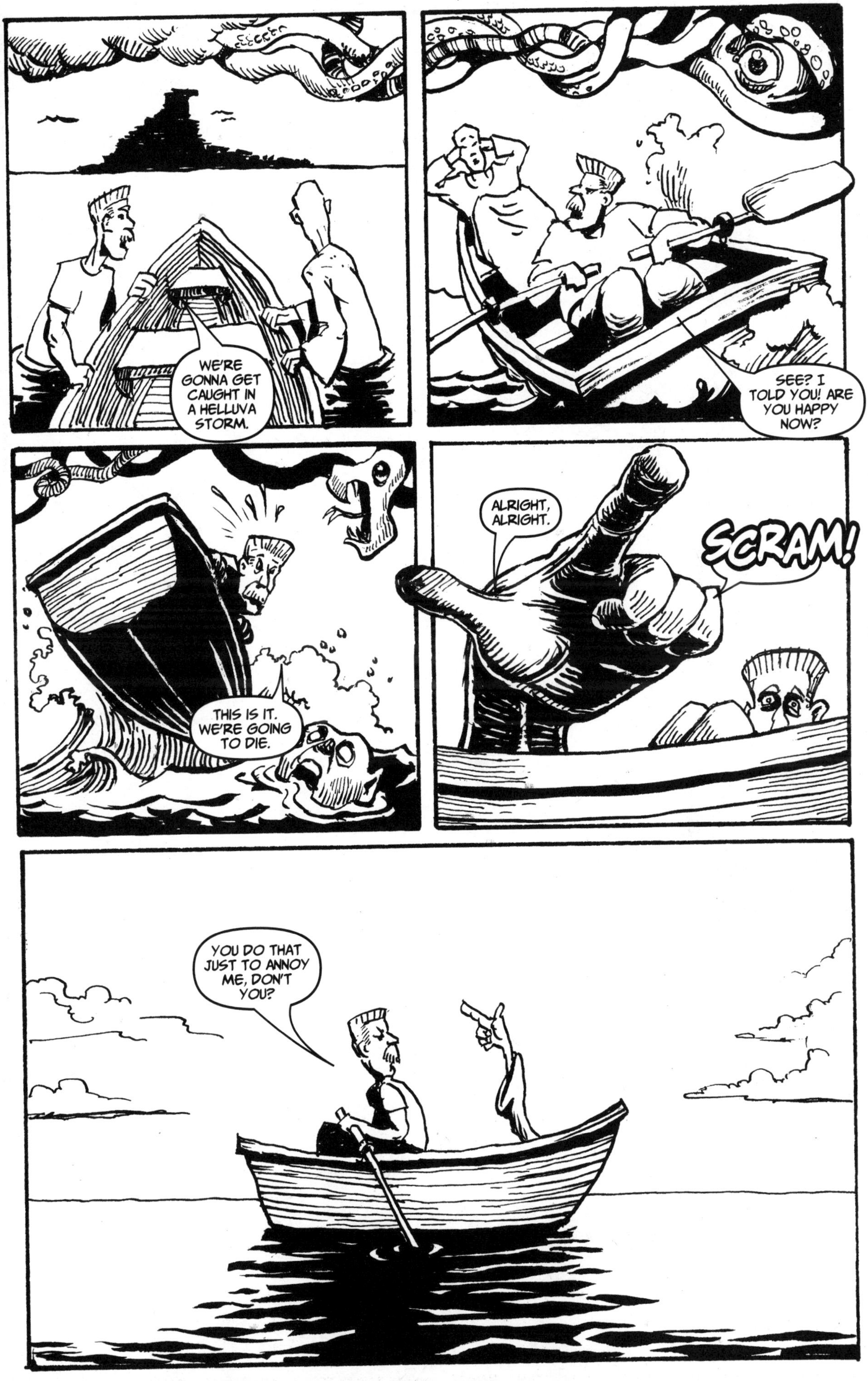
WE'RE GONNA GET CAUGHT IN A HELLUVA STORM.
SEE? I TOLD YOU! ARE YOU HAPPY NOW?
THIS IS IT. WE'RE GOING TO DIE.
ALRIGHT, ALRIGHT.
SCRAM!
YOU DO THAT JUST TO ANNOY ME, DON'T YOU?

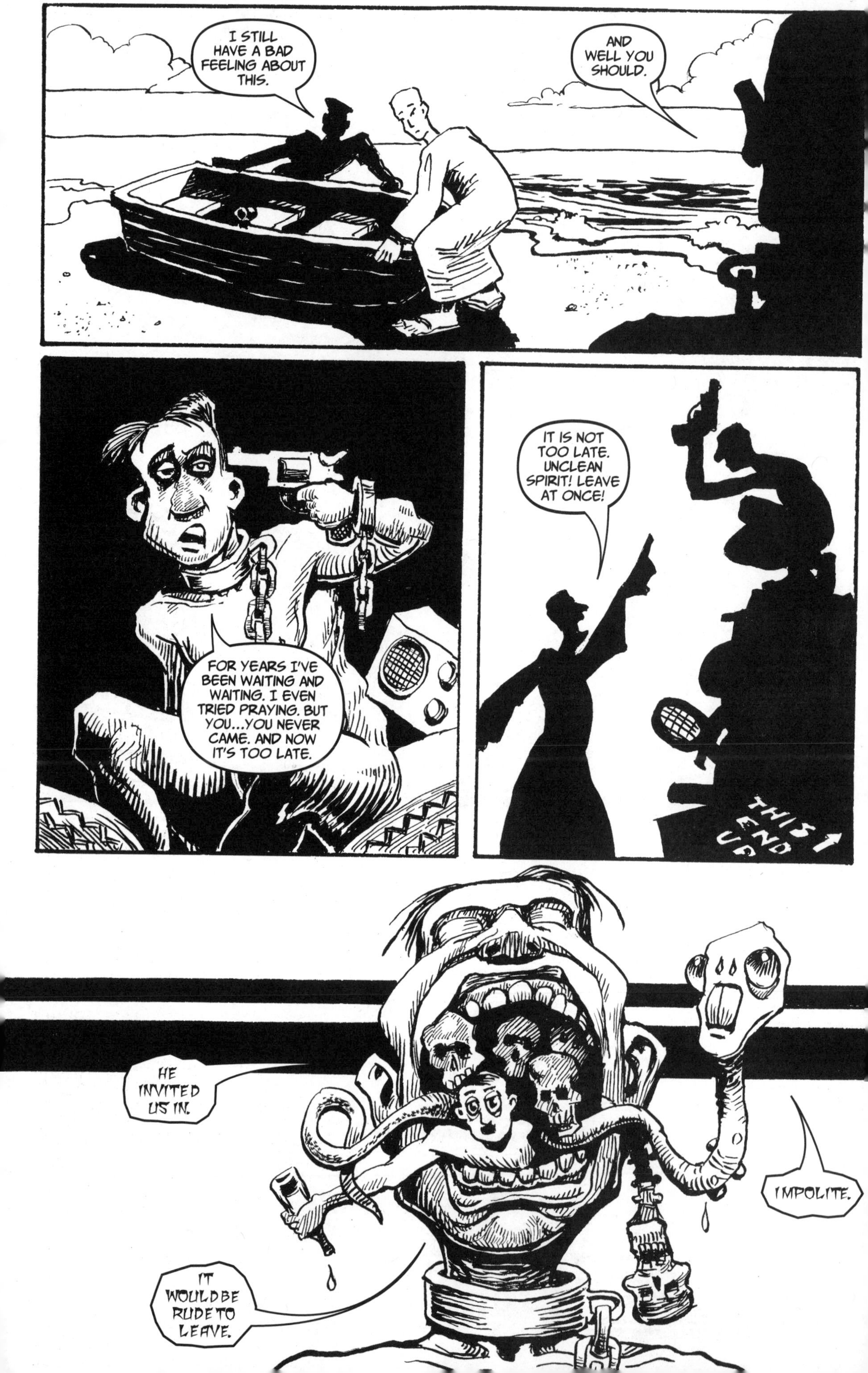
I STILL HAVE A BAD FEELING ABOUT THIS.
AND WELL YOU SHOULD.
FOR YEARS I'VE BEEN WAITING AND WAITING. I EVEN TRIED PRAYING. BUT YOU...YOU NEVER CAME. AND NOW IT'S TOO LATE.
IT IS NOT TOO LATE. UNCLEAN SPIRIT! LEAVE AT ONCE!
THIS END
HE INVITED US IN.
IT WOULD BE RUDE TO LEAVE.
IMPOLITE.

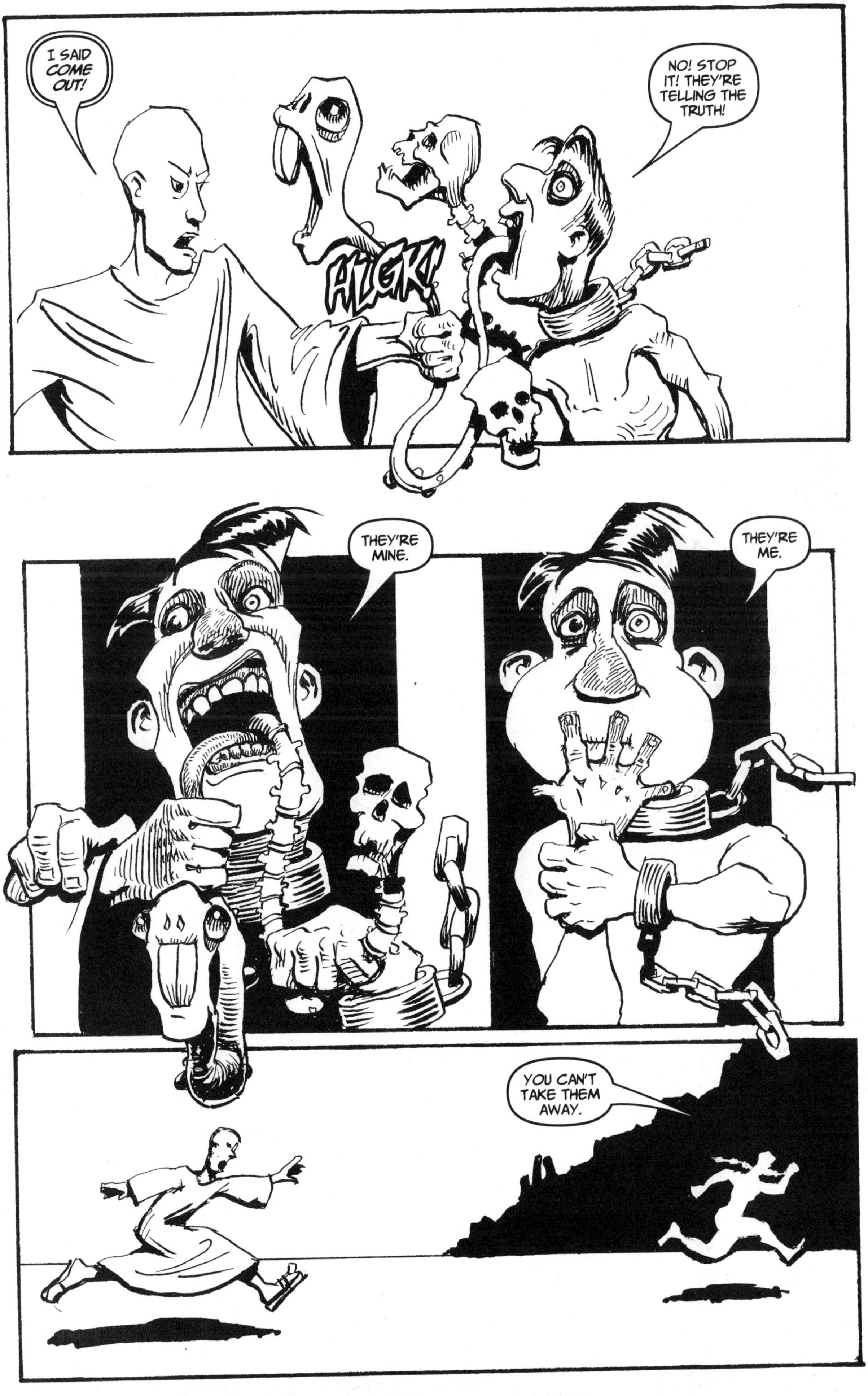
I SAID COME OUT!
AUGK!
NO! STOP IT! THEY'RE TELLING THE TRUTH!
THEY'RE MINE.
THEY'RE ME.
YOU CAN'T TAKE THEM AWAY.

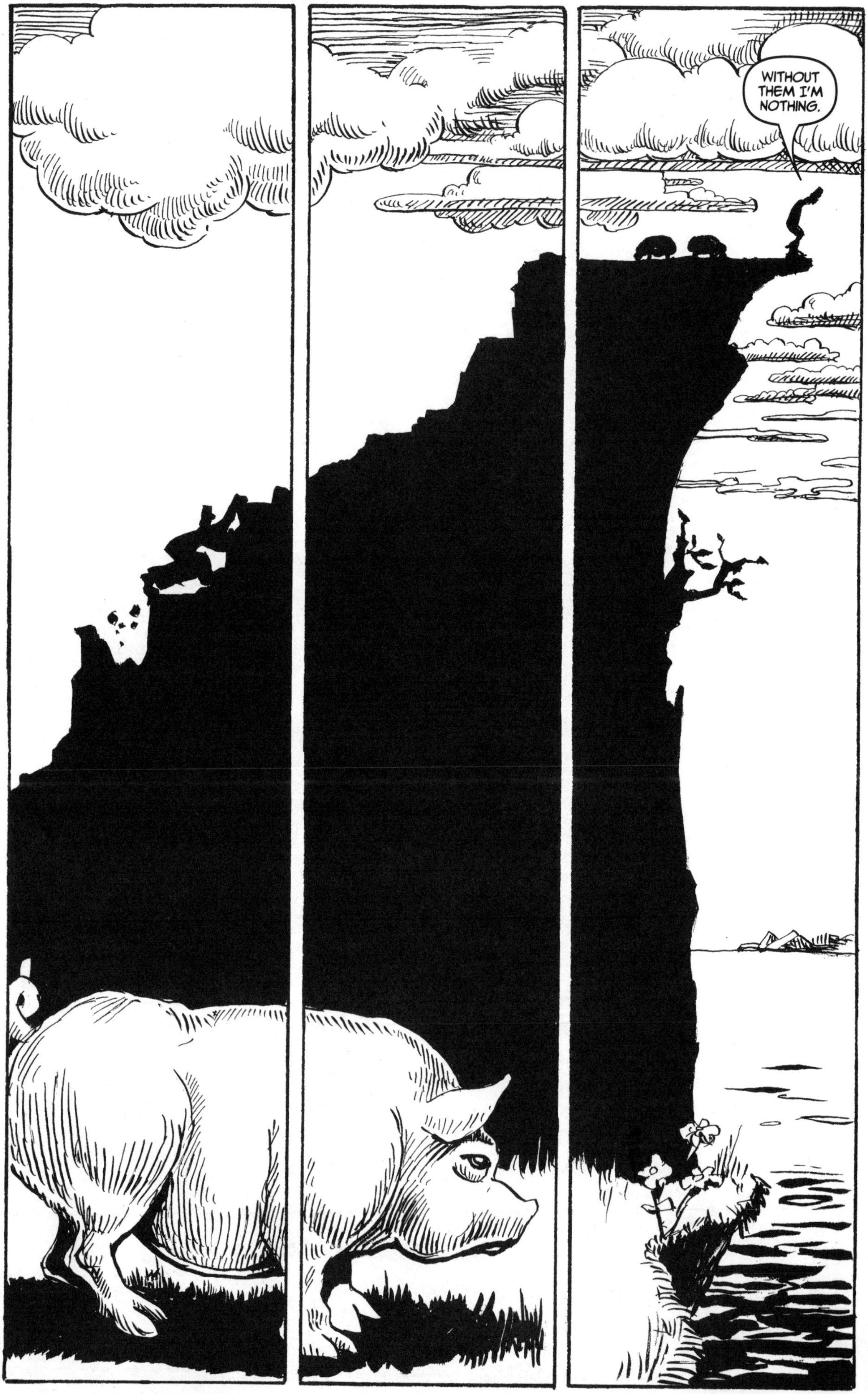
WITHOUT THEM I'M NOTHING.

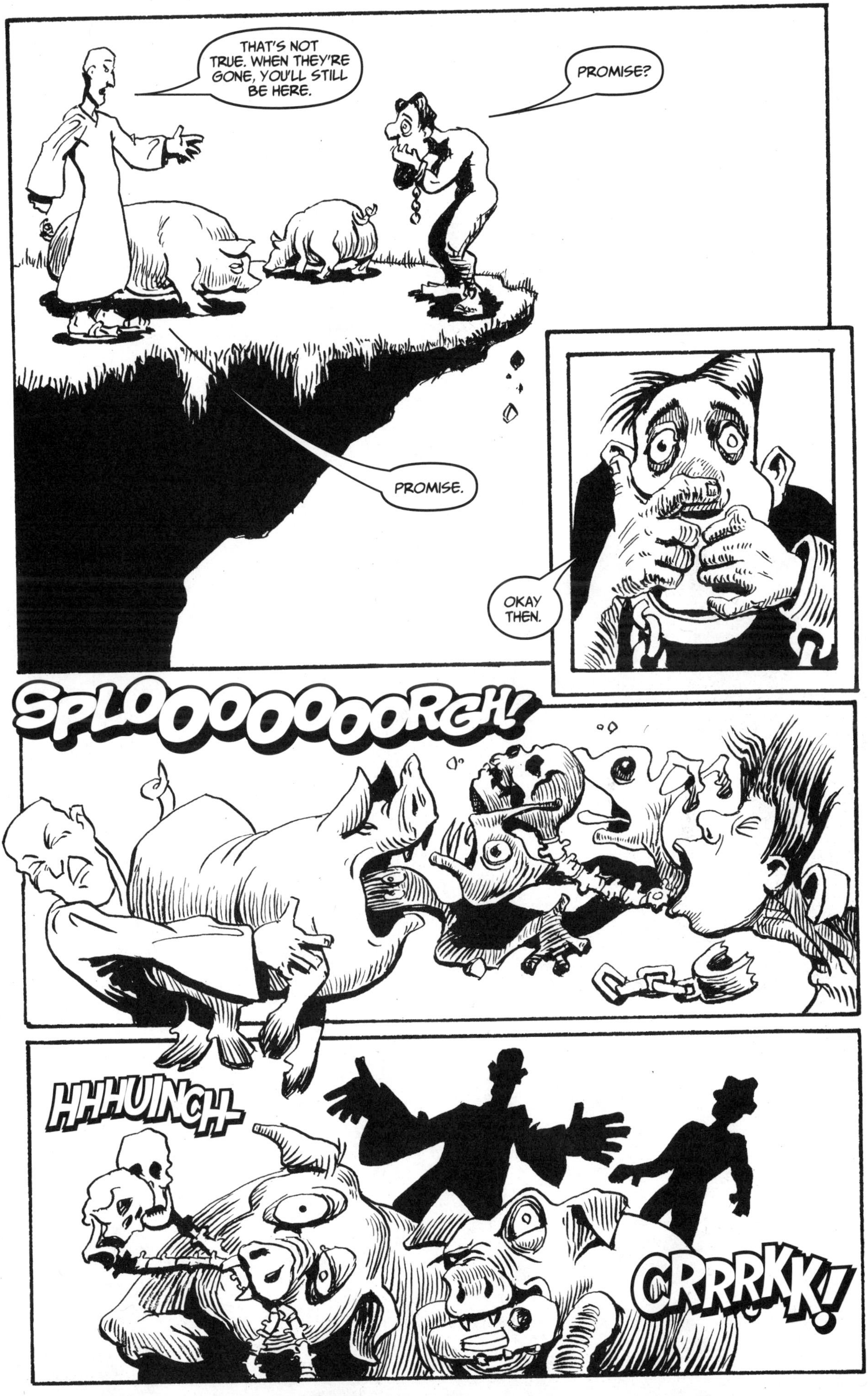
THAT'S NOT TRUE. WHEN THEY'RE GONE, YOU'LL STILL BE HERE.
PROMISE?
PROMISE.
OKAY THEN.
SPLOOOOOOOORGH!
HHHUINCH
CRRRKK!

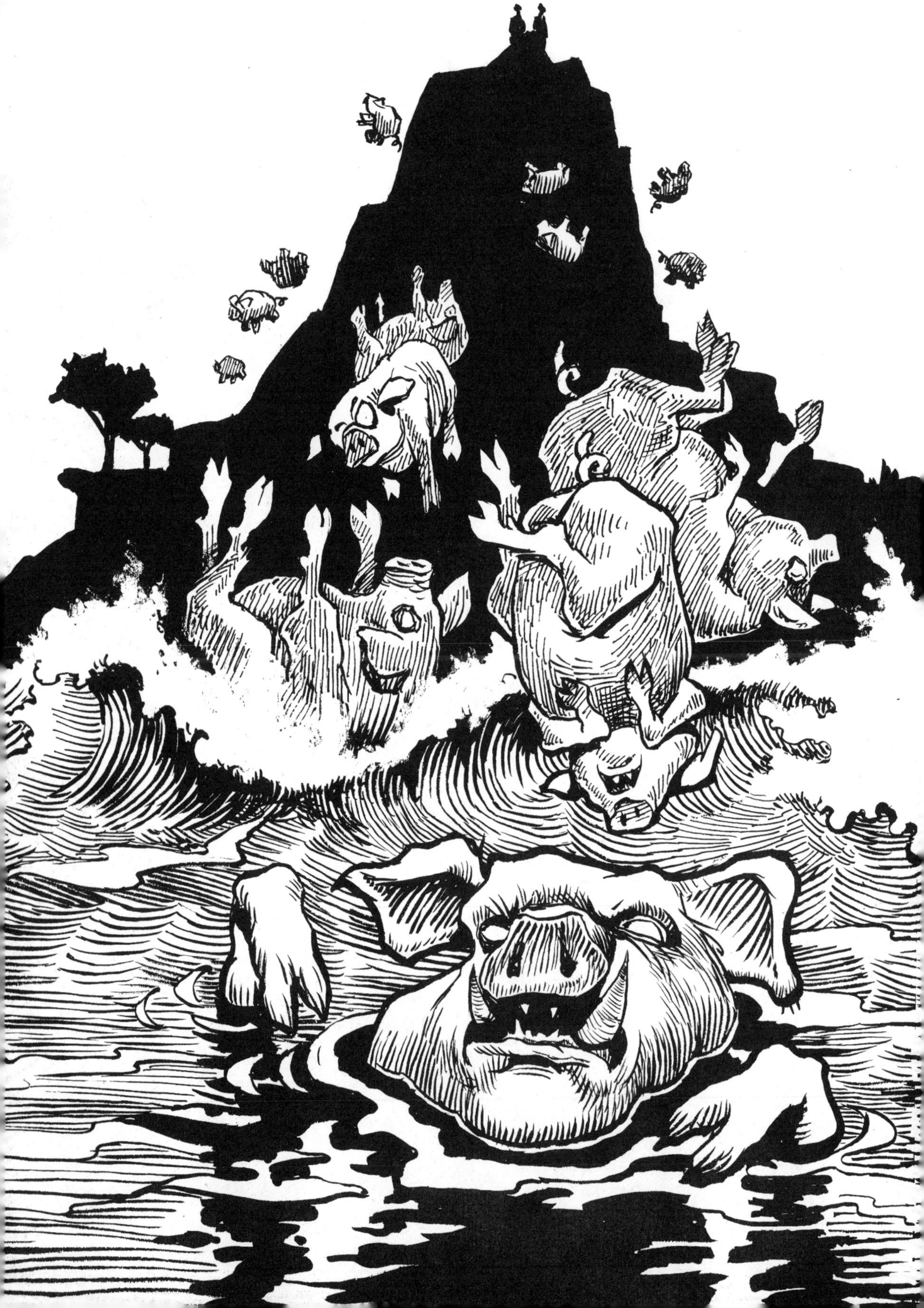

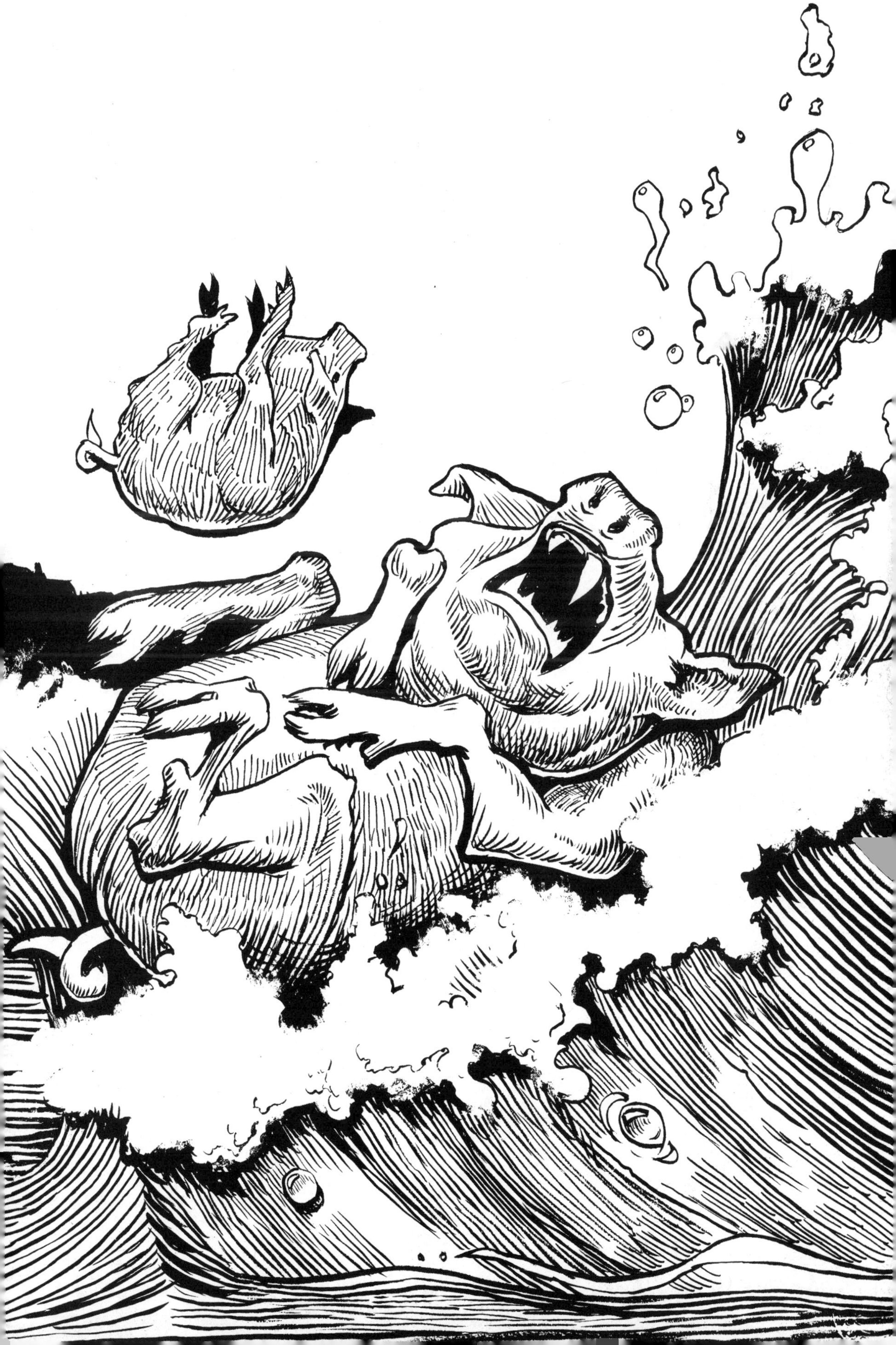

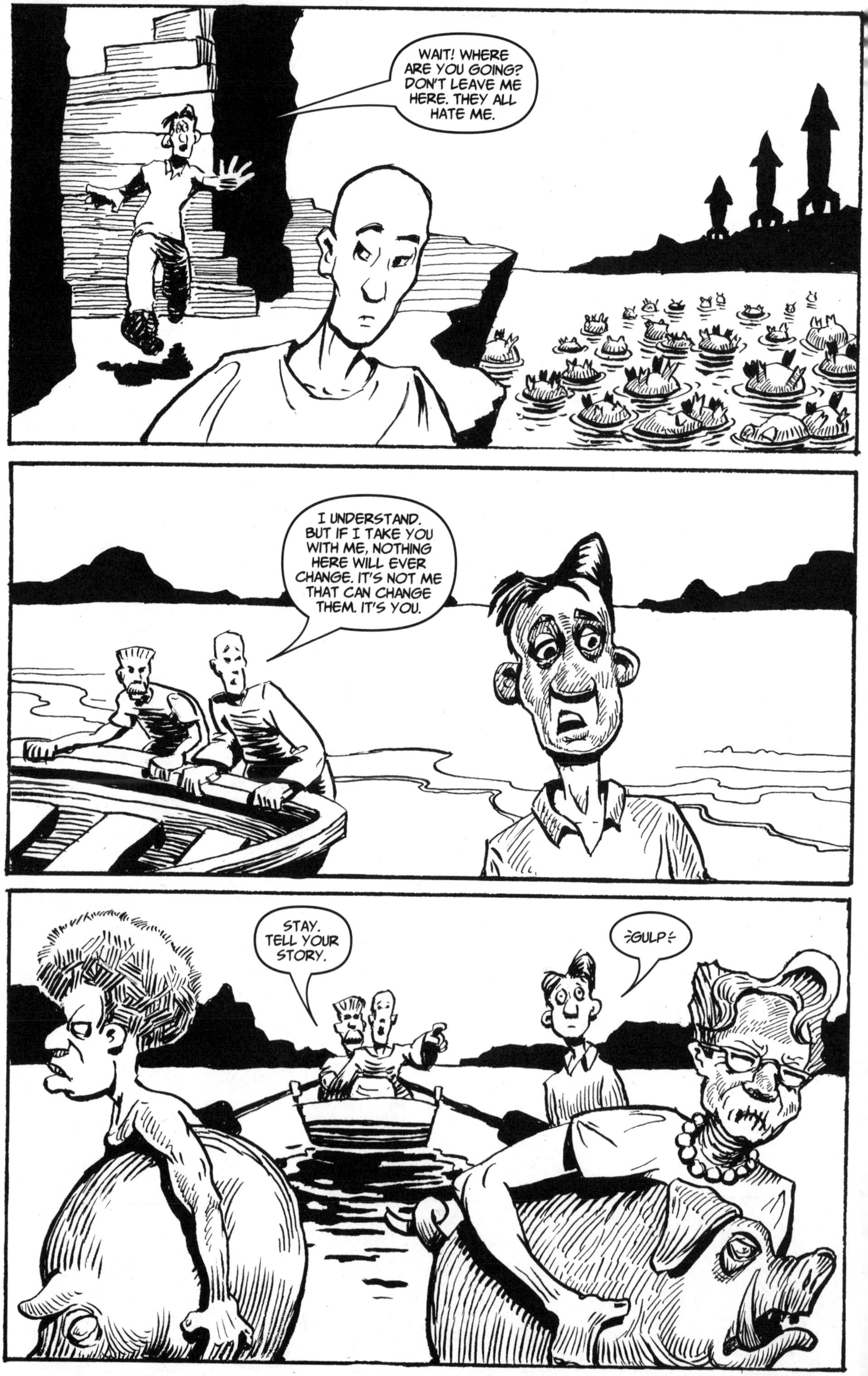
WAIT! WHERE ARE YOU GOING? DON'T LEAVE ME HERE. THEY ALL HATE ME.
I UNDERSTAND. BUT IF I TAKE YOU WITH ME, NOTHING HERE WILL EVER CHANGE. IT'S NOT ME THAT CAN CHANGE THEM. IT'S YOU.
STAY. TELL YOUR STORY.
GULP

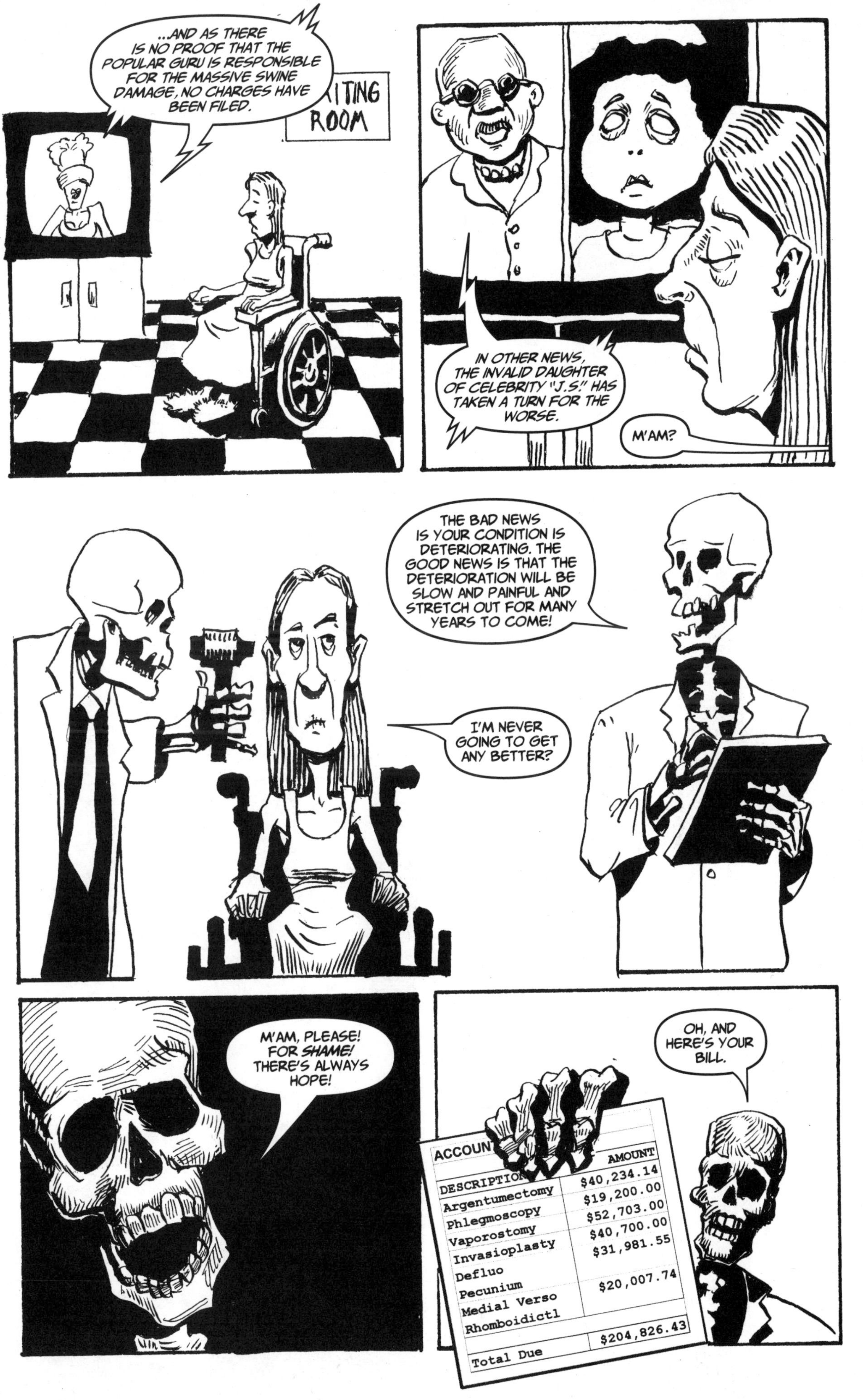
...AND AS THERE IS NO PROOF THAT THE POPULAR GURU IS RESPONSIBLE FOR THE MASSIVE SWINE DAMAGE, NO CHARGES HAVE BEEN FILED.
ROOM
IN OTHER NEWS, THE INVALID DAUGHTER OF CELEBRITY "J.S." HAS TAKEN A TURN FOR THE WORSE.
M'AM?
THE BAD NEWS IS YOUR CONDITION IS DETERIORATING. THE GOOD NEWS IS THAT THE DETERIORATION WILL BE SLOW AND PAINFUL AND STRETCH OUT FOR MANY YEARS TO COME!
I'M NEVER GOING TO GET ANY BETTER?
M'AM, PLEASE! FOR SHAME! THERE'S ALWAYS HOPE!
OH, AND HERE'S YOUR BILL.
ACCOUN
AMOUNT
DESCRIPTIO
Argentumectomy $40,234.14
Phlegmoscopy $19,200.00
Vaporostomy $52,703.00
Invasioplasty $40,700.00
Defluo Pecunium $31,981.55
Medial Verso Rhomboidictl $20,007.74
Total Due $204,826.43

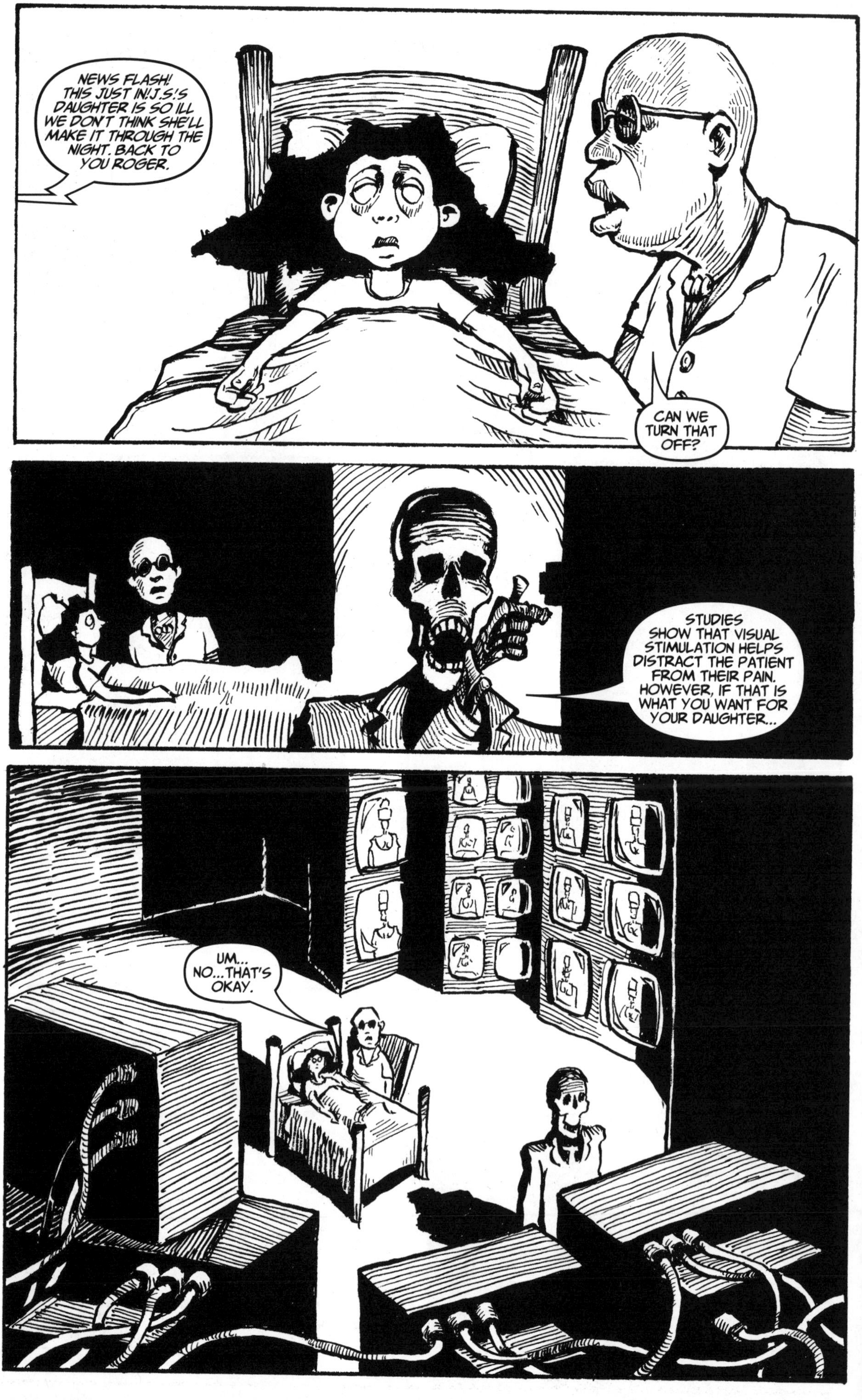
NEWS FLASH! THIS JUST IN! J.S.'S DAUGHTER IS SO ILL WE DON'T THINK SHE'LL MAKE IT THROUGH THE NIGHT. BACK TO YOU ROGER.
CAN WE TURN THAT OFF?
STUDIES SHOW THAT VISUAL STIMULATION HELPS DISTRACT THE PATIENT FROM THEIR PAIN. HOWEVER, IF THAT IS WHAT YOU WANT FOR YOUR DAUGHTER...
UM... NO...THAT'S OKAY.

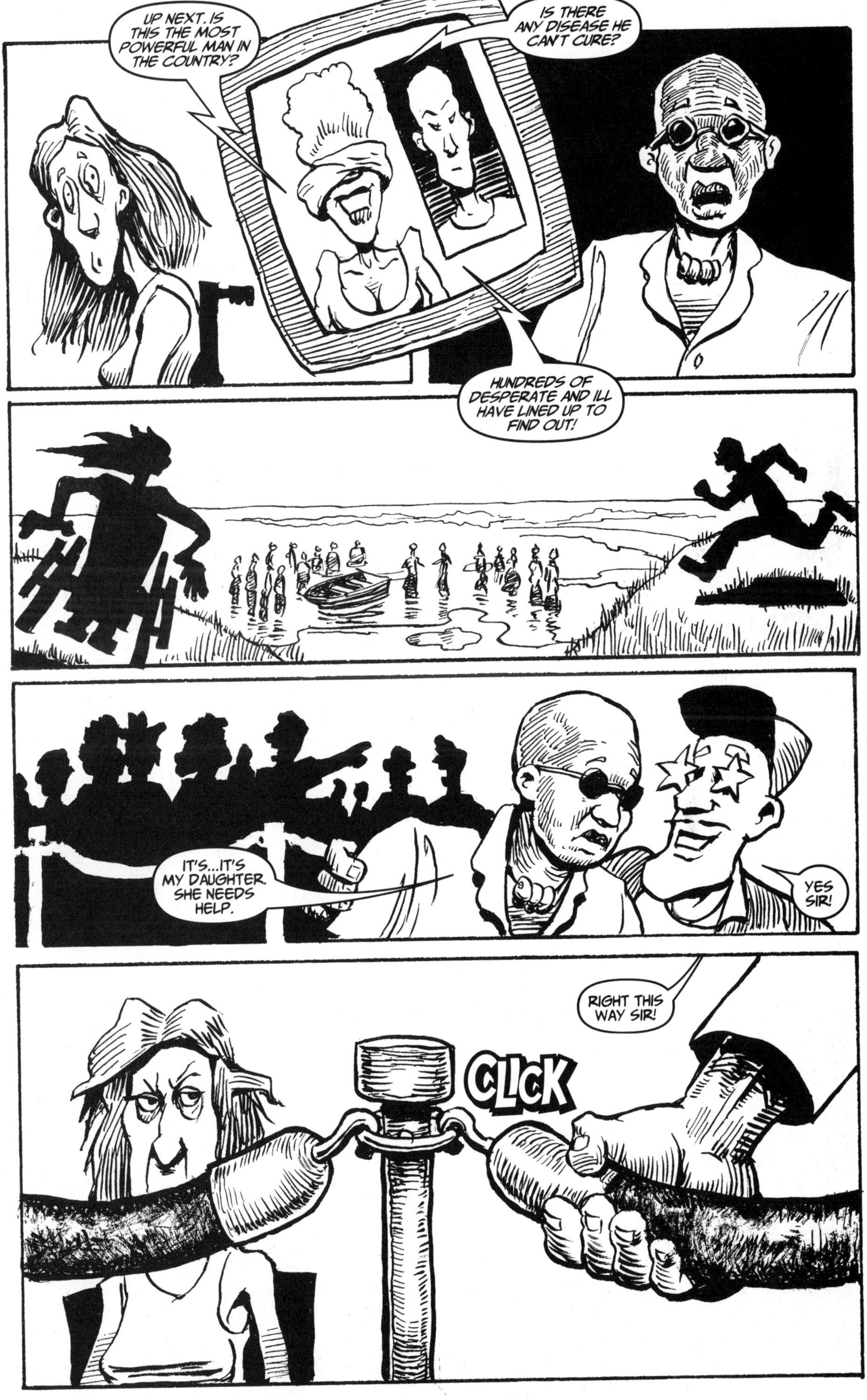
UP NEXT. IS THIS THE MOST POWERFUL MAN IN THE COUNTRY?
IS THERE ANY DISEASE HE CAN'T CURE?
HUNDREDS OF DESPERATE AND ILL HAVE LINED UP TO FIND OUT!
IT'S...IT'S MY DAUGHTER. SHE NEEDS HELP.
YES SIR!
RIGHT THIS WAY SIR!
CLICK

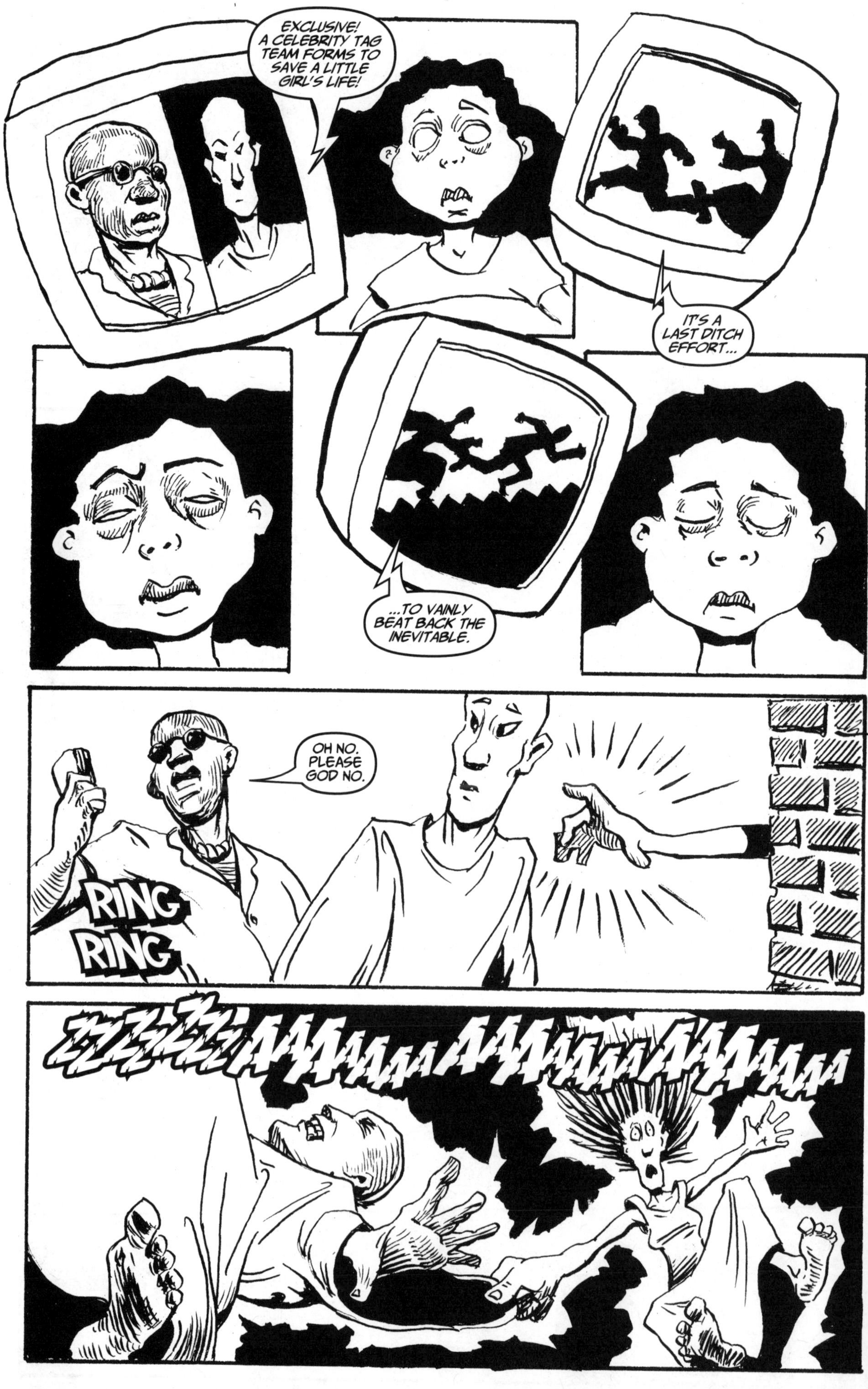
EXCLUSIVE! A CELEBRITY TAG TEAM FORMS TO SAVE A LITTLE GIRL'S LIFE!
IT'S A LAST DITCH EFFORT...
...TO VAINLY BEAT BACK THE INEVITABLE.
OH NO. PLEASE GOD NO.
RING RING
ZZZZZZAAAAaaaaaAAAAaaaaAAAAaaaaa

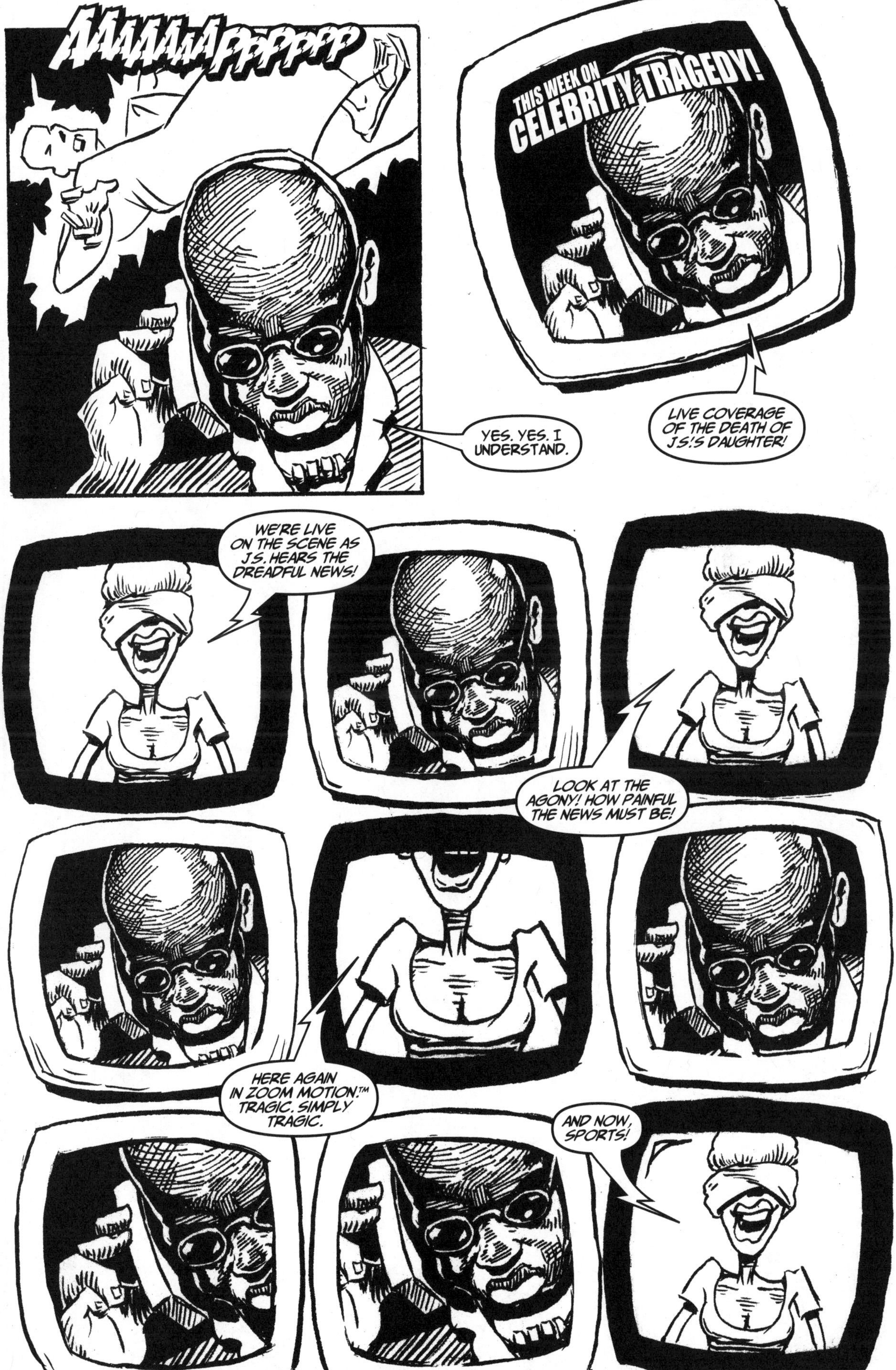

AAAAAAAPPPPPPP
THIS WEEK ON CELEBRITY TRAGEDY!
YES. YES. I UNDERSTAND.
LIVE COVERAGE OF THE DEATH OF J.S.'S DAUGHTER!
WE'RE LIVE ON THE SCENE AS J.S. HEARS THE DREADFUL NEWS!
LOOK AT THE AGONY! HOW PAINFUL THE NEWS MUST BE!
HERE AGAIN IN ZOOM MOTION.™ TRAGIC. SIMPLY TRAGIC.
AND NOW, SPORTS!

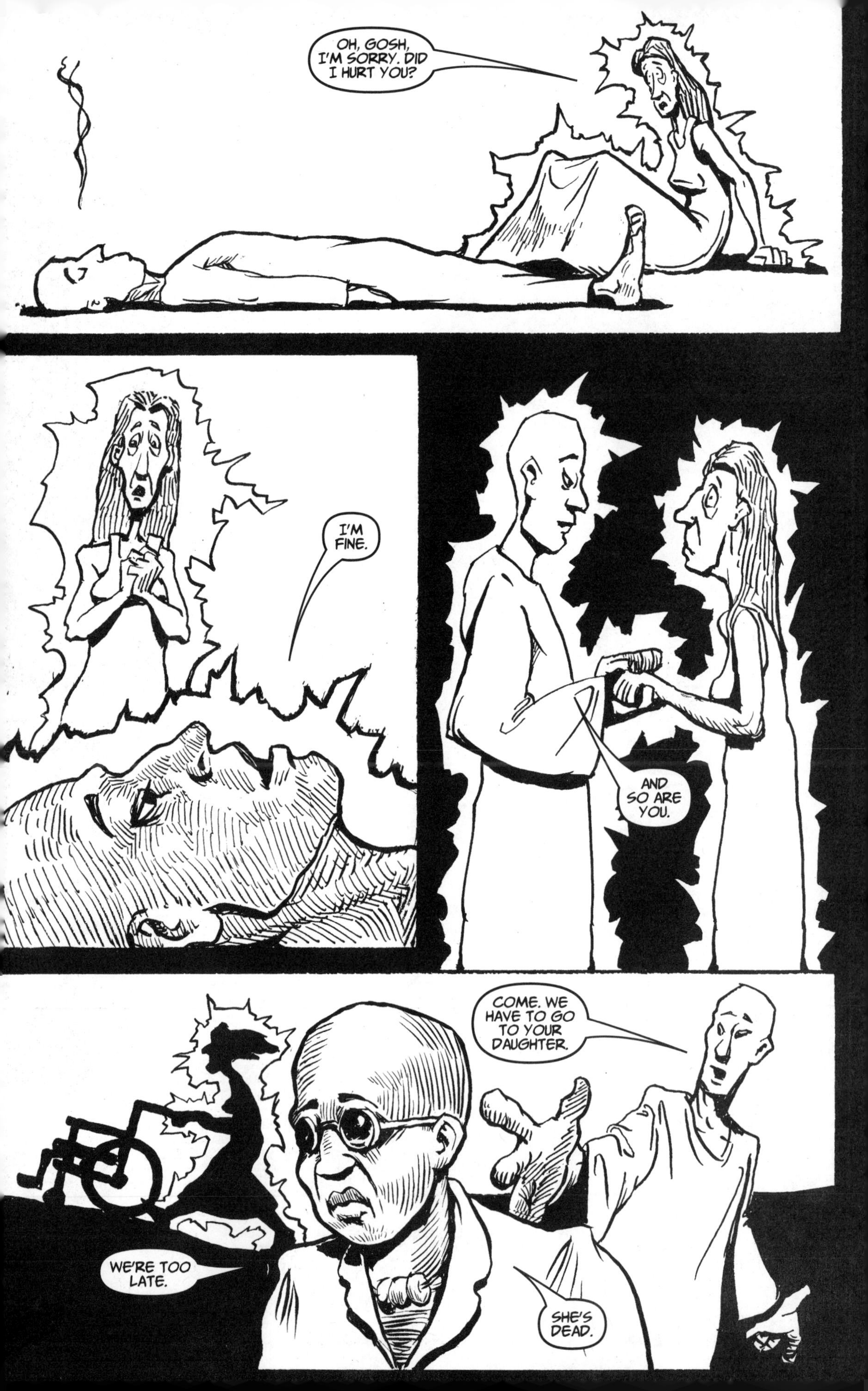
OH, GOSH, I'M SORRY. DID I HURT YOU?
I'M FINE.
AND SO ARE YOU.
COME. WE HAVE TO GO TO YOUR DAUGHTER.
WE'RE TOO LATE.
SHE'S DEAD.

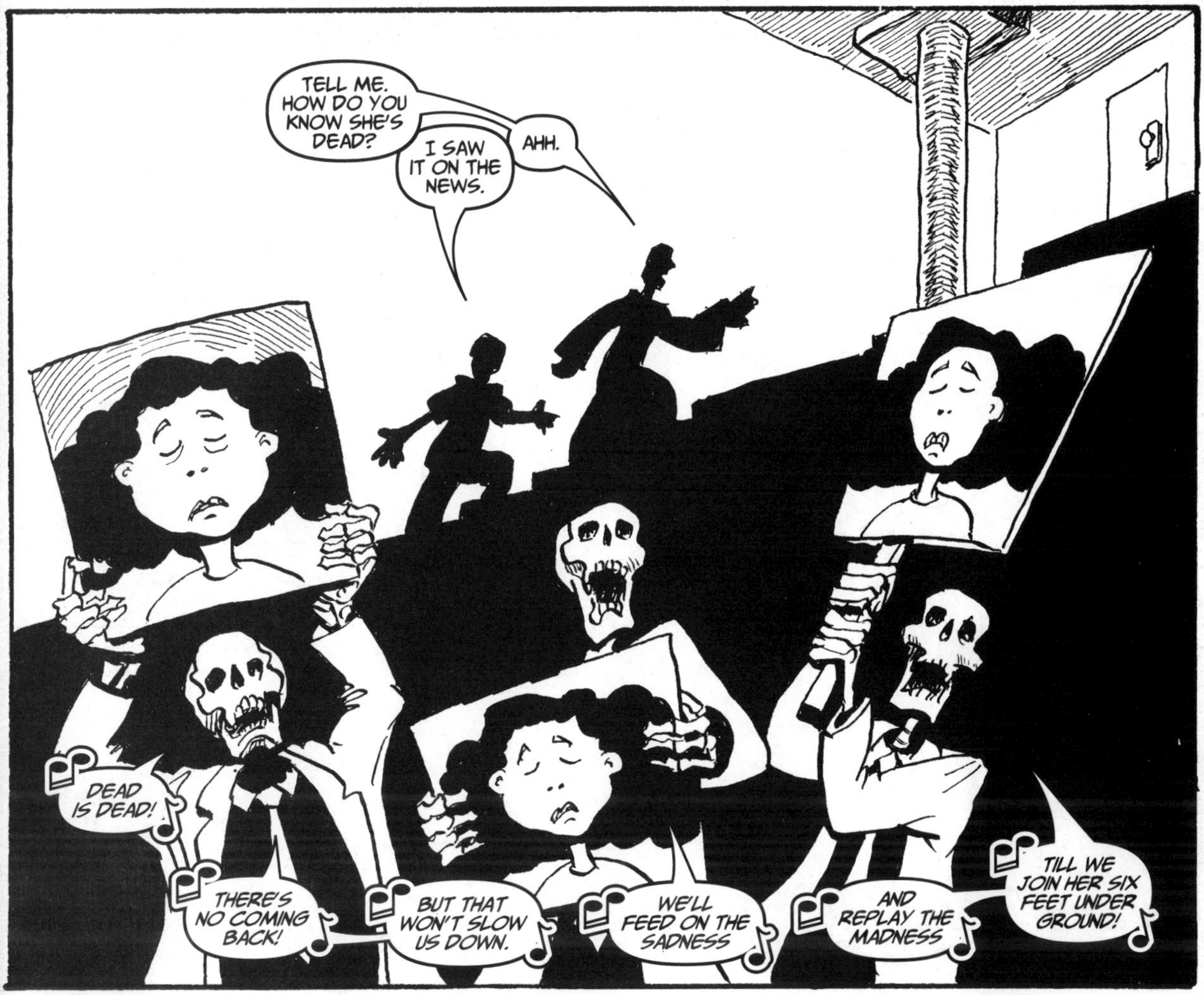
TELL ME. HOW DO YOU KNOW SHE'S DEAD?
I SAW IT ON THE NEWS.
AHH.
DEAD IS DEAD!
THERE'S NO COMING BACK!
BUT THAT WON'T SLOW US DOWN.
WE'LL FEED ON THE SADNESS
AND REPLAY THE MADNESS
TILL WE JOIN HER SIX FEET UNDER GROUND!

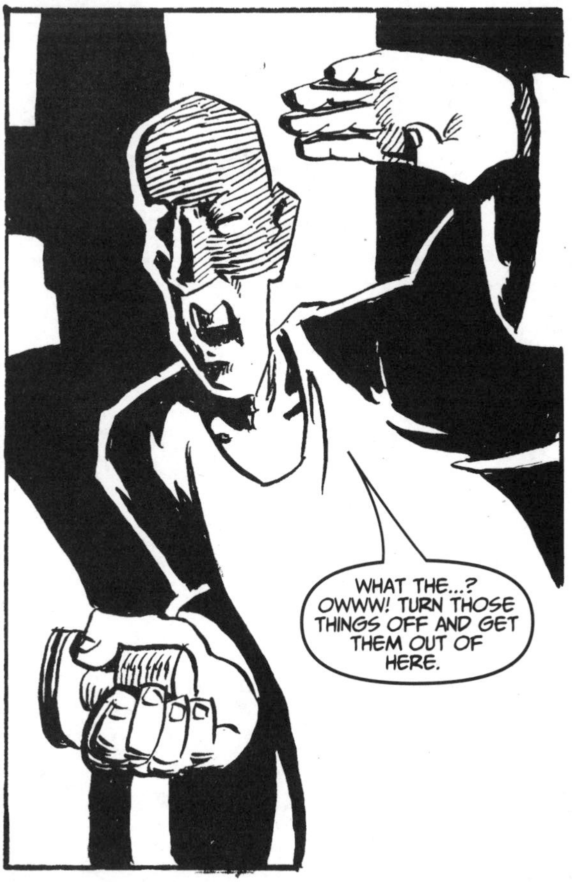
WHAT THE...? OWWW! TURN THOSE THINGS OFF AND GET THEM OUT OF HERE.

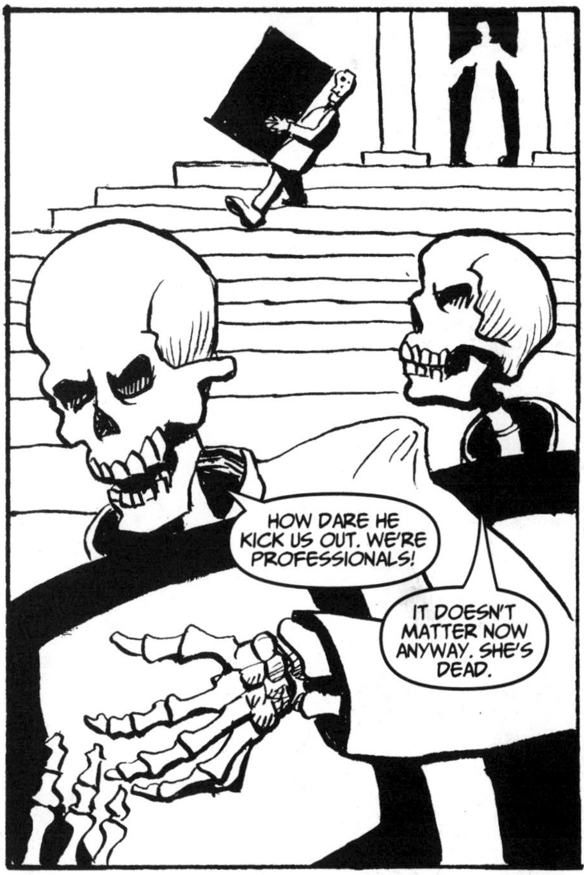
HOW DARE HE KICK US OUT. WE'RE PROFESSIONALS!
IT DOESN'T MATTER NOW ANYWAY. SHE'S DEAD.

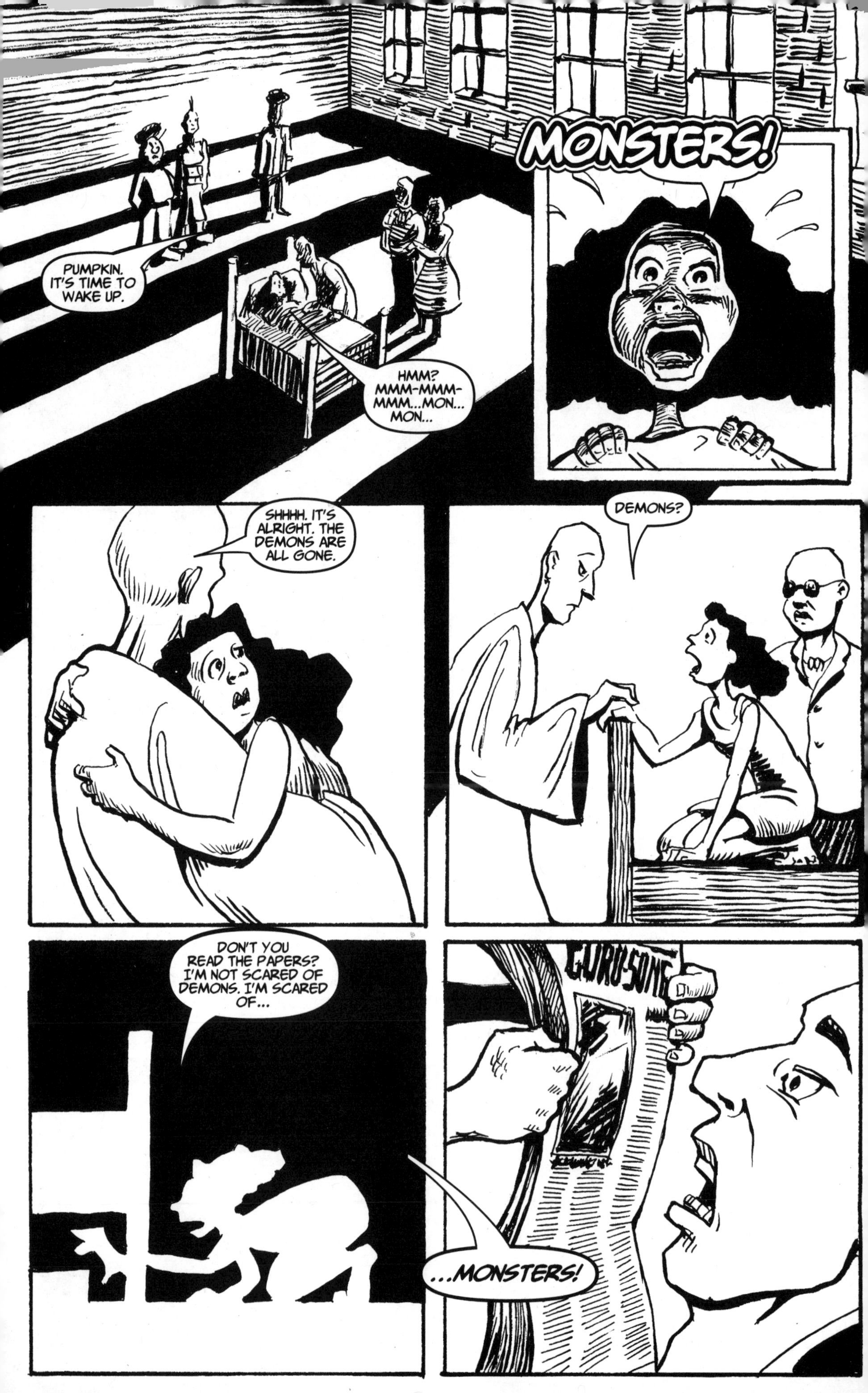
PUMPKIN. IT'S TIME TO WAKE UP.
HMM? MMM-MMM-MMM...MON... MON...
MONSTERS!
SHHHH. IT'S ALRIGHT. THE DEMONS ARE ALL GONE.
DEMONS?
DON'T YOU READ THE PAPERS? I'M NOT SCARED OF DEMONS. I'M SCARED OF...
...MONSTERS!

EXTRA ★ NEWS FLASH ★ EXTRA

VOL. IX . NO 1 DAILY

The End Times

GURU-SOME!

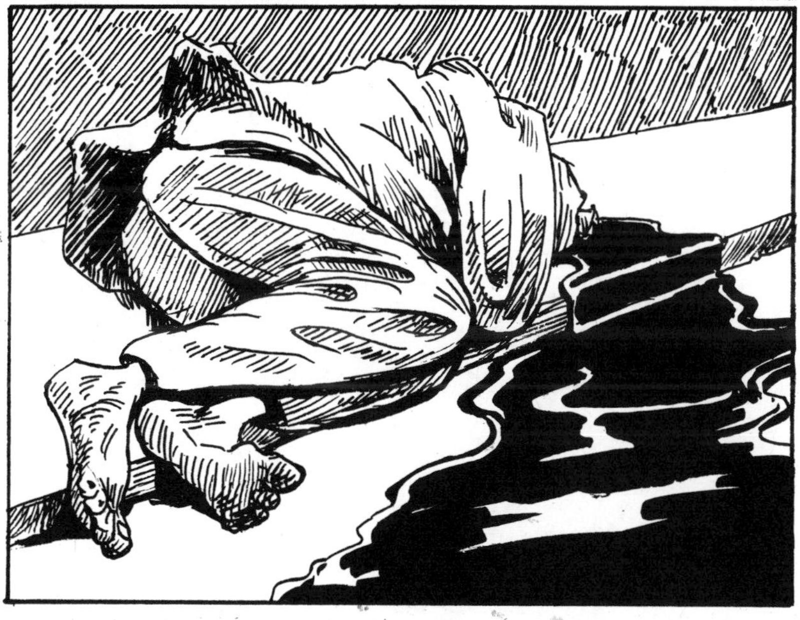

Baptizer Beheaded and Served On A Plate

In a bold political and strategic move, the administration today seperated the head and body of a cantankerous local doomsayer, known derisively by many as "The Baptizer" or simply "John."

Speculation about the severity of the decision has lead most leaders to applaud the effort as a manly and purposeful attempt to bring order and respect to a community that has become progressively whiney and ungrateful.

Although removing the head was not the administration's original intent, a series of backroom deals swiftly placed it at the forefront of a new shift in the balance of power.

One witness was quoted as saying "I wouldn't say the reasons for this action are particularly transparent, but neither are they inherently flawed. Clearly this kind of behaviour has it's roots in a deep love of country. We must all stand behind our king in this hour of rebellion and insurgency."

"The response has been generally quite favorable," said one senior official. "No one wants a leader who won't keep his promises"

"I guess his fifteen minutes were up."

The State Is Food

In response to growing unrest, the administration has been forced to outlaw communal meals until further notice. All consumables shall be prepared and dispensed according to officially sanctioned algorithms of supply and demand from authorized dispensaries. Severe penalties will be imposed on anyone feeding themselves or others without a permit.

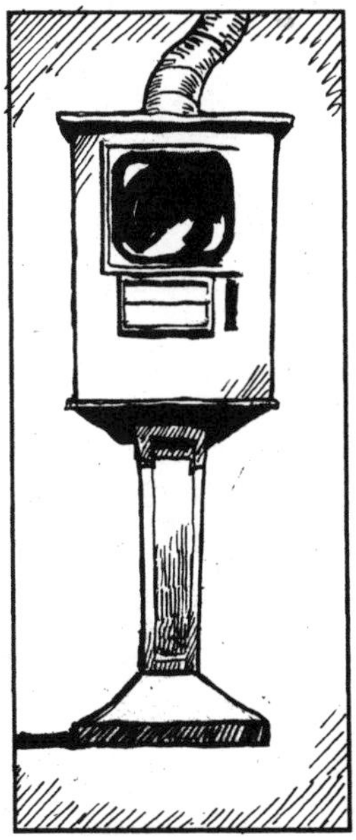

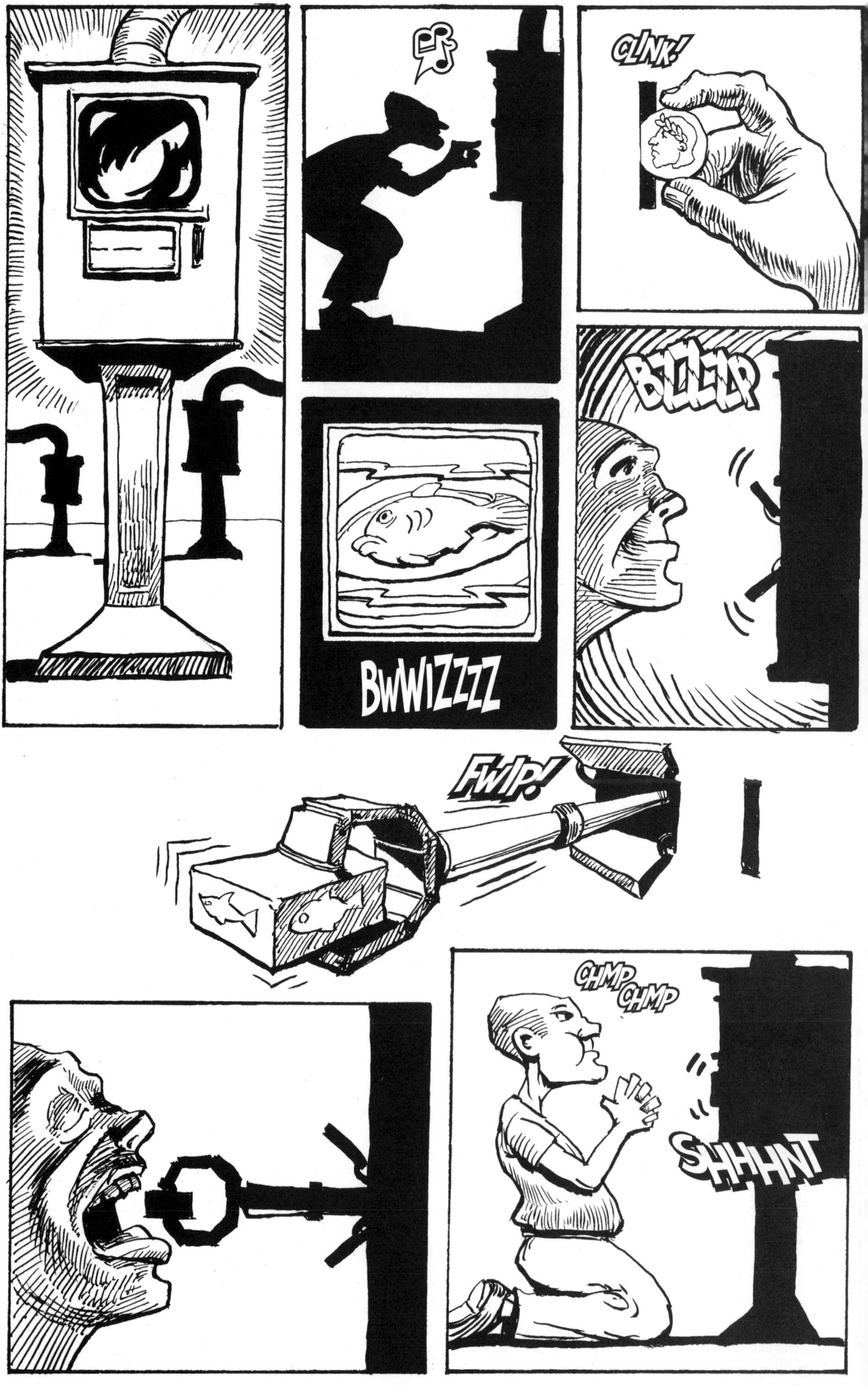
CLINK!
BZZZZP
BWWIZZZZ
FWIP!
CHMP CHMP
SHHHNT

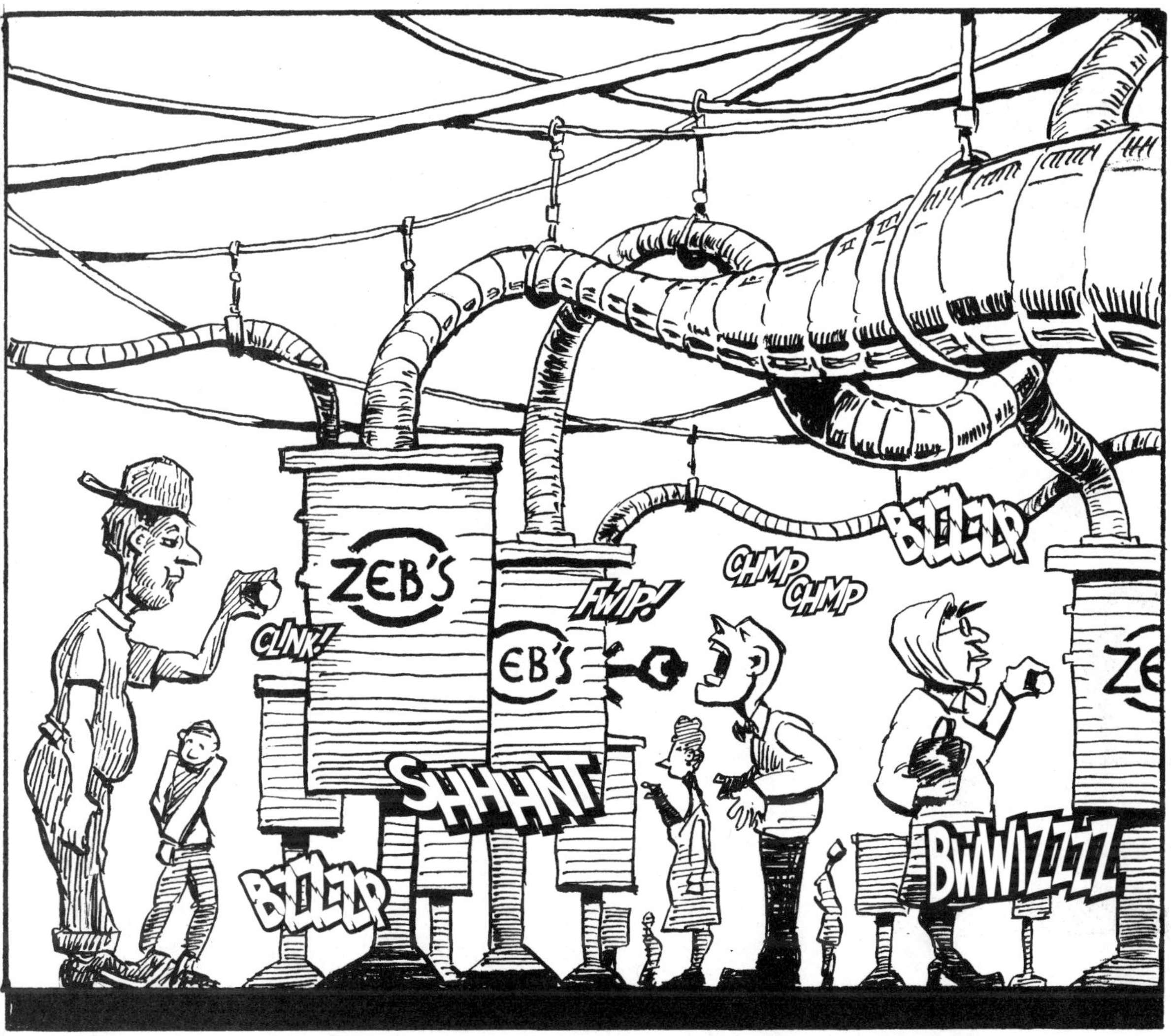
ZEB'S
EB'S
CLINK!
FWIP!
CHMP CHMP
BZZZZP
SHHHNT
BZZZZP
BWWIZZZZ

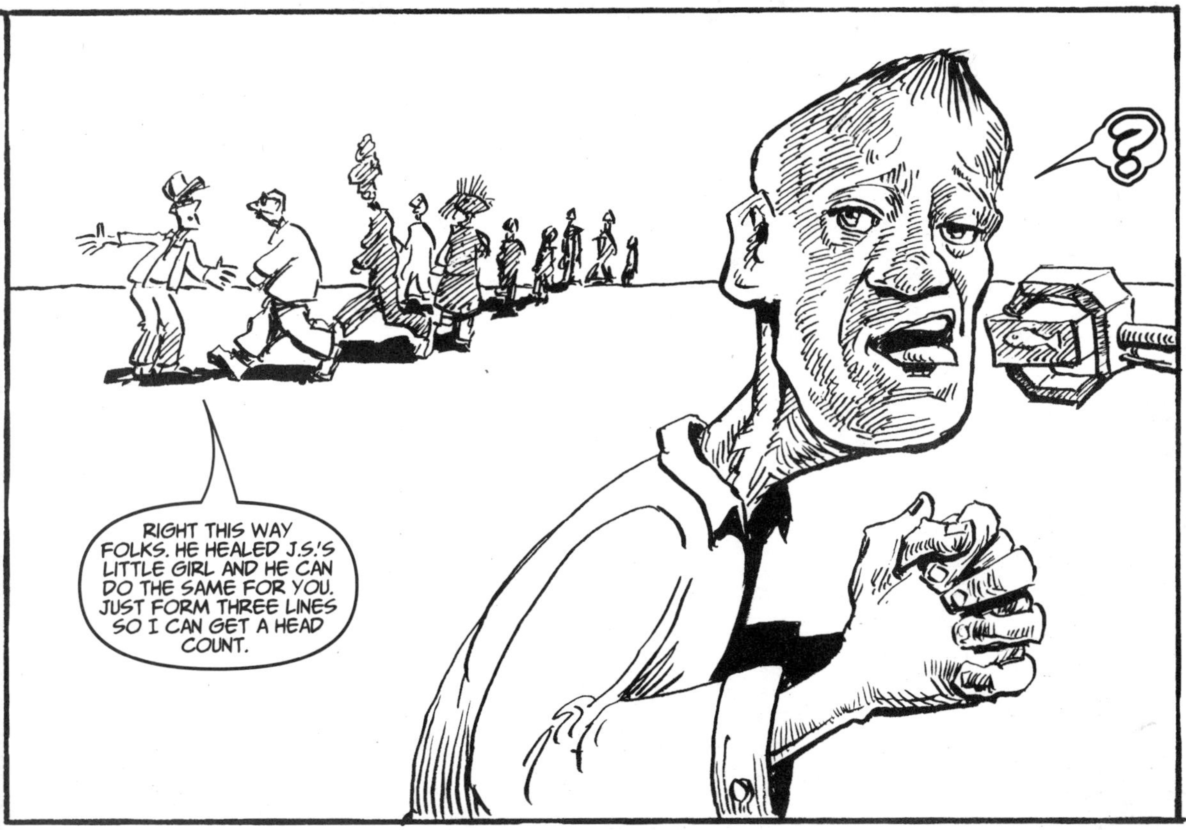
?
RIGHT THIS WAY FOLKS. HE HEALED J.S.'S LITTLE GIRL AND HE CAN DO THE SAME FOR YOU. JUST FORM THREE LINES SO I CAN GET A HEAD COUNT.

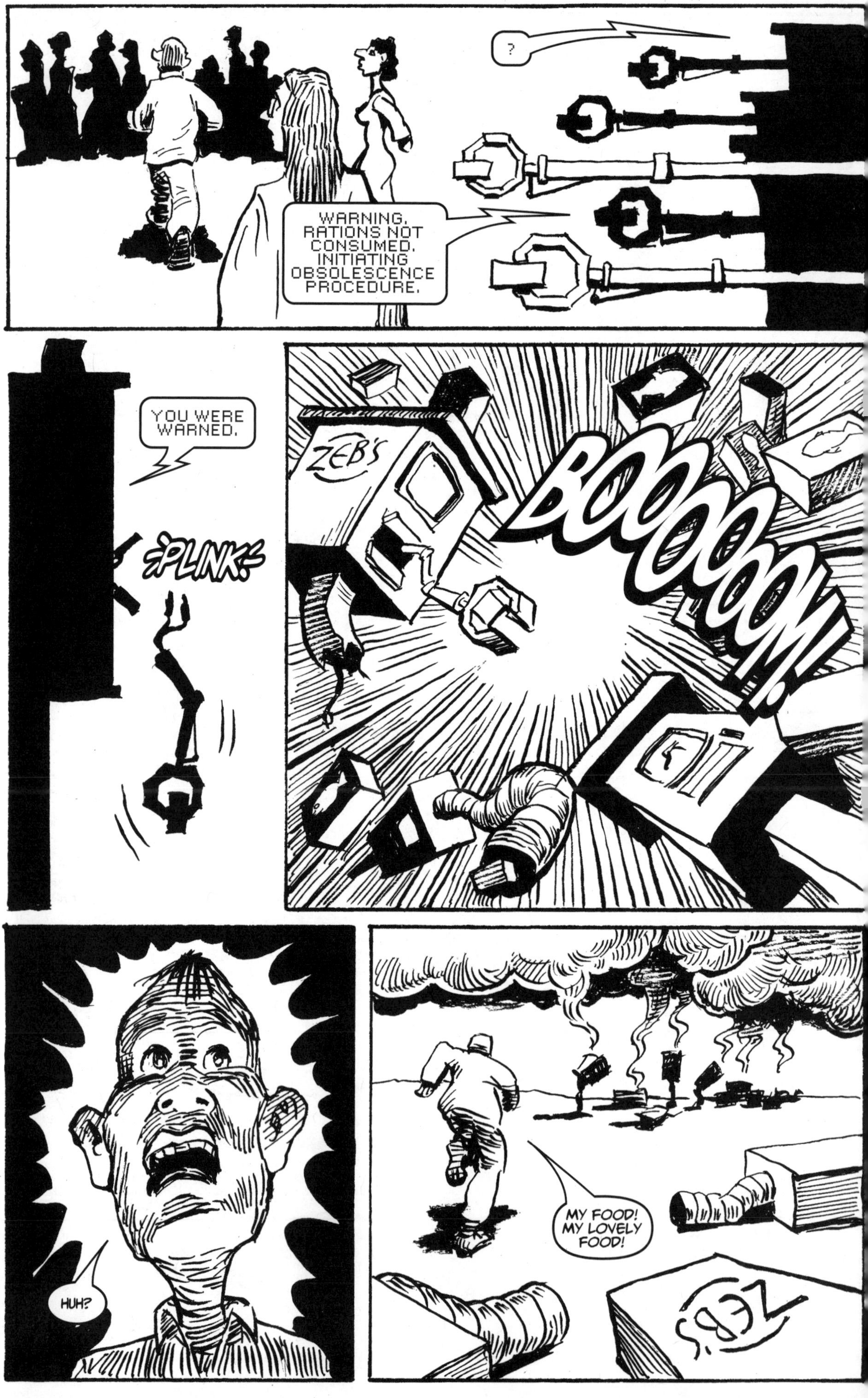
?
WARNING. RATIONS NOT CONSUMED. INITIATING OBSOLESCENCE PROCEDURE.
YOU WERE WARNED.
PLINK!
ZEB'S
BOOOOOM!
HUH?
MY FOOD! MY LOVELY FOOD!
ZEB'S

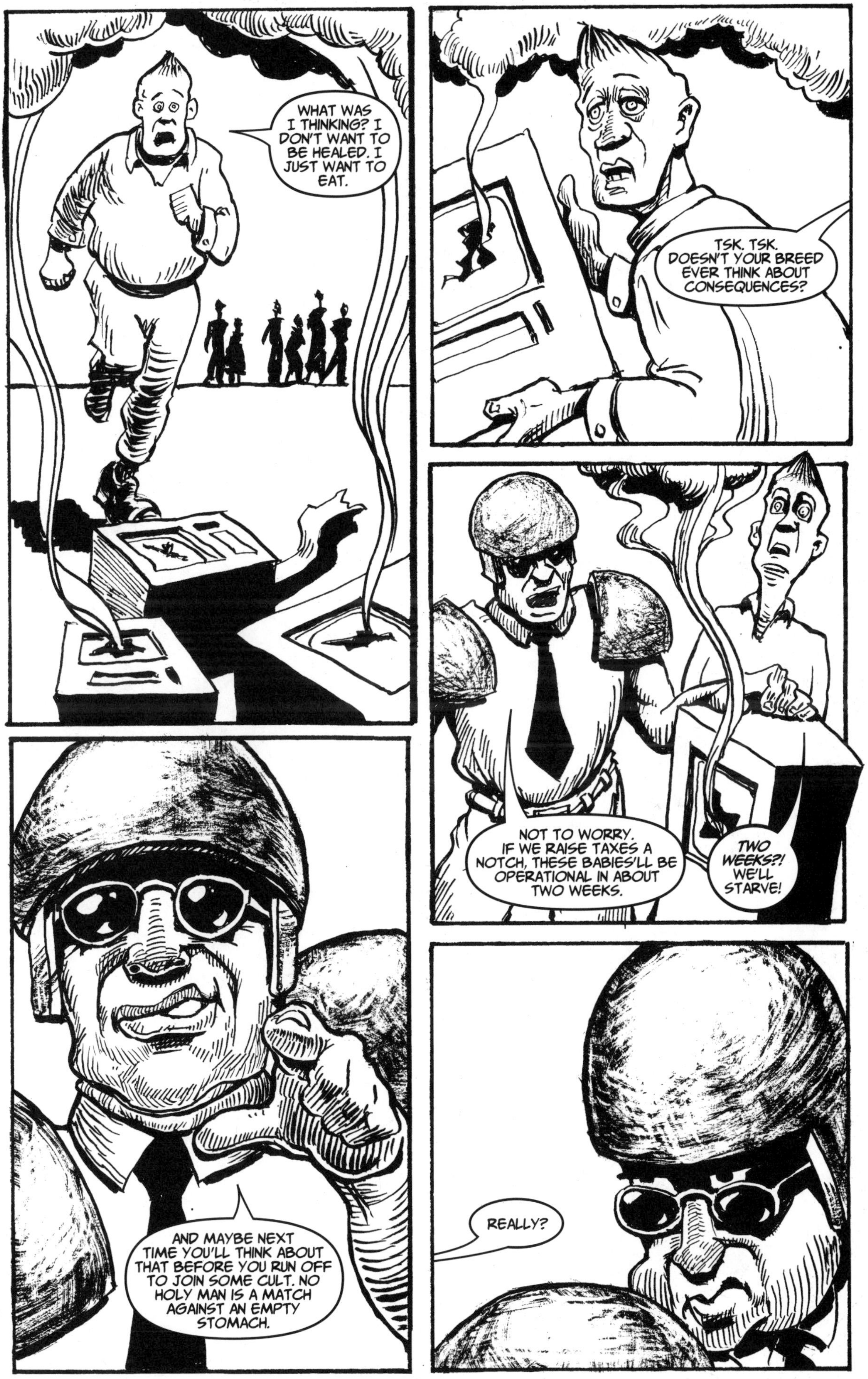
WHAT WAS I THINKING? I DON'T WANT TO BE HEALED. I JUST WANT TO EAT.
TSK. TSK. DOESN'T YOUR BREED EVER THINK ABOUT CONSEQUENCES?
NOT TO WORRY. IF WE RAISE TAXES A NOTCH, THESE BABIES'LL BE OPERATIONAL IN ABOUT TWO WEEKS.
TWO WEEKS?! WE'LL STARVE!
AND MAYBE NEXT TIME YOU'LL THINK ABOUT THAT BEFORE YOU RUN OFF TO JOIN SOME CULT. NO HOLY MAN IS A MATCH AGAINST AN EMPTY STOMACH.
REALLY?

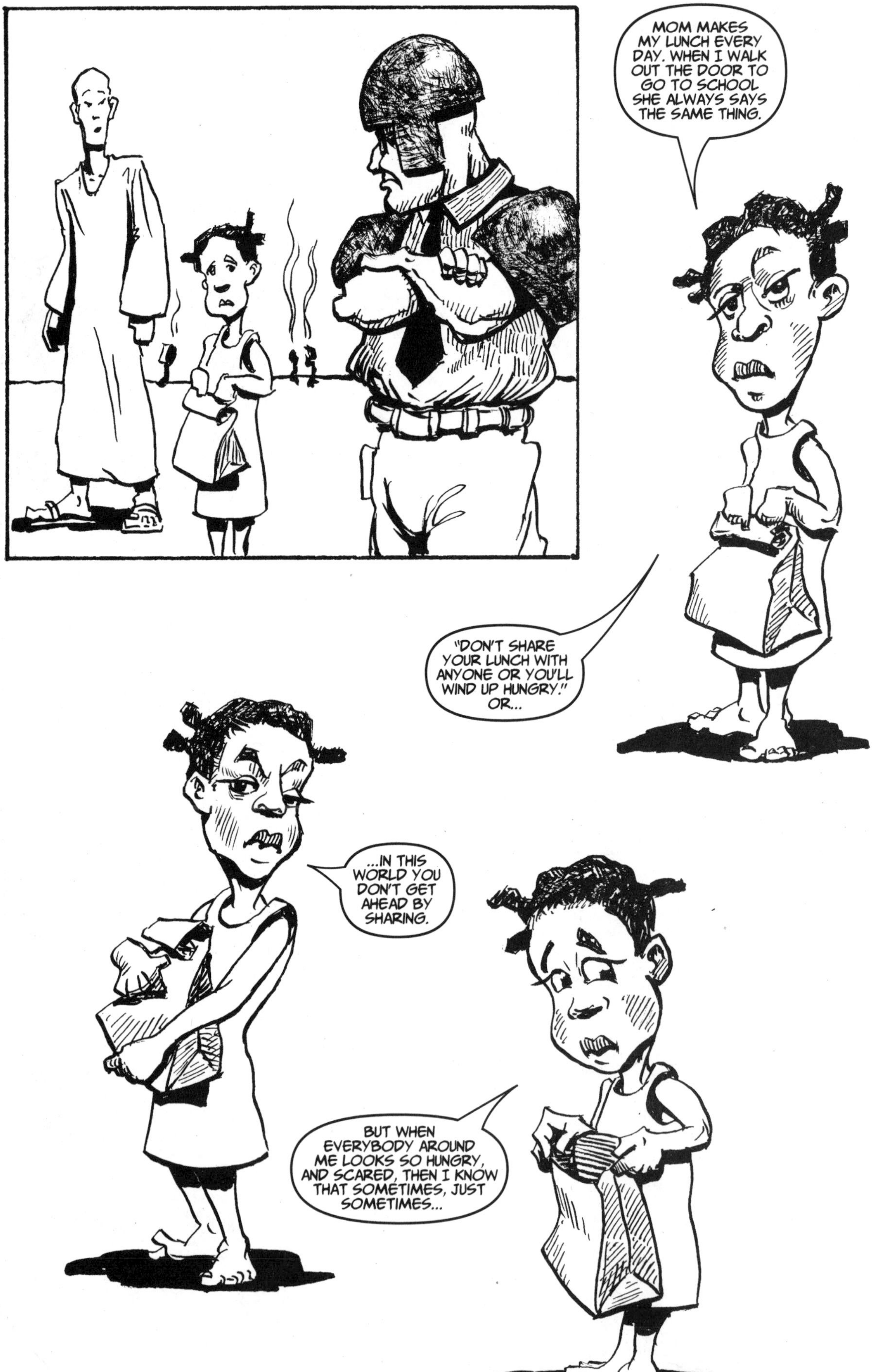
MOM MAKES MY LUNCH EVERY DAY. WHEN I WALK OUT THE DOOR TO GO TO SCHOOL SHE ALWAYS SAYS THE SAME THING.
"DON'T SHARE YOUR LUNCH WITH ANYONE OR YOU'LL WIND UP HUNGRY." OR...
...IN THIS WORLD YOU DON'T GET AHEAD BY SHARING.
BUT WHEN EVERYBODY AROUND ME LOOKS SO HUNGRY, AND SCARED, THEN I KNOW THAT SOMETIMES, JUST SOMETIMES...

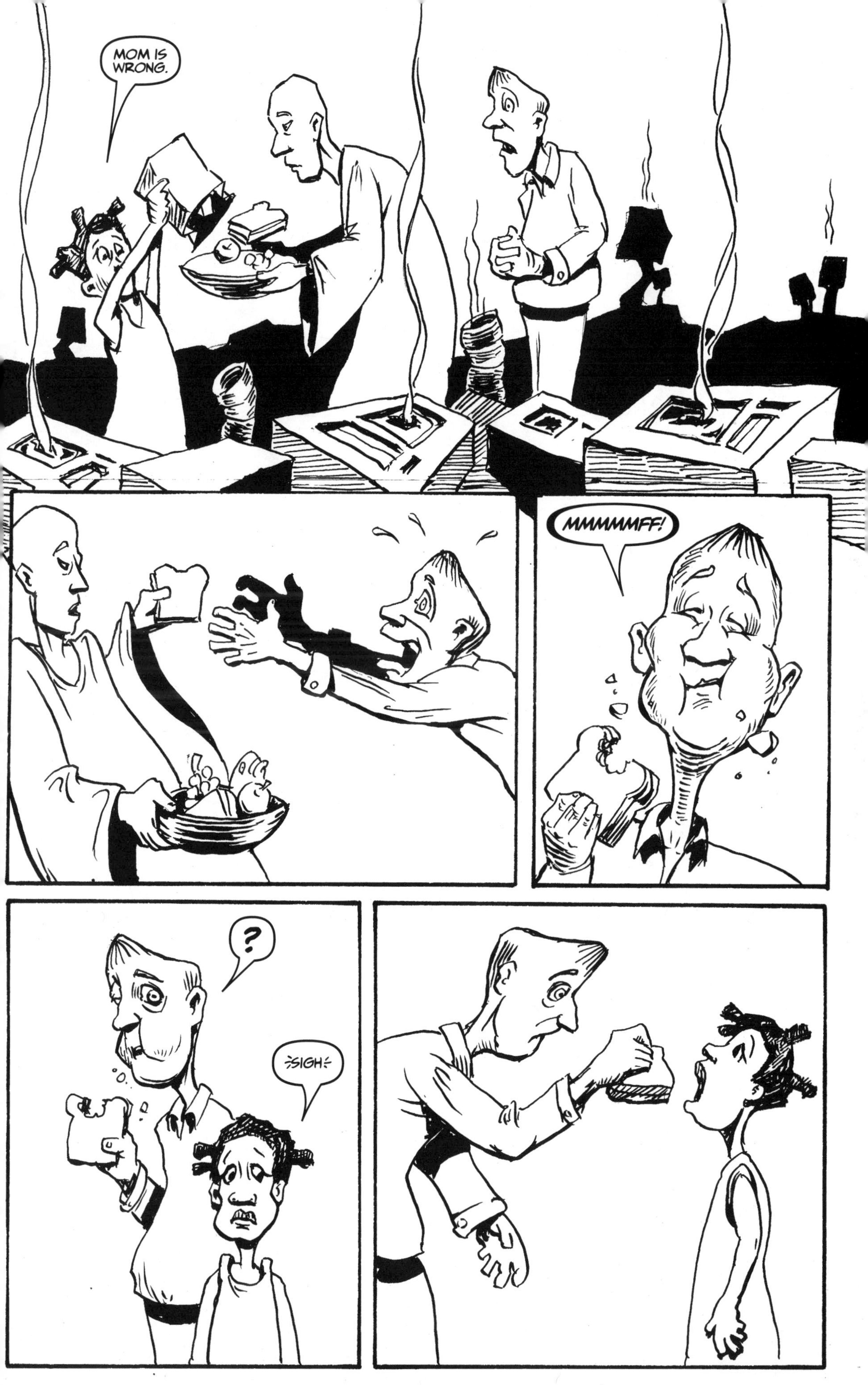
MOM IS WRONG.
MMMMMFF!
?
SIGH

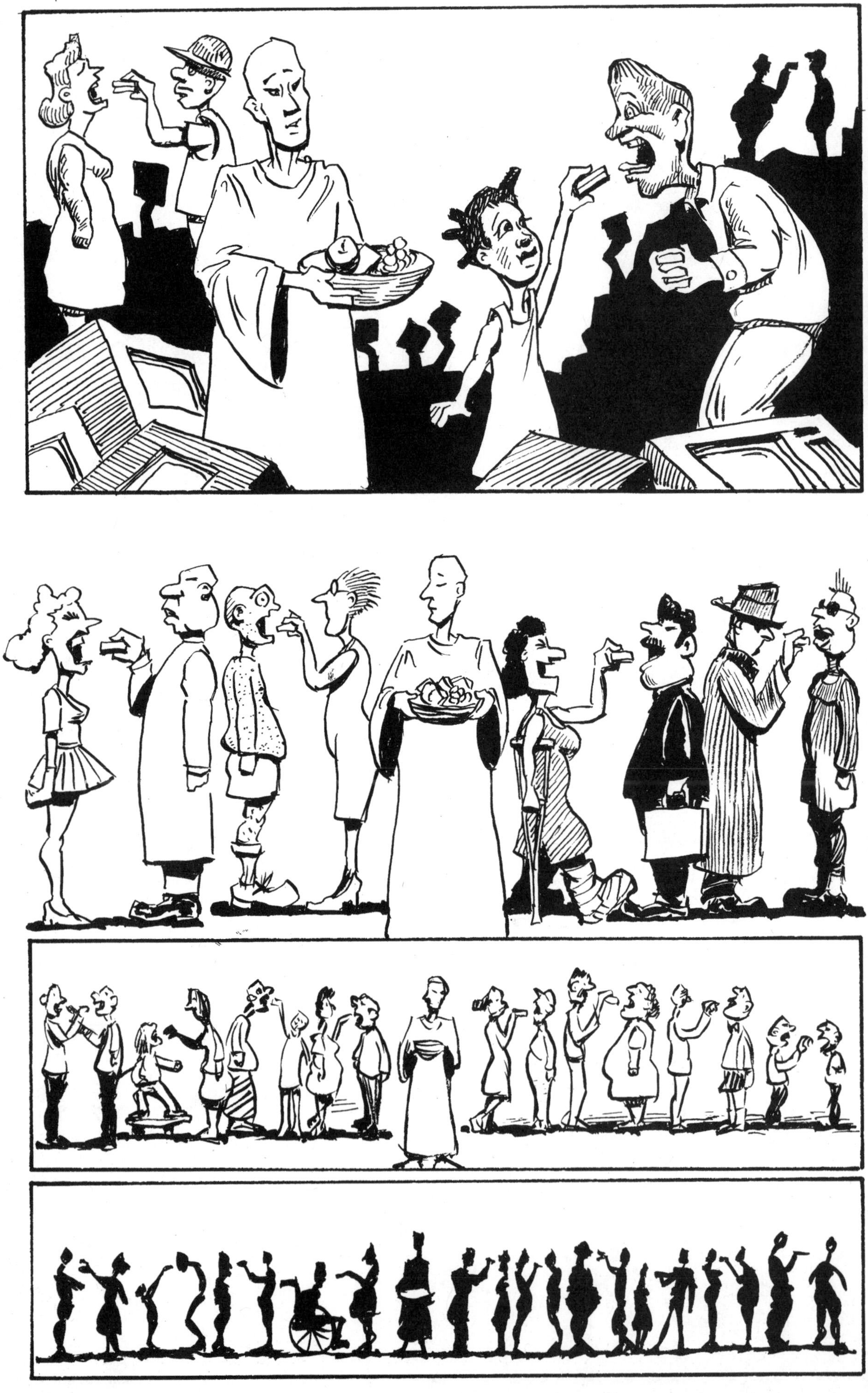

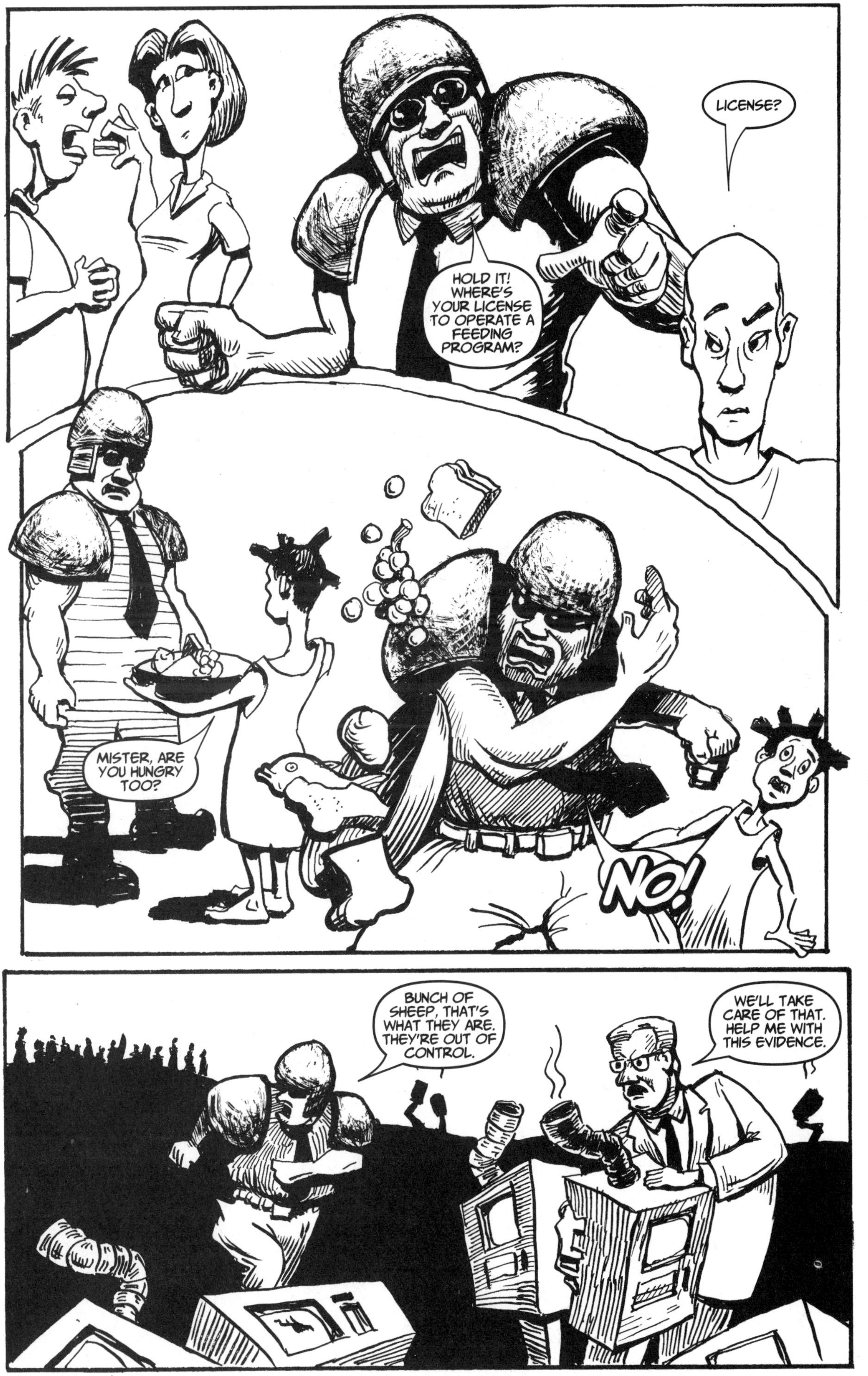
LICENSE?
HOLD IT! WHERE'S YOUR LICENSE TO OPERATE A FEEDING PROGRAM?
MISTER, ARE YOU HUNGRY TOO?
NO!
BUNCH OF SHEEP, THAT'S WHAT THEY ARE. THEY'RE OUT OF CONTROL.
WE'LL TAKE CARE OF THAT. HELP ME WITH THIS EVIDENCE.

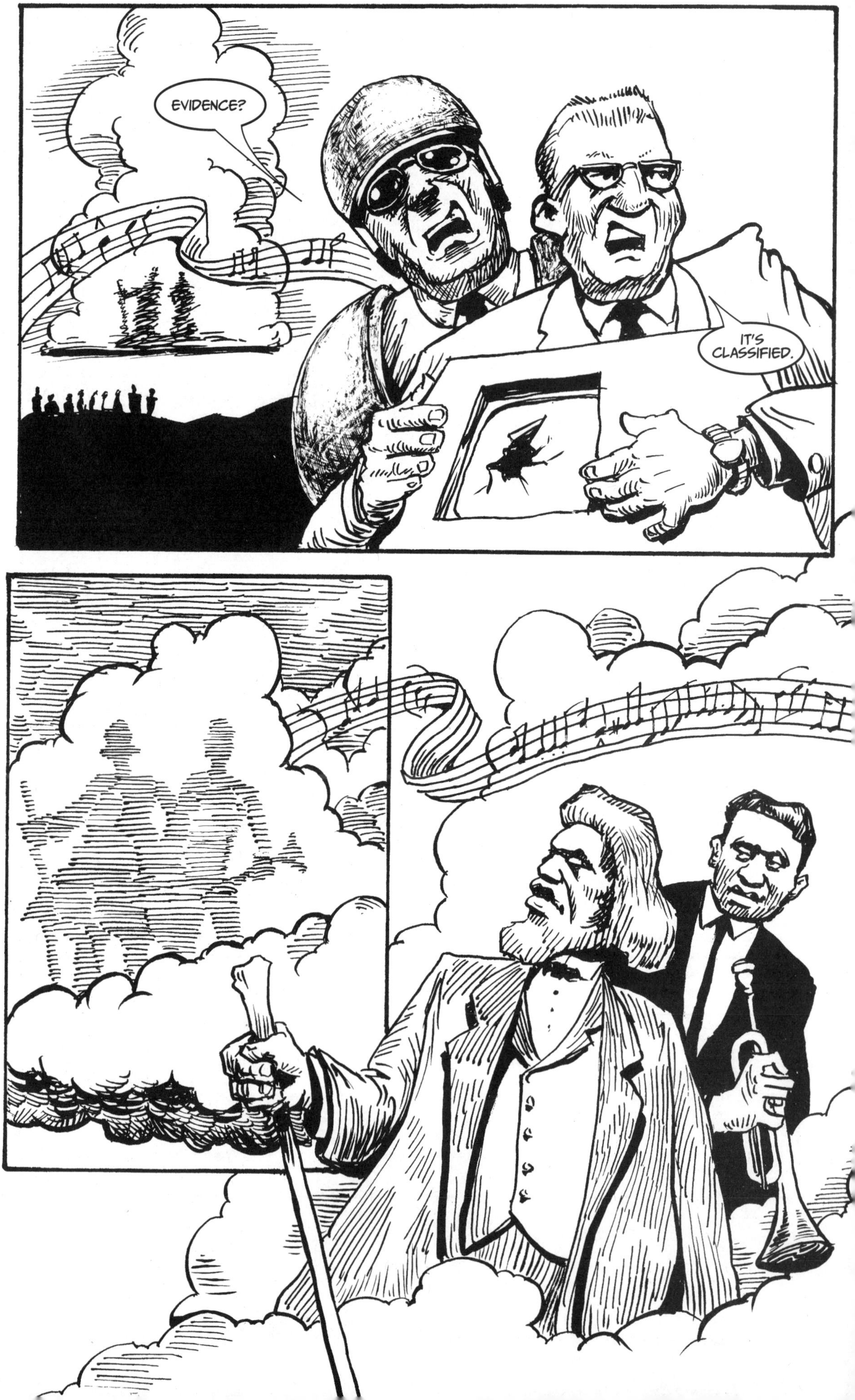
EVIDENCE?
IT'S CLASSIFIED.

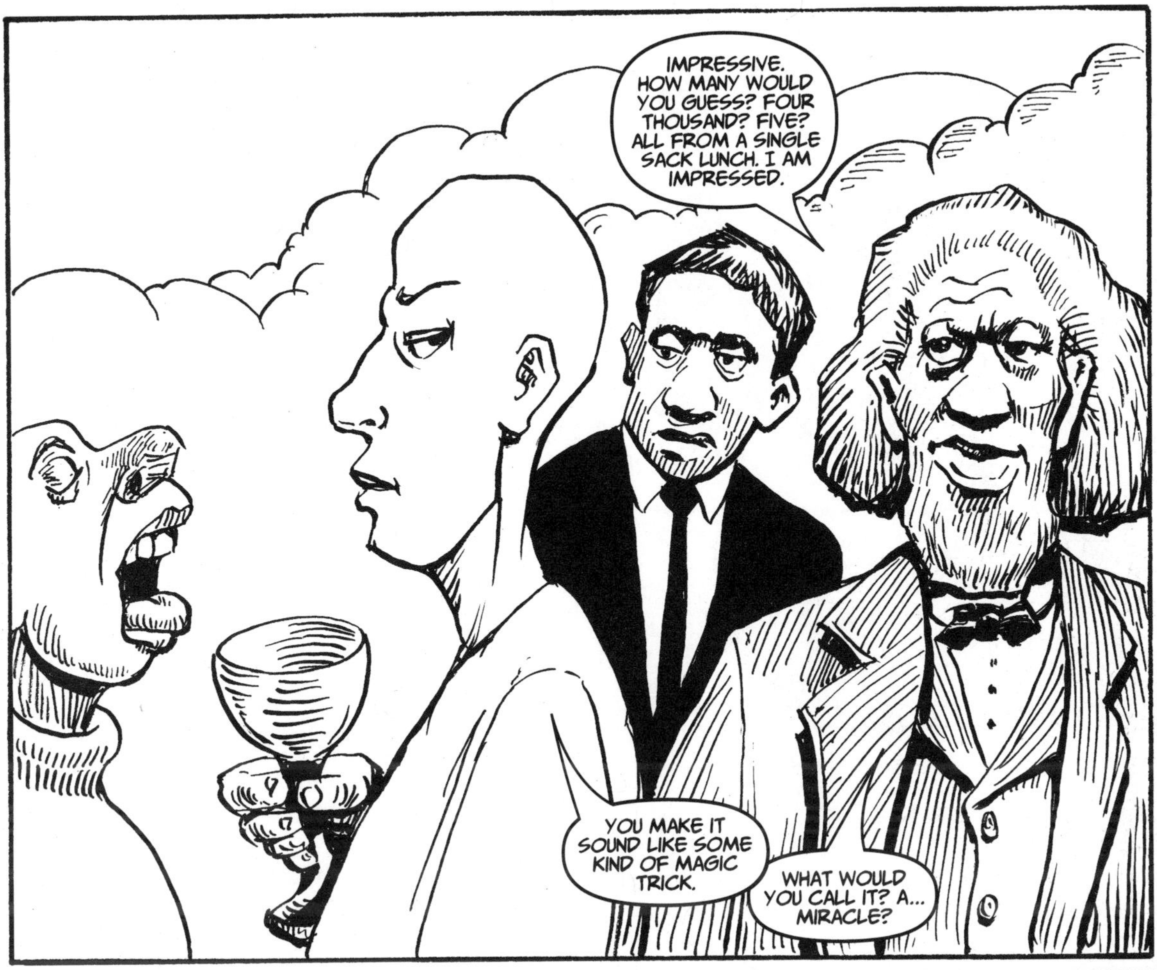
IMPRESSIVE. HOW MANY WOULD YOU GUESS? FOUR THOUSAND? FIVE? ALL FROM A SINGLE SACK LUNCH. I AM IMPRESSED.
YOU MAKE IT SOUND LIKE SOME KIND OF MAGIC TRICK.
WHAT WOULD YOU CALL IT? A... MIRACLE?

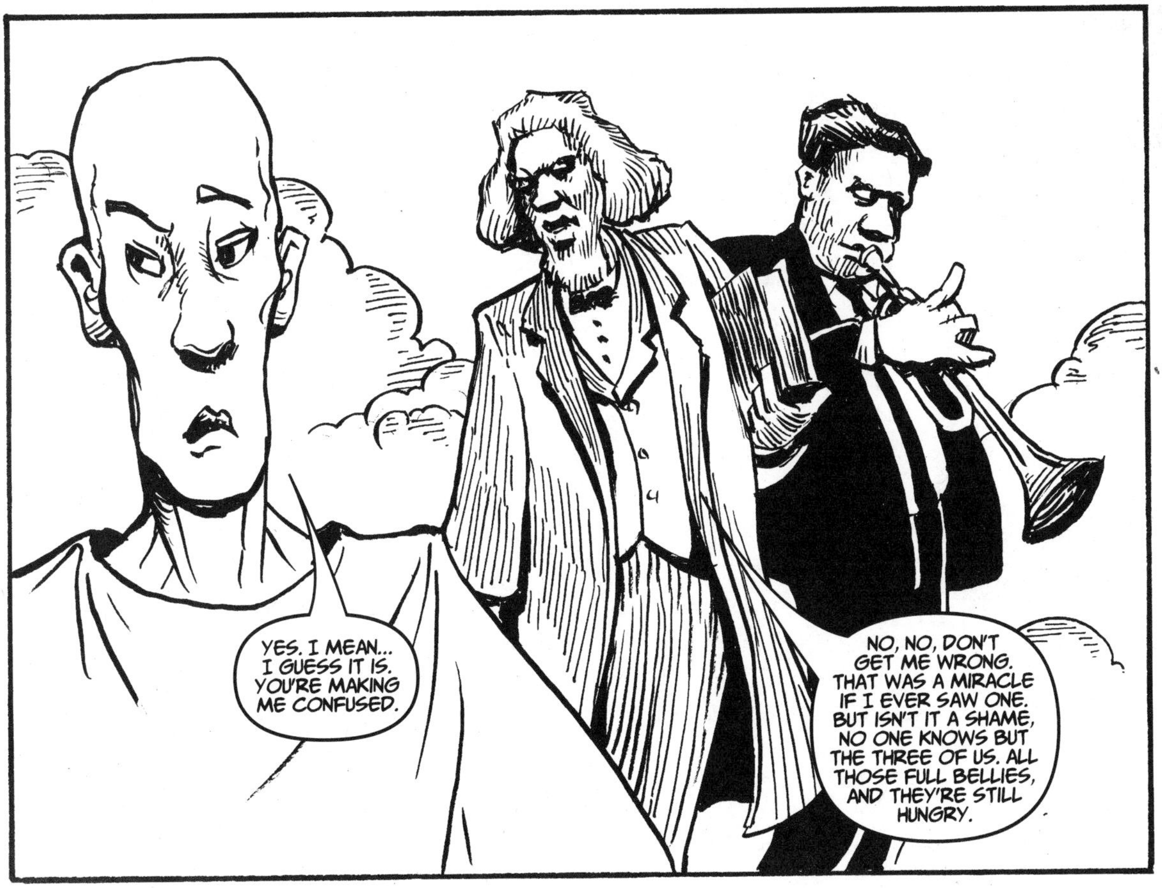
YES. I MEAN... I GUESS IT IS. YOU'RE MAKING ME CONFUSED.
NO, NO, DON'T GET ME WRONG. THAT WAS A MIRACLE IF I EVER SAW ONE. BUT ISN'T IT A SHAME, NO ONE KNOWS BUT THE THREE OF US. ALL THOSE FULL BELLIES, AND THEY'RE STILL HUNGRY.

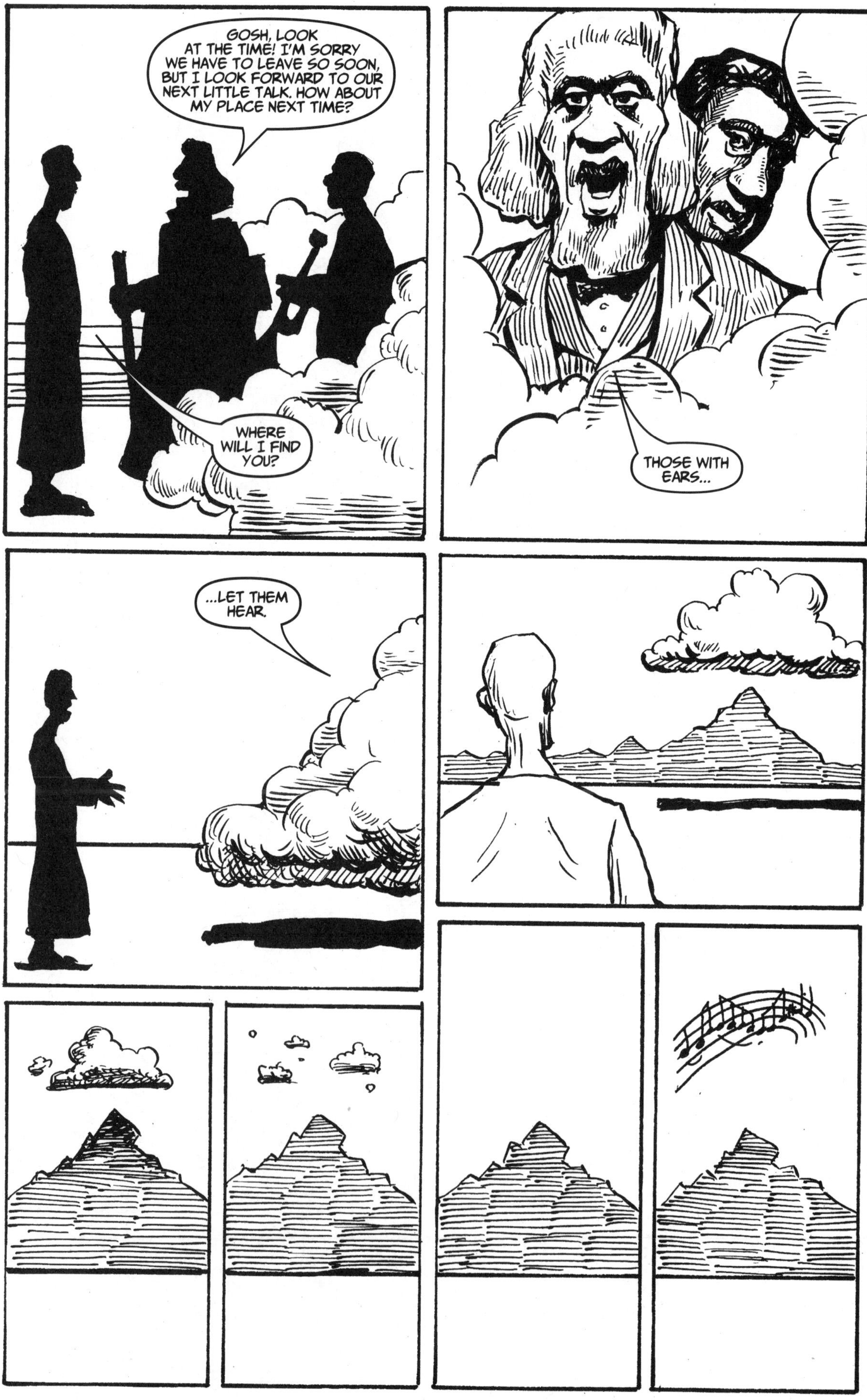
GOSH, LOOK AT THE TIME! I'M SORRY WE HAVE TO LEAVE SO SOON, BUT I LOOK FORWARD TO OUR NEXT LITTLE TALK. HOW ABOUT MY PLACE NEXT TIME?
WHERE WILL I FIND YOU?
THOSE WITH EARS...
...LET THEM HEAR.

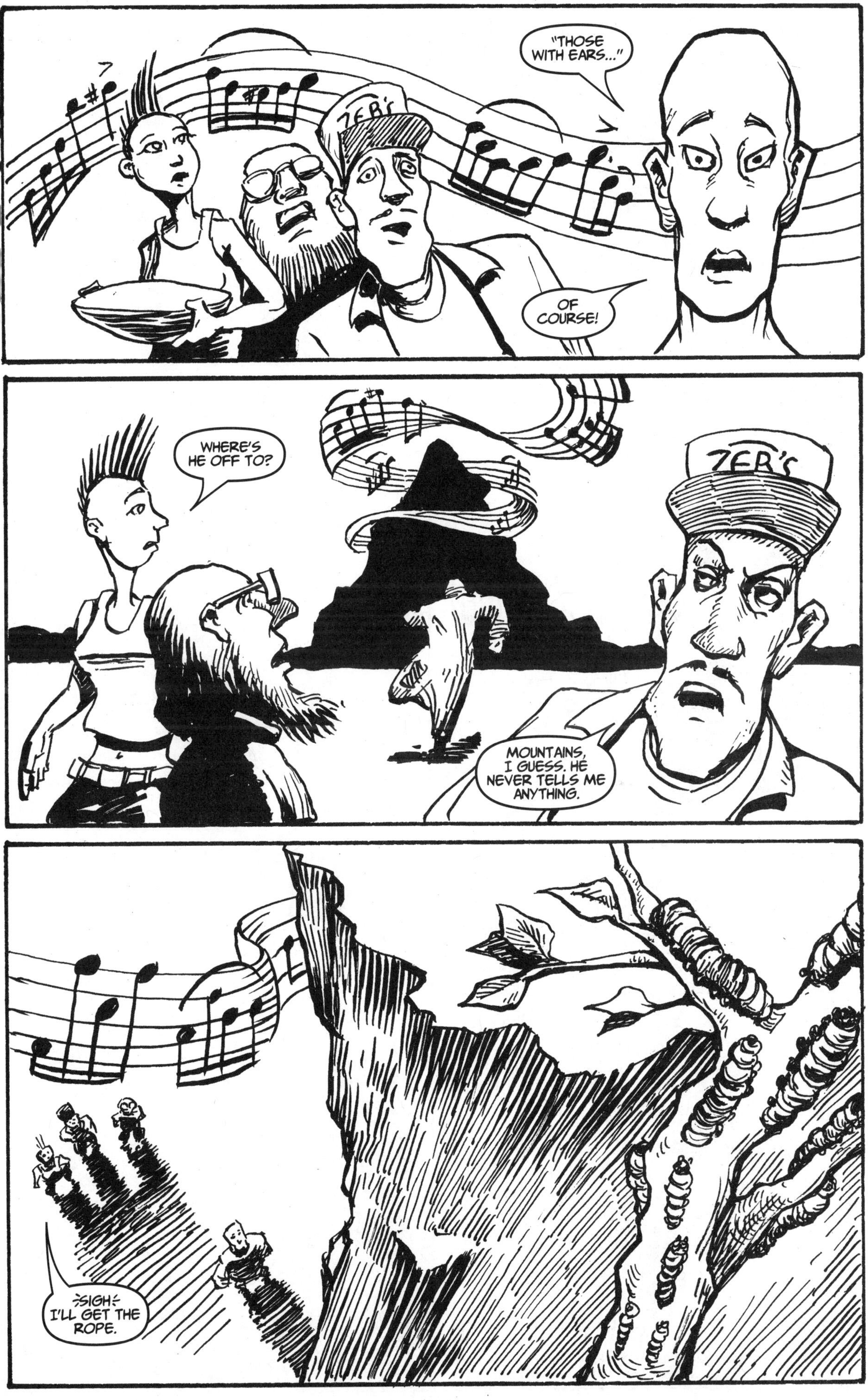
"THOSE WITH EARS..."
OF COURSE!
WHERE'S HE OFF TO?
MOUNTAINS, I GUESS. HE NEVER TELLS ME ANYTHING.
ZER'S
>SIGH< I'LL GET THE ROPE.

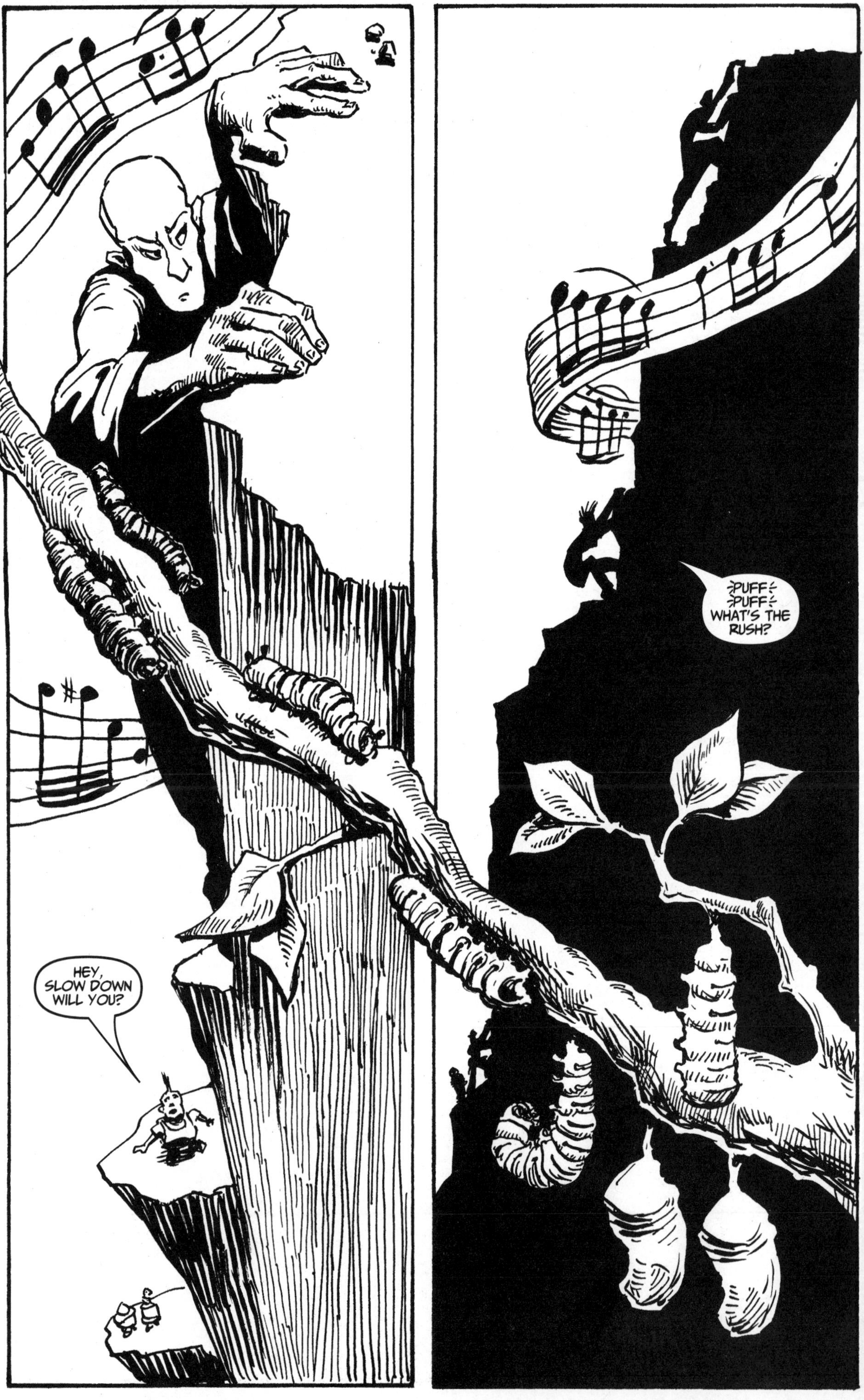
HEY, SLOW DOWN WILL YOU?
PUFF PUFF WHAT'S THE RUSH?

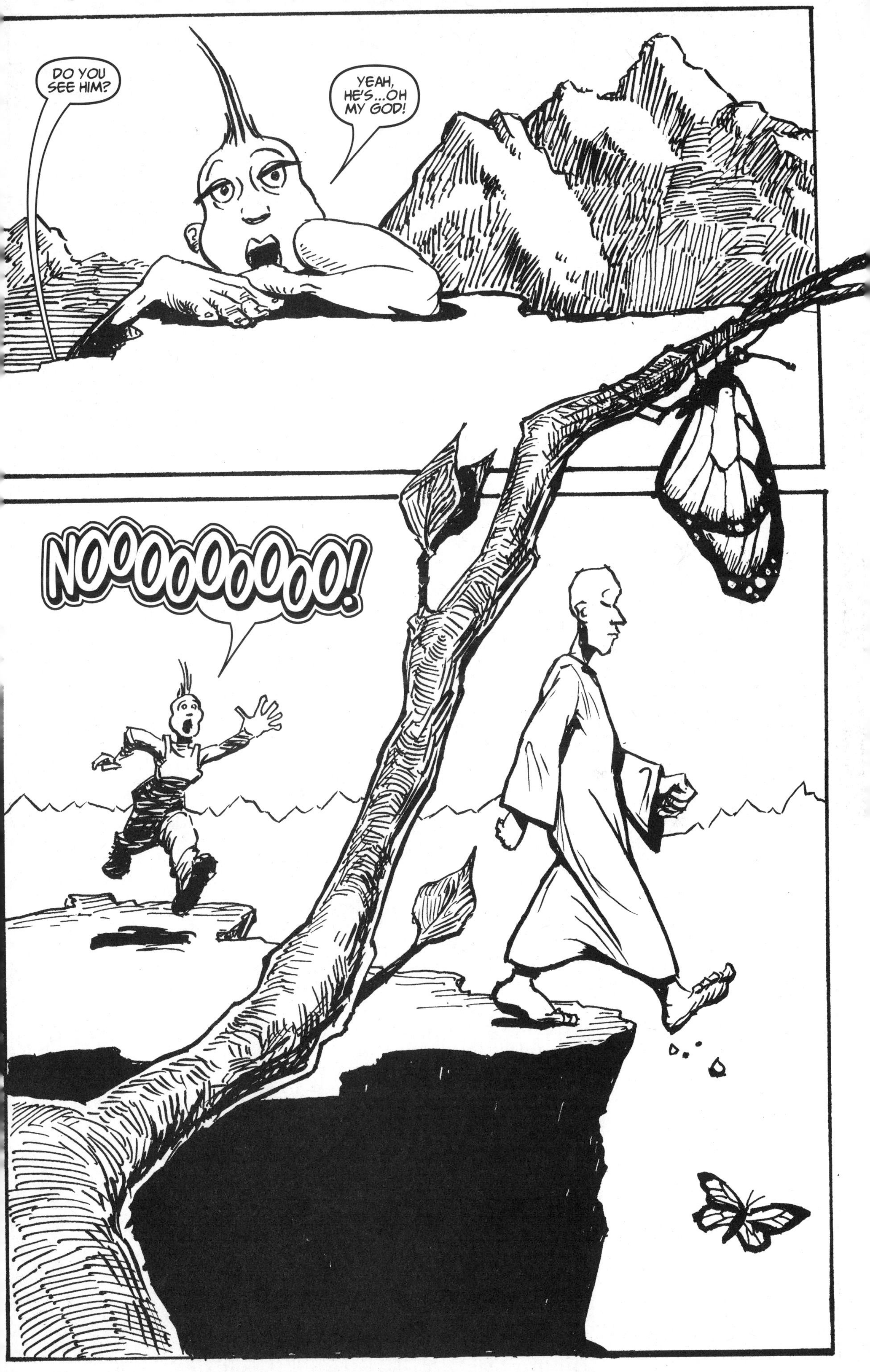
DO YOU SEE HIM?
YEAH, HE'S...OH MY GOD!
NOOOOOOOOOO!

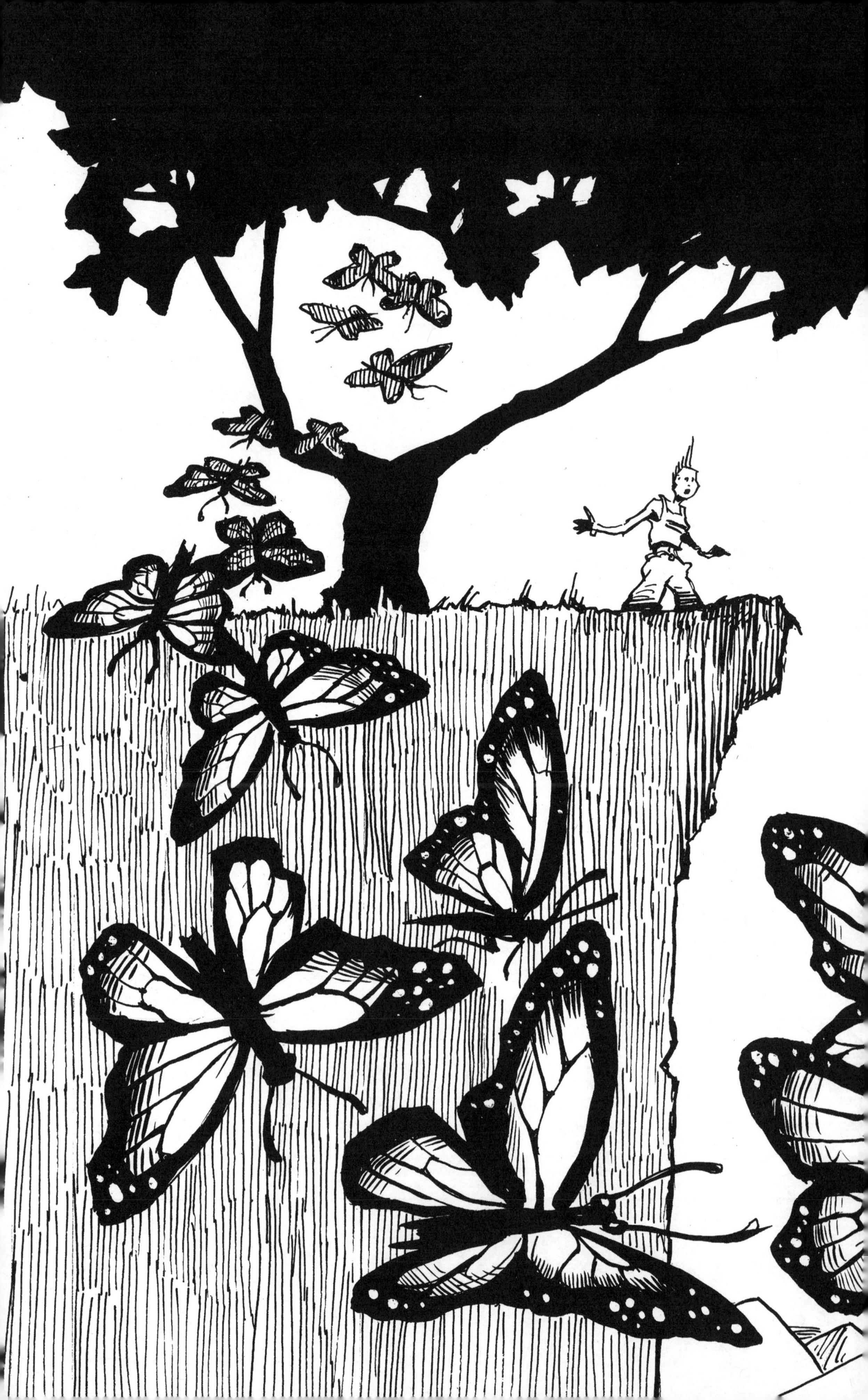

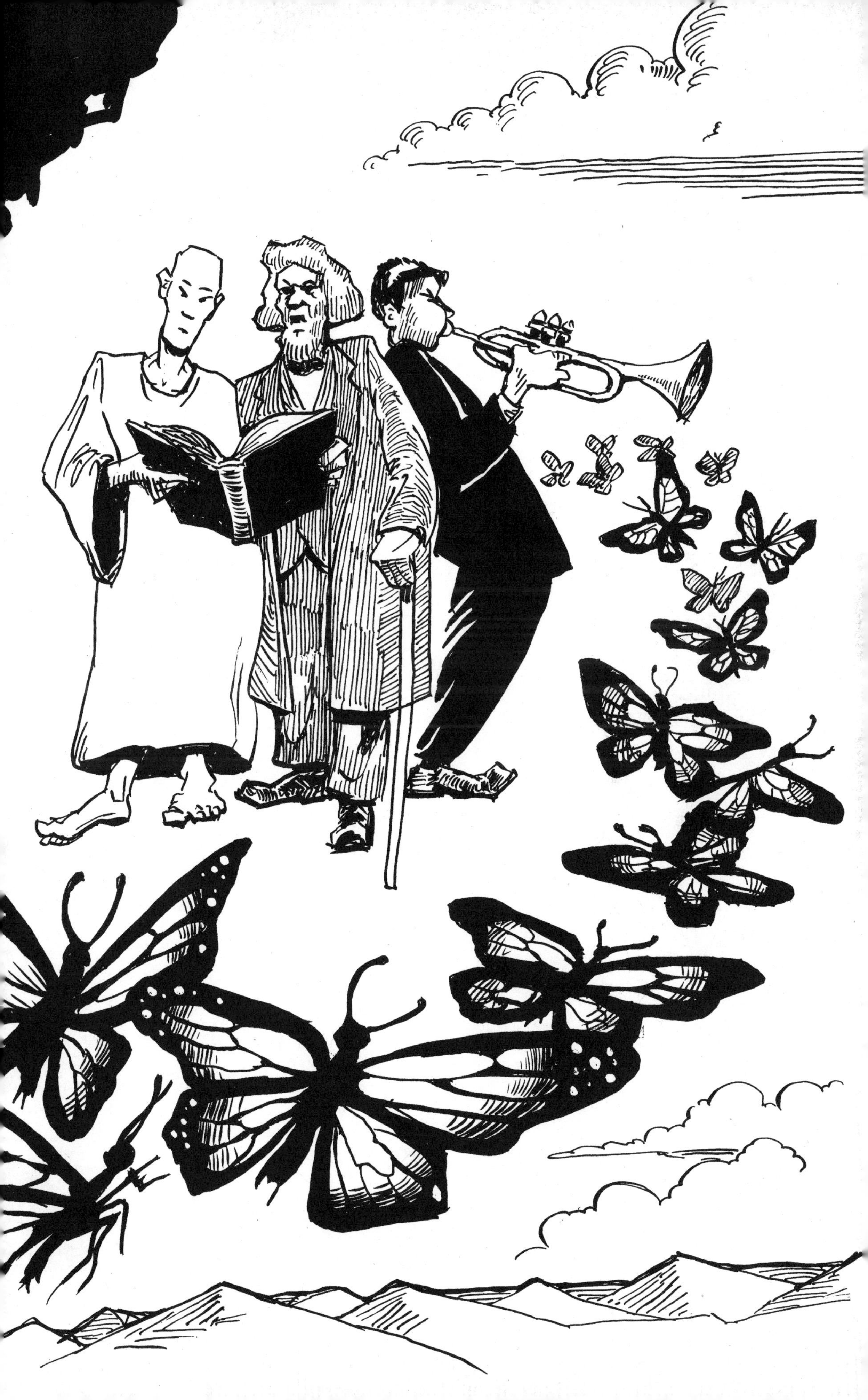

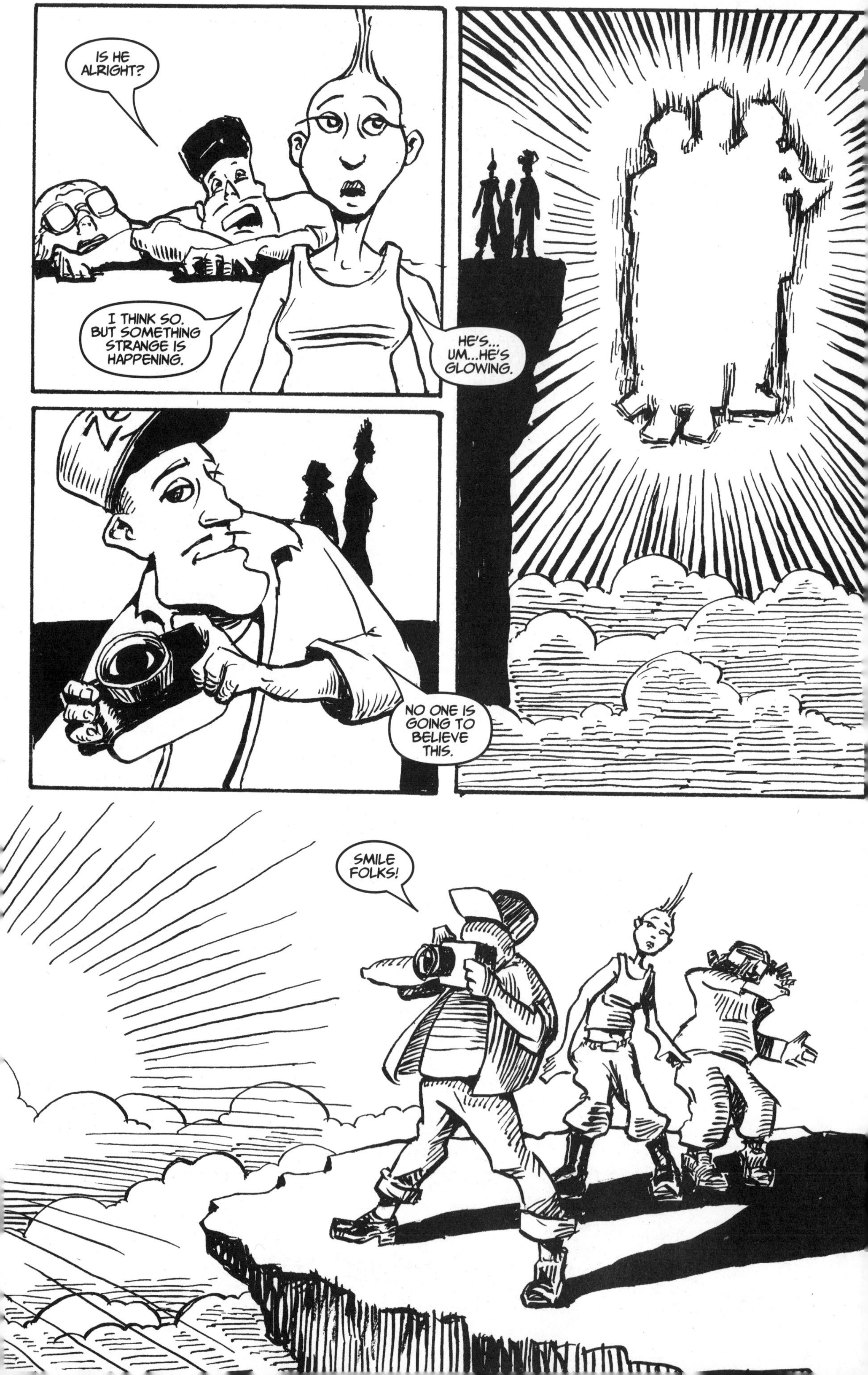
IS HE ALRIGHT?
I THINK SO. BUT SOMETHING STRANGE IS HAPPENING.
HE'S... UM...HE'S GLOWING.
NO ONE IS GOING TO BELIEVE THIS.
SMILE FOLKS!

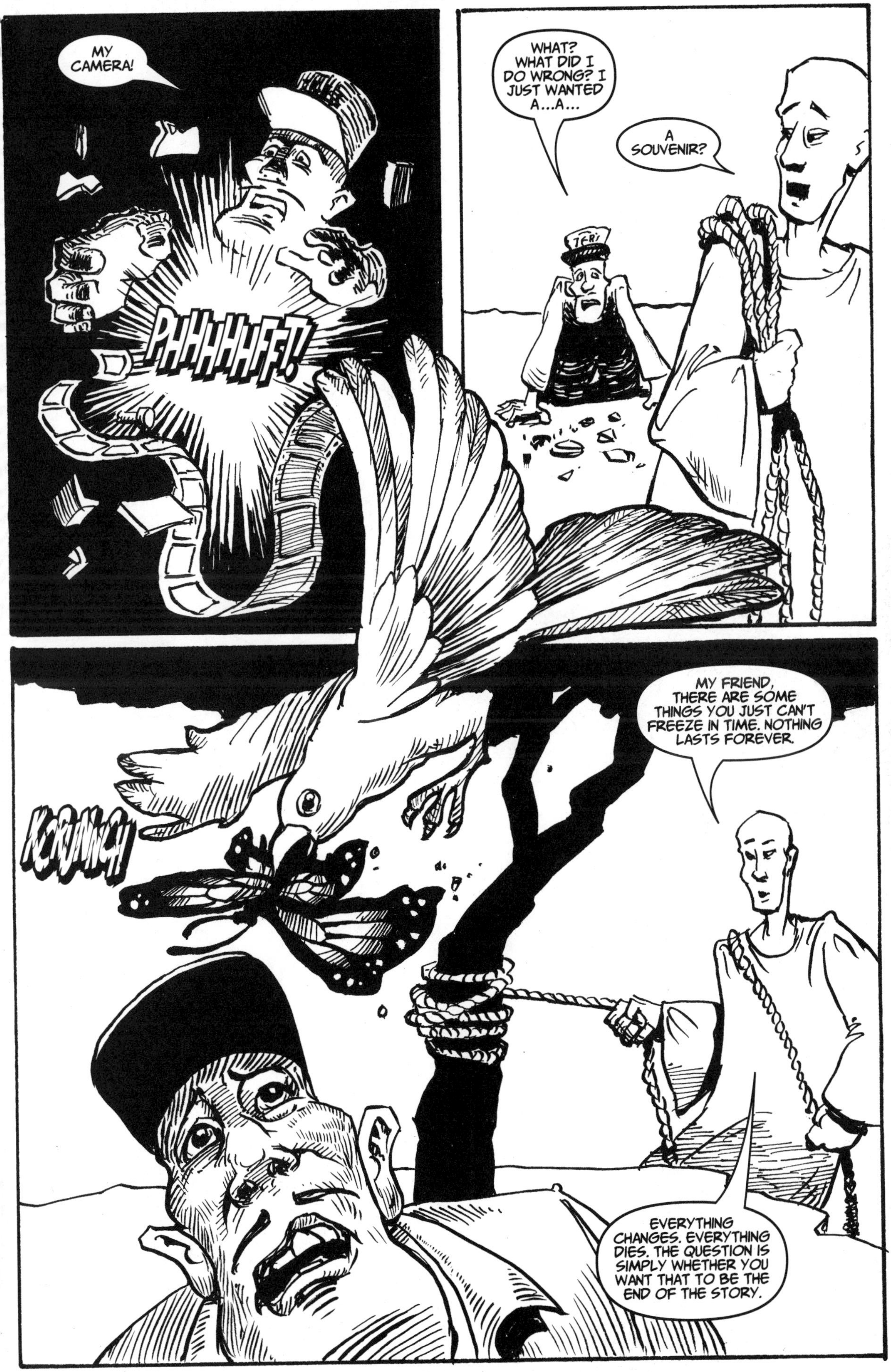
MY CAMERA!
PHHHHFFT!
WHAT? WHAT DID I DO WRONG? I JUST WANTED A...A...
A SOUVENIR?
MY FRIEND, THERE ARE SOME THINGS YOU JUST CAN'T FREEZE IN TIME. NOTHING LASTS FOREVER.
EVERYTHING CHANGES. EVERYTHING DIES. THE QUESTION IS SIMPLY WHETHER YOU WANT THAT TO BE THE END OF THE STORY.

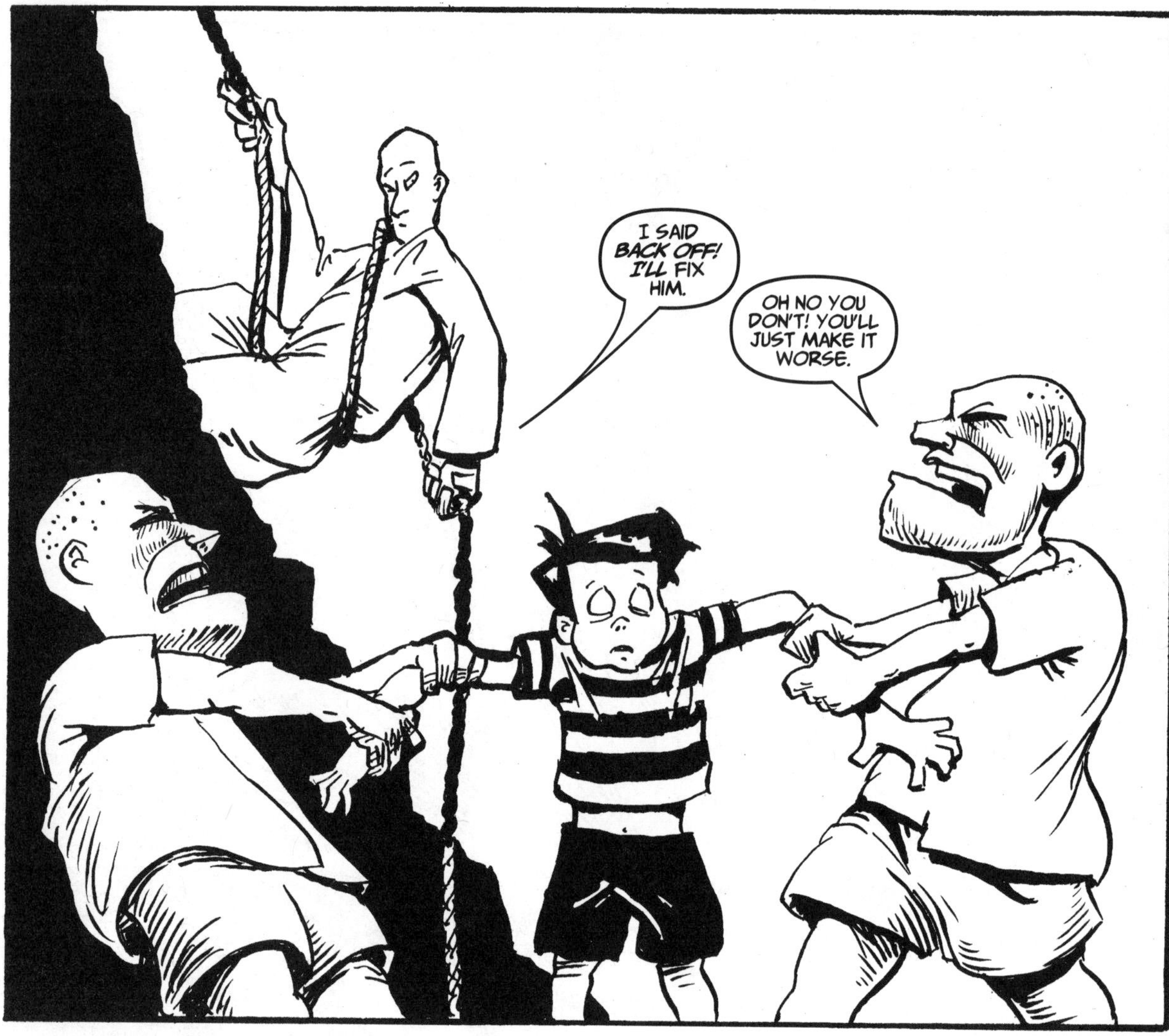

I SAID BACK OFF! I'LL FIX HIM.
OH NO YOU DON'T! YOU'LL JUST MAKE IT WORSE.

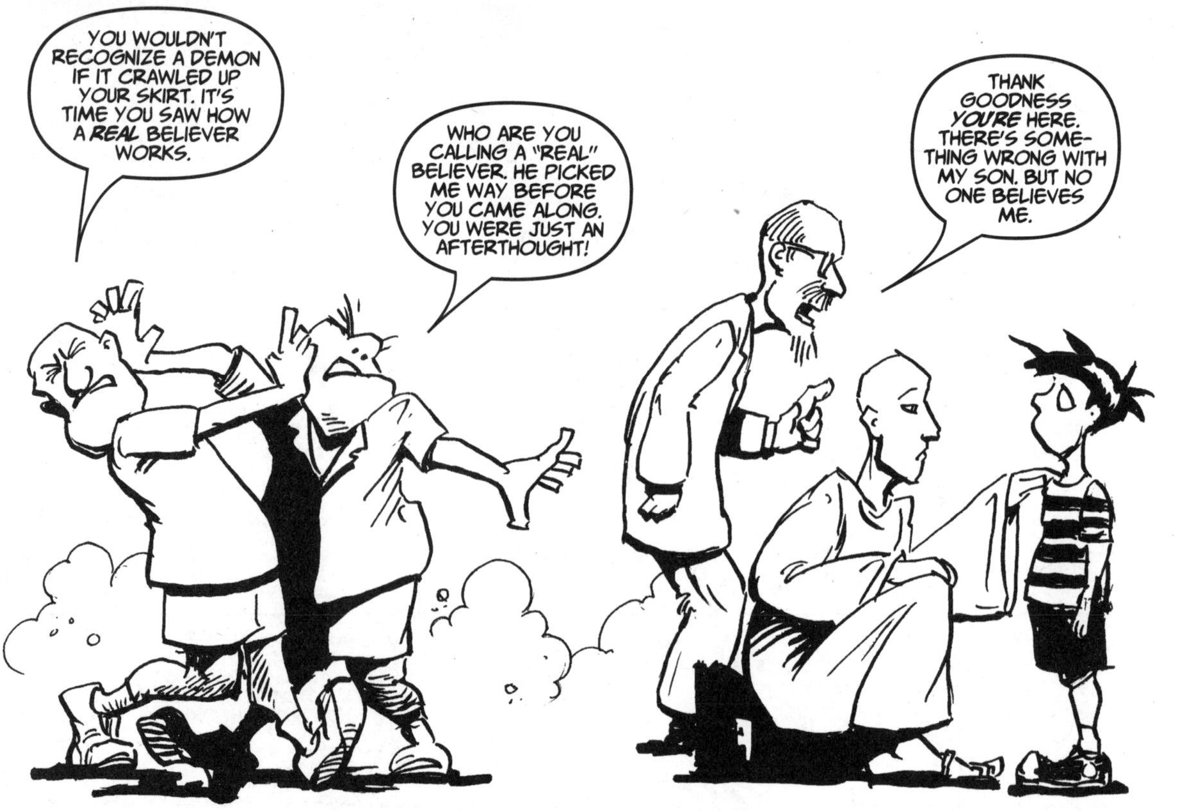

YOU WOULDN'T RECOGNIZE A DEMON IF IT CRAWLED UP YOUR SKIRT. IT'S TIME YOU SAW HOW A REAL BELIEVER WORKS.
WHO ARE YOU CALLING A "REAL" BELIEVER. HE PICKED ME WAY BEFORE YOU CAME ALONG. YOU WERE JUST AN AFTERTHOUGHT!
THANK GOODNESS YOU'RE HERE. THERE'S SOME-THING WRONG WITH MY SON. BUT NO ONE BELIEVES ME.

ANOTHER ONE? WHERE DO THEY KEEP COMING FROM?

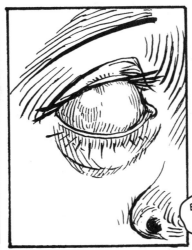

BACK OFF MIRACLE MAN.

I'M WILLING TO DESTROY THE BOY TO PROVE YOU WRONG. ARE YOU PREPARED TO DESTROY THE BOY TO PROVE YOU'RE RIGHT?

SPLIK!

LET'S CHECK!

≈UNGHH!≈

NOOOOO!

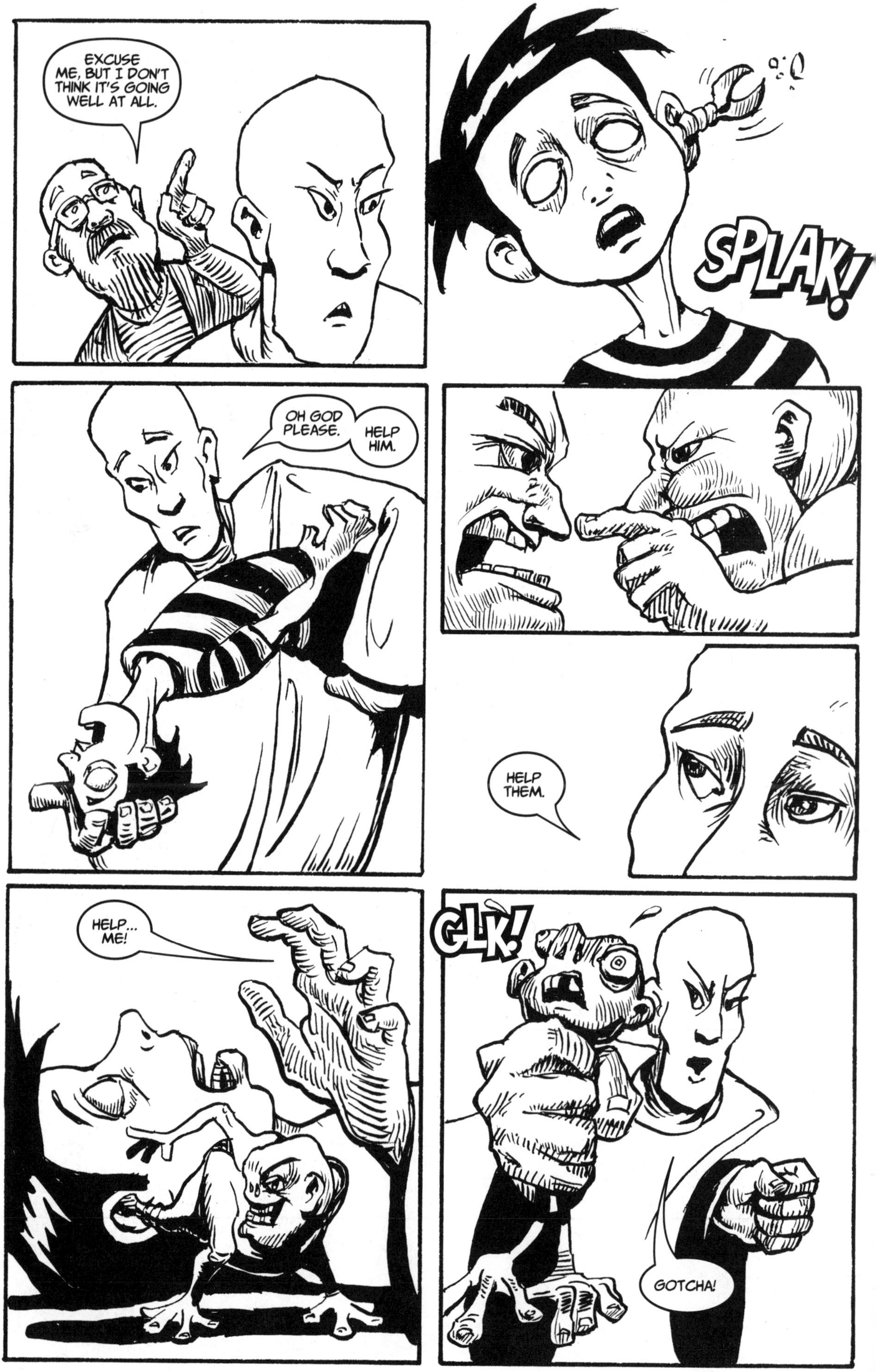
EXCUSE ME, BUT I DON'T THINK IT'S GOING WELL AT ALL.
SPLAK!
OH GOD PLEASE.
HELP HIM.
HELP THEM.
HELP... ME!
GLK!
GOTCHA!

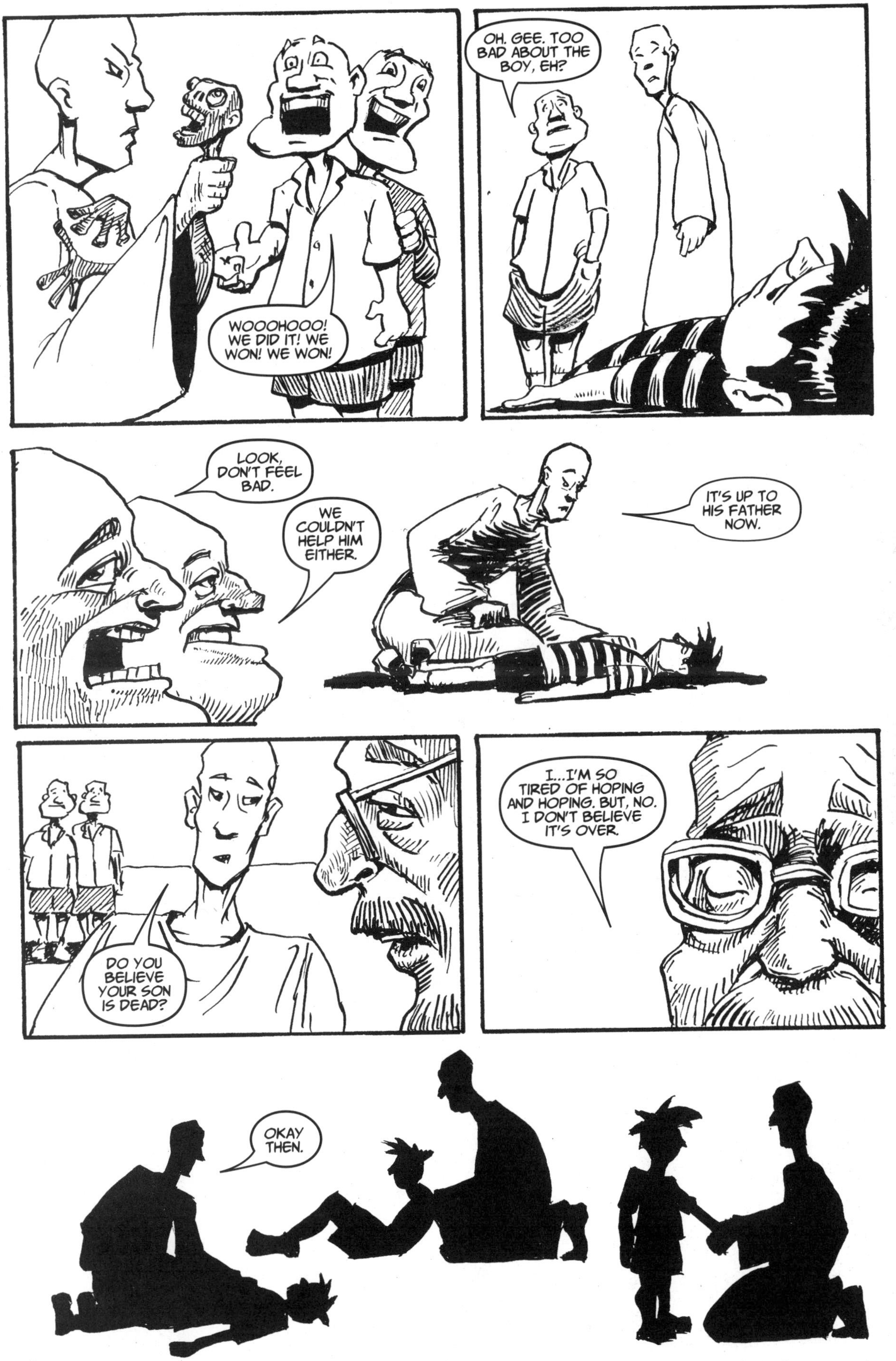
WOOOHOOO! WE DID IT! WE WON! WE WON!
OH. GEE. TOO BAD ABOUT THE BOY, EH?
LOOK, DON'T FEEL BAD.
WE COULDN'T HELP HIM EITHER.
IT'S UP TO HIS FATHER NOW.
DO YOU BELIEVE YOUR SON IS DEAD?
I...I'M SO TIRED OF HOPING AND HOPING. BUT, NO. I DON'T BELIEVE IT'S OVER.
OKAY THEN.

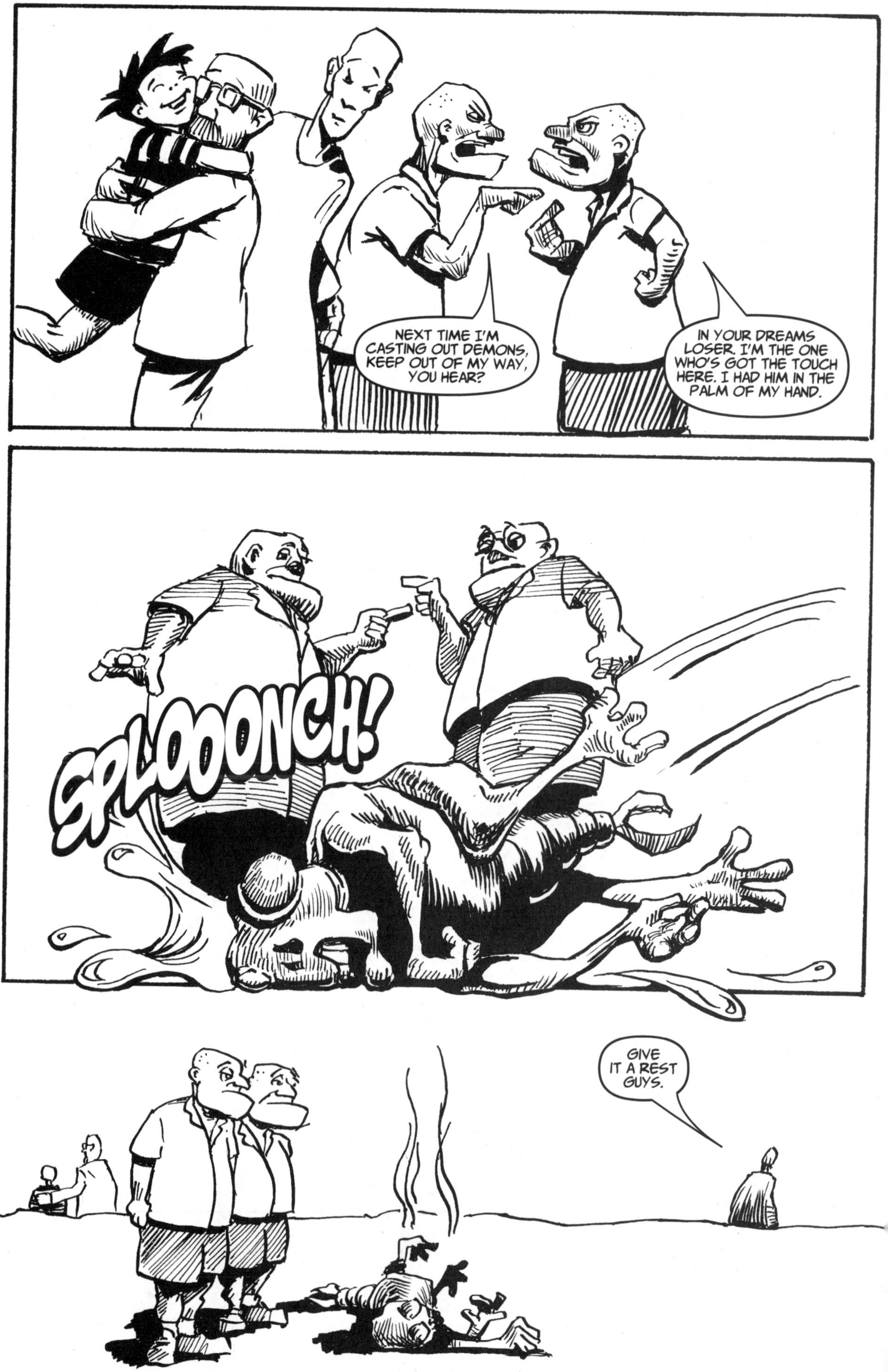
NEXT TIME I'M CASTING OUT DEMONS, KEEP OUT OF MY WAY, YOU HEAR?
IN YOUR DREAMS LOSER. I'M THE ONE WHO'S GOT THE TOUCH HERE. I HAD HIM IN THE PALM OF MY HAND.
SPLOOONCH!
GIVE IT A REST GUYS.

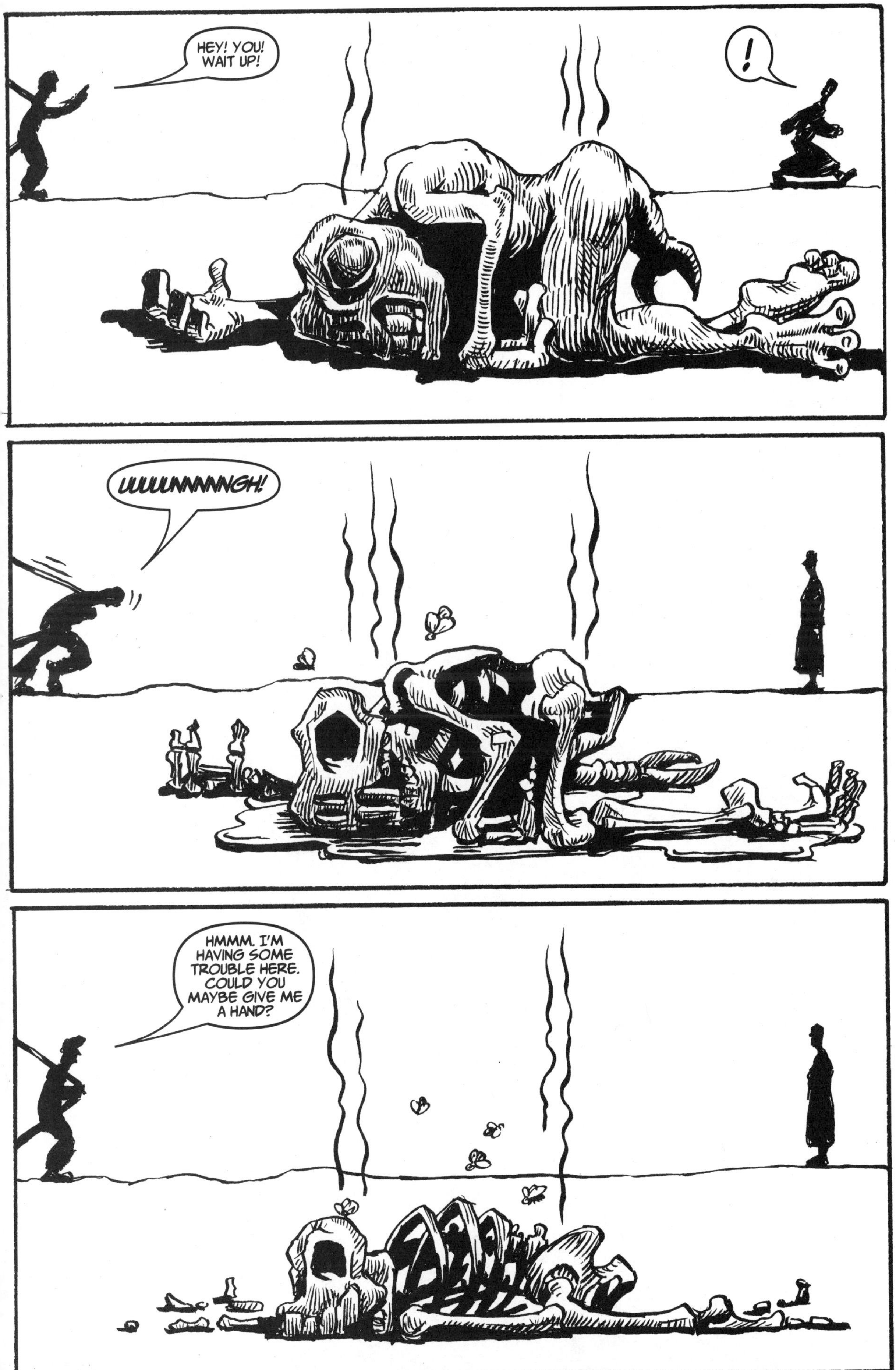
HEY! YOU! WAIT UP!
!
UUUUUNNNNNGH!
HMMM. I'M HAVING SOME TROUBLE HERE. COULD YOU MAYBE GIVE ME A HAND?

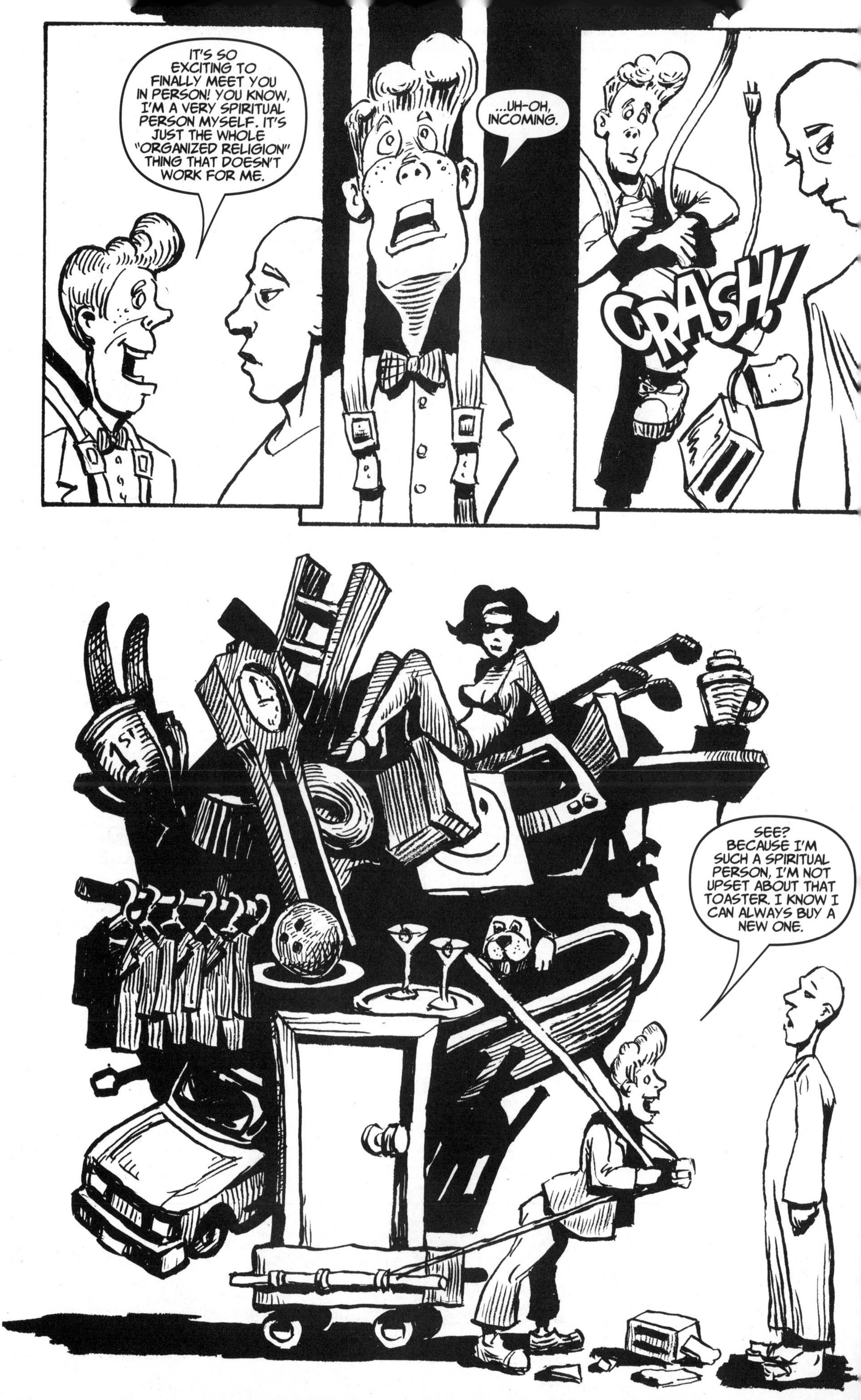
IT'S SO EXCITING TO FINALLY MEET YOU IN PERSON! YOU KNOW, I'M A VERY SPIRITUAL PERSON MYSELF. IT'S JUST THE WHOLE "ORGANIZED RELIGION" THING THAT DOESN'T WORK FOR ME.
...UH-OH, INCOMING.
CRASH!
SEE? BECAUSE I'M SUCH A SPIRITUAL PERSON, I'M NOT UPSET ABOUT THAT TOASTER. I KNOW I CAN ALWAYS BUY A NEW ONE.

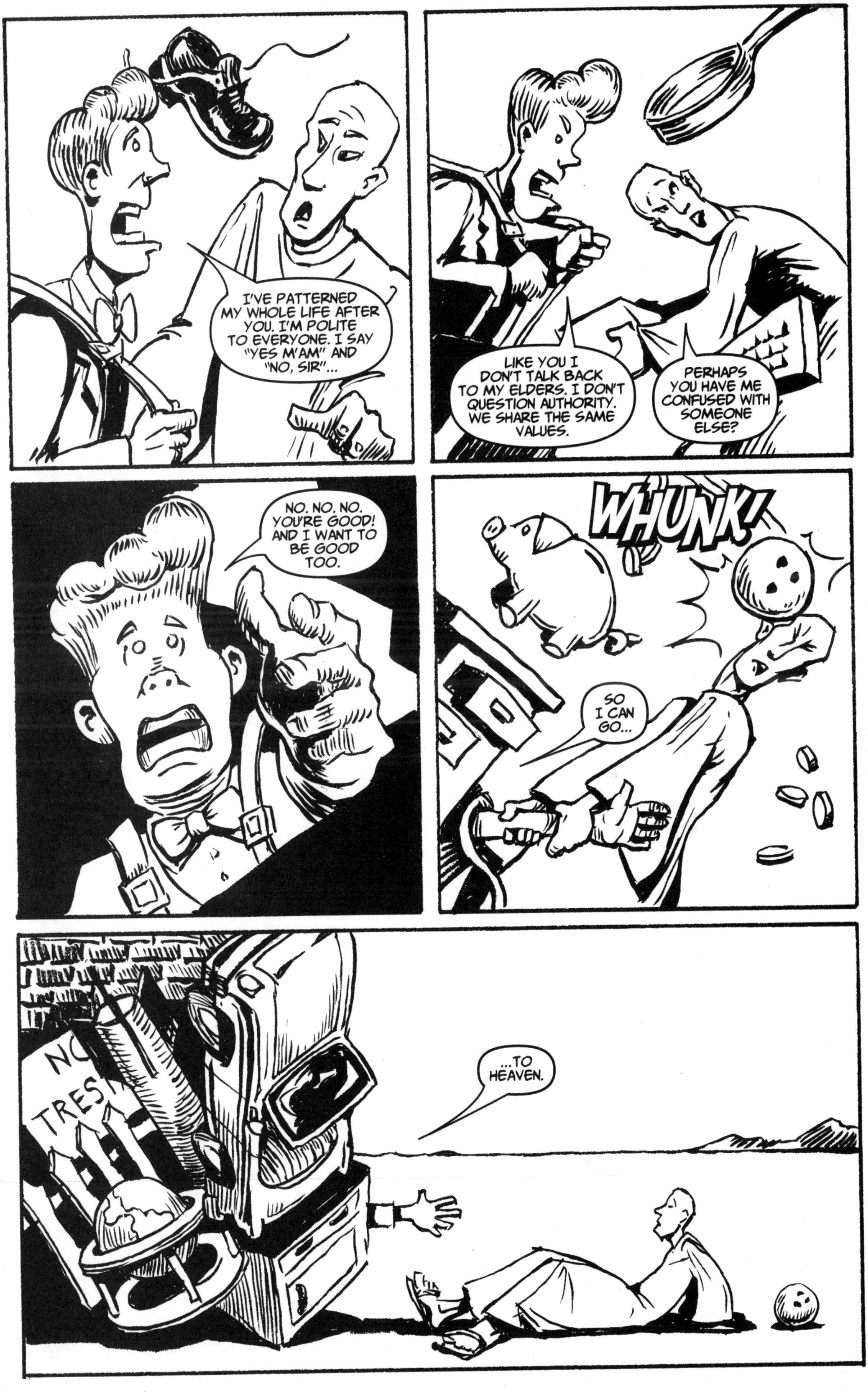
I'VE PATTERNED MY WHOLE LIFE AFTER YOU. I'M POLITE TO EVERYONE. I SAY "YES M'AM" AND "NO, SIR"...
LIKE YOU I DON'T TALK BACK TO MY ELDERS. I DON'T QUESTION AUTHORITY. WE SHARE THE SAME VALUES.
PERHAPS YOU HAVE ME CONFUSED WITH SOMEONE ELSE?
NO. NO. NO. YOU'RE GOOD! AND I WANT TO BE GOOD TOO.
WHUNK!
SO I CAN GO...
...TO HEAVEN.

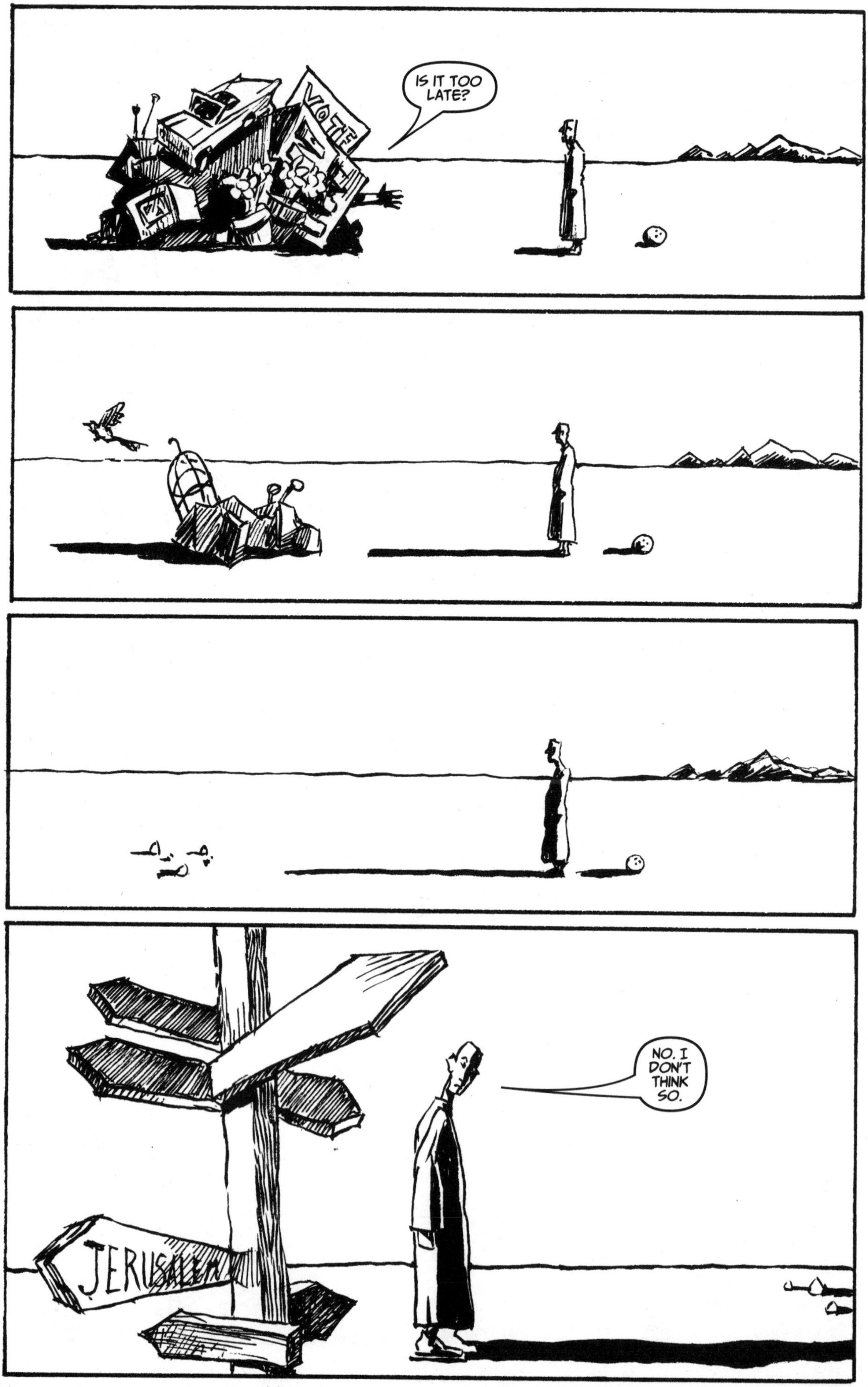
IS IT TOO LATE?
NO. I DON'T THINK SO.
JERUSALEM

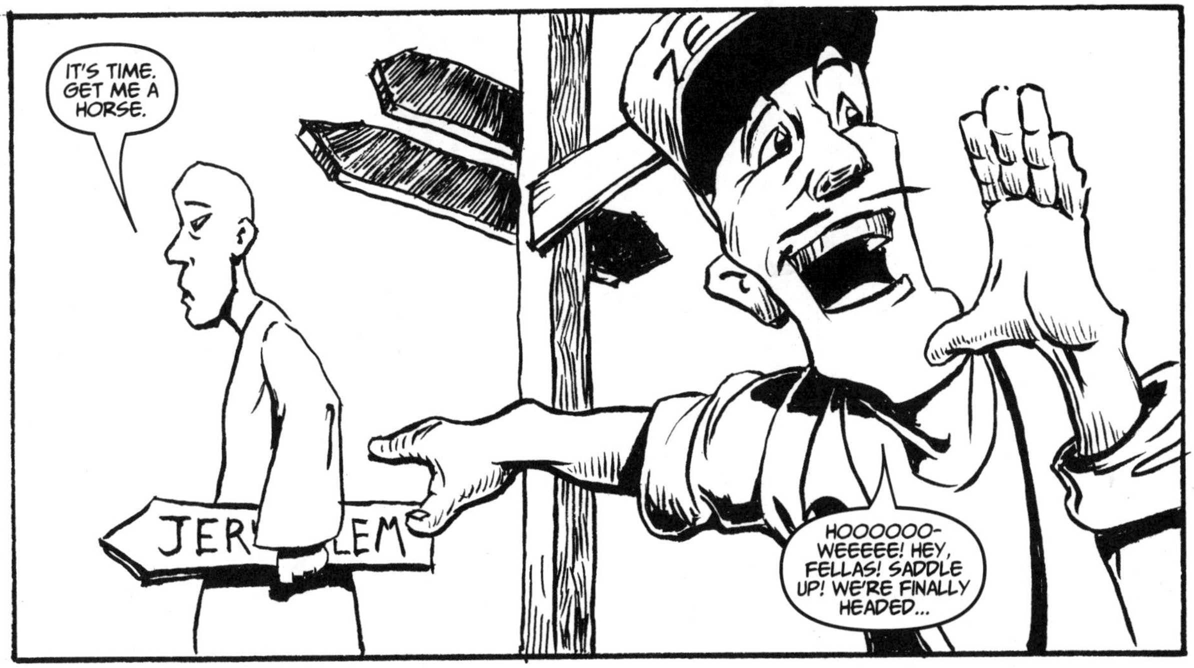
IT'S TIME. GET ME A HORSE.
HOOOOOO-WEEEEE! HEY, FELLAS! SADDLE UP! WE'RE FINALLY HEADED...

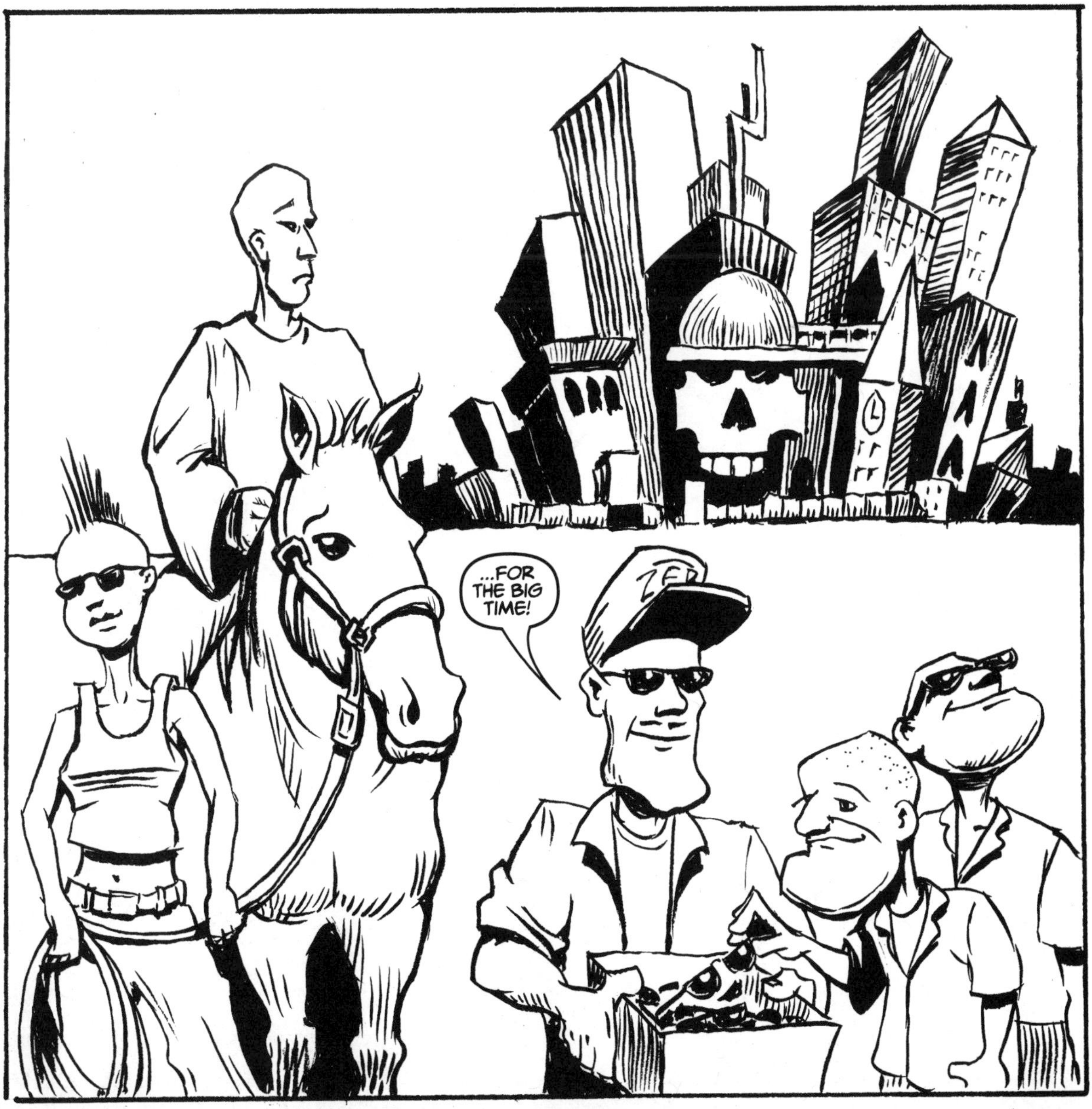
...FOR THE BIG TIME!

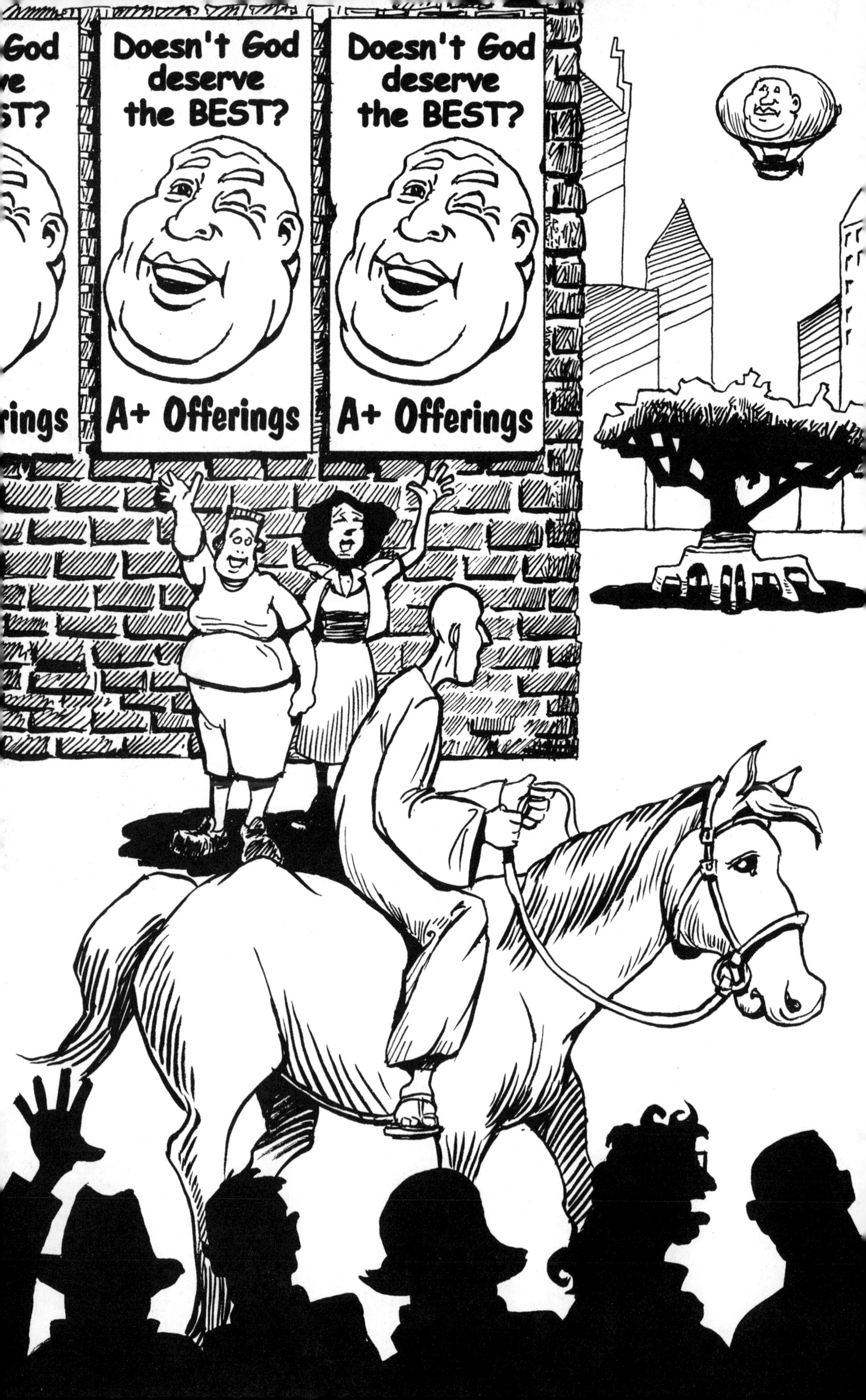
God
ve
ST?
rings
Doesn't God deserve the BEST?
A+ Offerings
Doesn't God deserve the BEST?
A+ Offerings

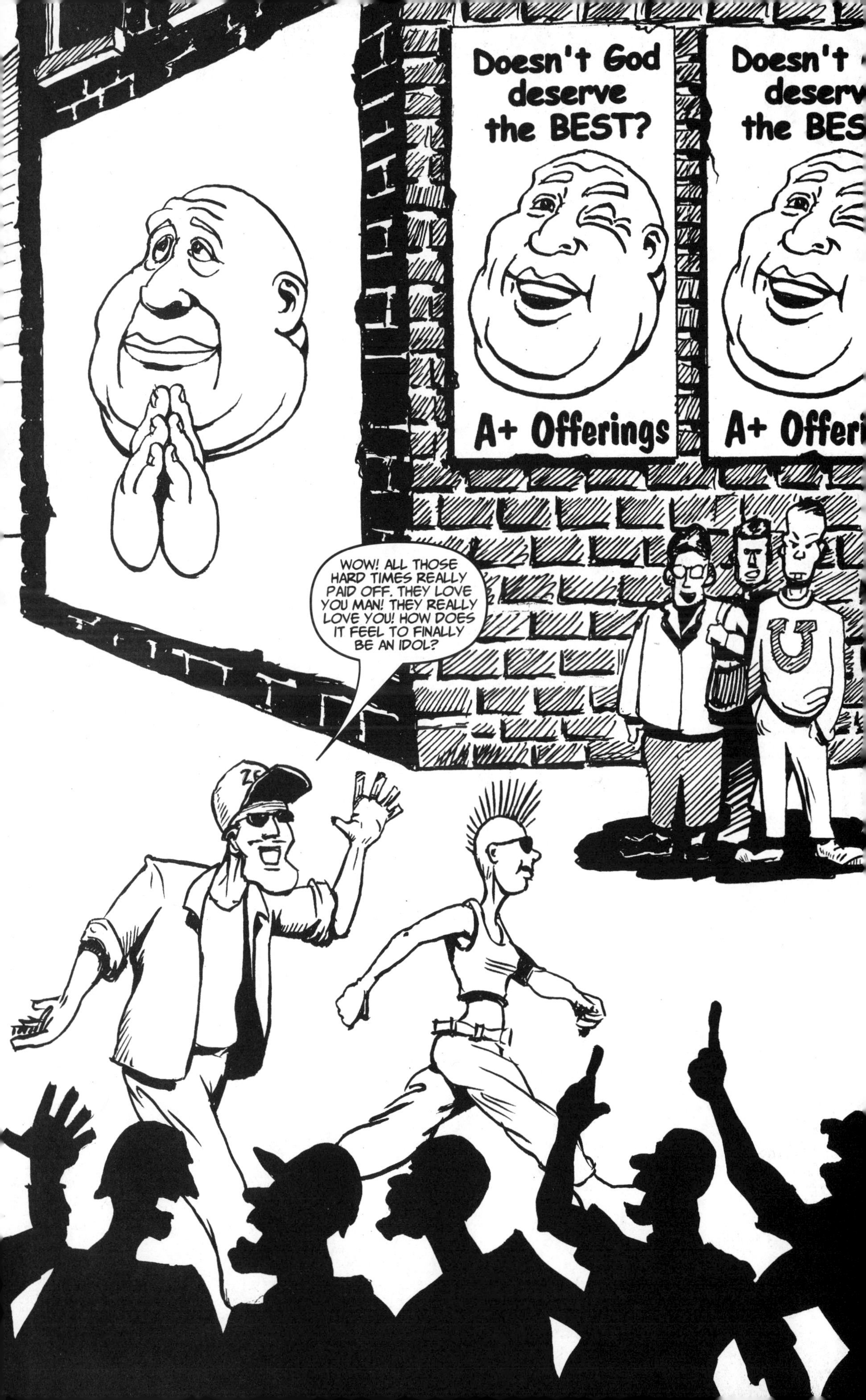
Doesn't God deserve the BEST?
A+ Offerings
WOW! ALL THOSE HARD TIMES REALLY PAID OFF. THEY LOVE YOU MAN! THEY REALLY LOVE YOU! HOW DOES IT FEEL TO FINALLY BE AN IDOL?

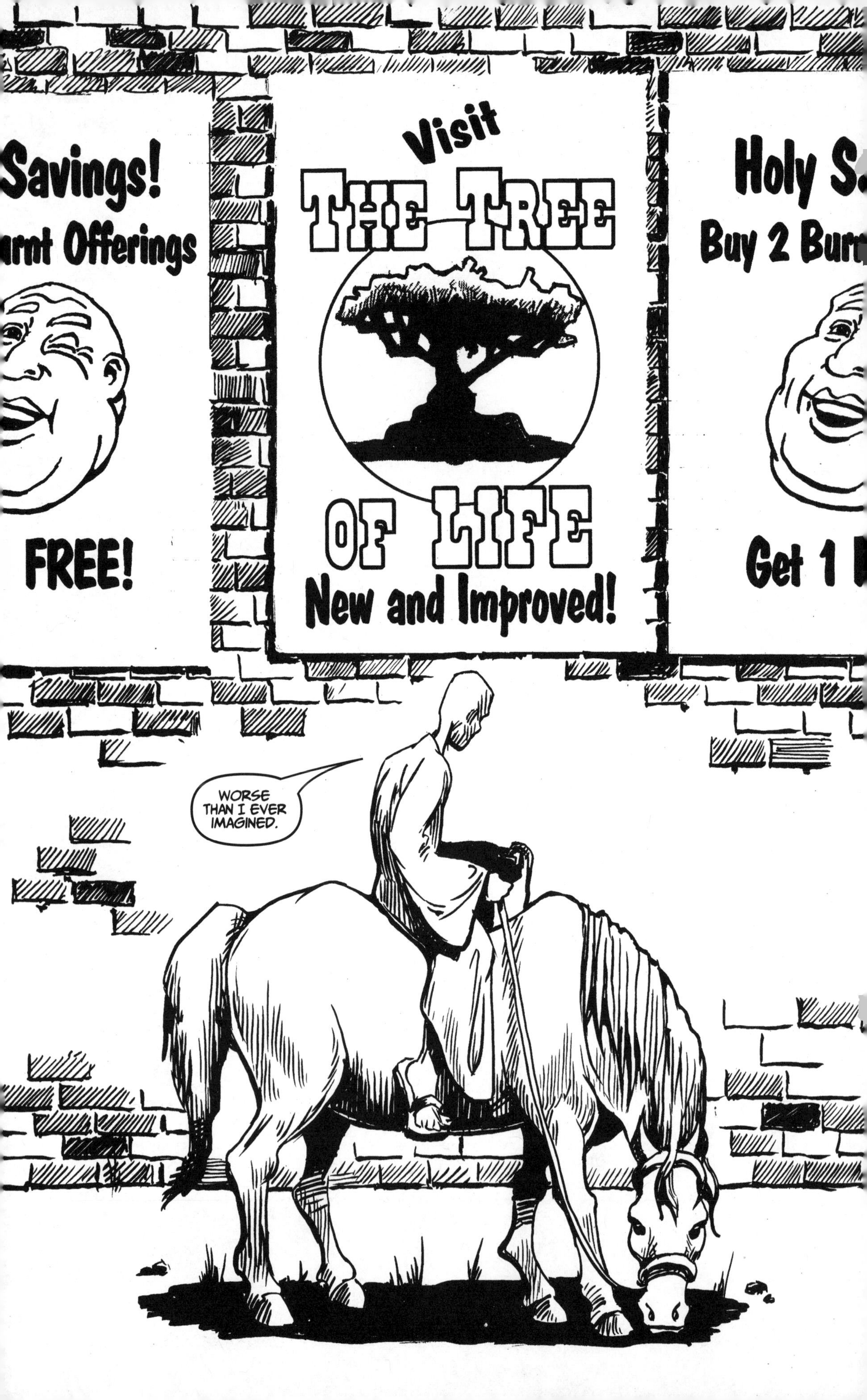

Savings!
rnt Offerings
FREE!
Visit
THE TREE
OF LIFE
New and Improved!
Holy S
Buy 2 Bur
Get 1
WORSE THAN I EVER IMAGINED.

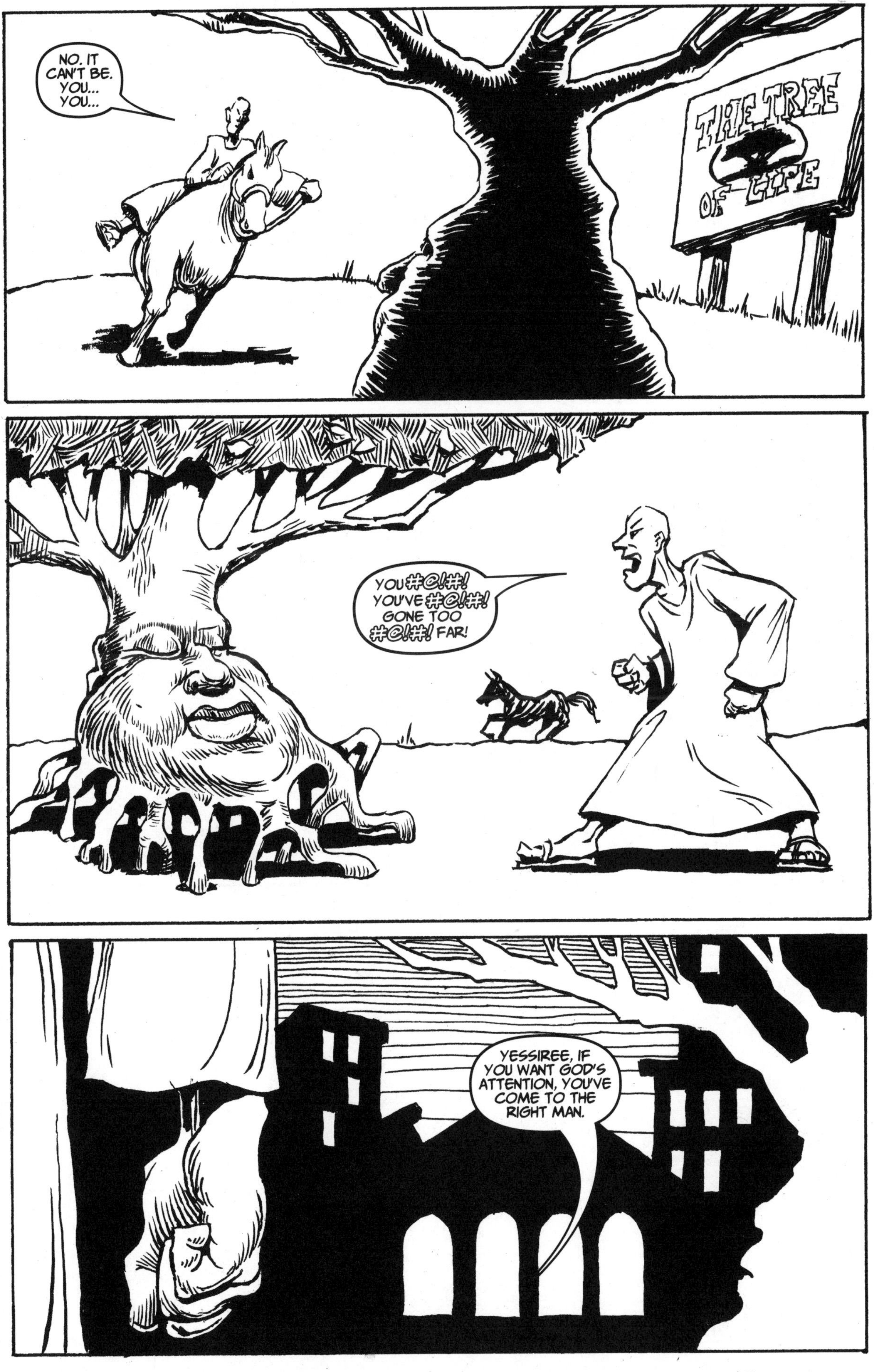
NO. IT CAN'T BE. YOU... YOU...
THE TREE OF LIFE
YOU #@!#! YOU'VE #@!#! GONE TOO #@!#! FAR!
YESSIREE, IF YOU WANT GOD'S ATTENTION, YOU'VE COME TO THE RIGHT MAN.

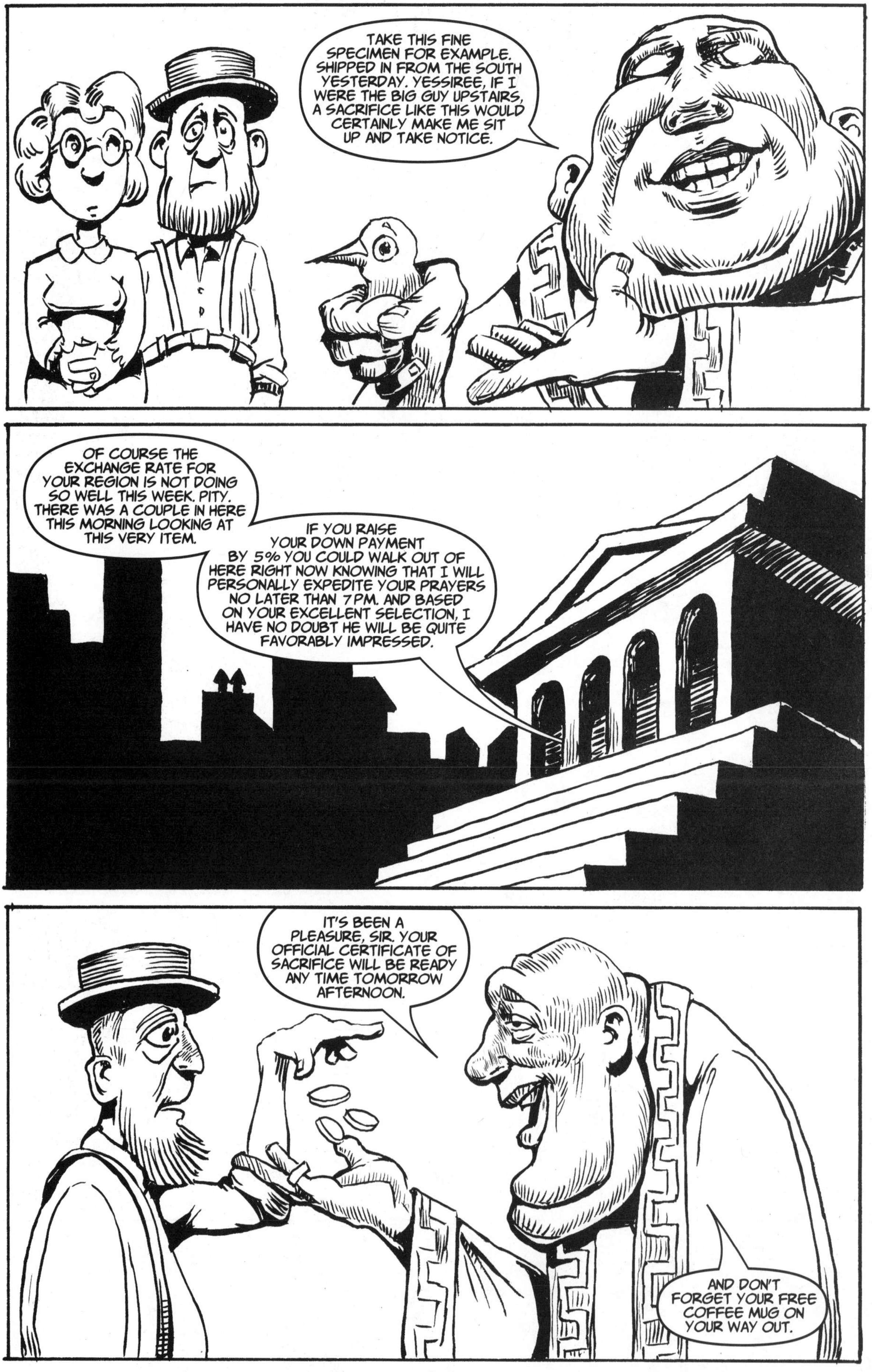
TAKE THIS FINE SPECIMEN FOR EXAMPLE. SHIPPED IN FROM THE SOUTH YESTERDAY. YESSIREE, IF I WERE THE BIG GUY UPSTAIRS, A SACRIFICE LIKE THIS WOULD CERTAINLY MAKE ME SIT UP AND TAKE NOTICE.
OF COURSE THE EXCHANGE RATE FOR YOUR REGION IS NOT DOING SO WELL THIS WEEK. PITY. THERE WAS A COUPLE IN HERE THIS MORNING LOOKING AT THIS VERY ITEM.
IF YOU RAISE YOUR DOWN PAYMENT BY 5% YOU COULD WALK OUT OF HERE RIGHT NOW KNOWING THAT I WILL PERSONALLY EXPEDITE YOUR PRAYERS NO LATER THAN 7PM. AND BASED ON YOUR EXCELLENT SELECTION, I HAVE NO DOUBT HE WILL BE QUITE FAVORABLY IMPRESSED.
IT'S BEEN A PLEASURE, SIR. YOUR OFFICIAL CERTIFICATE OF SACRIFICE WILL BE READY ANY TIME TOMORROW AFTERNOON.
AND DON'T FORGET YOUR FREE COFFEE MUG ON YOUR WAY OUT.

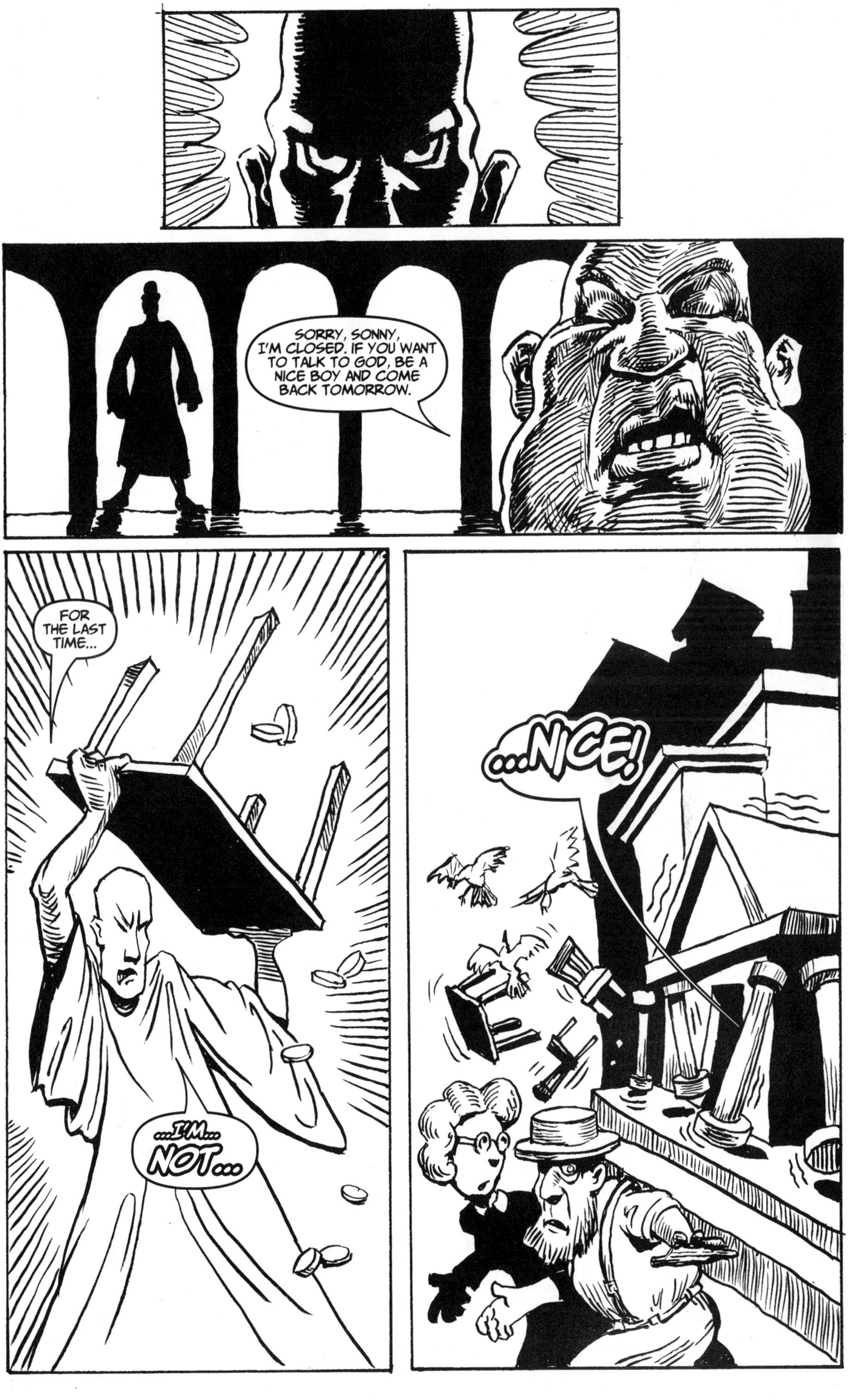
SORRY, SONNY, I'M CLOSED. IF YOU WANT TO TALK TO GOD, BE A NICE BOY AND COME BACK TOMORROW.
FOR THE LAST TIME...
...I'M... NOT...
...NICE!

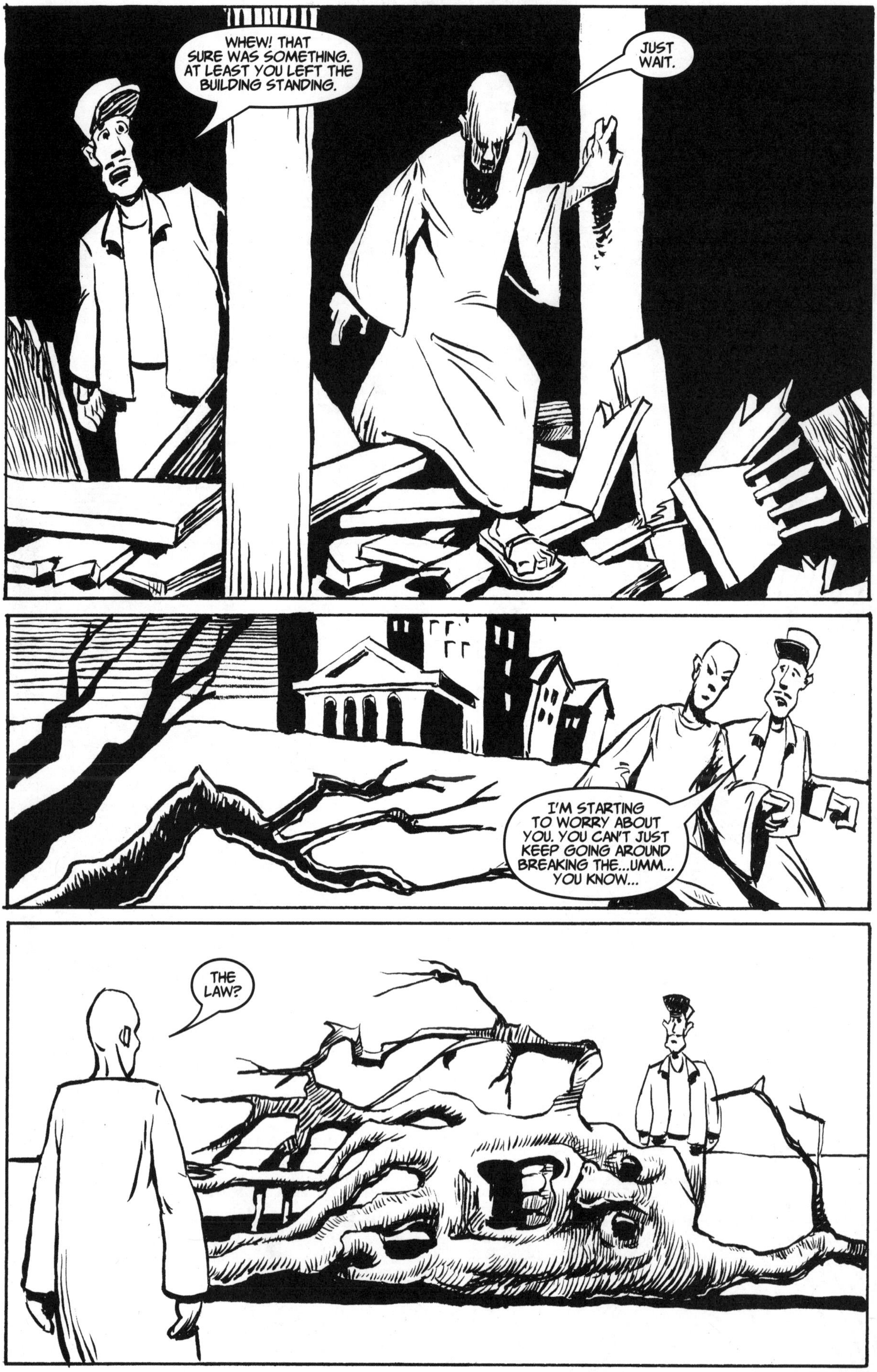
WHEW! THAT SURE WAS SOMETHING. AT LEAST YOU LEFT THE BUILDING STANDING.
JUST WAIT.
I'M STARTING TO WORRY ABOUT YOU. YOU CAN'T JUST KEEP GOING AROUND BREAKING THE...UMM... YOU KNOW...
THE LAW?

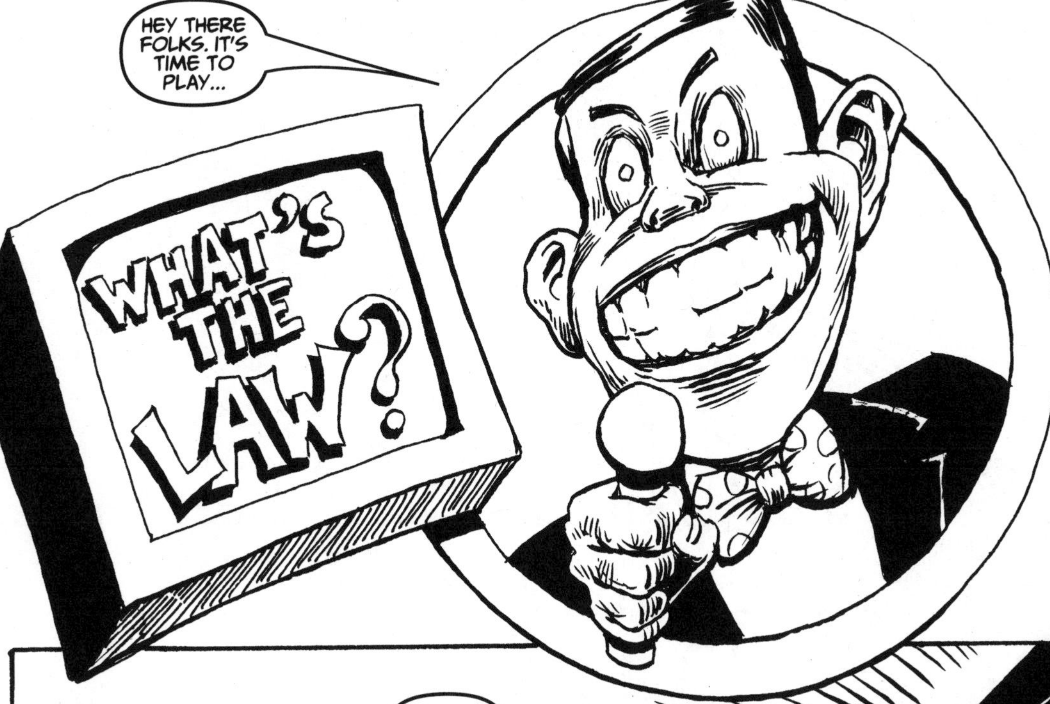
HEY THERE FOLKS. IT'S TIME TO PLAY...
WHAT'S THE LAW?

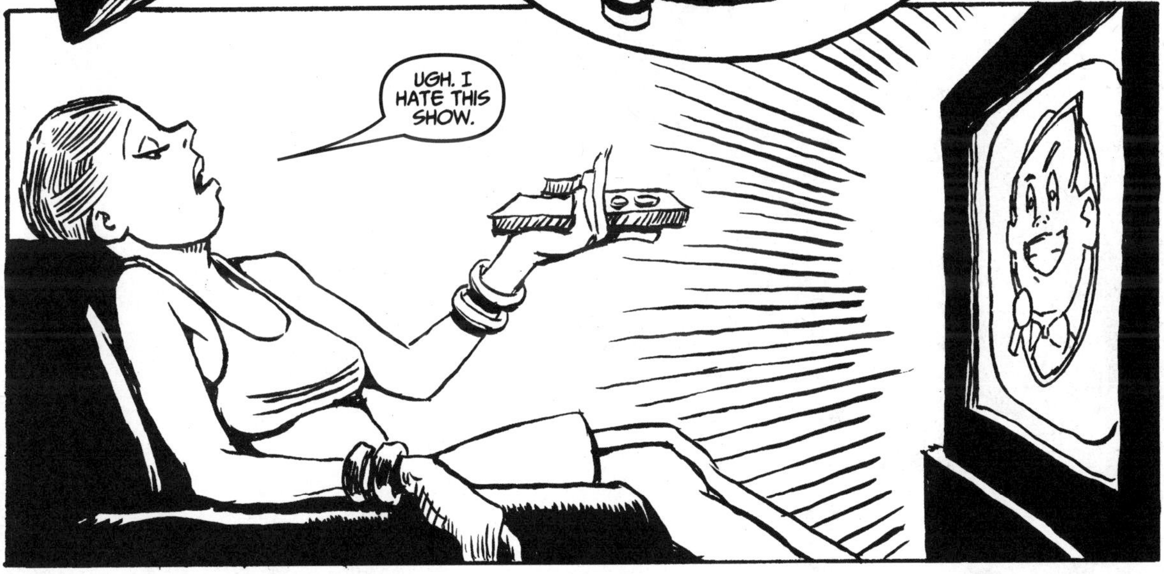
UGH. I HATE THIS SHOW.

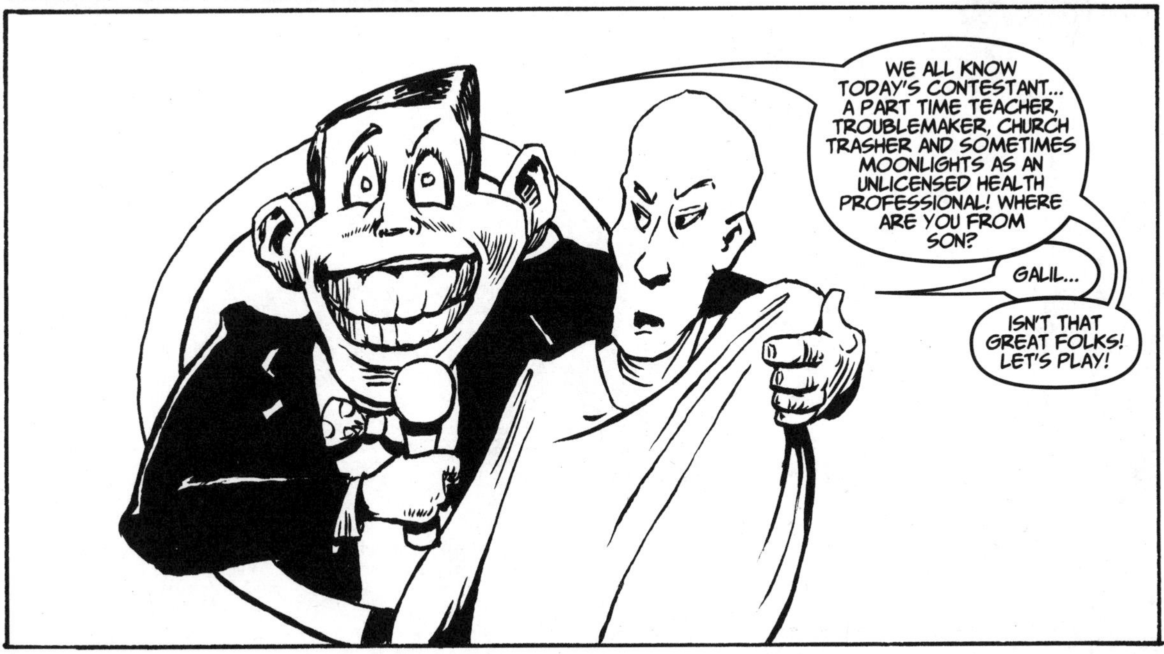
WE ALL KNOW TODAY'S CONTESTANT... A PART TIME TEACHER, TROUBLEMAKER, CHURCH TRASHER AND SOMETIMES MOONLIGHTS AS AN UNLICENSED HEALTH PROFESSIONAL! WHERE ARE YOU FROM SON?
GALIL...
ISN'T THAT GREAT FOLKS! LET'S PLAY!

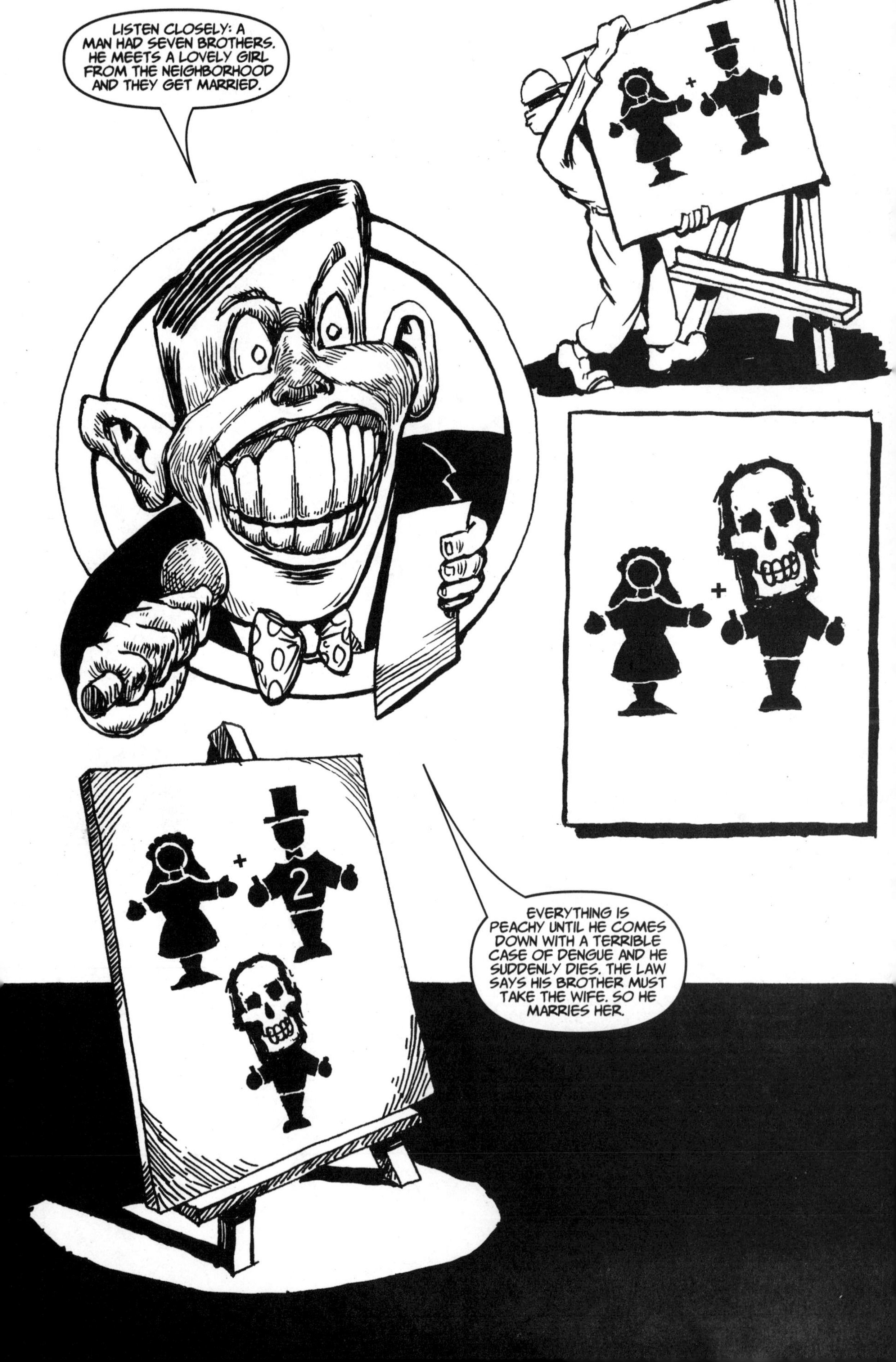
LISTEN CLOSELY: A MAN HAD SEVEN BROTHERS. HE MEETS A LOVELY GIRL FROM THE NEIGHBORHOOD AND THEY GET MARRIED.
+
+
+
2
EVERYTHING IS PEACHY UNTIL HE COMES DOWN WITH A TERRIBLE CASE OF DENGUE AND HE SUDDENLY DIES. THE LAW SAYS HIS BROTHER MUST TAKE THE WIFE. SO HE MARRIES HER.

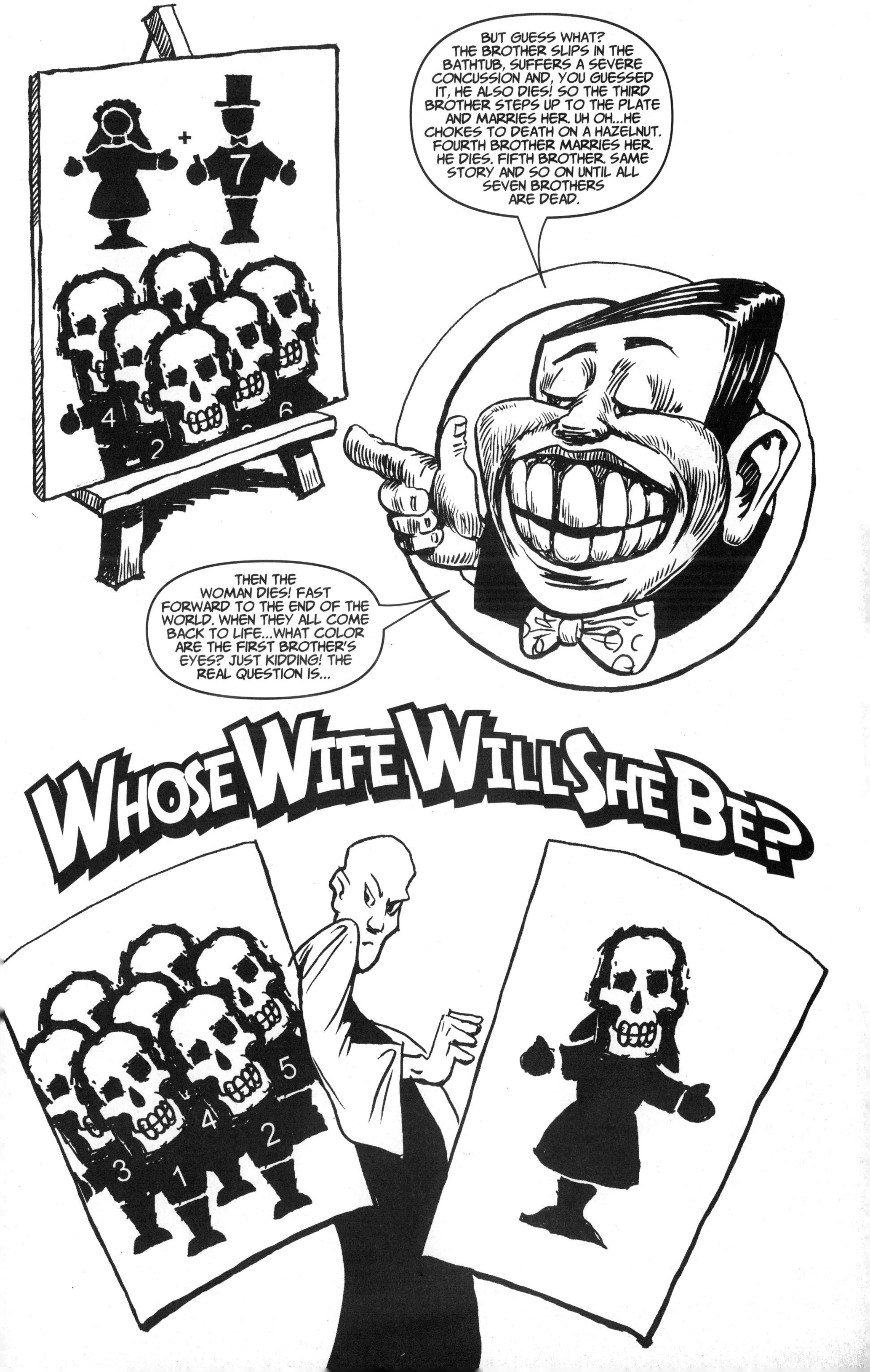
BUT GUESS WHAT? THE BROTHER SLIPS IN THE BATHTUB, SUFFERS A SEVERE CONCUSSION AND, YOU GUESSED IT, HE ALSO DIES! SO THE THIRD BROTHER STEPS UP TO THE PLATE AND MARRIES HER. UH OH...HE CHOKES TO DEATH ON A HAZELNUT. FOURTH BROTHER MARRIES HER. HE DIES. FIFTH BROTHER. SAME STORY AND SO ON UNTIL ALL SEVEN BROTHERS ARE DEAD.
THEN THE WOMAN DIES! FAST FORWARD TO THE END OF THE WORLD. WHEN THEY ALL COME BACK TO LIFE...WHAT COLOR ARE THE FIRST BROTHER'S EYES? JUST KIDDING! THE REAL QUESTION IS...
WHOSE WIFE WILL SHE BE?

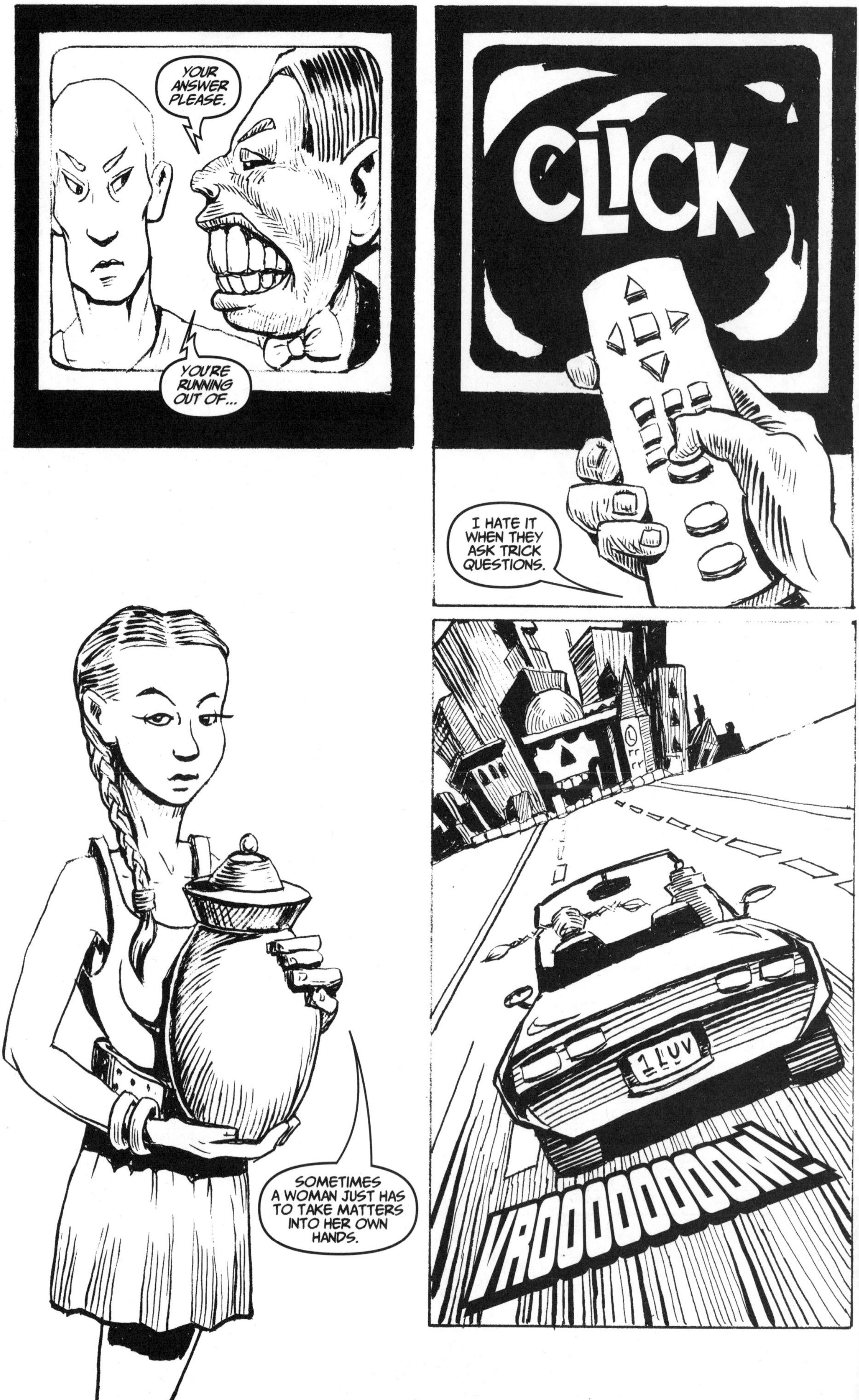

YOUR ANSWER PLEASE.
YOU'RE RUNNING OUT OF...
CLICK
I HATE IT WHEN THEY ASK TRICK QUESTIONS.
SOMETIMES A WOMAN JUST HAS TO TAKE MATTERS INTO HER OWN HANDS.
1LUV
VROOOOOOOOM!

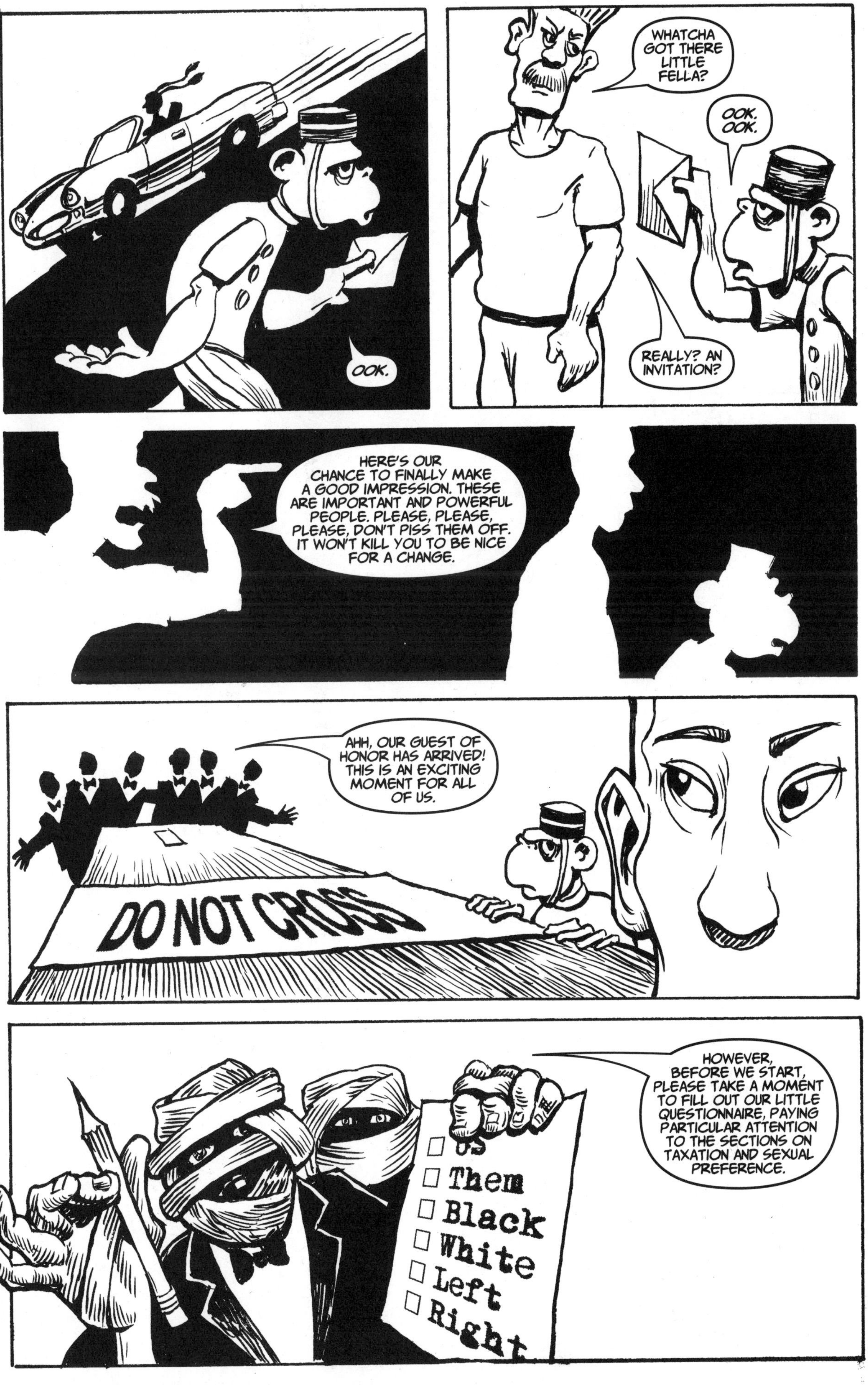
OOK.
WHATCHA GOT THERE LITTLE FELLA?
OOK. OOK.
REALLY? AN INVITATION?
HERE'S OUR CHANCE TO FINALLY MAKE A GOOD IMPRESSION. THESE ARE IMPORTANT AND POWERFUL PEOPLE. PLEASE, PLEASE, PLEASE, DON'T PISS THEM OFF. IT WON'T KILL YOU TO BE NICE FOR A CHANGE.
AHH, OUR GUEST OF HONOR HAS ARRIVED! THIS IS AN EXCITING MOMENT FOR ALL OF US.
DO NOT CROSS
HOWEVER, BEFORE WE START, PLEASE TAKE A MOMENT TO FILL OUT OUR LITTLE QUESTIONNAIRE, PAYING PARTICULAR ATTENTION TO THE SECTIONS ON TAXATION AND SEXUAL PREFERENCE.
Them
Black
White
Left
Right

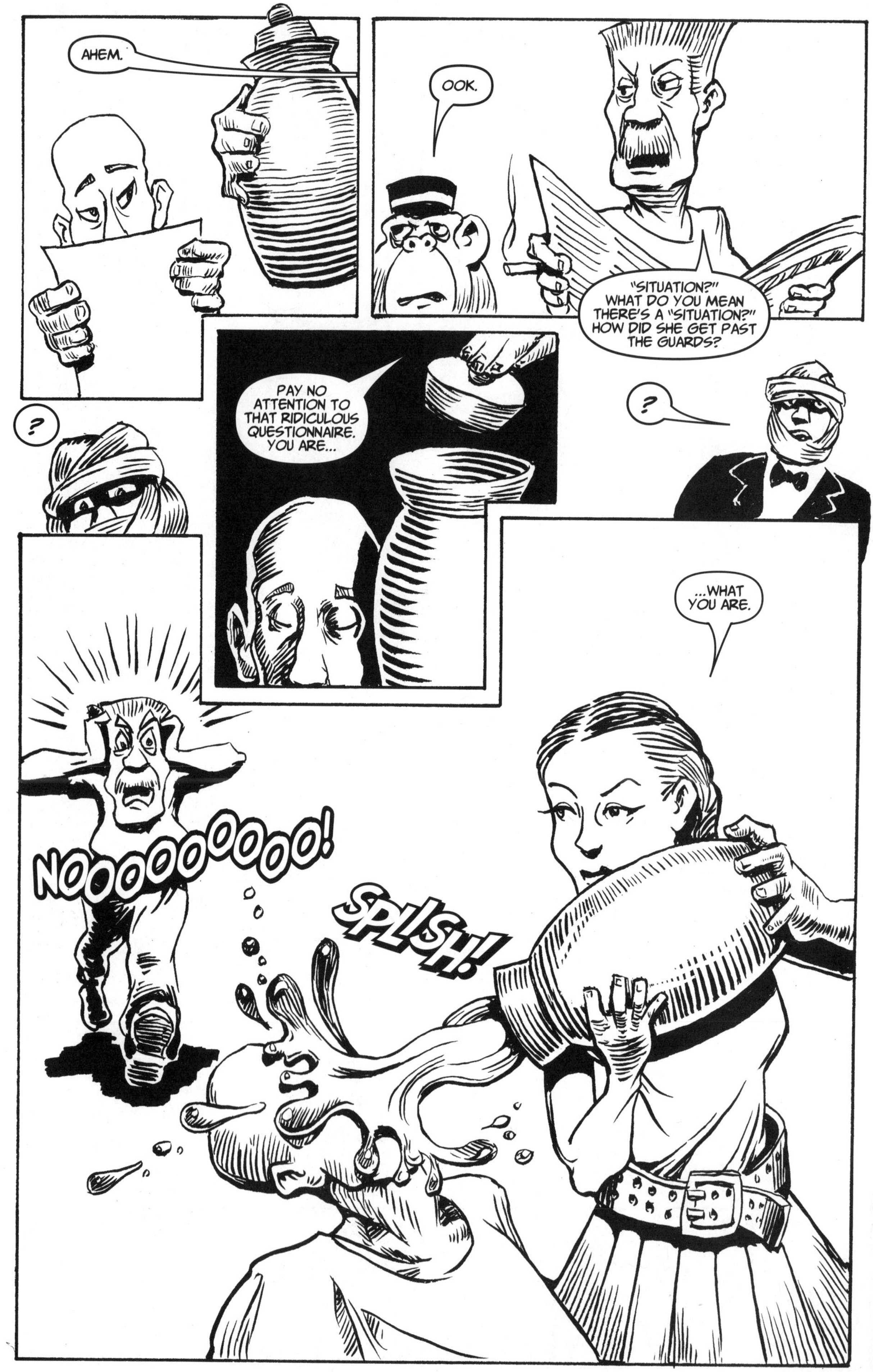
AHEM.
OOK.
"SITUATION?" WHAT DO YOU MEAN THERE'S A "SITUATION?" HOW DID SHE GET PAST THE GUARDS?
?
PAY NO ATTENTION TO THAT RIDICULOUS QUESTIONNAIRE. YOU ARE...
?
...WHAT YOU ARE.
NOOOOOOOOOO!
SPLISH!

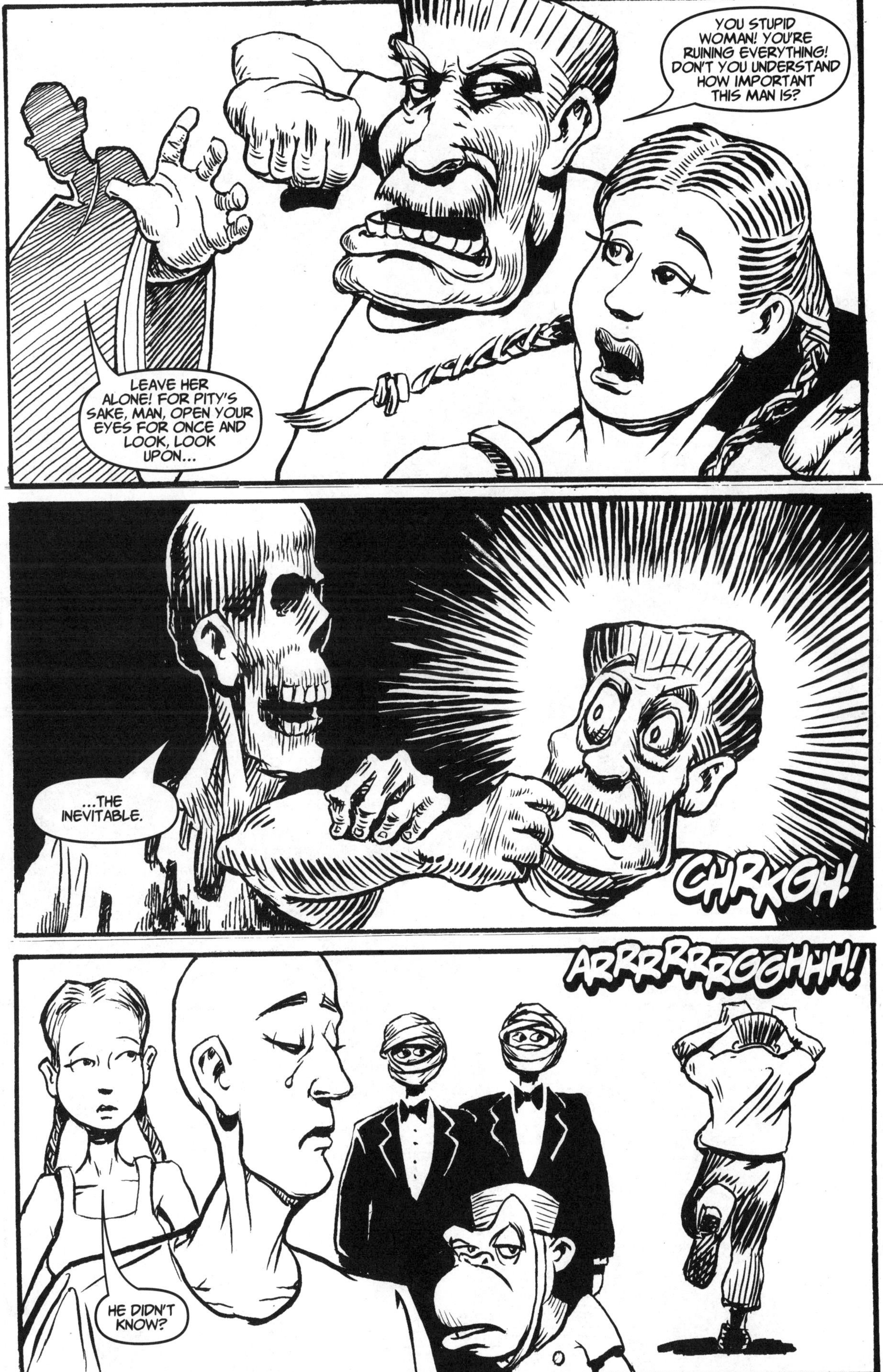
YOU STUPID WOMAN! YOU'RE RUINING EVERYTHING! DON'T YOU UNDERSTAND HOW IMPORTANT THIS MAN IS?
LEAVE HER ALONE! FOR PITY'S SAKE, MAN, OPEN YOUR EYES FOR ONCE AND LOOK, LOOK UPON...
...THE INEVITABLE.
CHRKGH!
ARRRRRRGGHHH!
HE DIDN'T KNOW?

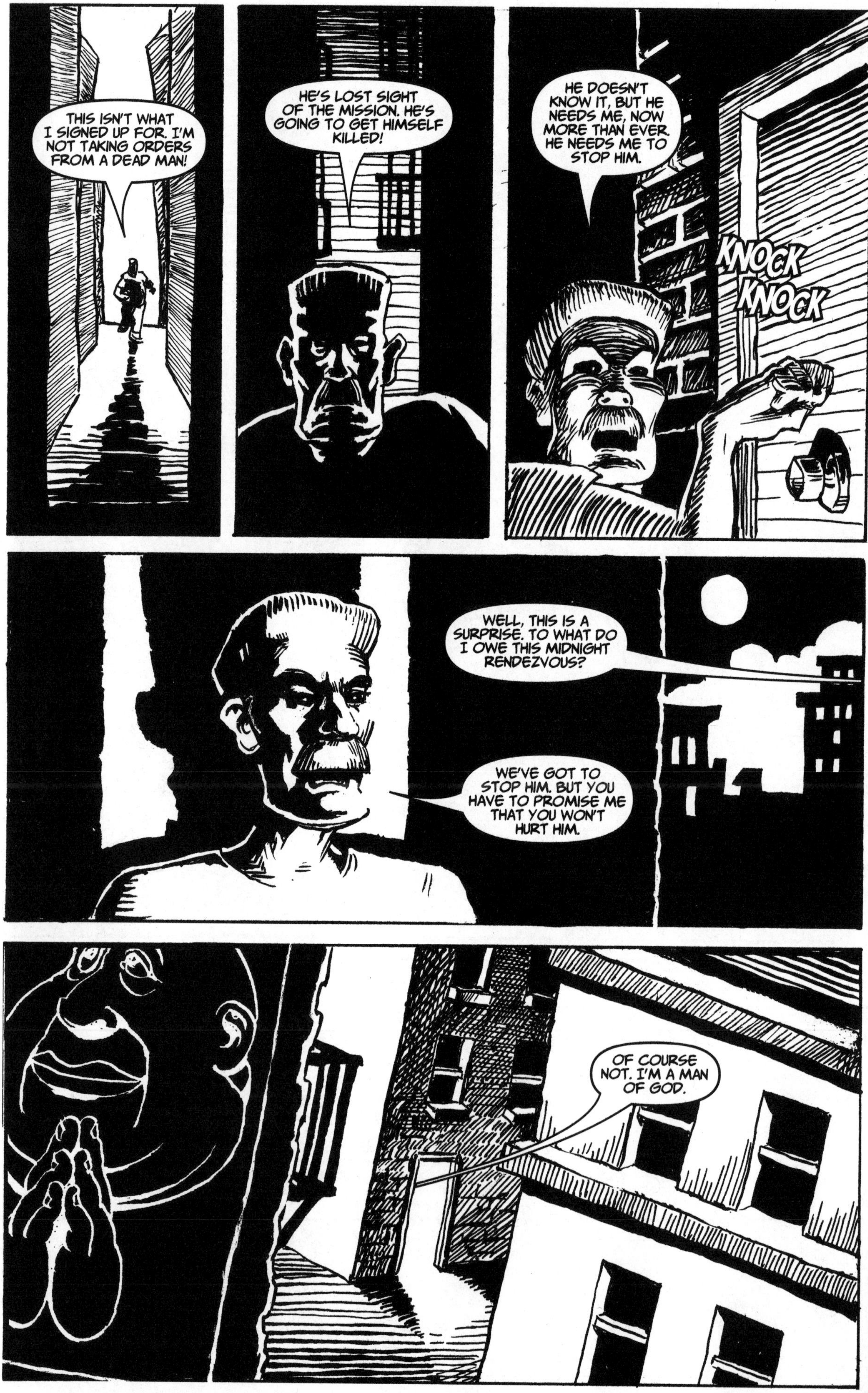
THIS ISN'T WHAT I SIGNED UP FOR. I'M NOT TAKING ORDERS FROM A DEAD MAN!
HE'S LOST SIGHT OF THE MISSION. HE'S GOING TO GET HIMSELF KILLED!
HE DOESN'T KNOW IT, BUT HE NEEDS ME, NOW MORE THAN EVER. HE NEEDS ME TO STOP HIM.
KNOCK KNOCK
WELL, THIS IS A SURPRISE. TO WHAT DO I OWE THIS MIDNIGHT RENDEZVOUS?
WE'VE GOT TO STOP HIM. BUT YOU HAVE TO PROMISE ME THAT YOU WON'T HURT HIM.
OF COURSE NOT. I'M A MAN OF GOD.

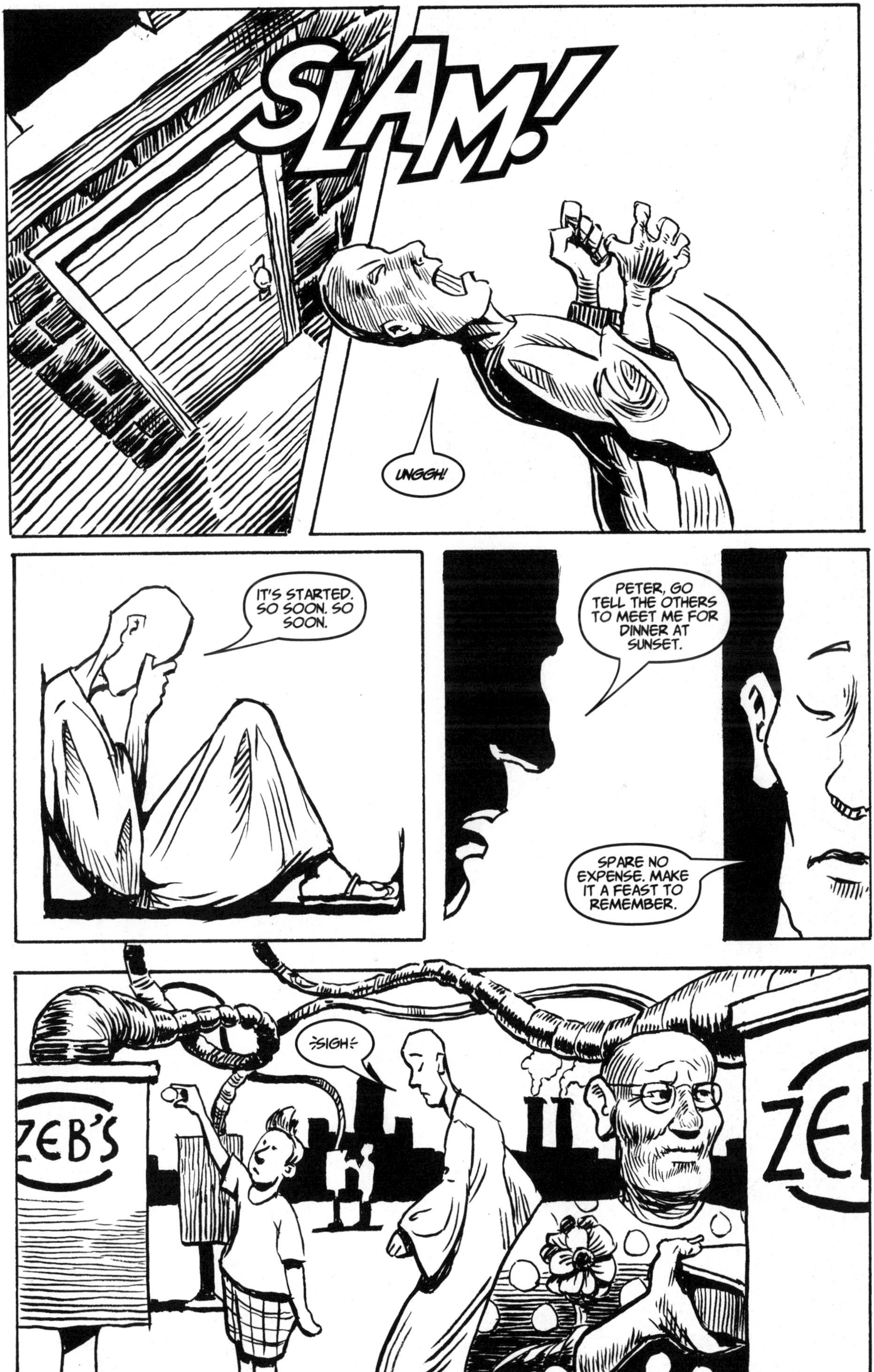
SLAM!
UNGGH!
IT'S STARTED. SO SOON. SO SOON.
PETER, GO TELL THE OTHERS TO MEET ME FOR DINNER AT SUNSET.
SPARE NO EXPENSE. MAKE IT A FEAST TO REMEMBER.
SIGH
ZEB'S
ZEB

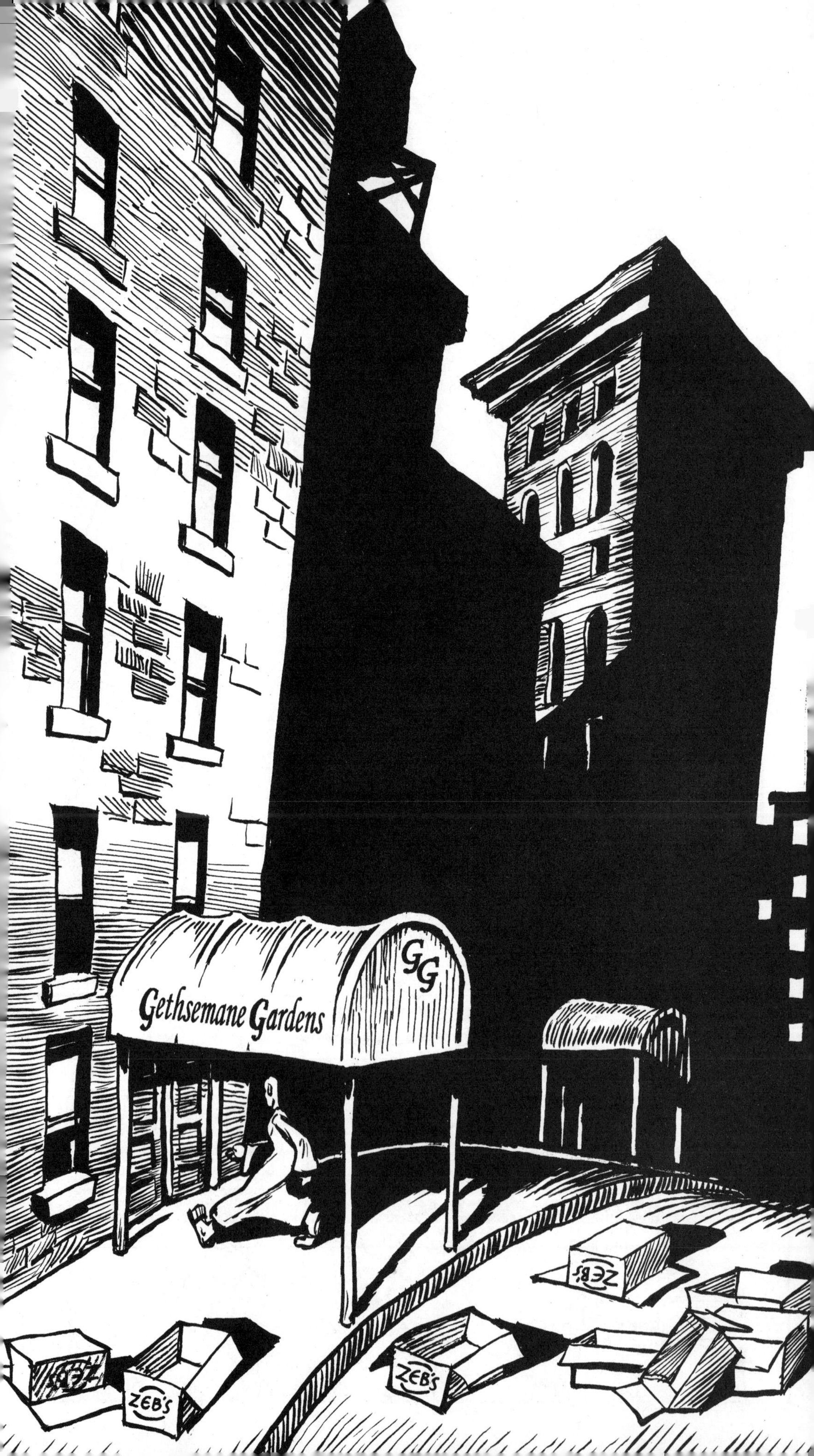

GG
Gethsemane Gardens
ZEB'S
ZEB'S
ZEB'S

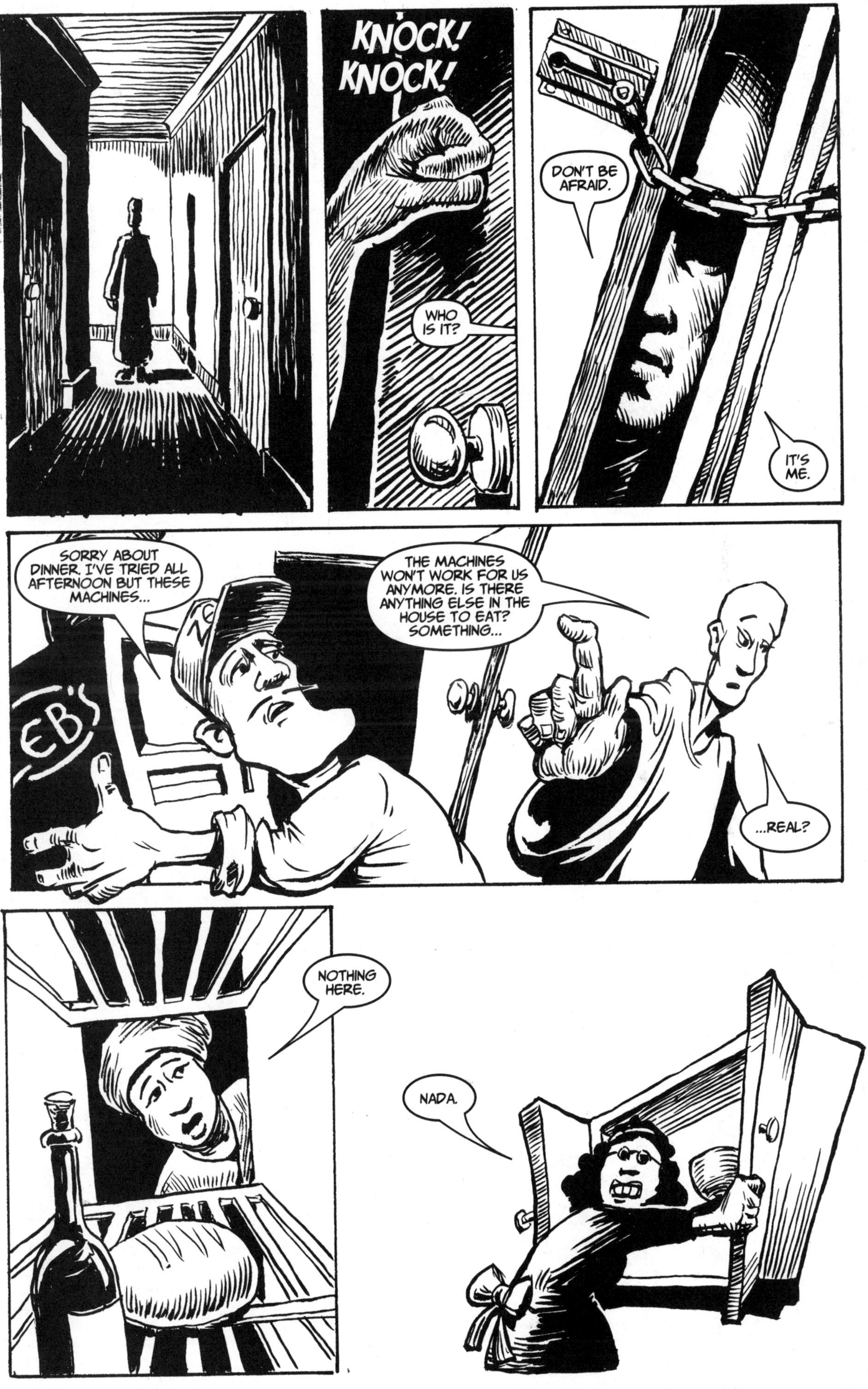
KNOCK! KNOCK!
WHO IS IT?
DON'T BE AFRAID.
IT'S ME.
SORRY ABOUT DINNER. I'VE TRIED ALL AFTERNOON BUT THESE MACHINES...
EB'S
THE MACHINES WON'T WORK FOR US ANYMORE. IS THERE ANYTHING ELSE IN THE HOUSE TO EAT? SOMETHING...
...REAL?
NOTHING HERE.
NADA.

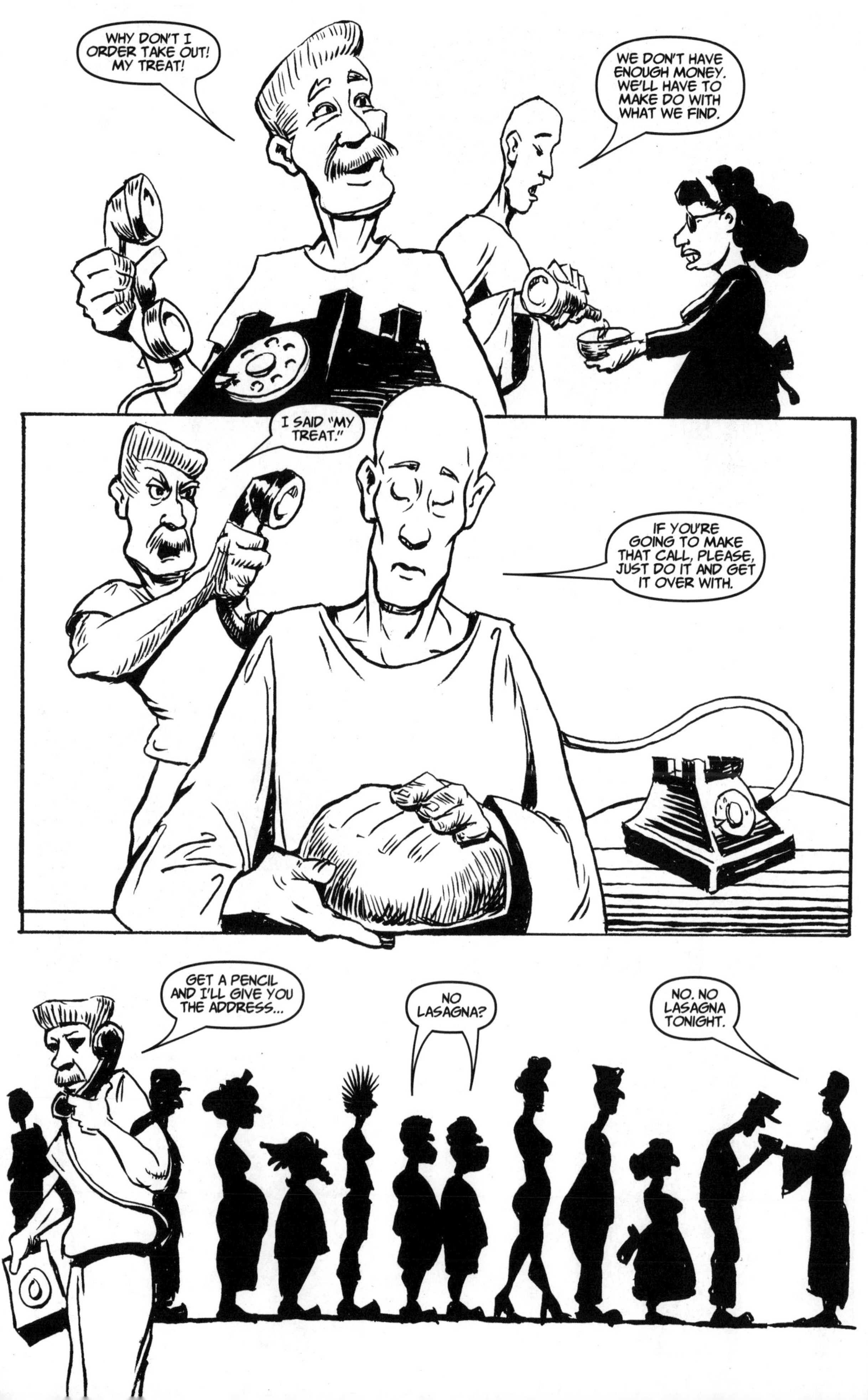

WHY DON'T I ORDER TAKE OUT! MY TREAT!
WE DON'T HAVE ENOUGH MONEY. WE'LL HAVE TO MAKE DO WITH WHAT WE FIND.
I SAID "MY TREAT."
IF YOU'RE GOING TO MAKE THAT CALL, PLEASE, JUST DO IT AND GET IT OVER WITH.
GET A PENCIL AND I'LL GIVE YOU THE ADDRESS...
NO LASAGNA?
NO. NO LASAGNA TONIGHT.

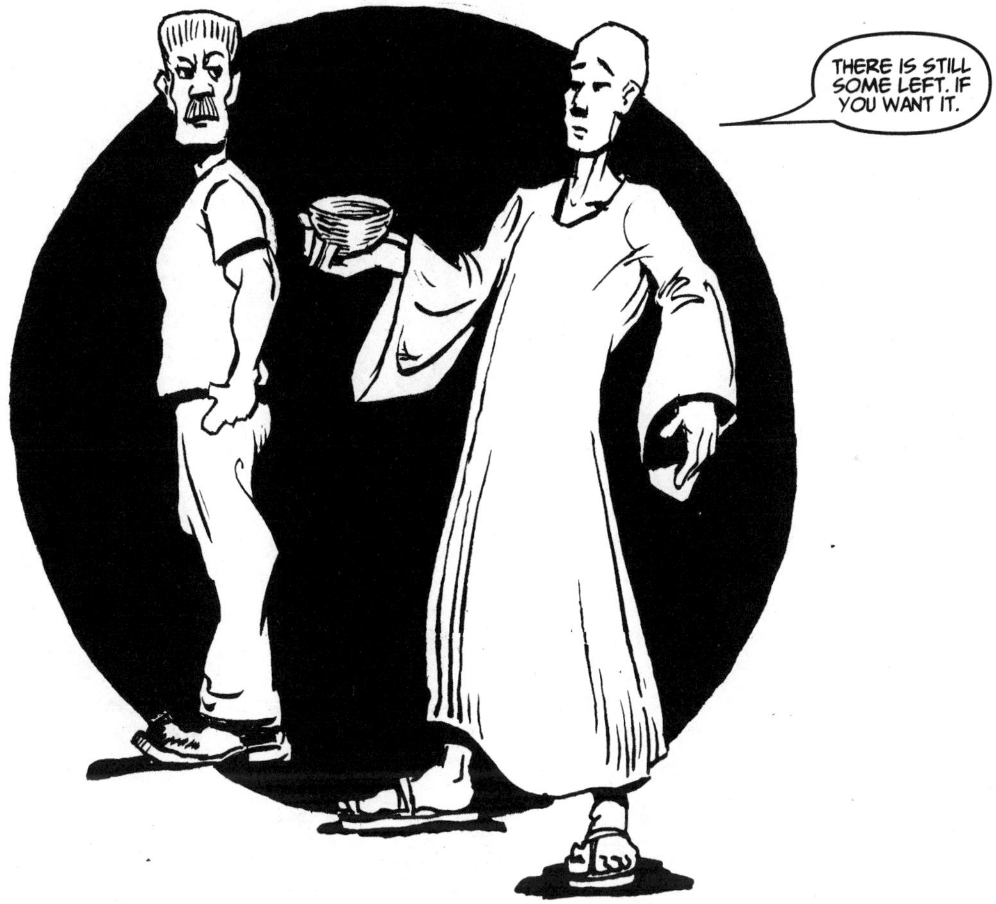
THERE IS STILL SOME LEFT. IF YOU WANT IT.

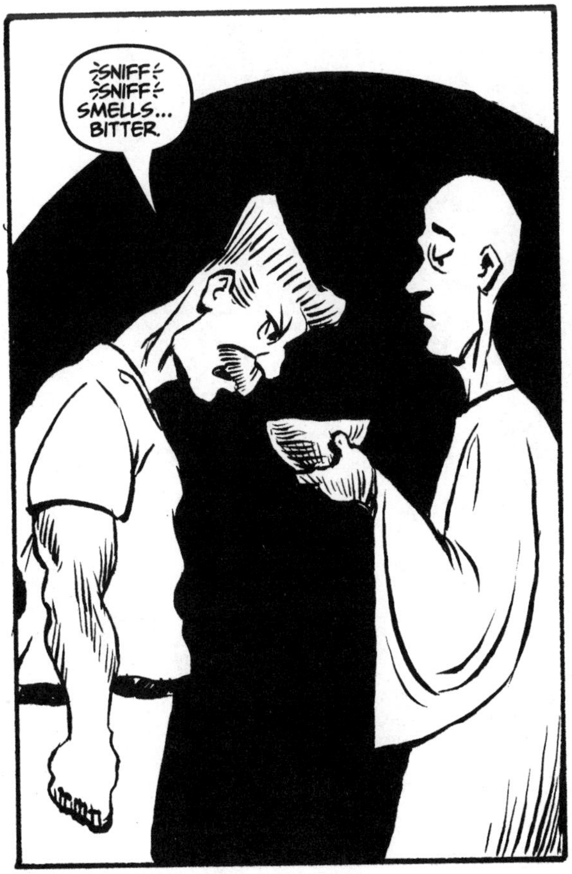
SNIFF SNIFF SMELLS... BITTER.

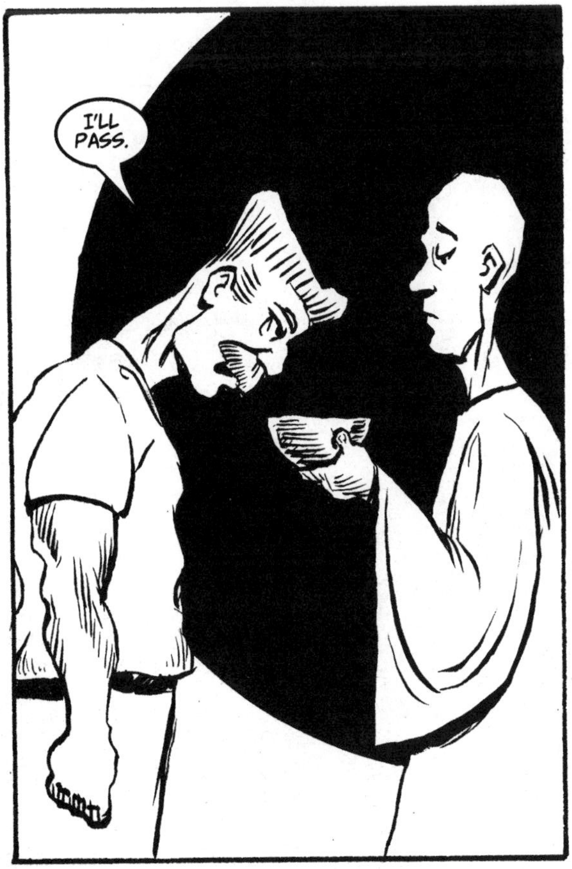
I'LL PASS.

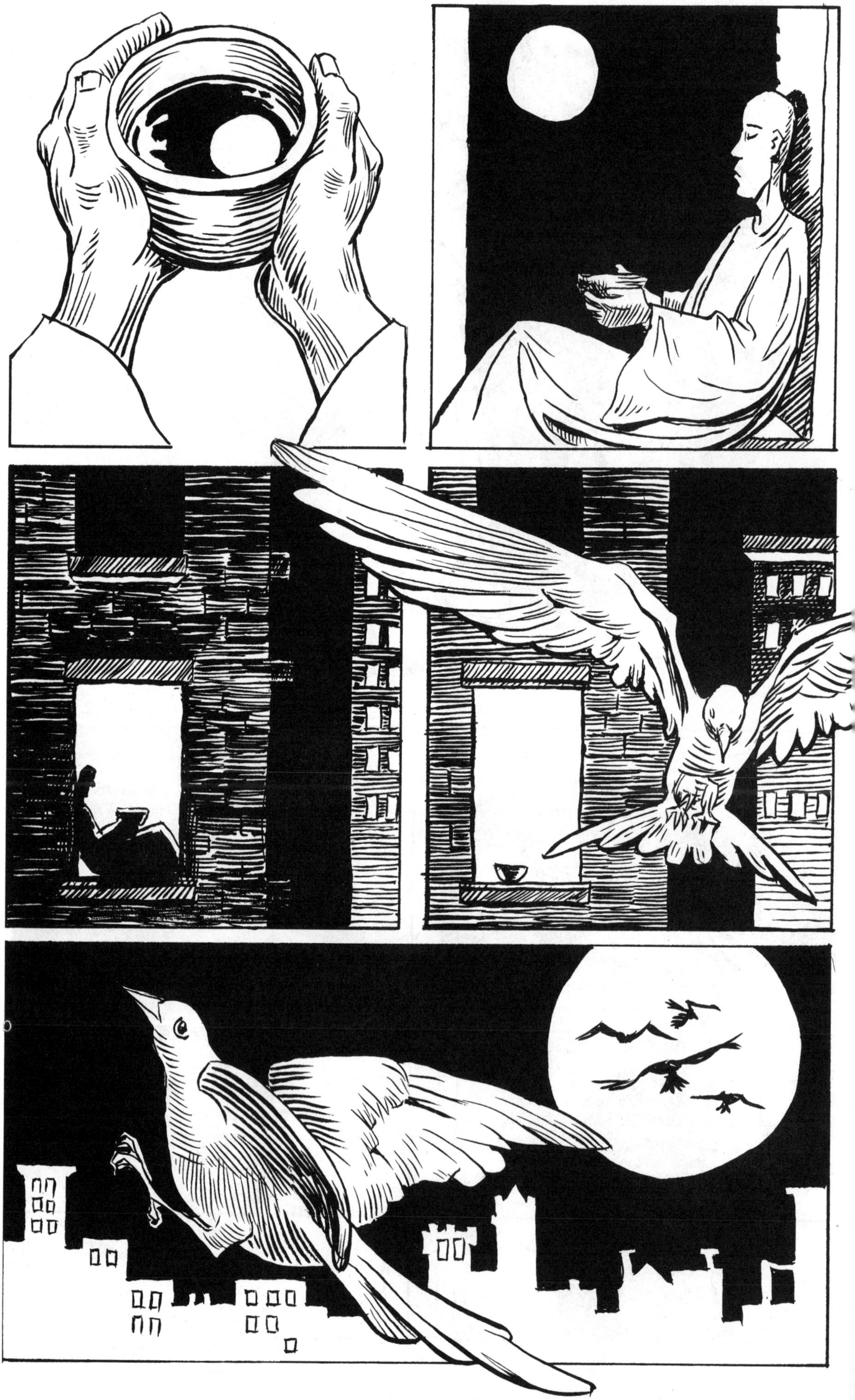

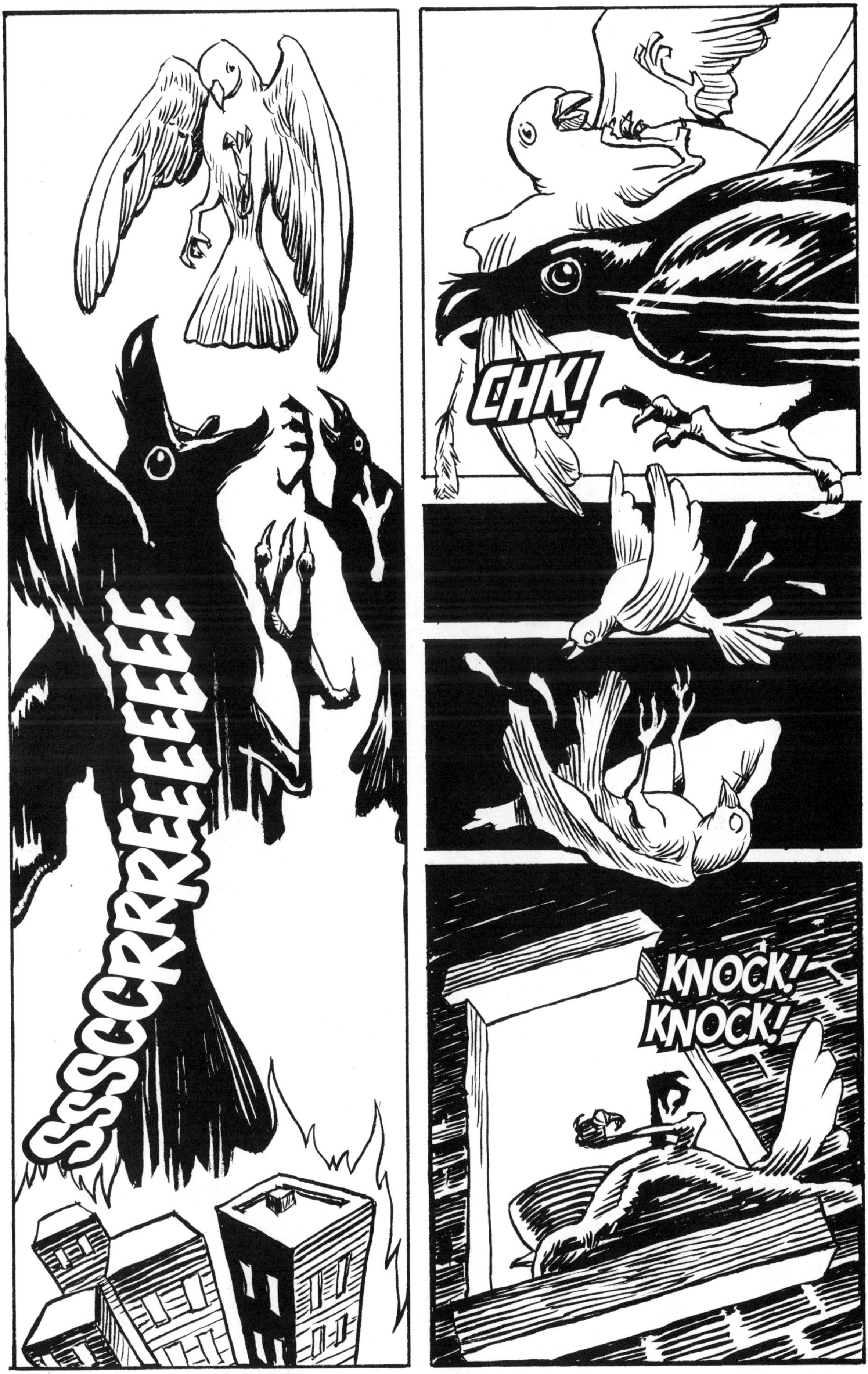
SSSCRREEEEEEE
CHK!
KNOCK! KNOCK!

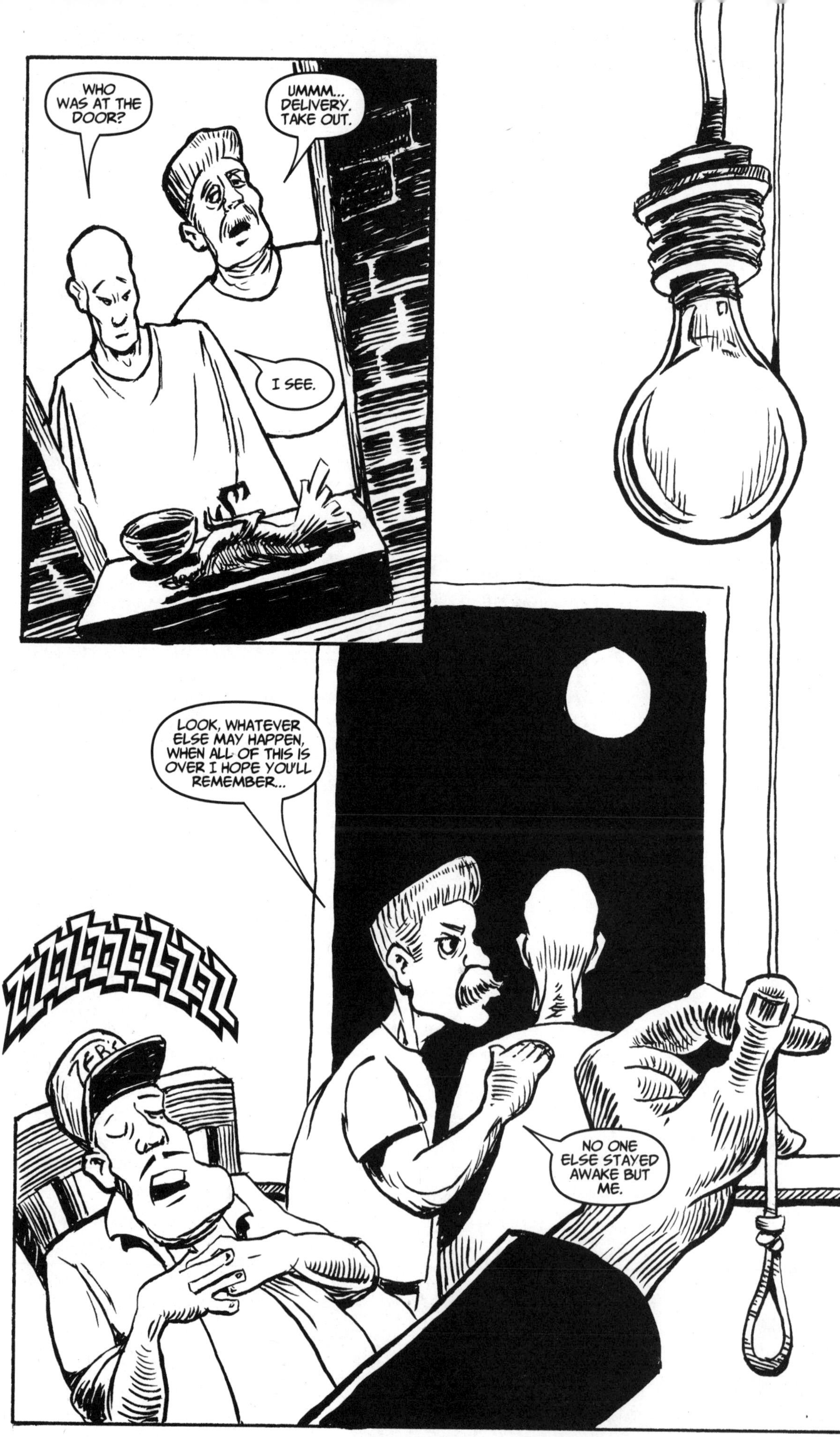
WHO WAS AT THE DOOR?
UMMM... DELIVERY. TAKE OUT.
I SEE.
LOOK, WHATEVER ELSE MAY HAPPEN, WHEN ALL OF THIS IS OVER I HOPE YOU'LL REMEMBER...
ZZZZZZZZZZ
NO ONE ELSE STAYED AWAKE BUT ME.

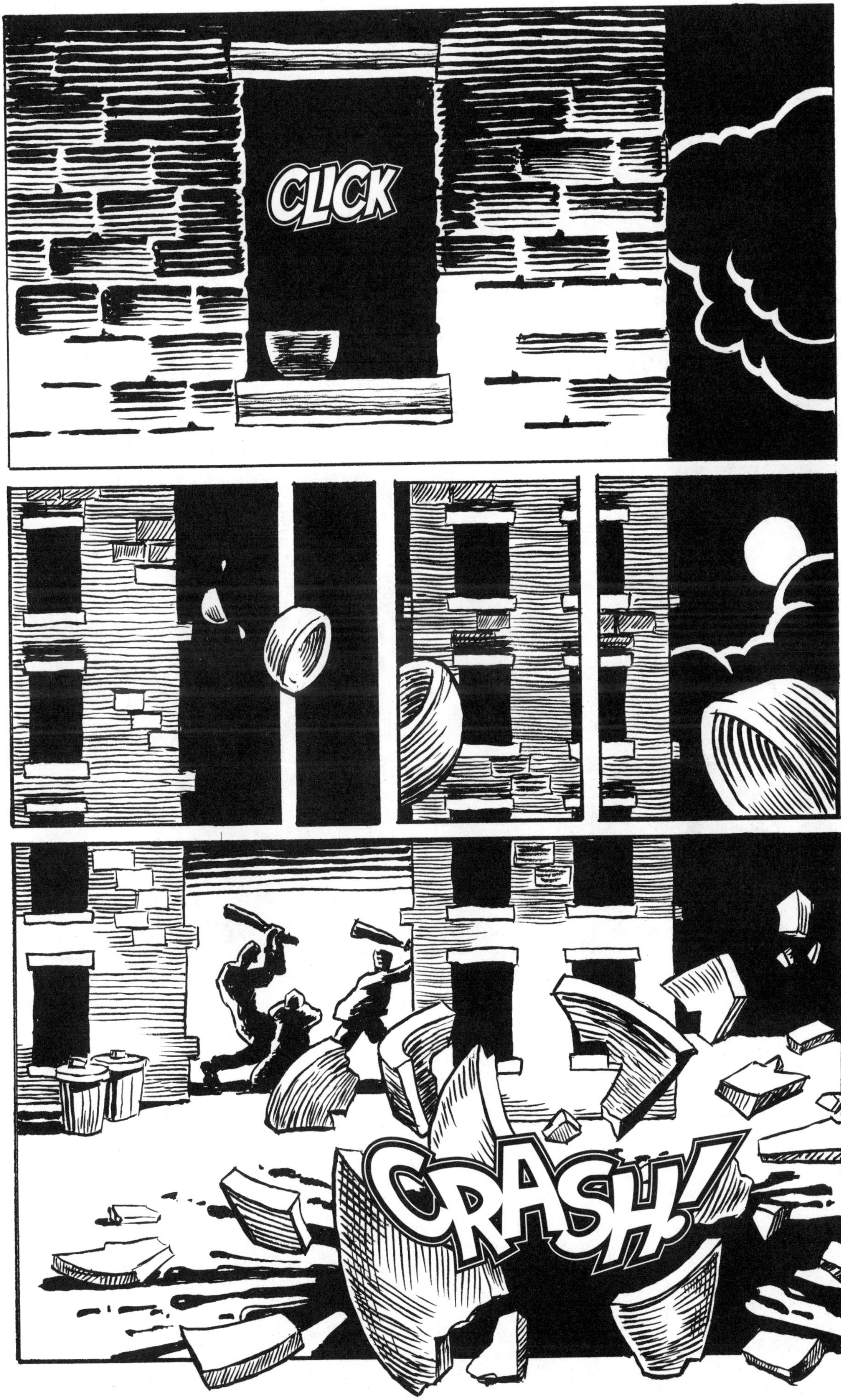
CLICK
CRASH!

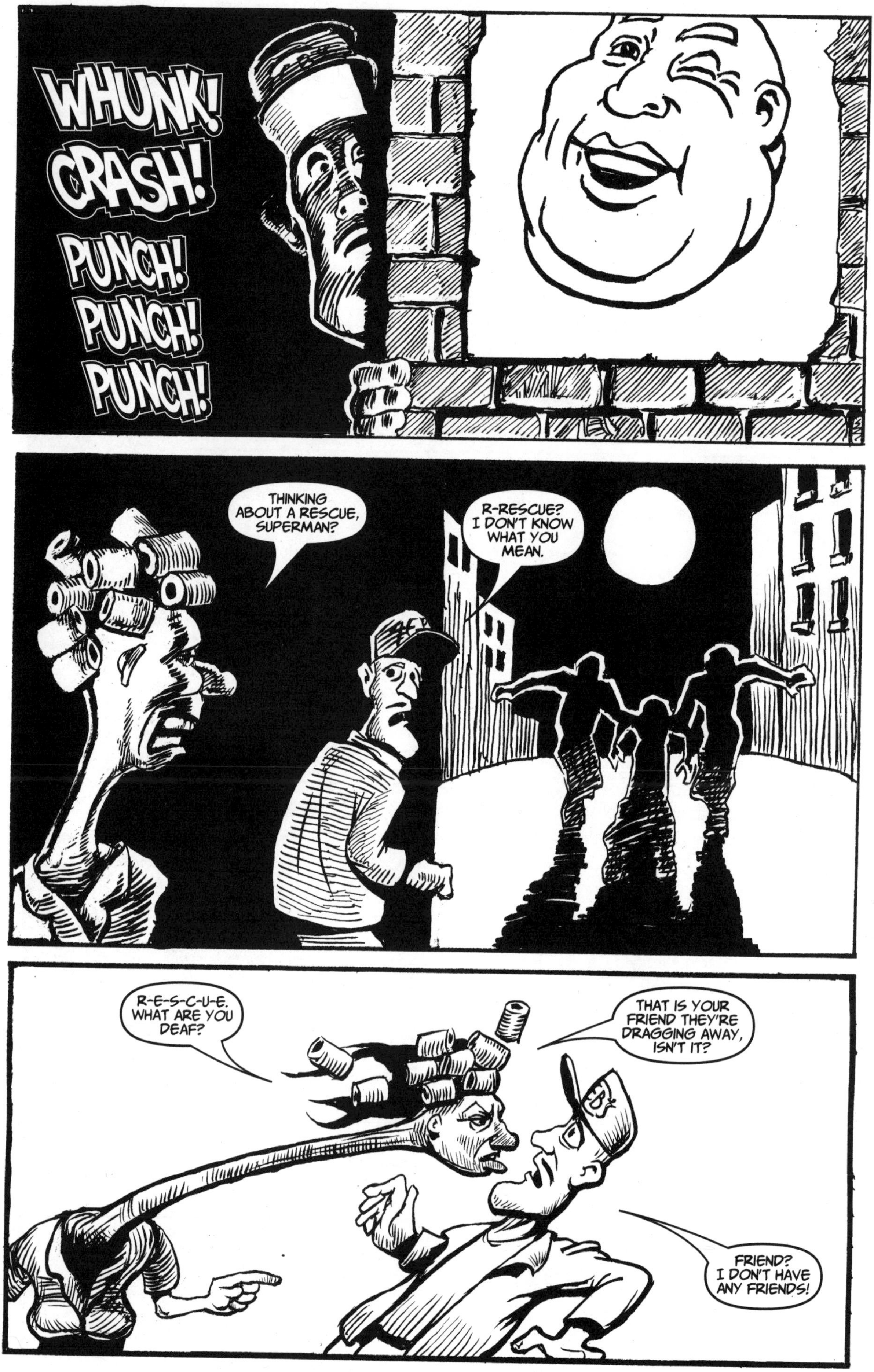
WHUNK!
CRASH!
PUNCH!
PUNCH!
PUNCH!
THINKING ABOUT A RESCUE, SUPERMAN?
R-RESCUE? I DON'T KNOW WHAT YOU MEAN.
R-E-S-C-U-E. WHAT ARE YOU DEAF?
THAT IS YOUR FRIEND THEY'RE DRAGGING AWAY, ISN'T IT?
FRIEND? I DON'T HAVE ANY FRIENDS!

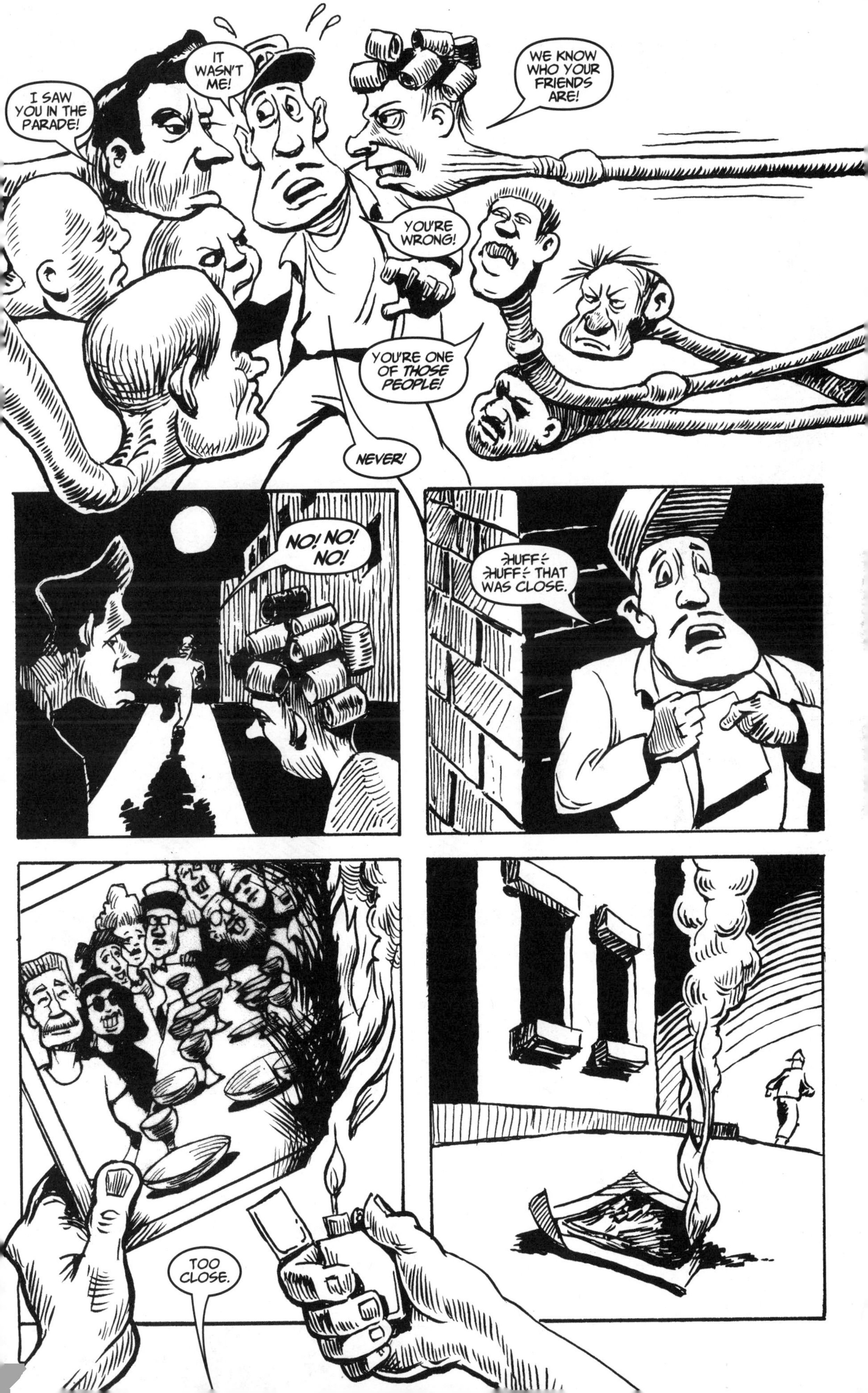
I SAW YOU IN THE PARADE!
IT WASN'T ME!
WE KNOW WHO YOUR FRIENDS ARE!
YOU'RE WRONG!
YOU'RE ONE OF THOSE PEOPLE!
NEVER!
NO! NO! NO!
HUFF HUFF THAT WAS CLOSE.
TOO CLOSE.

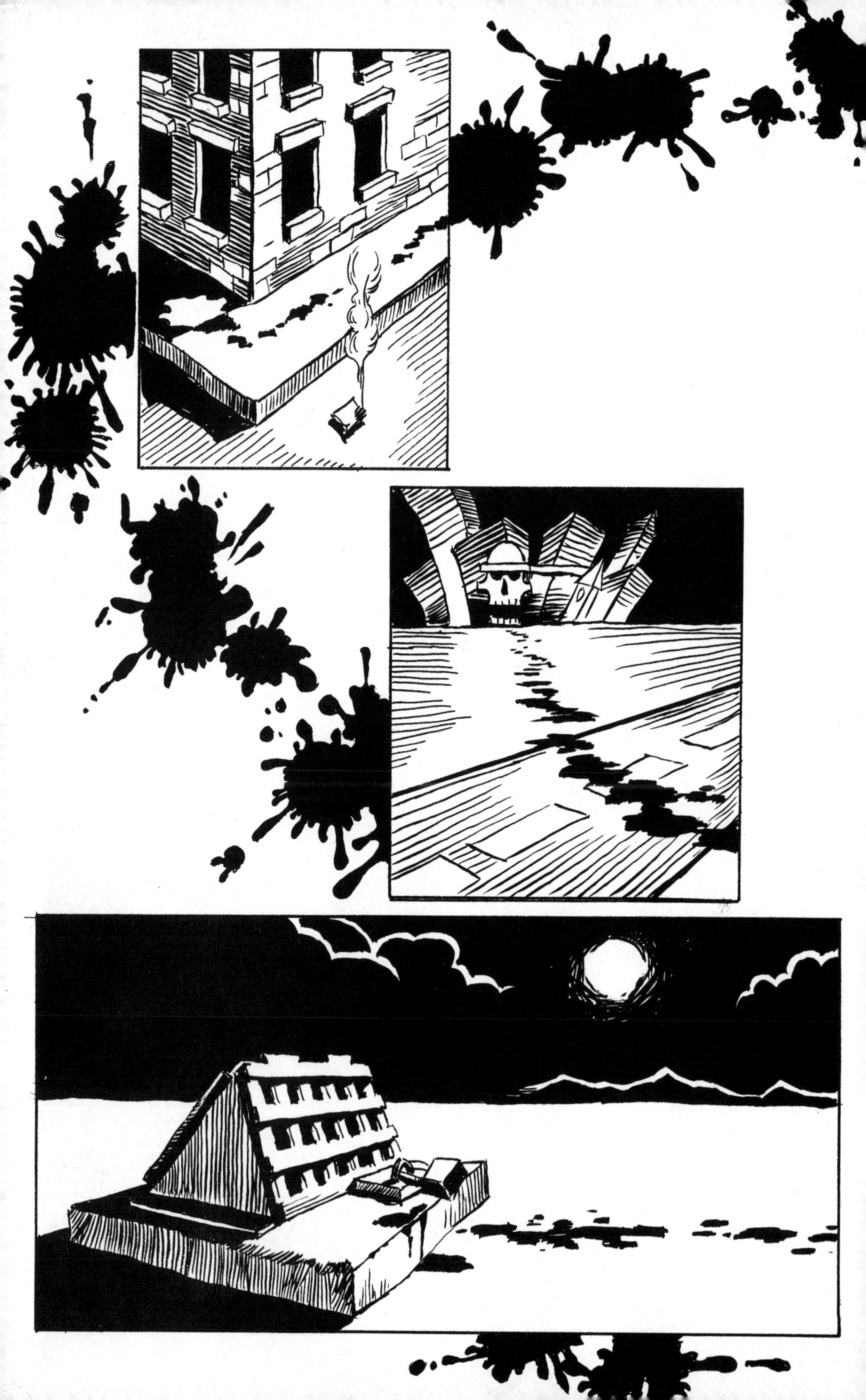

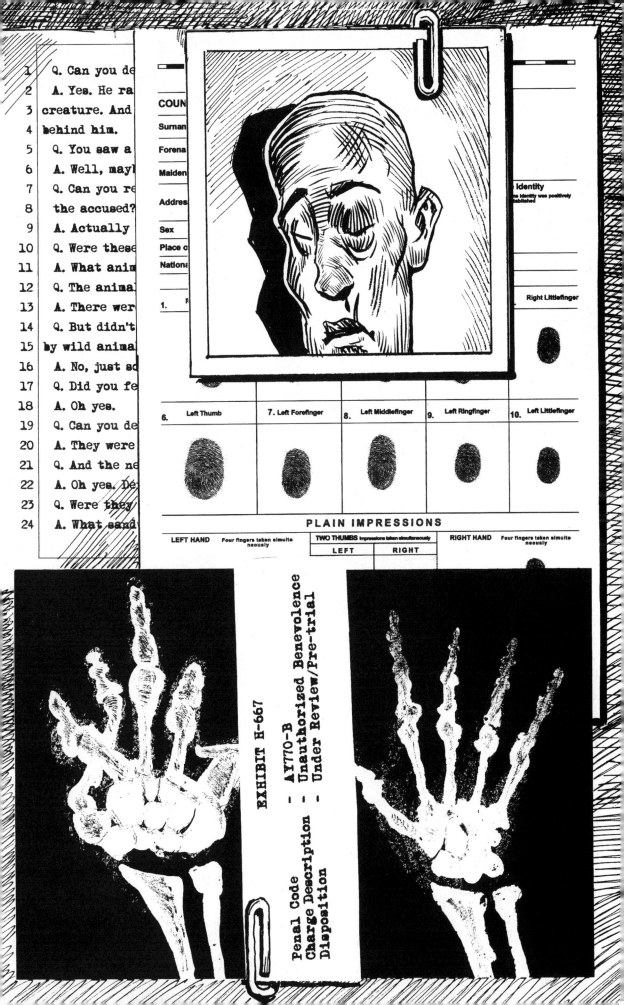

1 Q. Can you de
2 A. Yes. He ra
3 creature. And
4 behind him.
5 Q. You saw a
6 A. Well, mayl
7 Q. Can you re
8 the accused?
9 A. Actually
10 Q. Were these
11 A. What anim
12 Q. The animal
13 A. There wer
14 Q. But didn't
15 by wild anima
16 A. No, just so
17 Q. Did you fe
18 A. Oh yes.
19 Q. Can you de
20 A. They were
21 Q. And the ne
22 A. Oh yes. De
23 Q. Were they
24 A. What sand

COUN
Surnan
Forena
Maiden
Addres
Sex
Place o
Nationa

Identity
e identity was positively
ablished

1.

Right Littlefinger

| 6. Left Thumb | 7. Left Forefinger | 8. Left Middlefinger | 9. Left Ringfinger | 10. Left Littlefinger |

PLAIN IMPRESSIONS

LEFT HAND Four fingers taken simultaneously

TWO THUMBS Impressions taken simultaneously

| LEFT | RIGHT |

RIGHT HAND Four fingers taken simultaneously

EXHIBIT H-667

Penal Code   = AY770-B
Charge Description = Unauthorized Benevolence
Disposition   = Under Review/Pre-trial

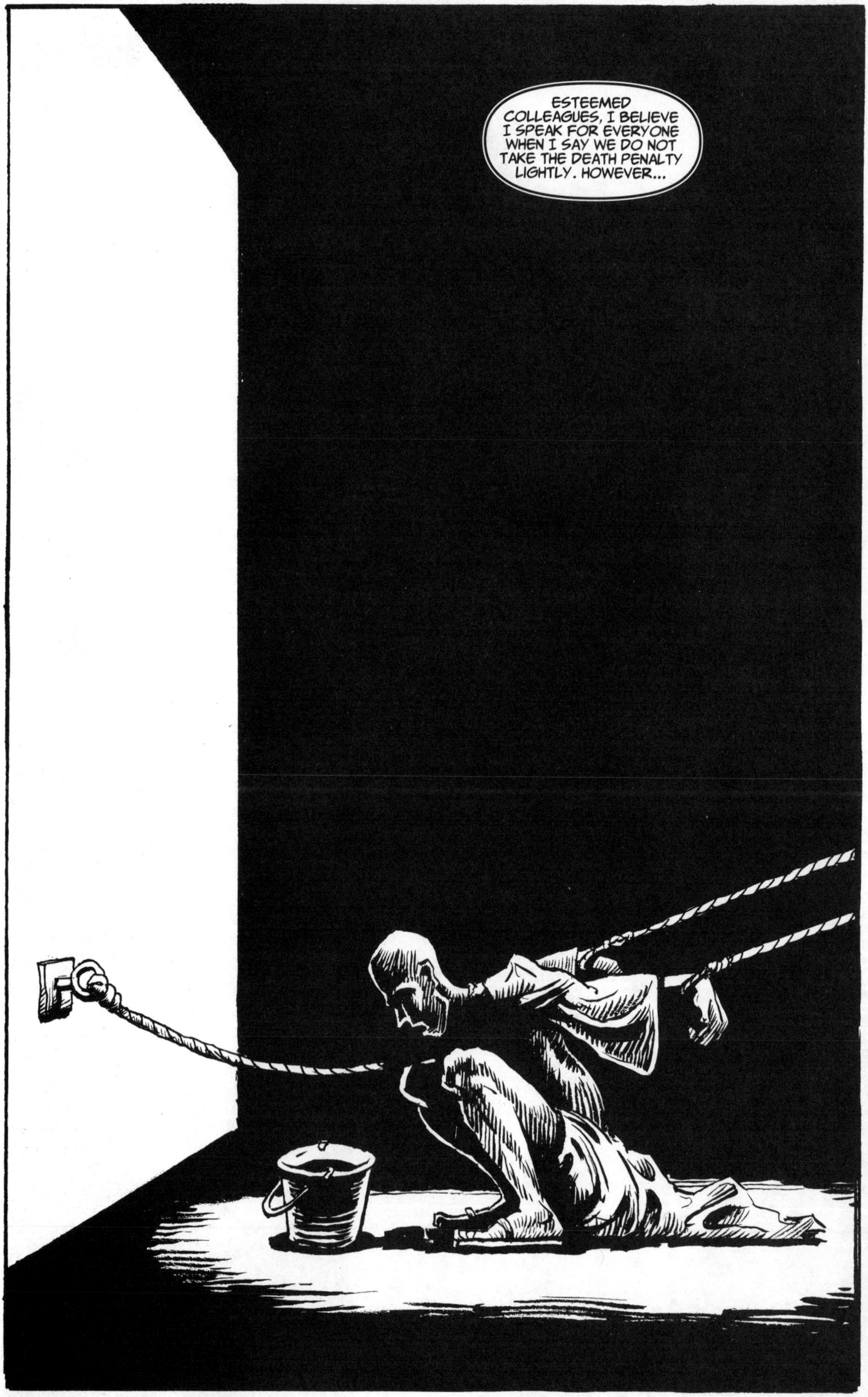
ESTEEMED COLLEAGUES, I BELIEVE I SPEAK FOR EVERYONE WHEN I SAY WE DO NOT TAKE THE DEATH PENALTY LIGHTLY. HOWEVER...

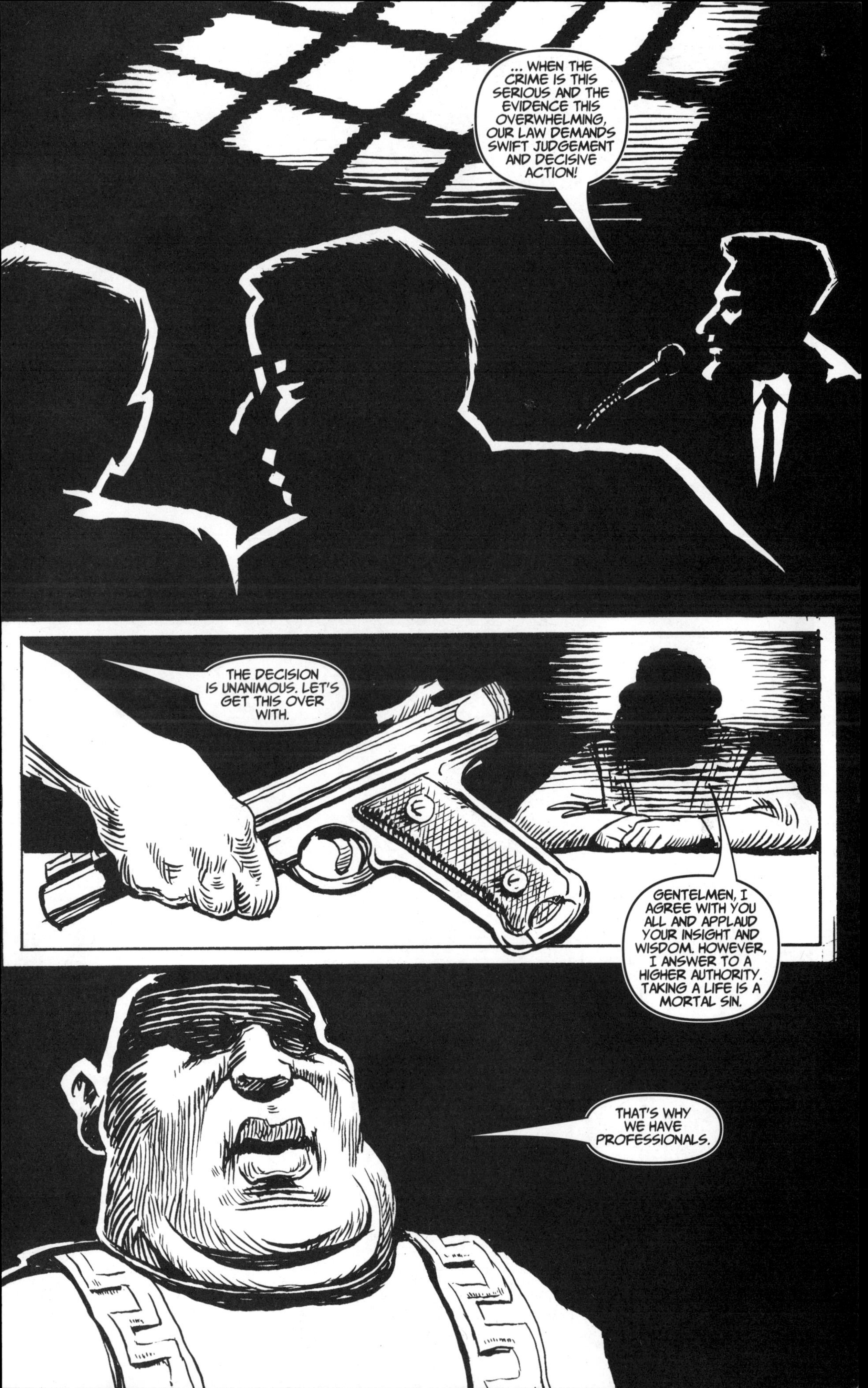
... WHEN THE CRIME IS THIS SERIOUS AND THE EVIDENCE THIS OVERWHELMING, OUR LAW DEMANDS SWIFT JUDGEMENT AND DECISIVE ACTION!
THE DECISION IS UNANIMOUS. LET'S GET THIS OVER WITH.
GENTELMEN, I AGREE WITH YOU ALL AND APPLAUD YOUR INSIGHT AND WISDOM. HOWEVER, I ANSWER TO A HIGHER AUTHORITY. TAKING A LIFE IS A MORTAL SIN.
THAT'S WHY WE HAVE PROFESSIONALS.

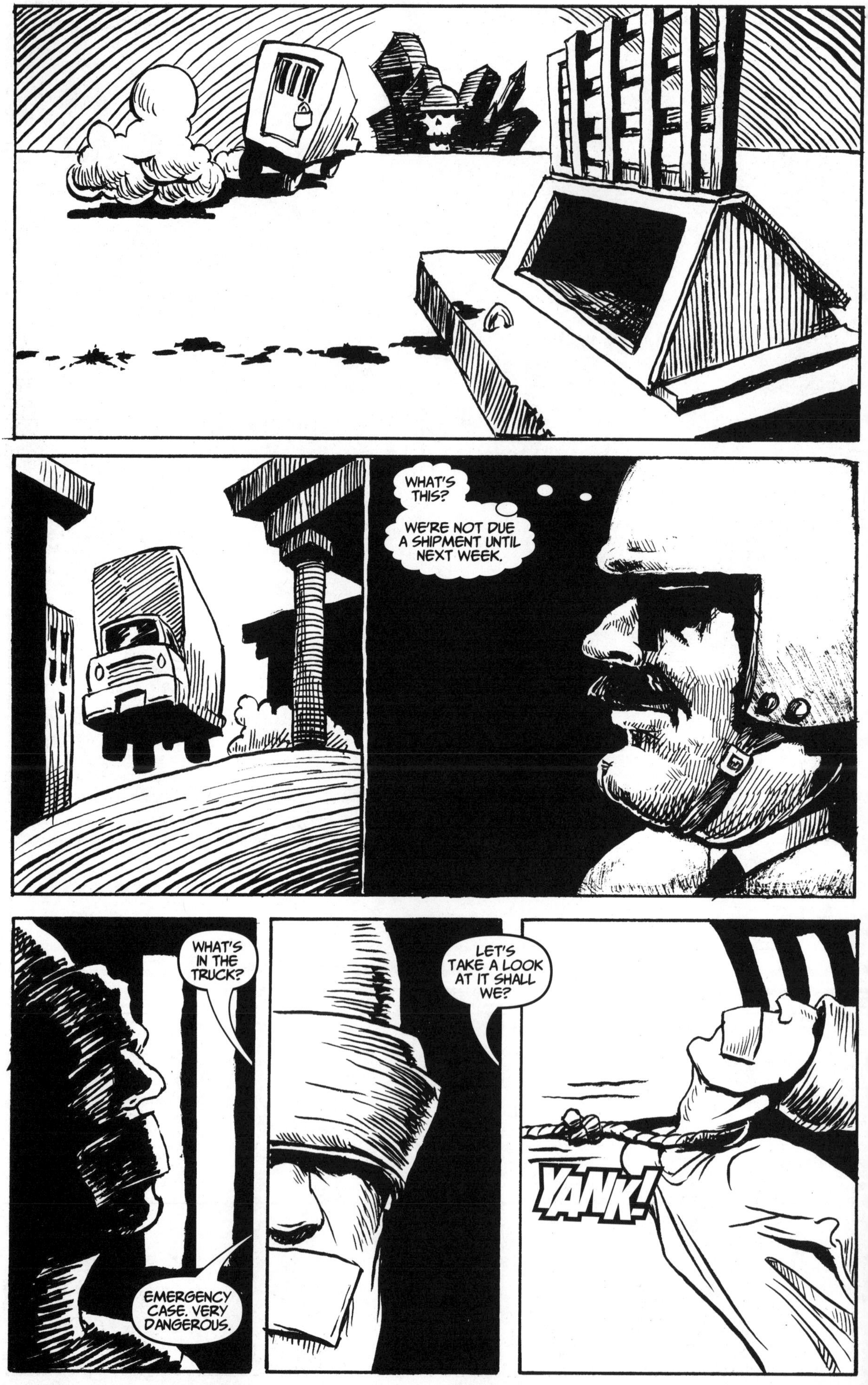
WHAT'S THIS?
WE'RE NOT DUE A SHIPMENT UNTIL NEXT WEEK.
WHAT'S IN THE TRUCK?
EMERGENCY CASE. VERY DANGEROUS.
LET'S TAKE A LOOK AT IT SHALL WE?
YANK!

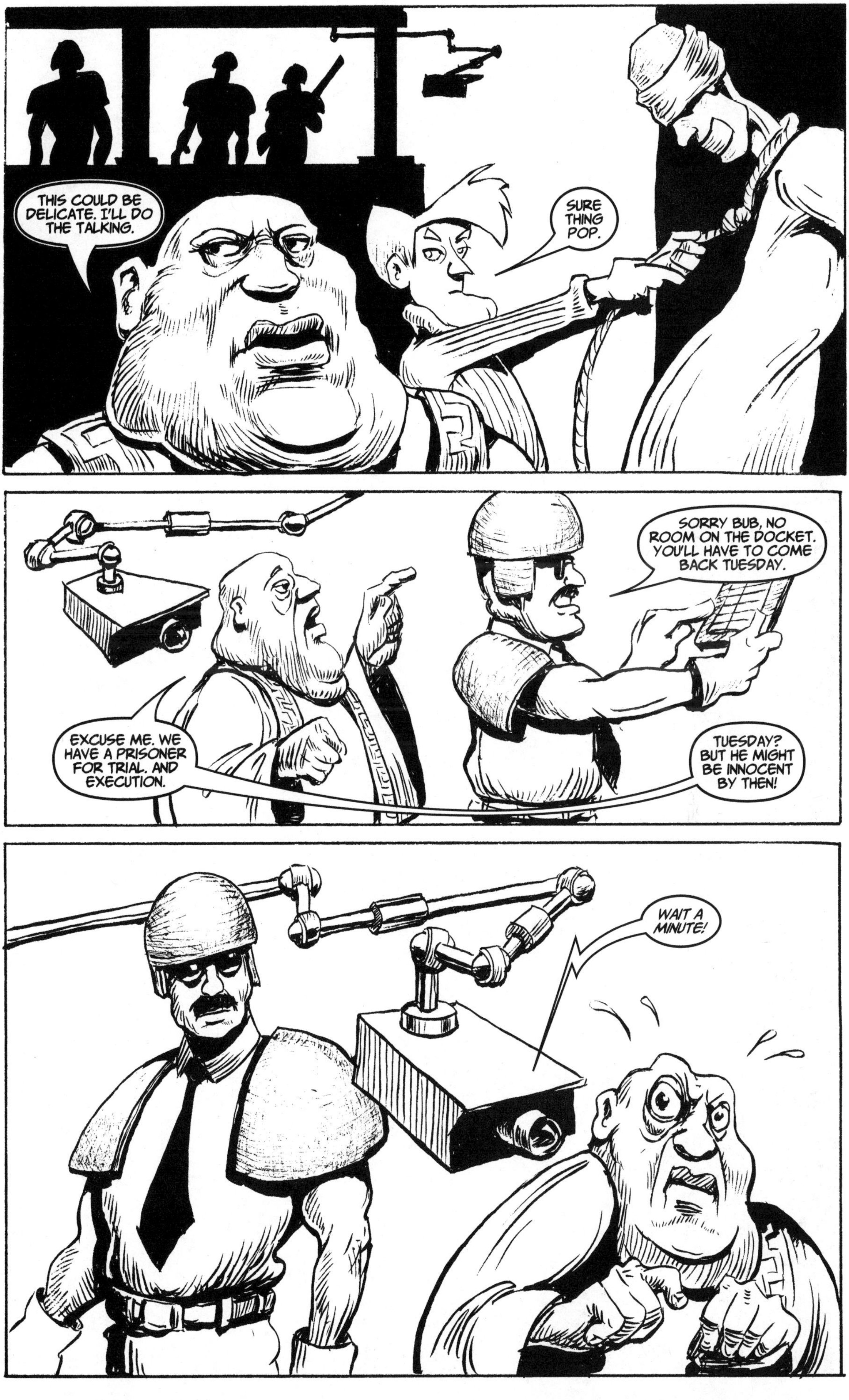
THIS COULD BE DELICATE. I'LL DO THE TALKING.
SURE THING POP.
EXCUSE ME. WE HAVE A PRISONER FOR TRIAL. AND EXECUTION.
SORRY BUB, NO ROOM ON THE DOCKET. YOU'LL HAVE TO COME BACK TUESDAY.
TUESDAY? BUT HE MIGHT BE INNOCENT BY THEN!
WAIT A MINUTE!

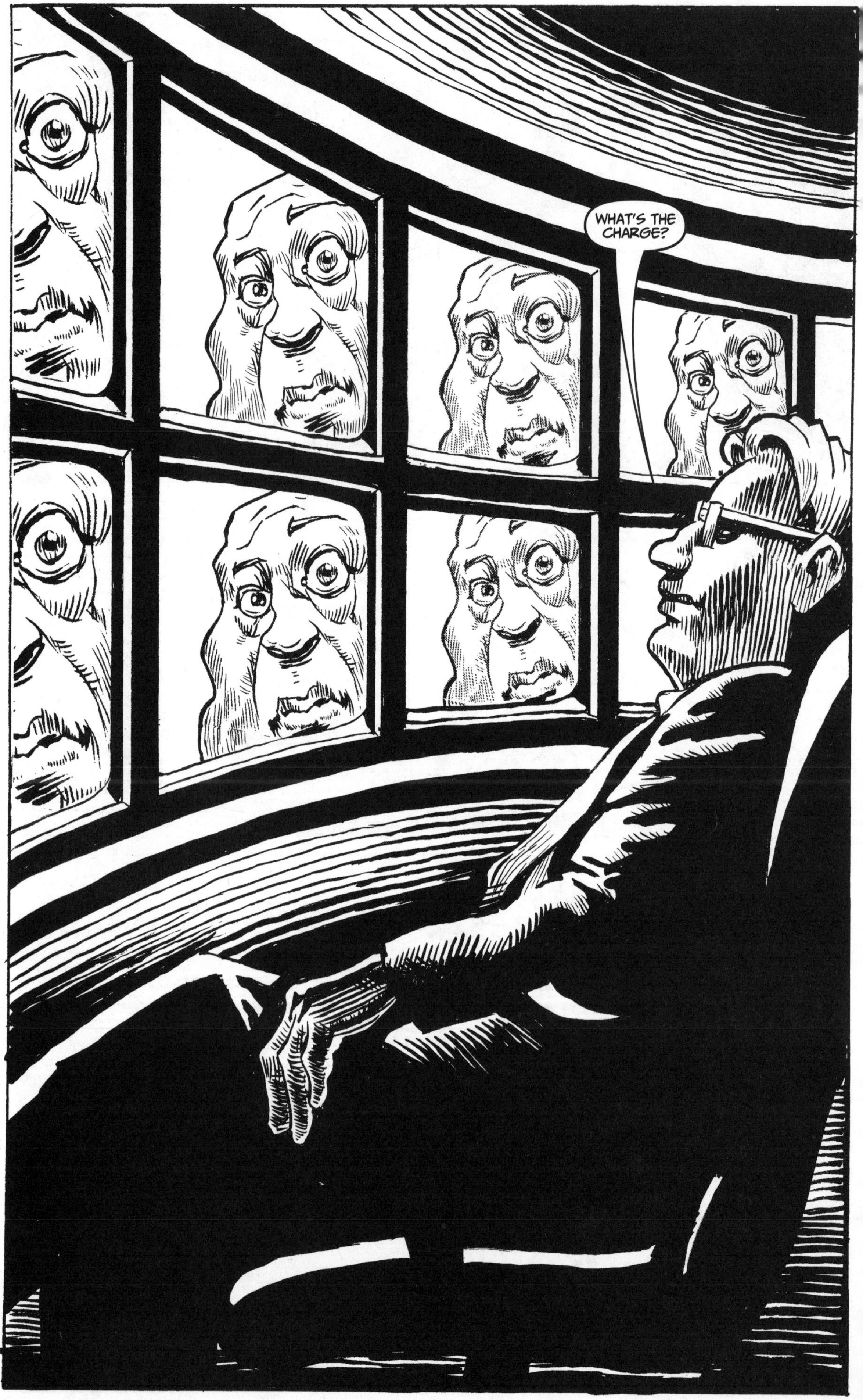
WHAT'S THE CHARGE?

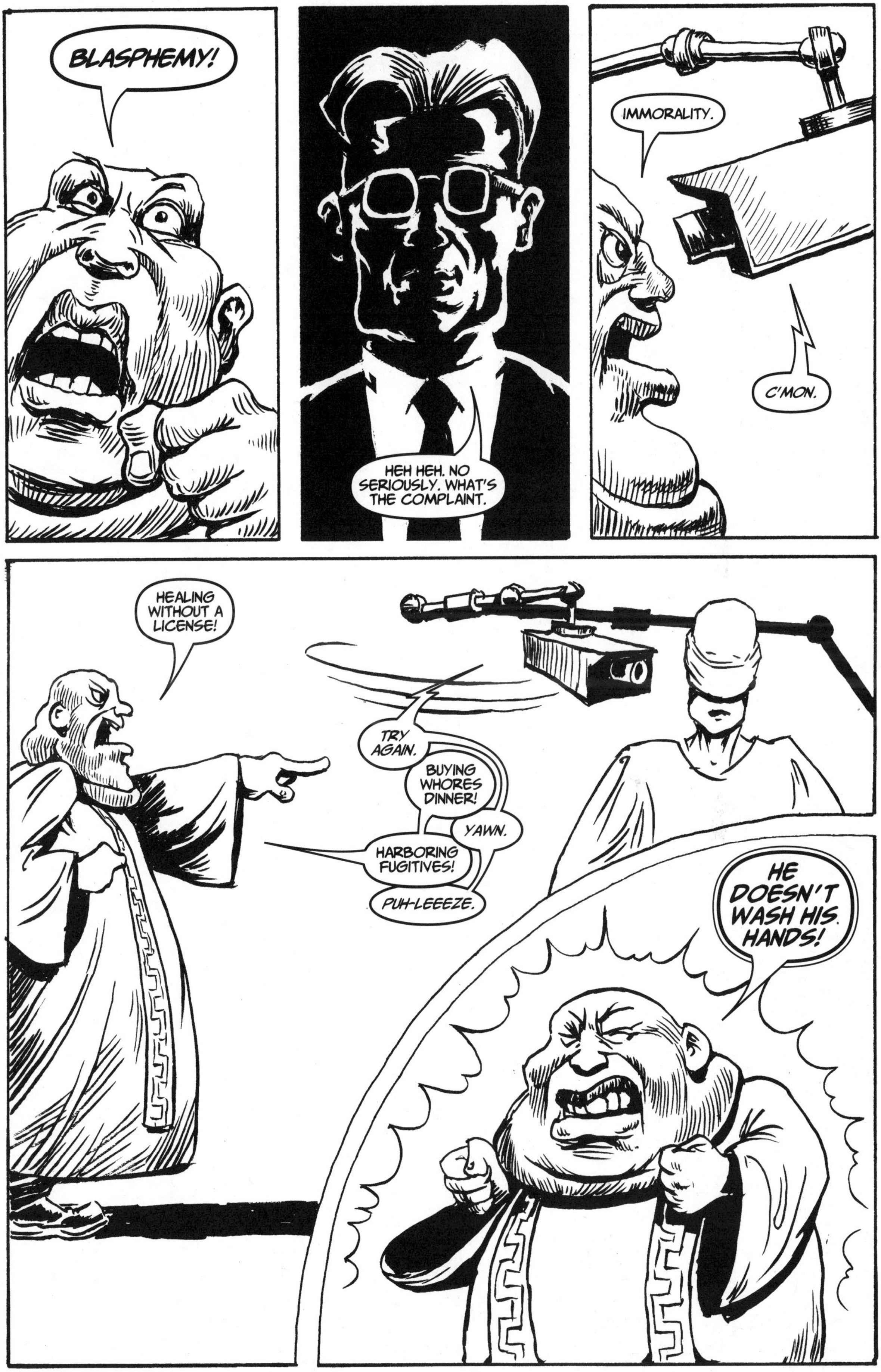
BLASPHEMY!
HEH HEH. NO SERIOUSLY. WHAT'S THE COMPLAINT.
IMMORALITY.
C'MON.
HEALING WITHOUT A LICENSE!
TRY AGAIN.
BUYING WHORES DINNER!
YAWN.
HARBORING FUGITIVES!
PUH-LEEEZE.
HE DOESN'T WASH HIS HANDS!

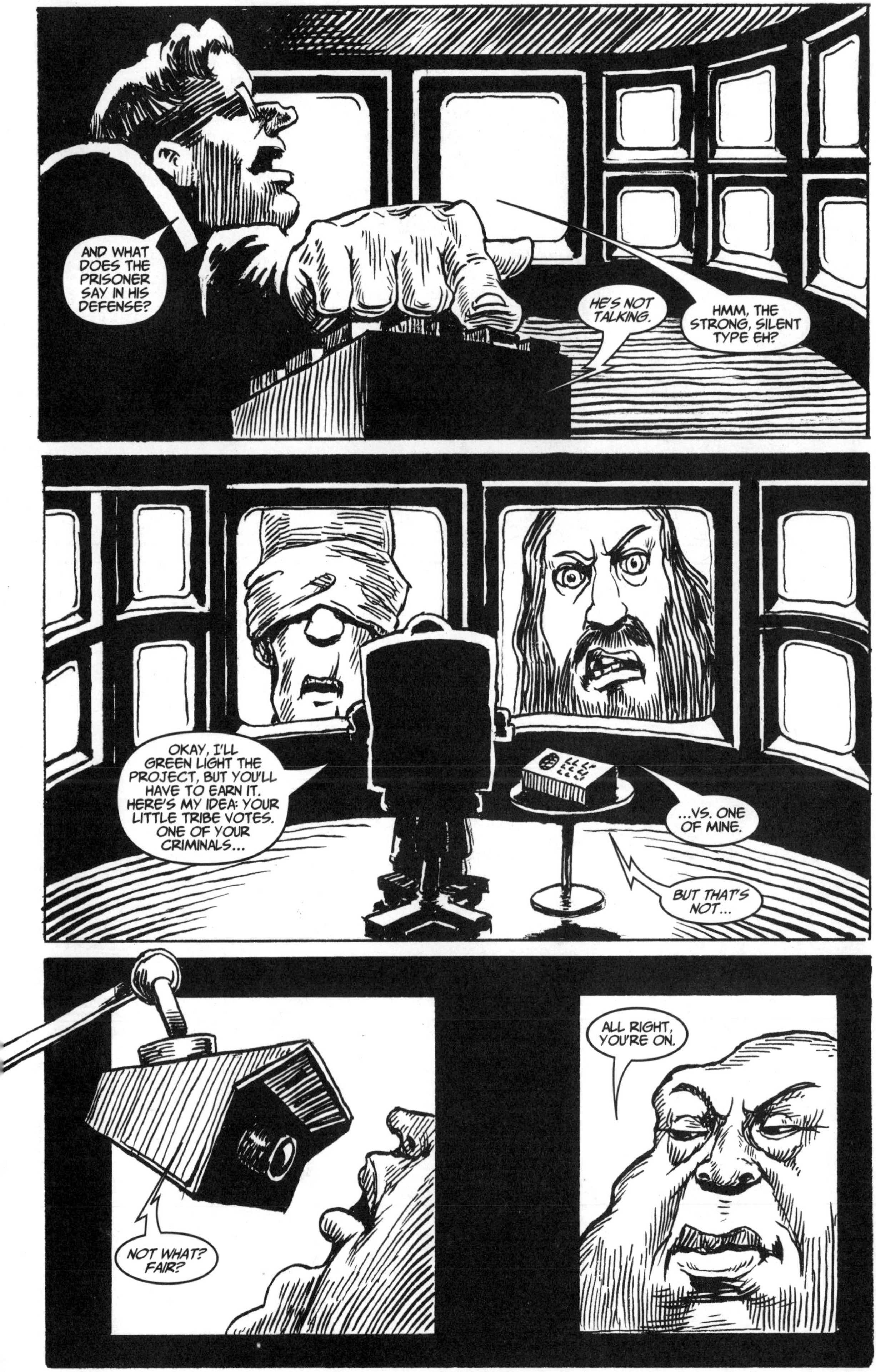
AND WHAT DOES THE PRISONER SAY IN HIS DEFENSE?
HE'S NOT TALKING.
HMM, THE STRONG, SILENT TYPE EH?
OKAY, I'LL GREEN LIGHT THE PROJECT, BUT YOU'LL HAVE TO EARN IT. HERE'S MY IDEA: YOUR LITTLE TRIBE VOTES. ONE OF YOUR CRIMINALS...
...VS. ONE OF MINE.
BUT THAT'S NOT...
NOT WHAT? FAIR?
ALL RIGHT, YOU'RE ON.

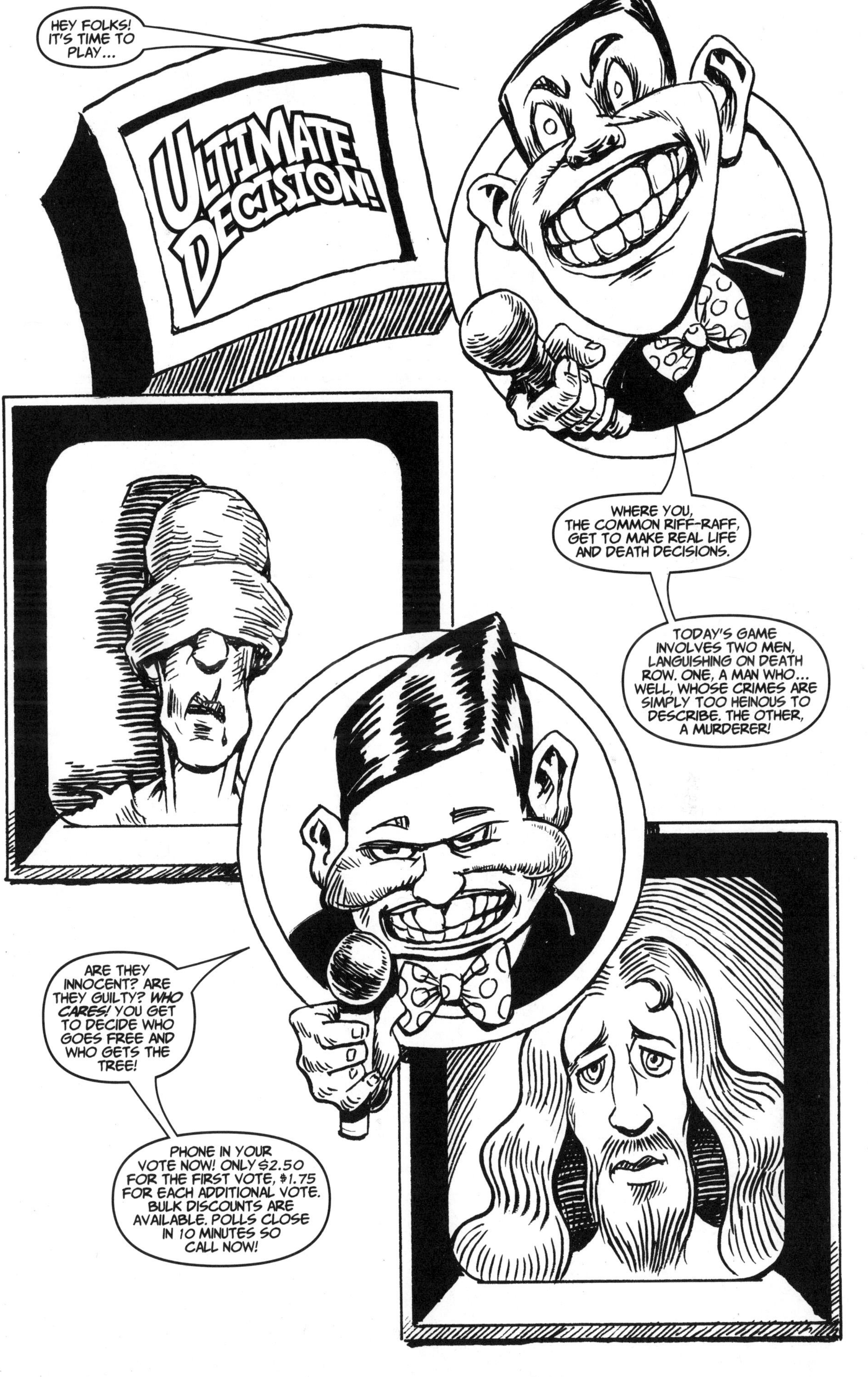
HEY FOLKS! IT'S TIME TO PLAY...
ULTIMATE DECISION!
WHERE YOU, THE COMMON RIFF-RAFF, GET TO MAKE REAL LIFE AND DEATH DECISIONS.
TODAY'S GAME INVOLVES TWO MEN, LANGUISHING ON DEATH ROW. ONE, A MAN WHO... WELL, WHOSE CRIMES ARE SIMPLY TOO HEINOUS TO DESCRIBE. THE OTHER, A MURDERER!
ARE THEY INNOCENT? ARE THEY GUILTY? *WHO CARES!* YOU GET TO DECIDE WHO GOES FREE AND WHO GETS THE TREE!
PHONE IN YOUR VOTE NOW! ONLY $2.50 FOR THE FIRST VOTE, $1.75 FOR EACH ADDITIONAL VOTE. BULK DISCOUNTS ARE AVAILABLE. POLLS CLOSE IN 10 MINUTES SO CALL NOW!

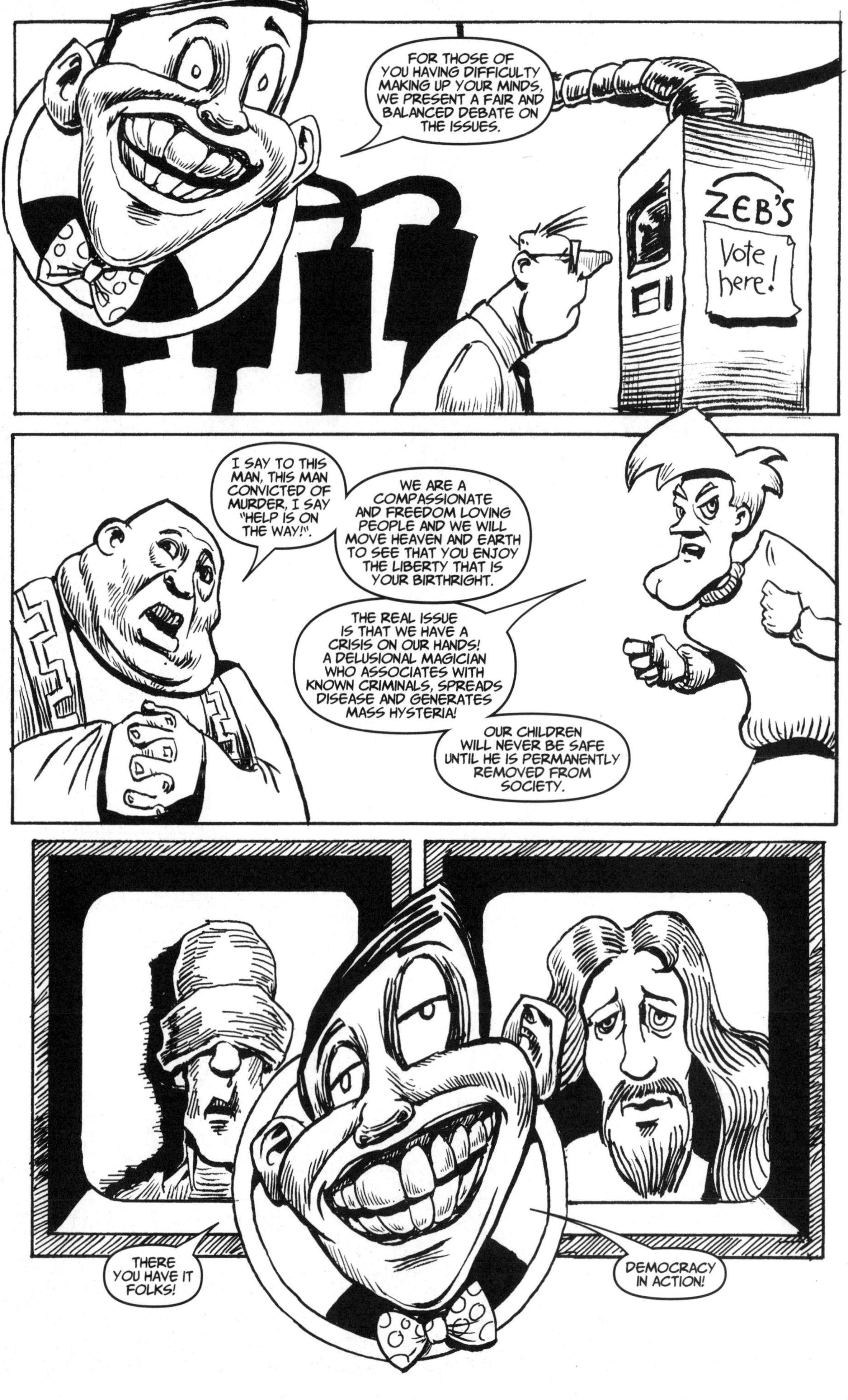
FOR THOSE OF YOU HAVING DIFFICULTY MAKING UP YOUR MINDS, WE PRESENT A FAIR AND BALANCED DEBATE ON THE ISSUES.
ZEB'S
Vote here!
I SAY TO THIS MAN, THIS MAN CONVICTED OF MURDER, I SAY "HELP IS ON THE WAY!".
WE ARE A COMPASSIONATE AND FREEDOM LOVING PEOPLE AND WE WILL MOVE HEAVEN AND EARTH TO SEE THAT YOU ENJOY THE LIBERTY THAT IS YOUR BIRTHRIGHT.
THE REAL ISSUE IS THAT WE HAVE A CRISIS ON OUR HANDS! A DELUSIONAL MAGICIAN WHO ASSOCIATES WITH KNOWN CRIMINALS, SPREADS DISEASE AND GENERATES MASS HYSTERIA!
OUR CHILDREN WILL NEVER BE SAFE UNTIL HE IS PERMANENTLY REMOVED FROM SOCIETY.
THERE YOU HAVE IT FOLKS!
DEMOCRACY IN ACTION!

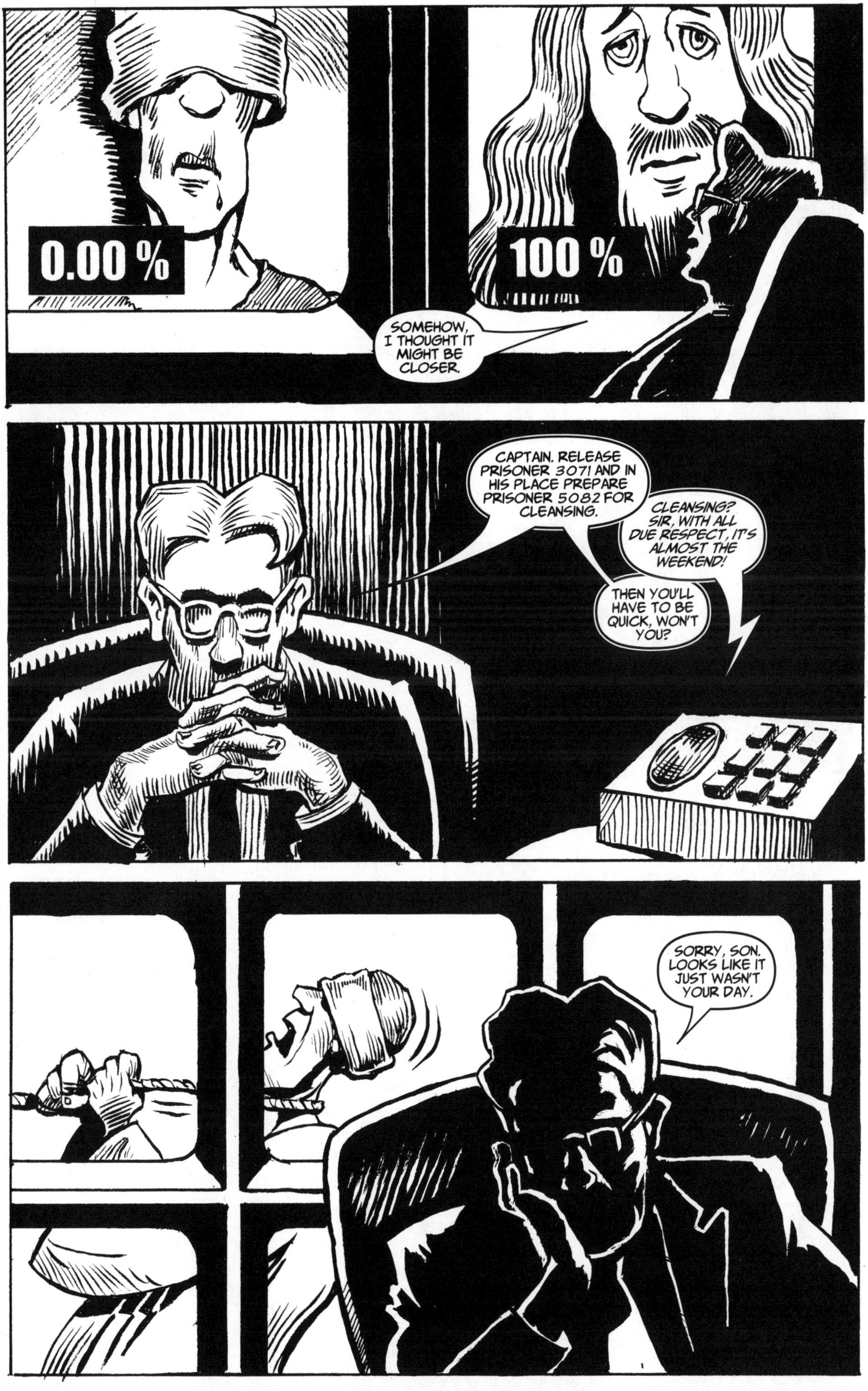
0.00 %
100 %
SOMEHOW, I THOUGHT IT MIGHT BE CLOSER.
CAPTAIN. RELEASE PRISONER 3071 AND IN HIS PLACE PREPARE PRISONER 5082 FOR CLEANSING.
CLEANSING? SIR, WITH ALL DUE RESPECT, IT'S ALMOST THE WEEKEND!
THEN YOU'LL HAVE TO BE QUICK, WON'T YOU?
SORRY, SON. LOOKS LIKE IT JUST WASN'T YOUR DAY.

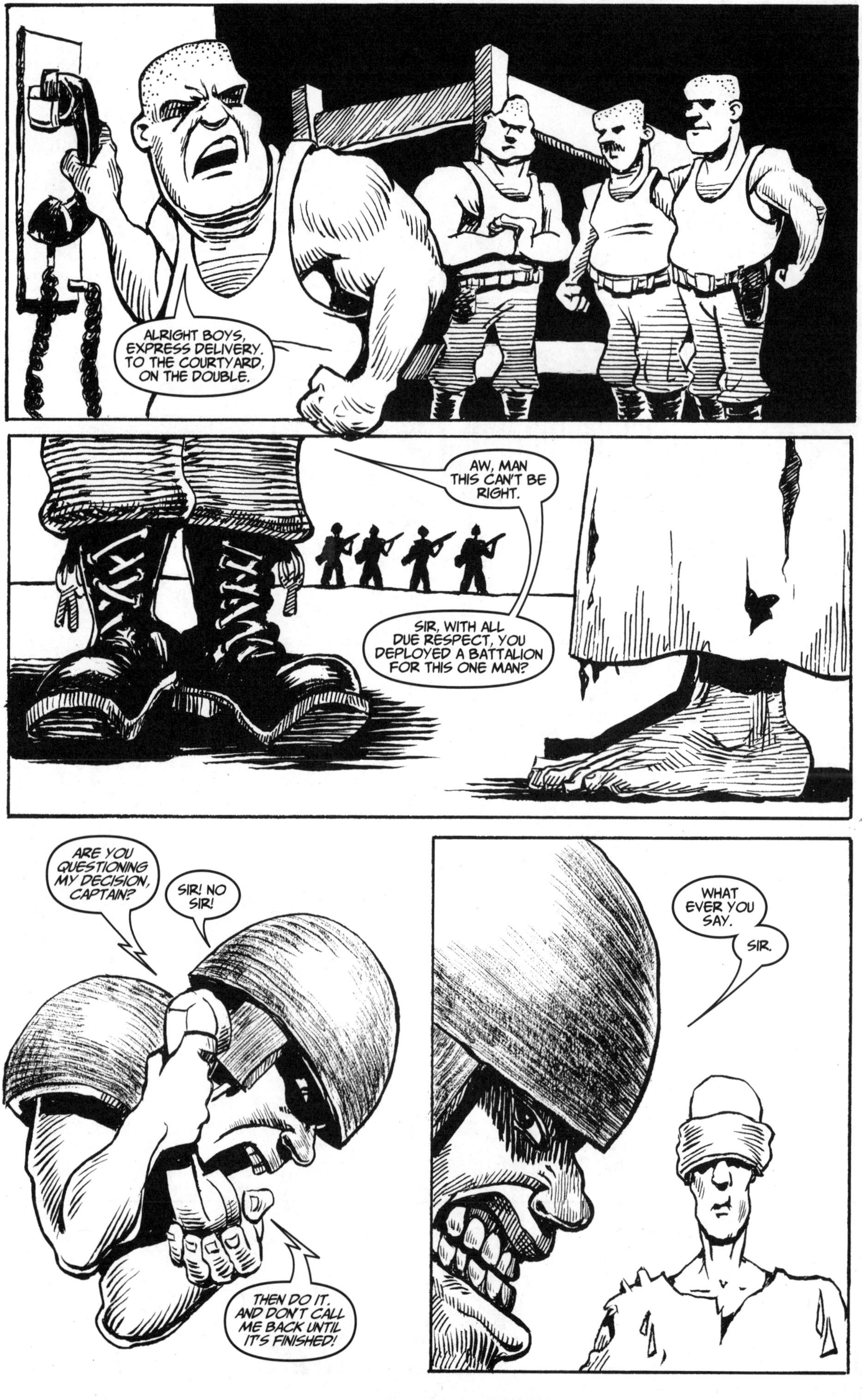
ALRIGHT BOYS, EXPRESS DELIVERY. TO THE COURTYARD, ON THE DOUBLE.
AW, MAN THIS CAN'T BE RIGHT.
SIR, WITH ALL DUE RESPECT, YOU DEPLOYED A BATTALION FOR THIS ONE MAN?
ARE YOU QUESTIONING MY DECISION, CAPTAIN?
SIR! NO SIR!
THEN DO IT. AND DON'T CALL ME BACK UNTIL IT'S FINISHED!
WHAT EVER YOU SAY.
SIR.

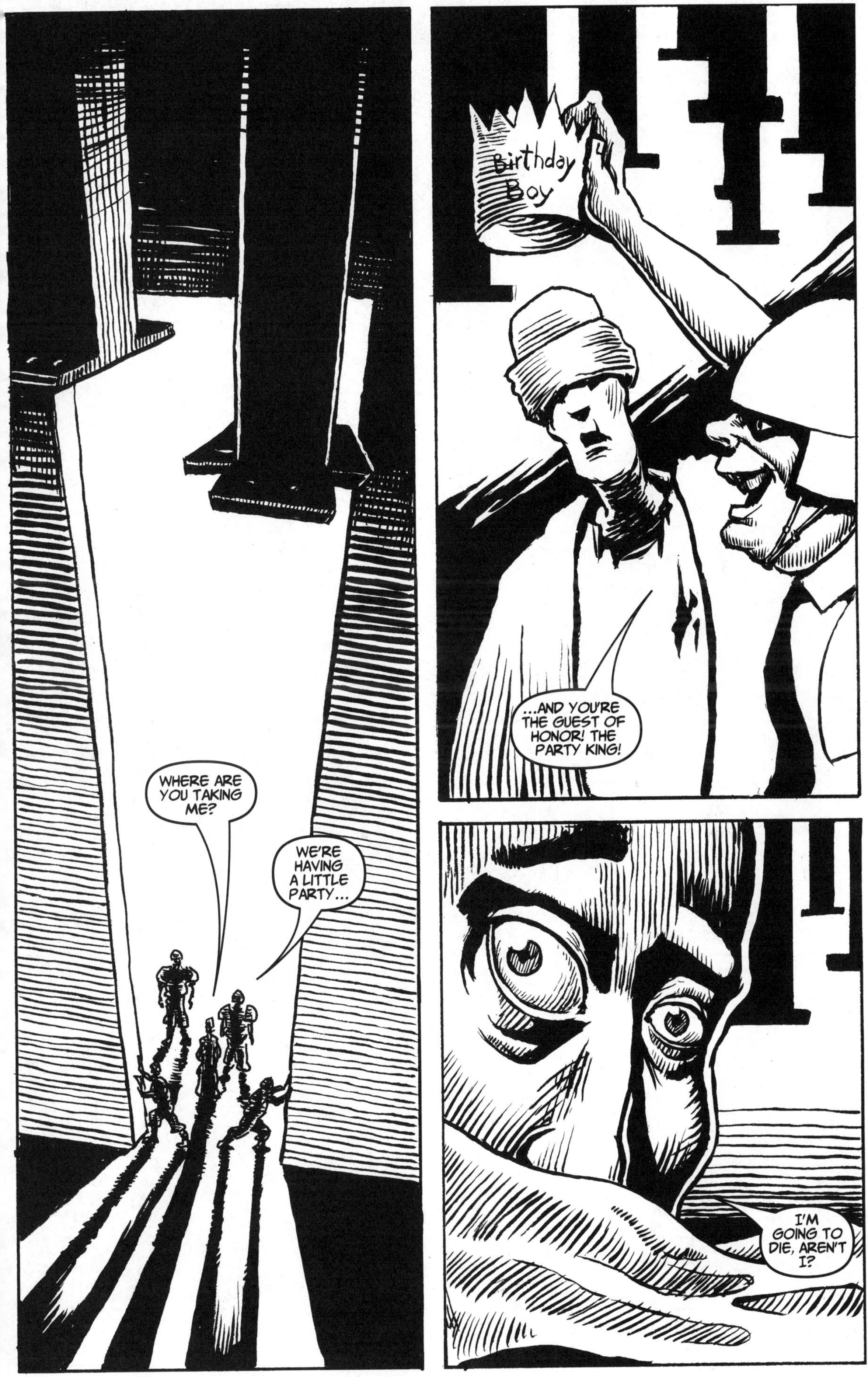

WHERE ARE YOU TAKING ME?
WE'RE HAVING A LITTLE PARTY...
Birthday Boy
...AND YOU'RE THE GUEST OF HONOR! THE PARTY KING!
I'M GOING TO DIE, AREN'T I?

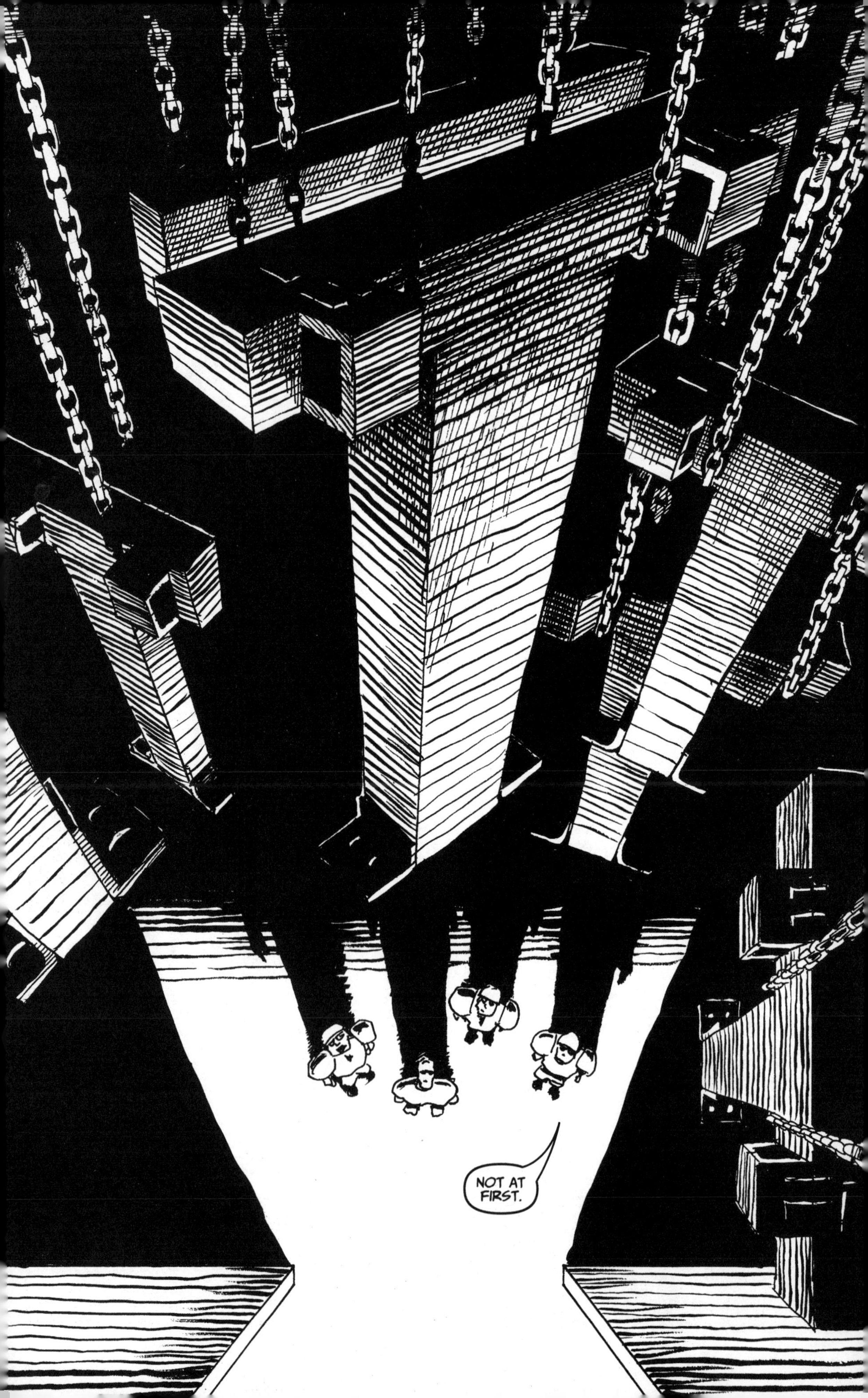
NOT AT FIRST.

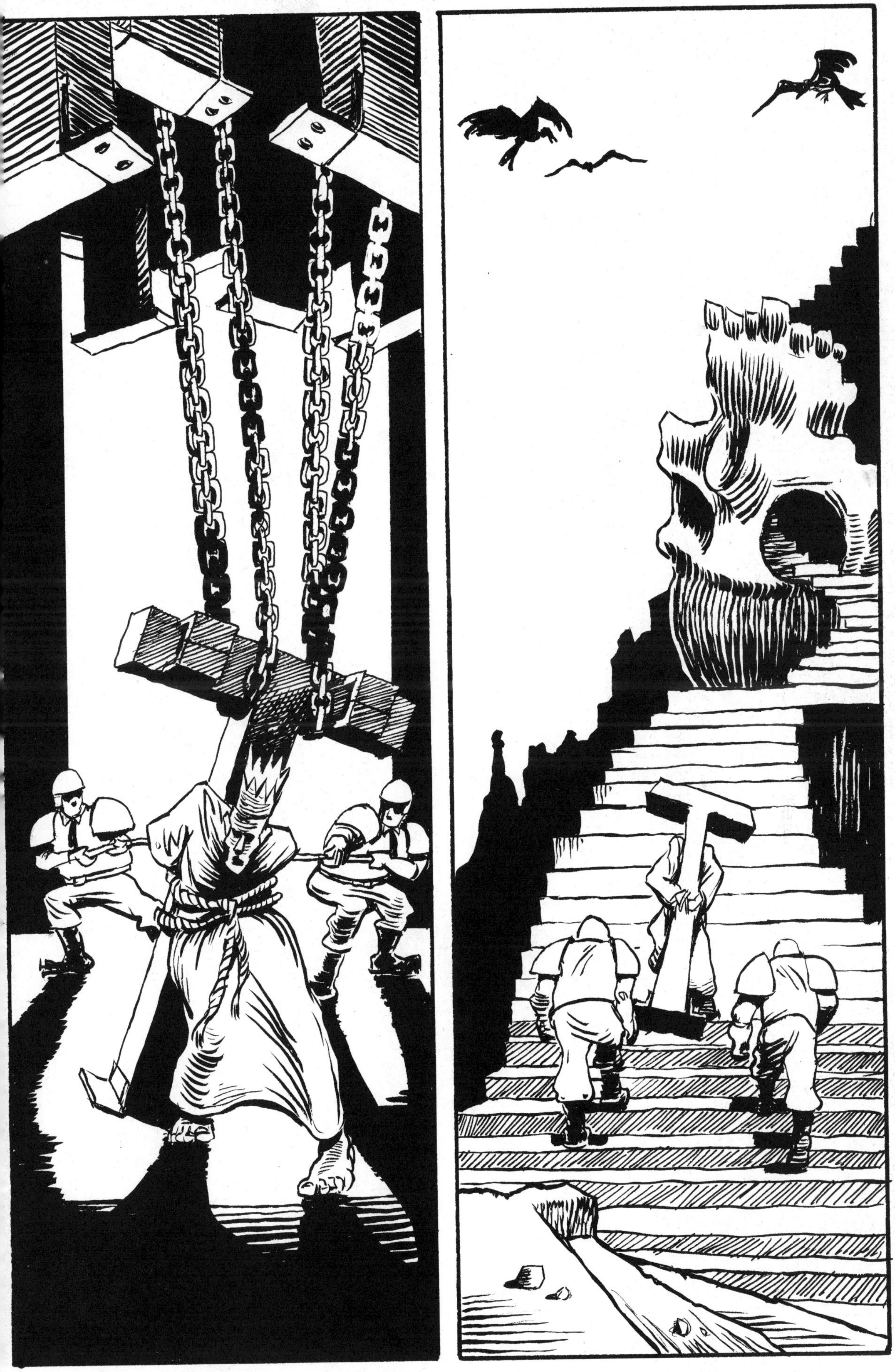

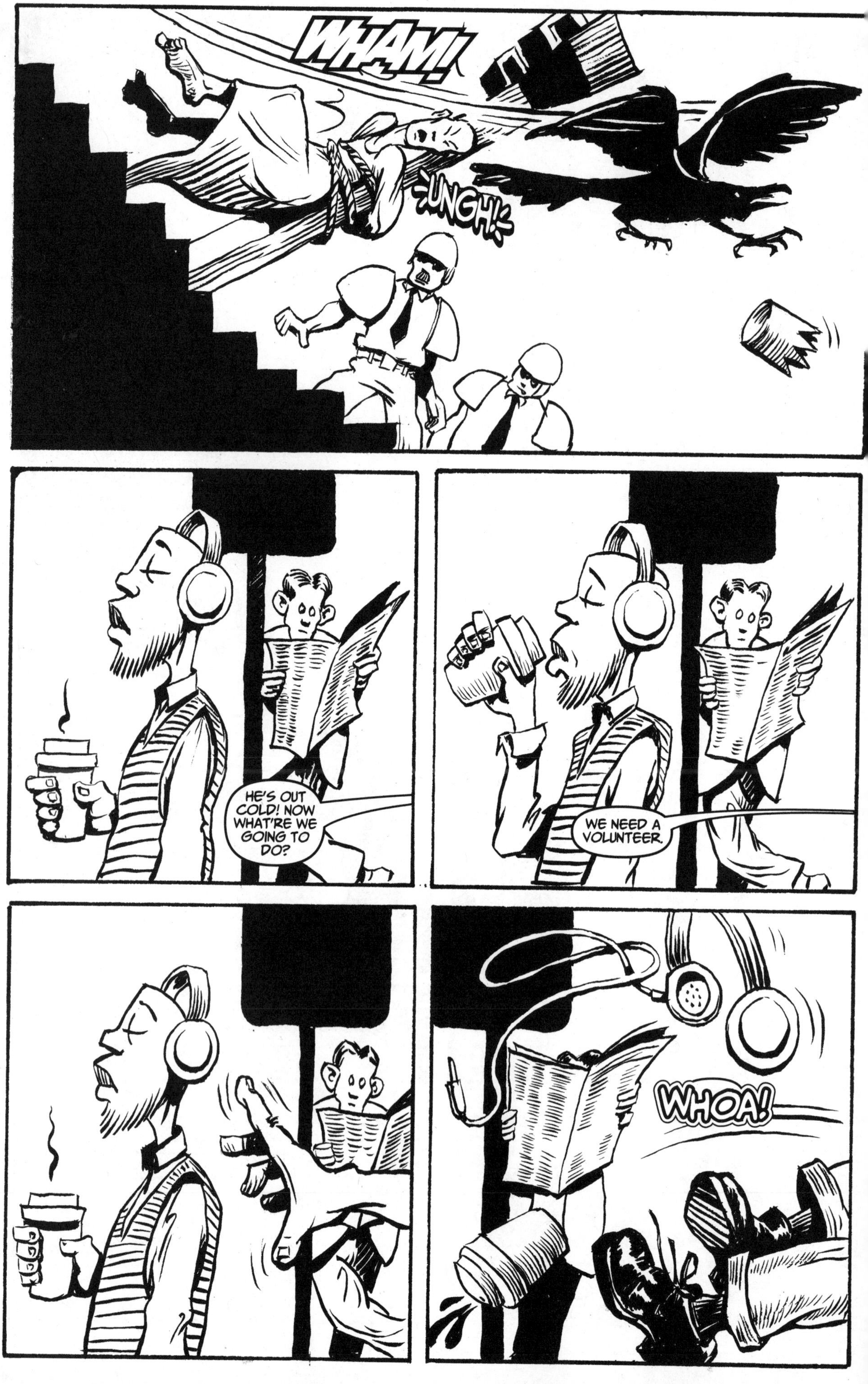
WHAM!
UNGH!
HE'S OUT COLD! NOW WHAT'RE WE GOING TO DO?
WE NEED A VOLUNTEER.
WHOA!

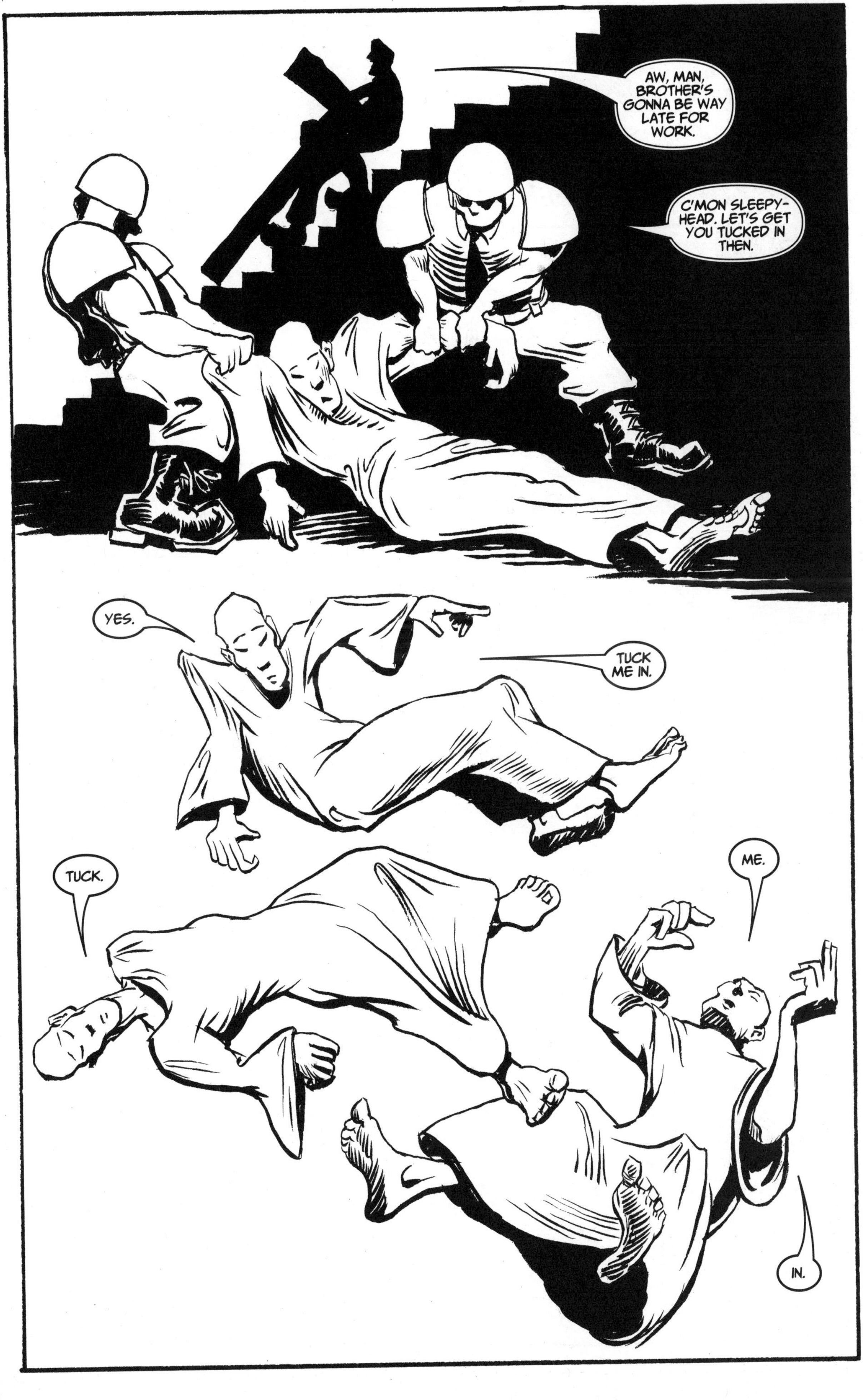
AW, MAN, BROTHER'S GONNA BE WAY LATE FOR WORK.
C'MON SLEEPY-HEAD. LET'S GET YOU TUCKED IN THEN.
YES.
TUCK ME IN.
TUCK.
ME.
IN.

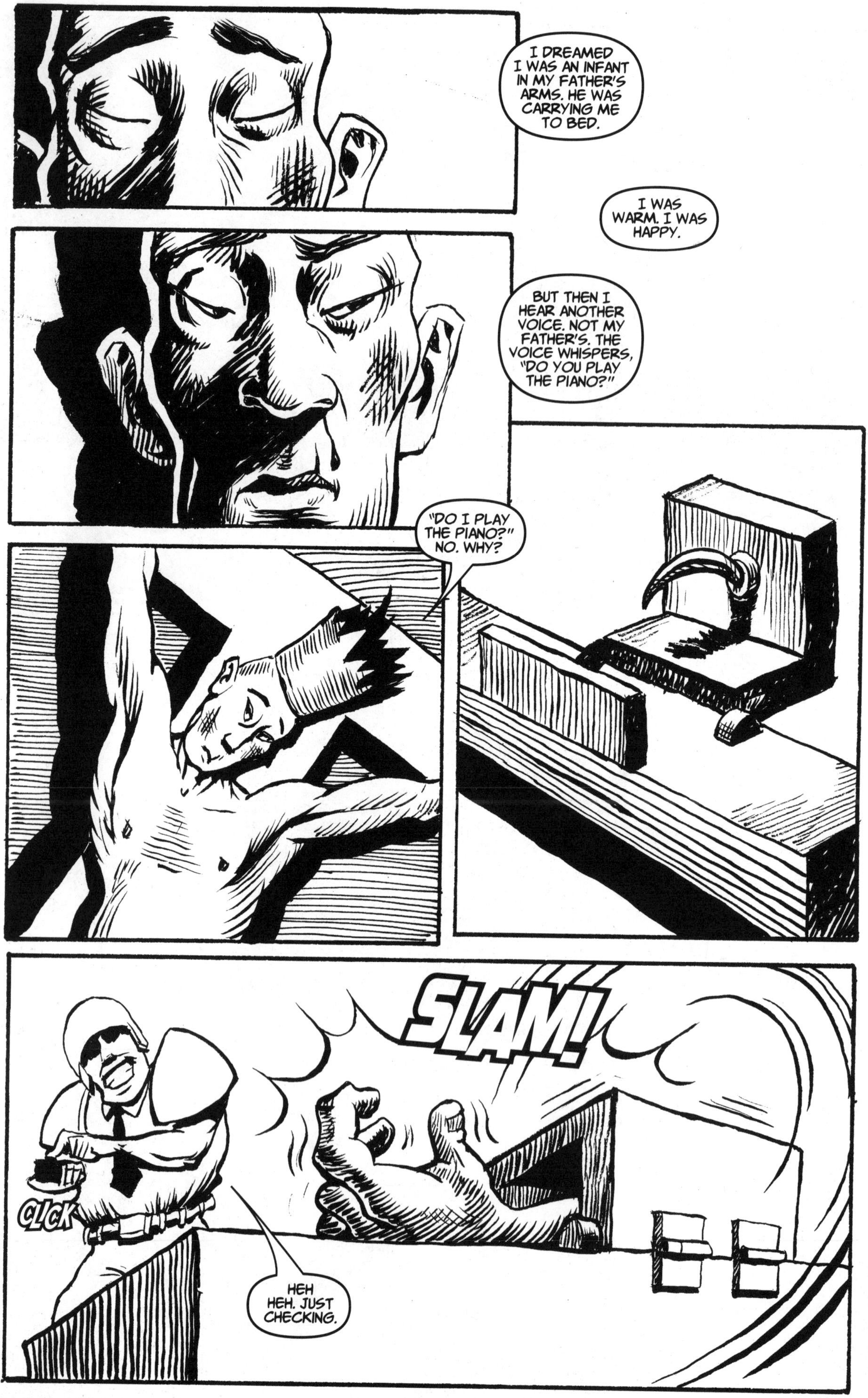
I DREAMED I WAS AN INFANT IN MY FATHER'S ARMS. HE WAS CARRYING ME TO BED.
I WAS WARM. I WAS HAPPY.
BUT THEN I HEAR ANOTHER VOICE. NOT MY FATHER'S. THE VOICE WHISPERS, "DO YOU PLAY THE PIANO?"
"DO I PLAY THE PIANO?" NO. WHY?
SLAM!
CLICK
HEH HEH. JUST CHECKING.

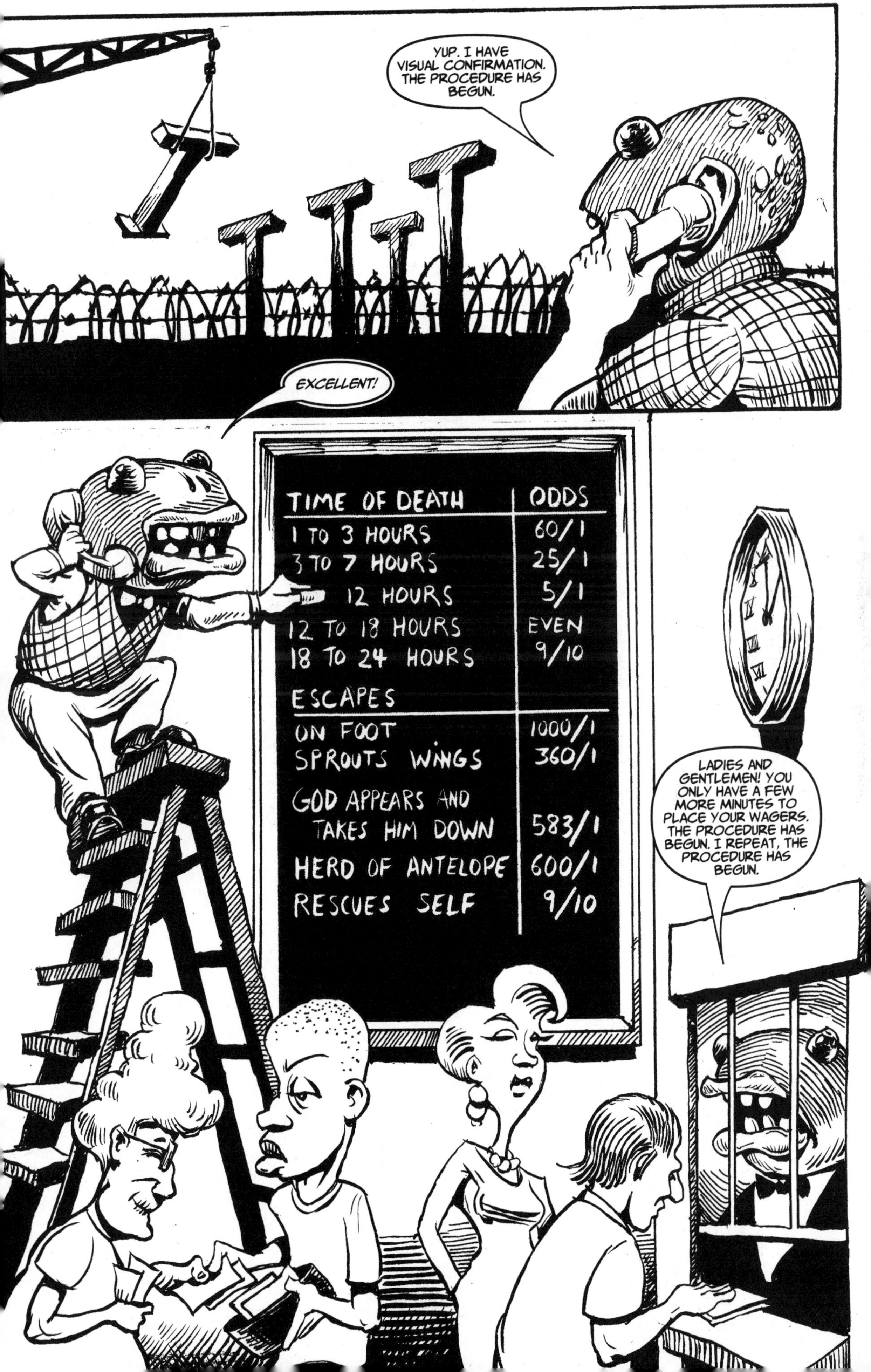
YUP. I HAVE VISUAL CONFIRMATION. THE PROCEDURE HAS BEGUN.
EXCELLENT!
TIME OF DEATH ODDS
1 TO 3 HOURS 60/1
3 TO 7 HOURS 25/1
12 HOURS 5/1
12 TO 18 HOURS EVEN
18 TO 24 HOURS 9/10
ESCAPES
ON FOOT 1000/1
SPROUTS WINGS 360/1
GOD APPEARS AND TAKES HIM DOWN 583/1
HERD OF ANTELOPE 600/1
RESCUES SELF 9/10
LADIES AND GENTLEMEN! YOU ONLY HAVE A FEW MORE MINUTES TO PLACE YOUR WAGERS. THE PROCEDURE HAS BEGUN. I REPEAT, THE PROCEDURE HAS BEGUN.

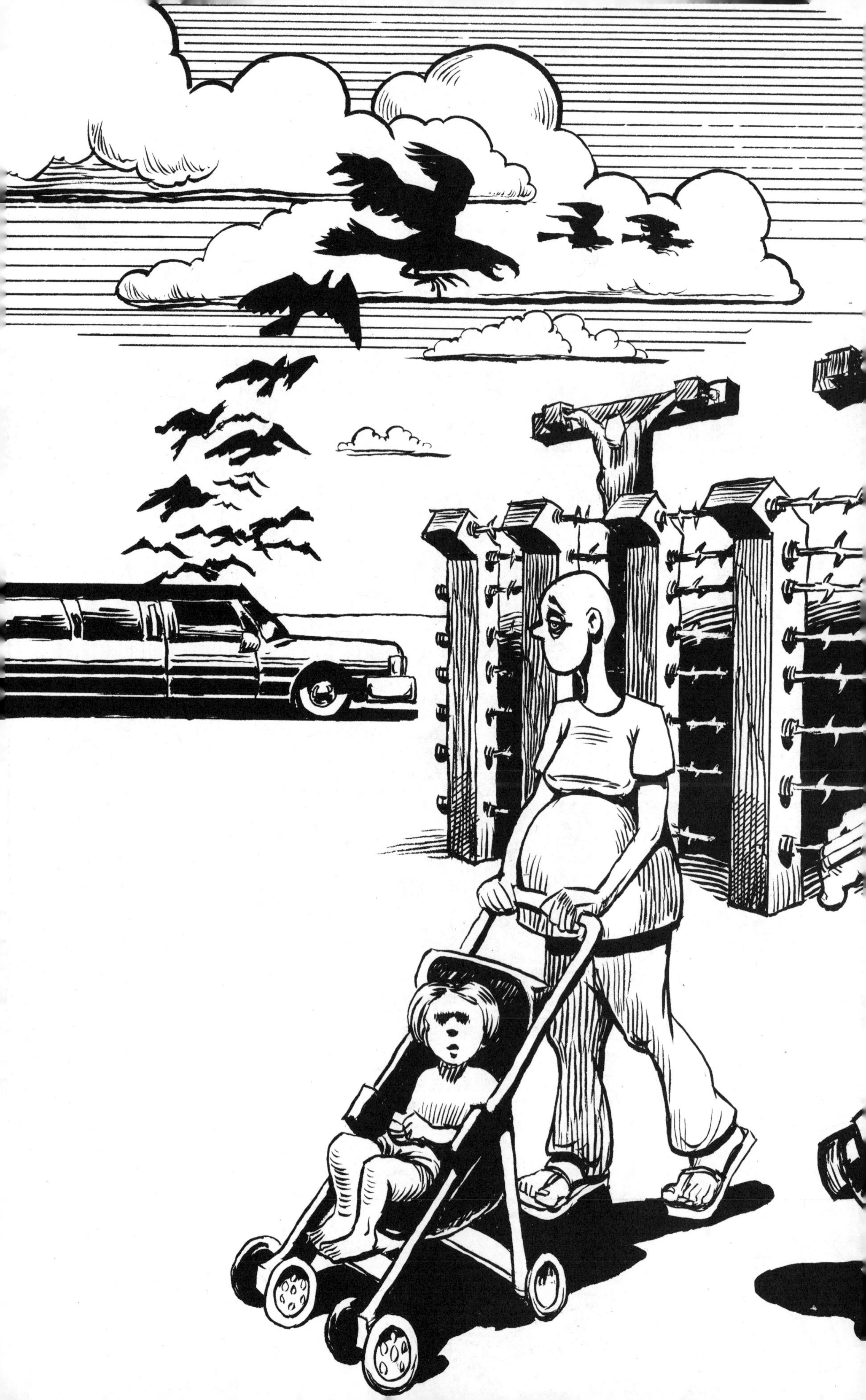

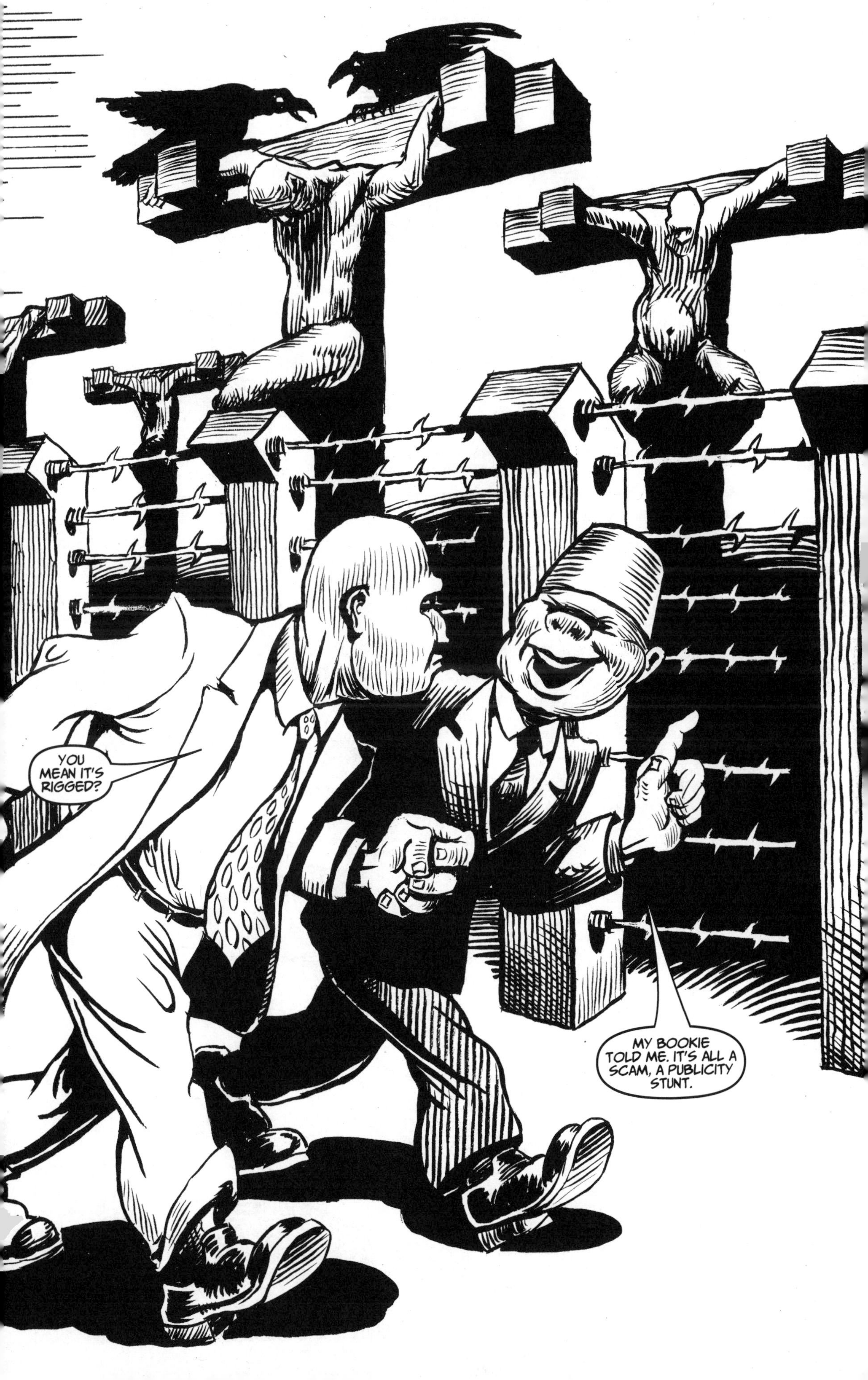
YOU MEAN IT'S RIGGED?
MY BOOKIE TOLD ME. IT'S ALL A SCAM, A PUBLICITY STUNT.

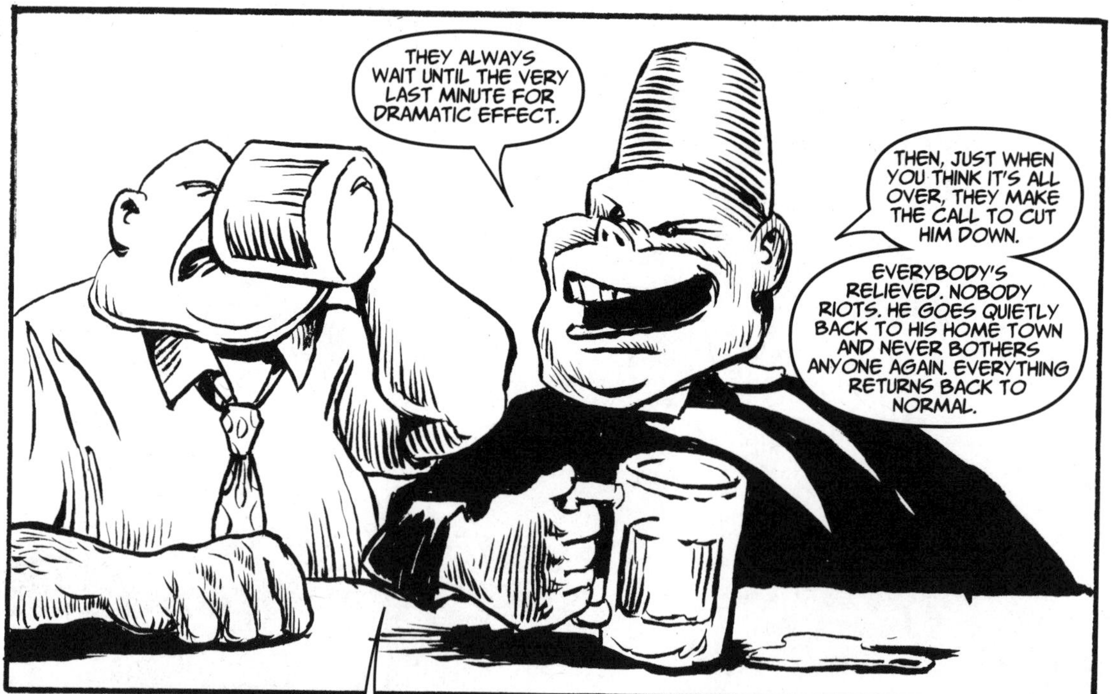
THEY ALWAYS WAIT UNTIL THE VERY LAST MINUTE FOR DRAMATIC EFFECT.
THEN, JUST WHEN YOU THINK IT'S ALL OVER, THEY MAKE THE CALL TO CUT HIM DOWN.
EVERYBODY'S RELIEVED. NOBODY RIOTS. HE GOES QUIETLY BACK TO HIS HOME TOWN AND NEVER BOTHERS ANYONE AGAIN. EVERYTHING RETURNS BACK TO NORMAL.
MARK MY WORDS, THAT PHONE IS GOING TO RING ANY MINUTE NOW.

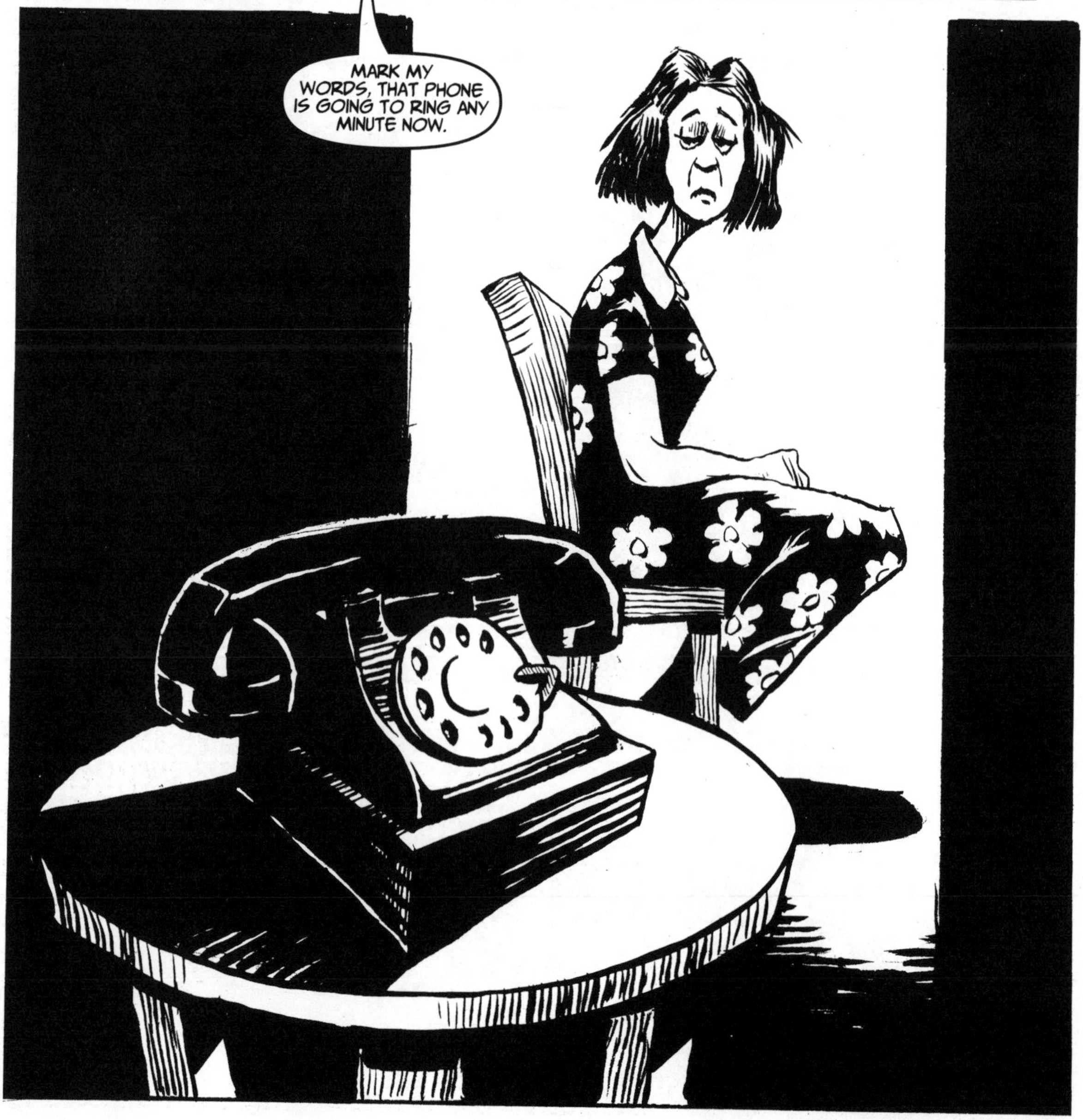

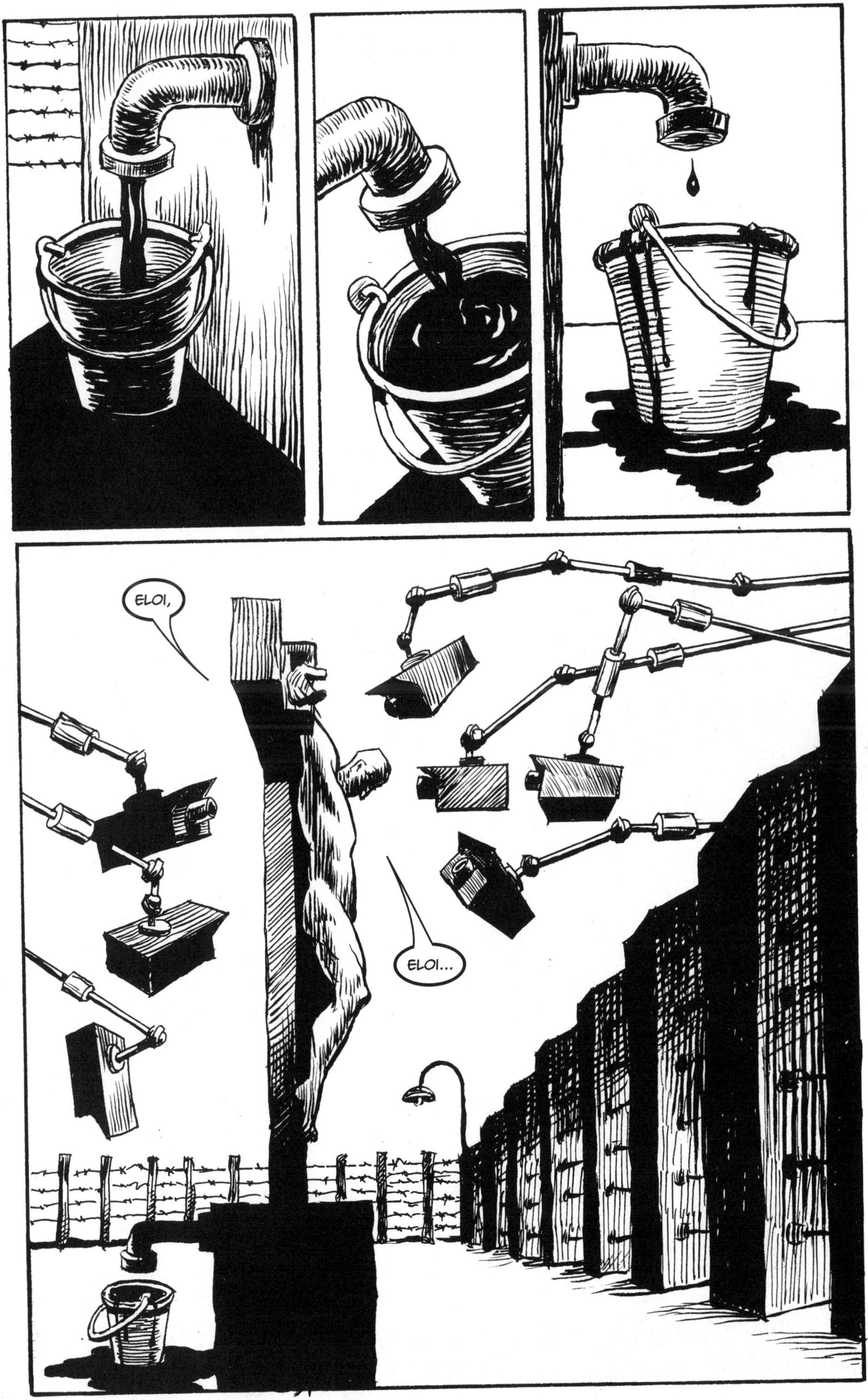
ELOI,
ELOI...

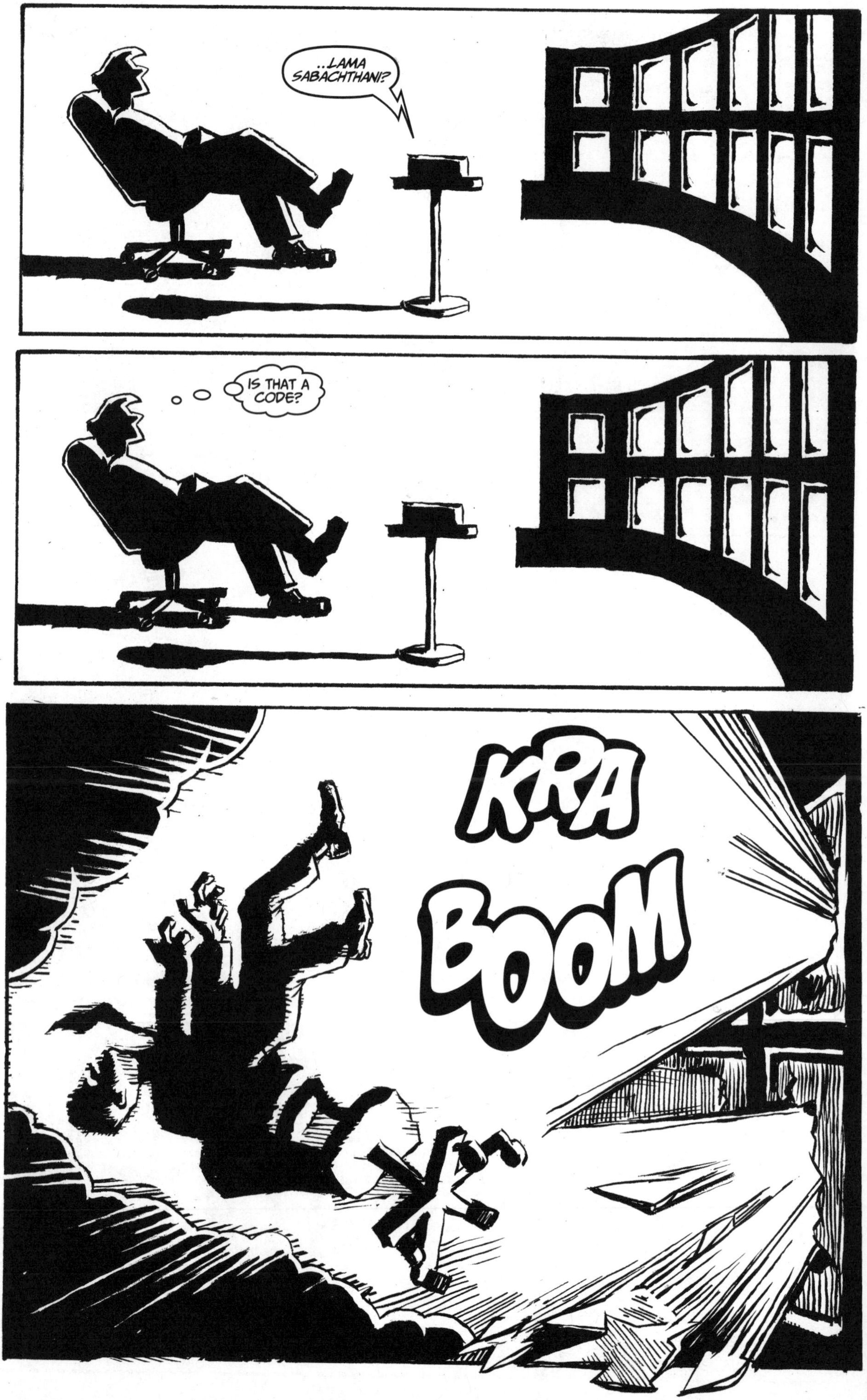
..LAMA SABACHTHANI?
IS THAT A CODE?
KRA BOOM

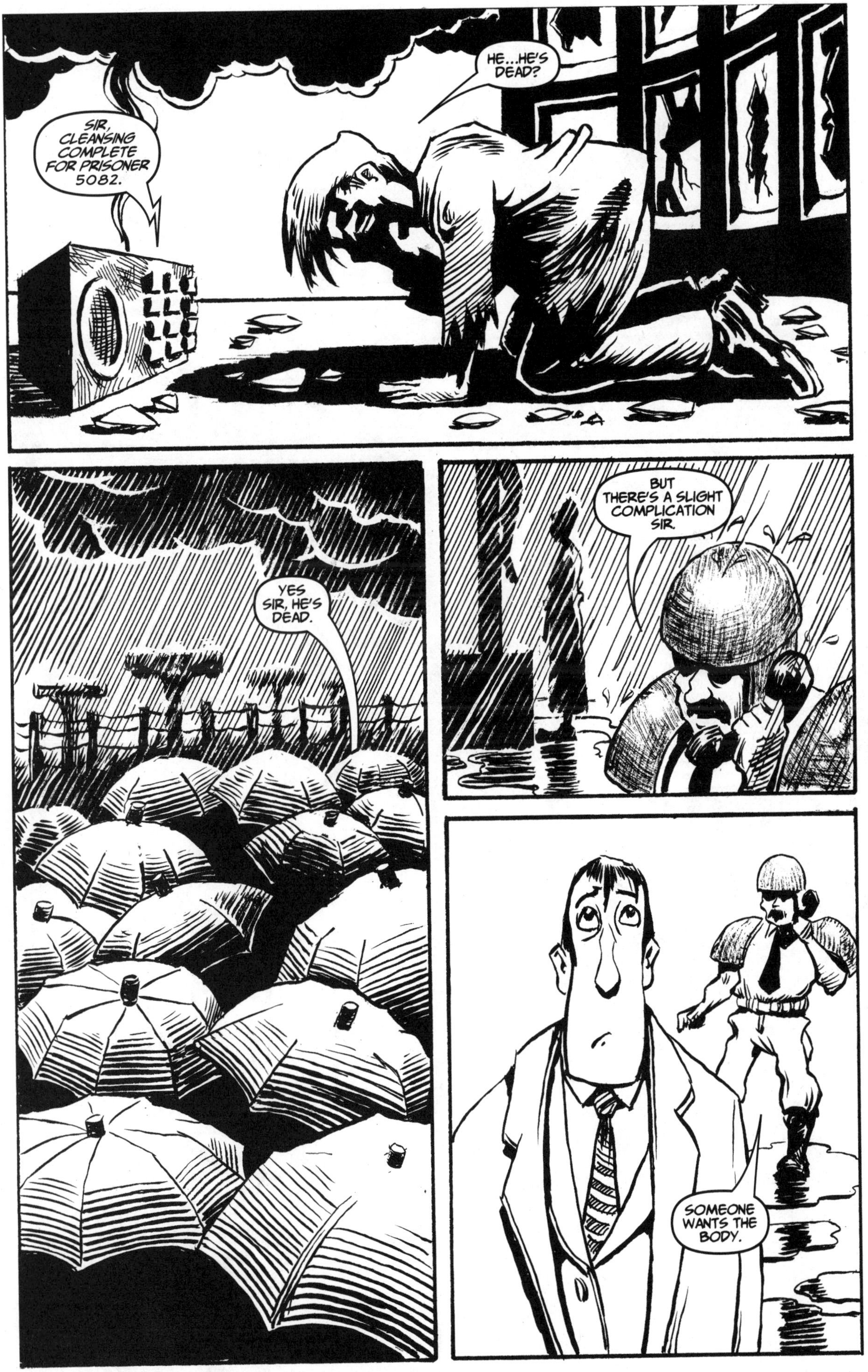
SIR, CLEANSING COMPLETE FOR PRISONER 5082.
HE...HE'S DEAD?
YES SIR, HE'S DEAD.
BUT THERE'S A SLIGHT COMPLICATION SIR.
SOMEONE WANTS THE BODY.

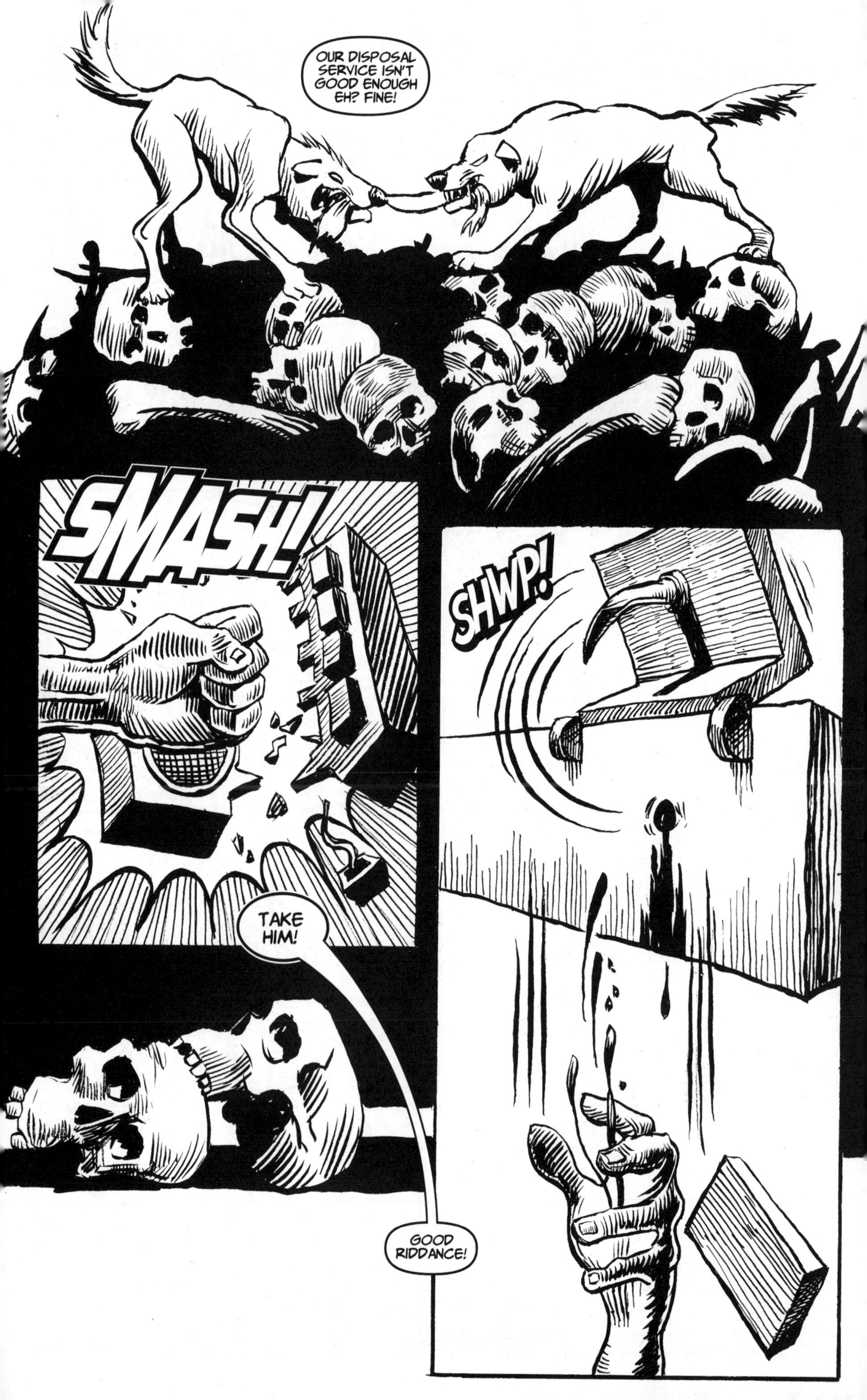
OUR DISPOSAL SERVICE ISN'T GOOD ENOUGH EH? FINE!
SMASH!
SHWP!
TAKE HIM!
GOOD RIDDANCE!

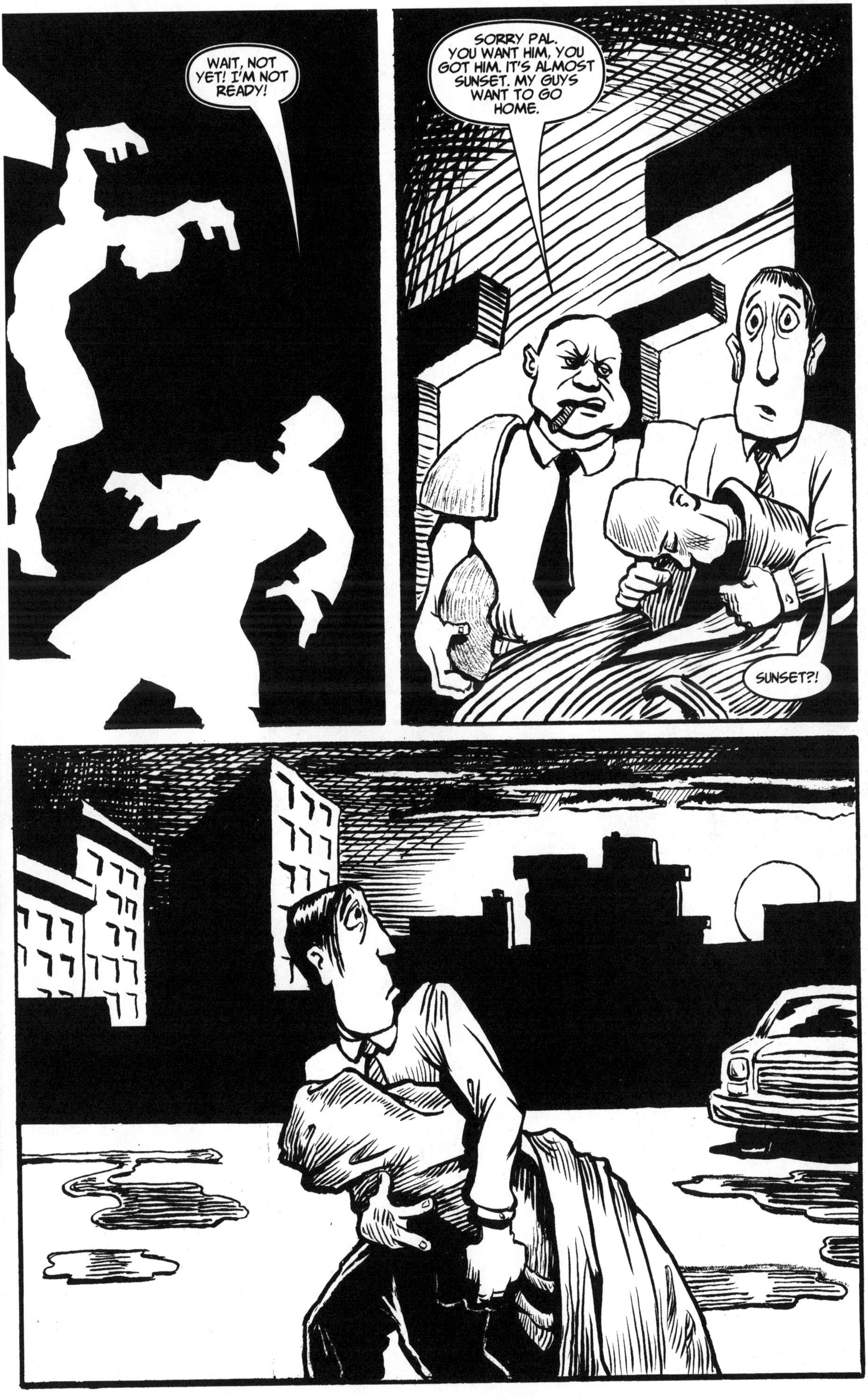
WAIT, NOT YET! I'M NOT READY!
SORRY PAL. YOU WANT HIM, YOU GOT HIM. IT'S ALMOST SUNSET. MY GUYS WANT TO GO HOME.
SUNSET?!

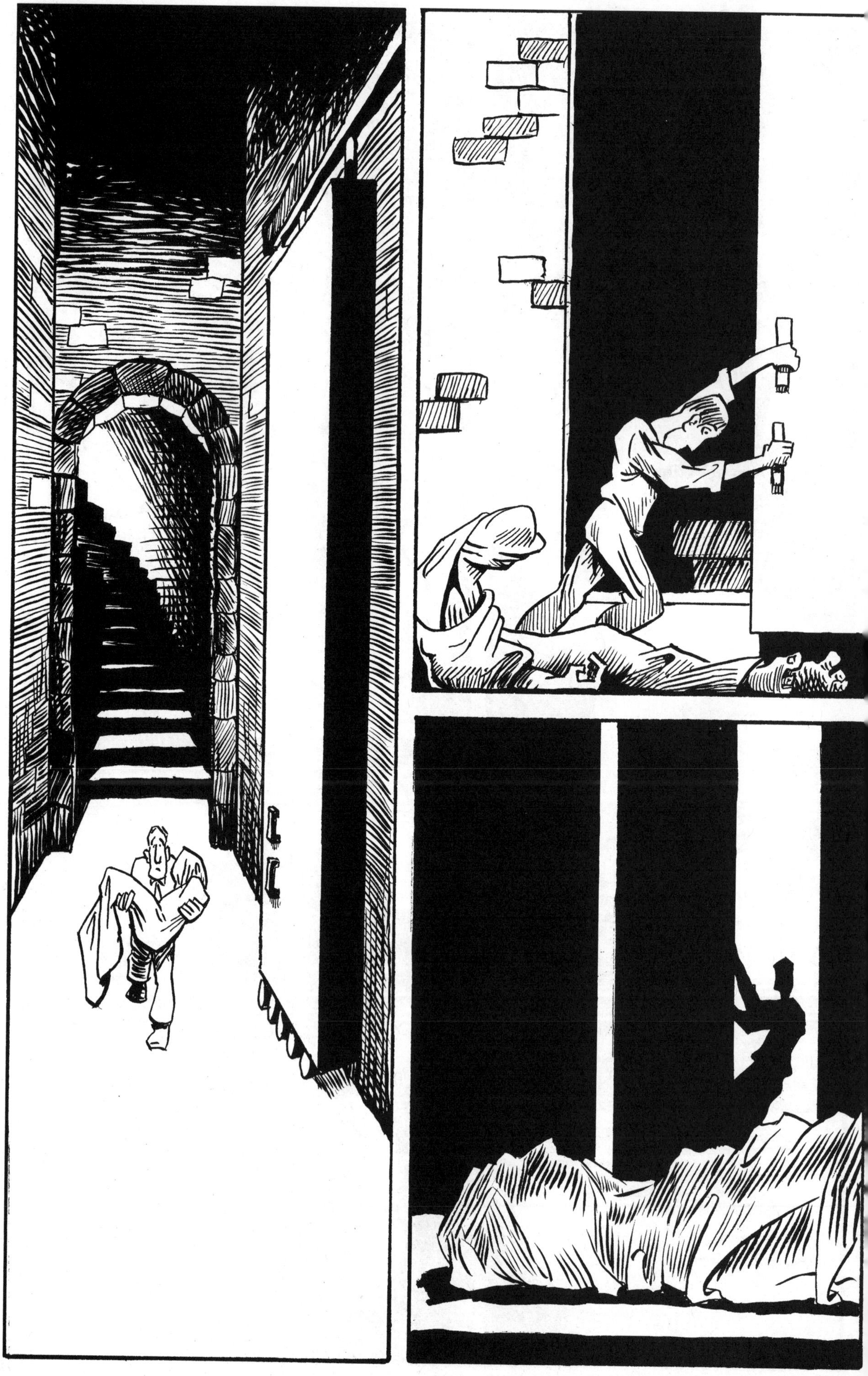

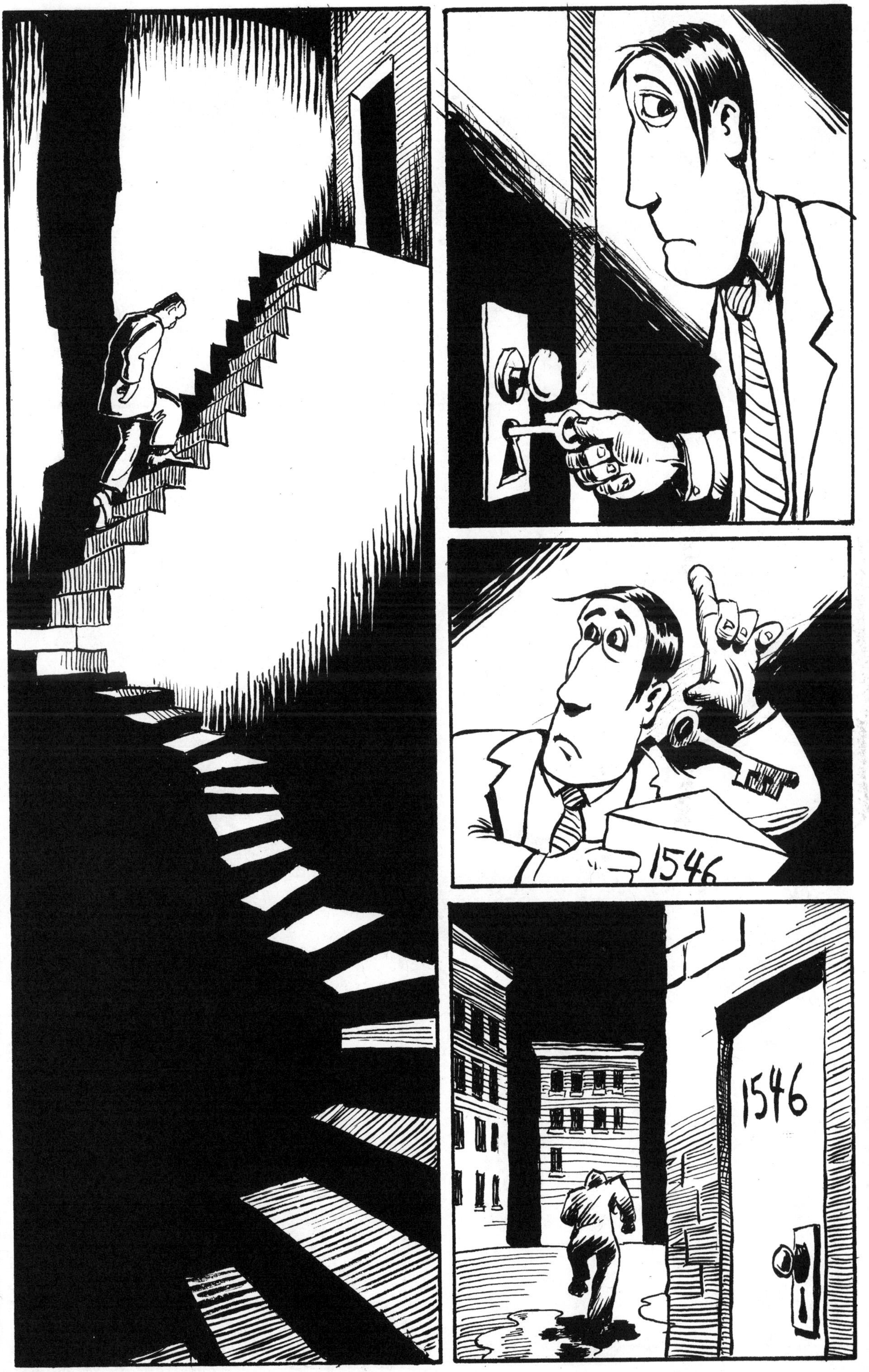

1546
1546

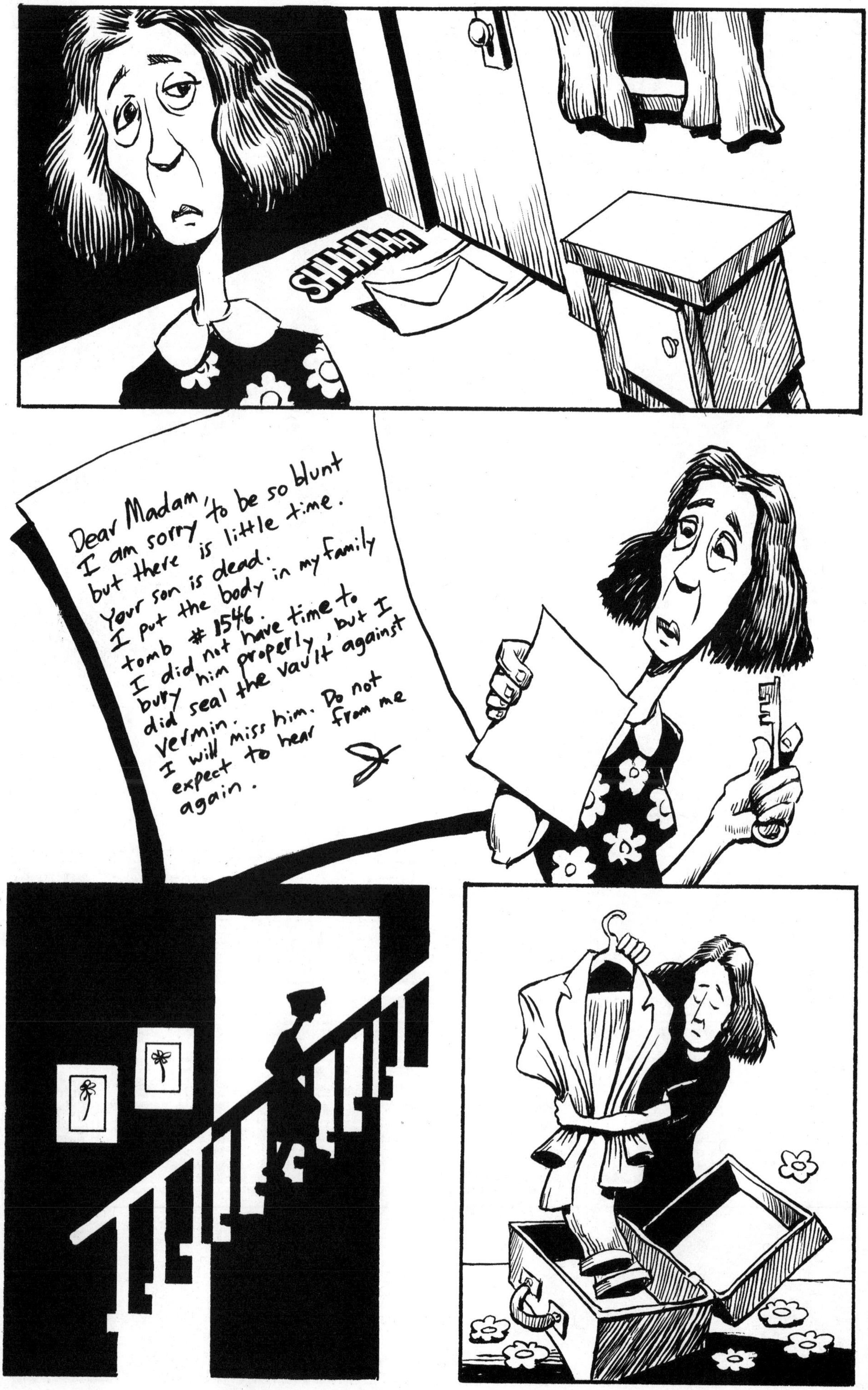
SHHHHHH
Dear Madam,
I am sorry to be so blunt
but there is little time.
Your son is dead.
I put the body in my family
tomb # 1546.
I did not have time to
bury him properly, but I
did seal the vault against
vermin.
I will miss him. Do not
expect to hear from me
again.

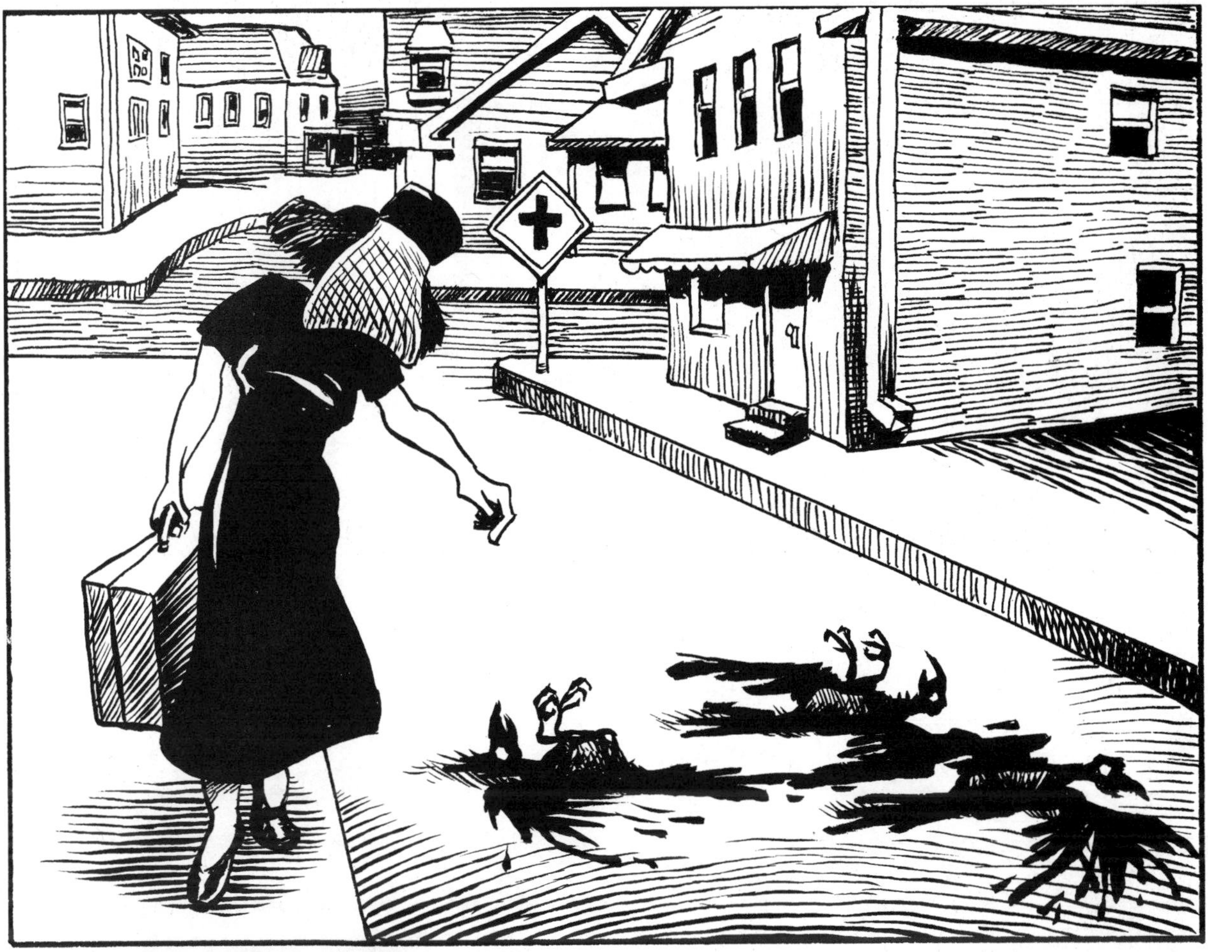

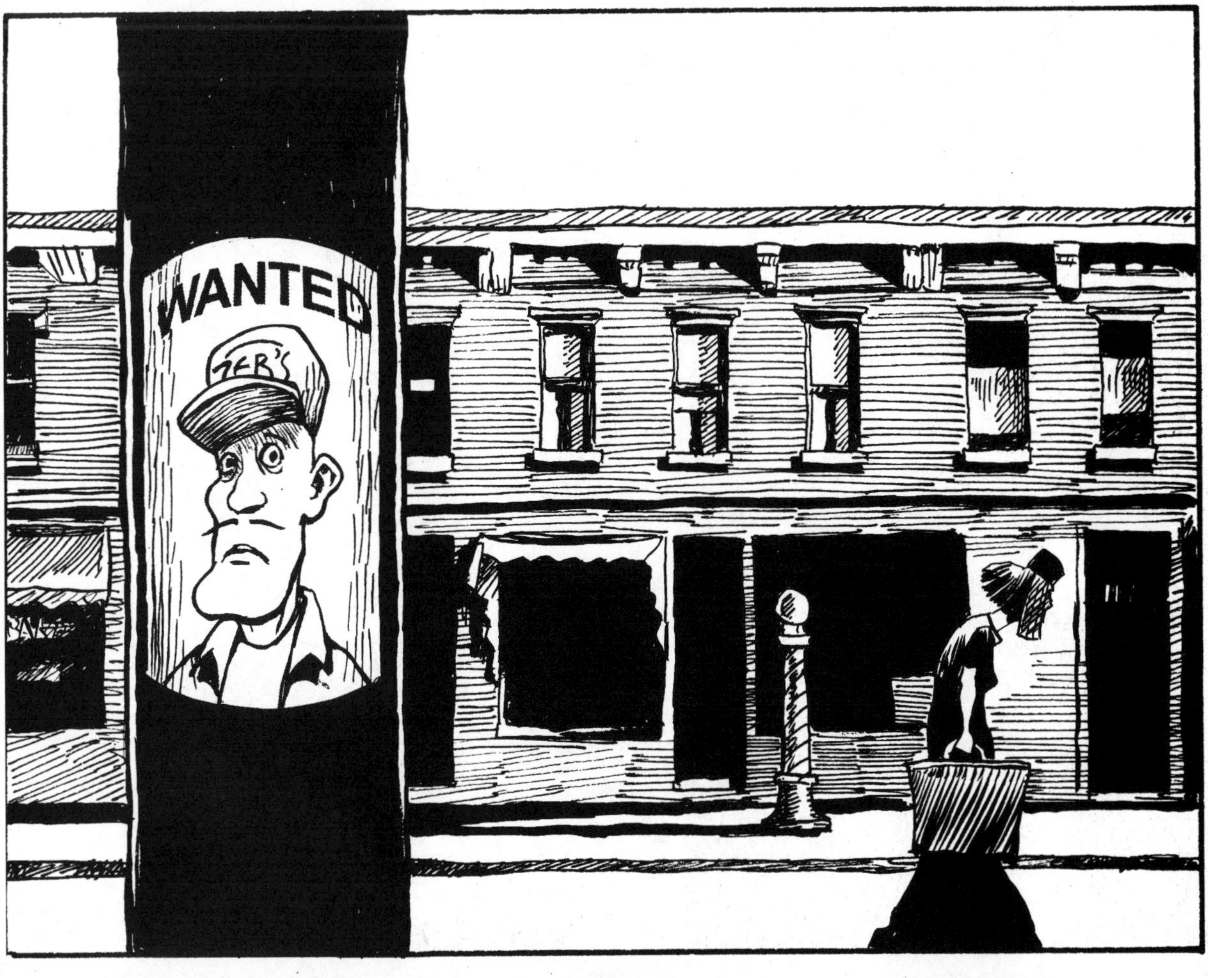
WANTED
ZEB'S

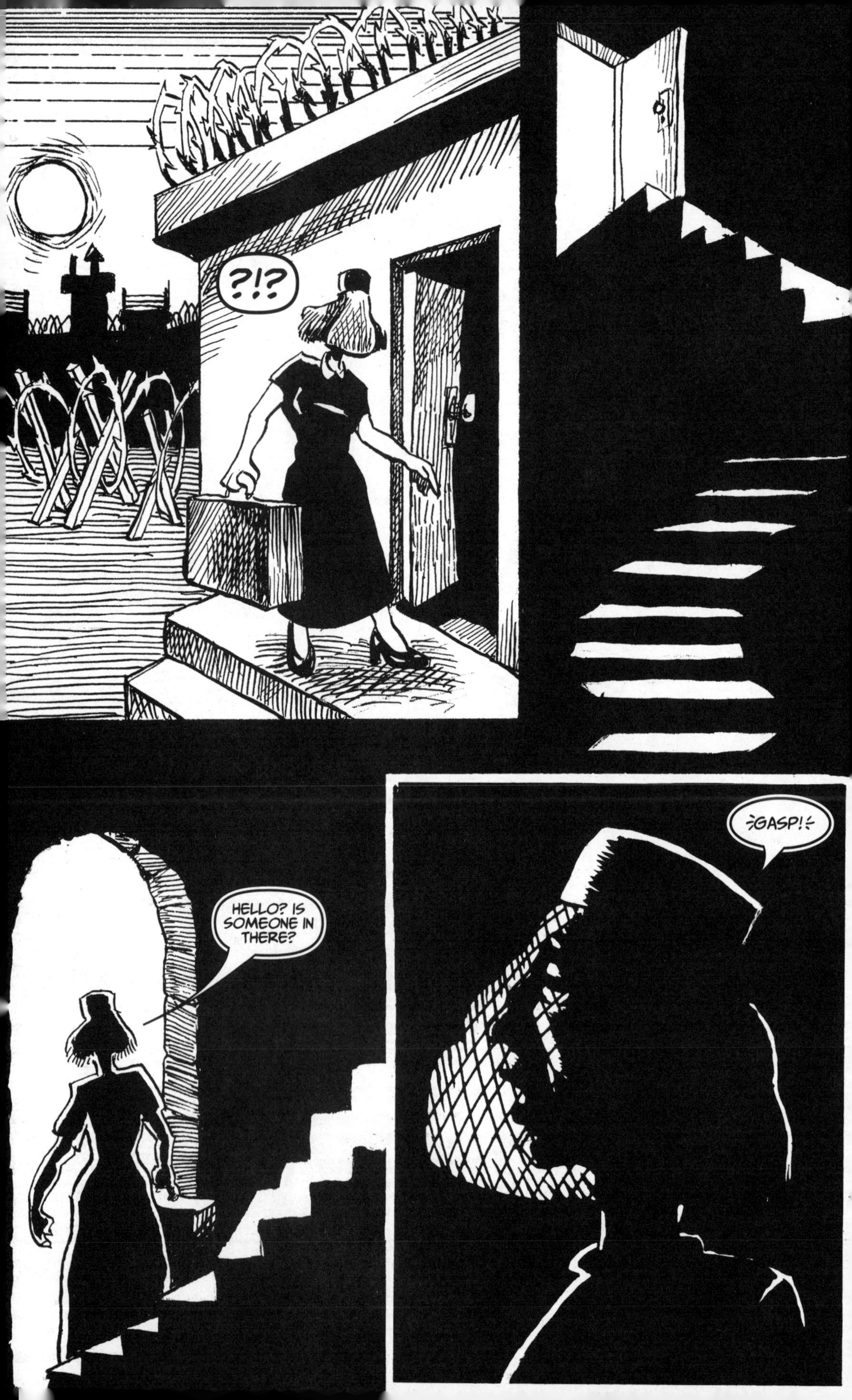
?!?
HELLO? IS SOMEONE IN THERE?
GASP!

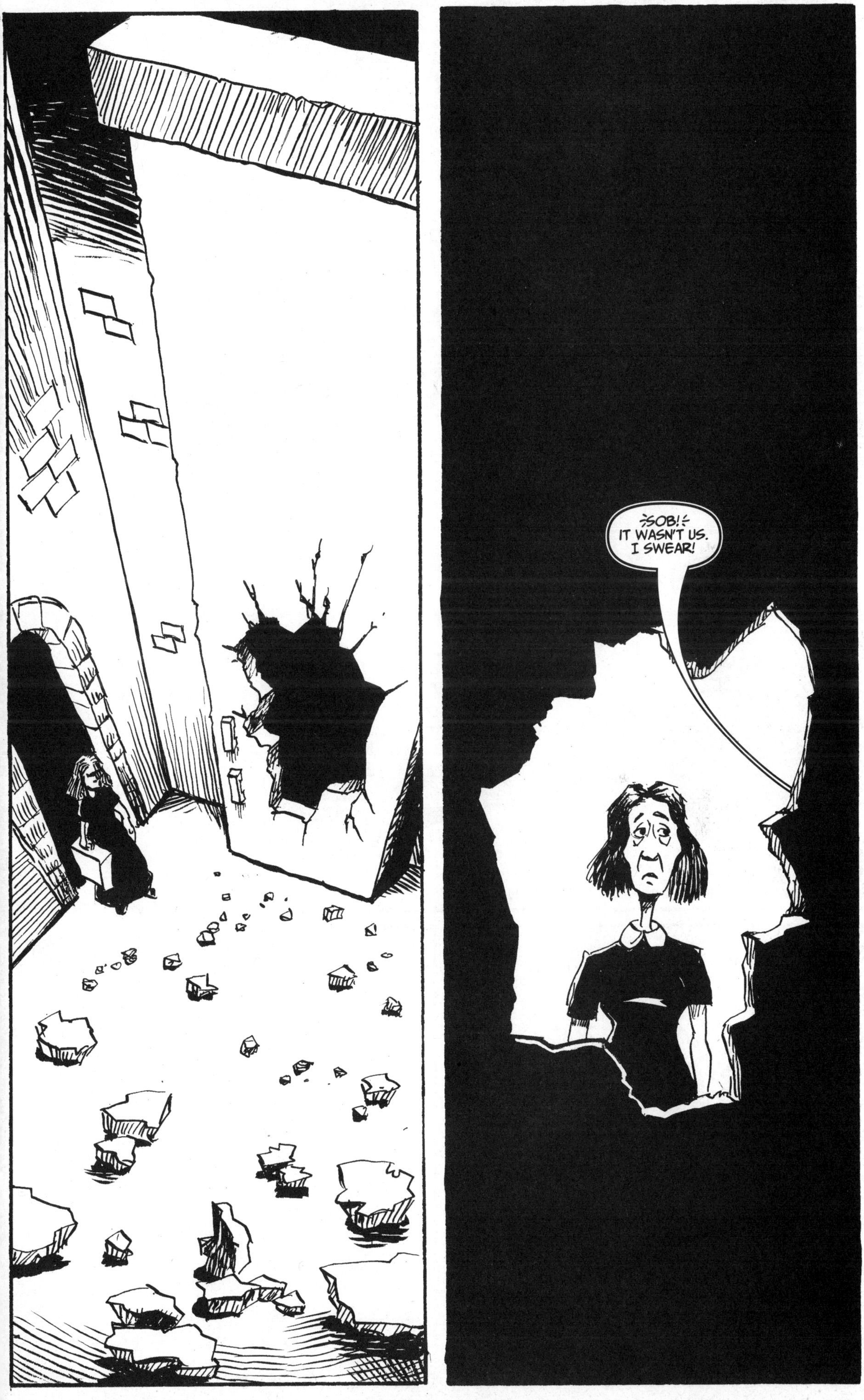

SOB!
IT WASN'T US.
I SWEAR!

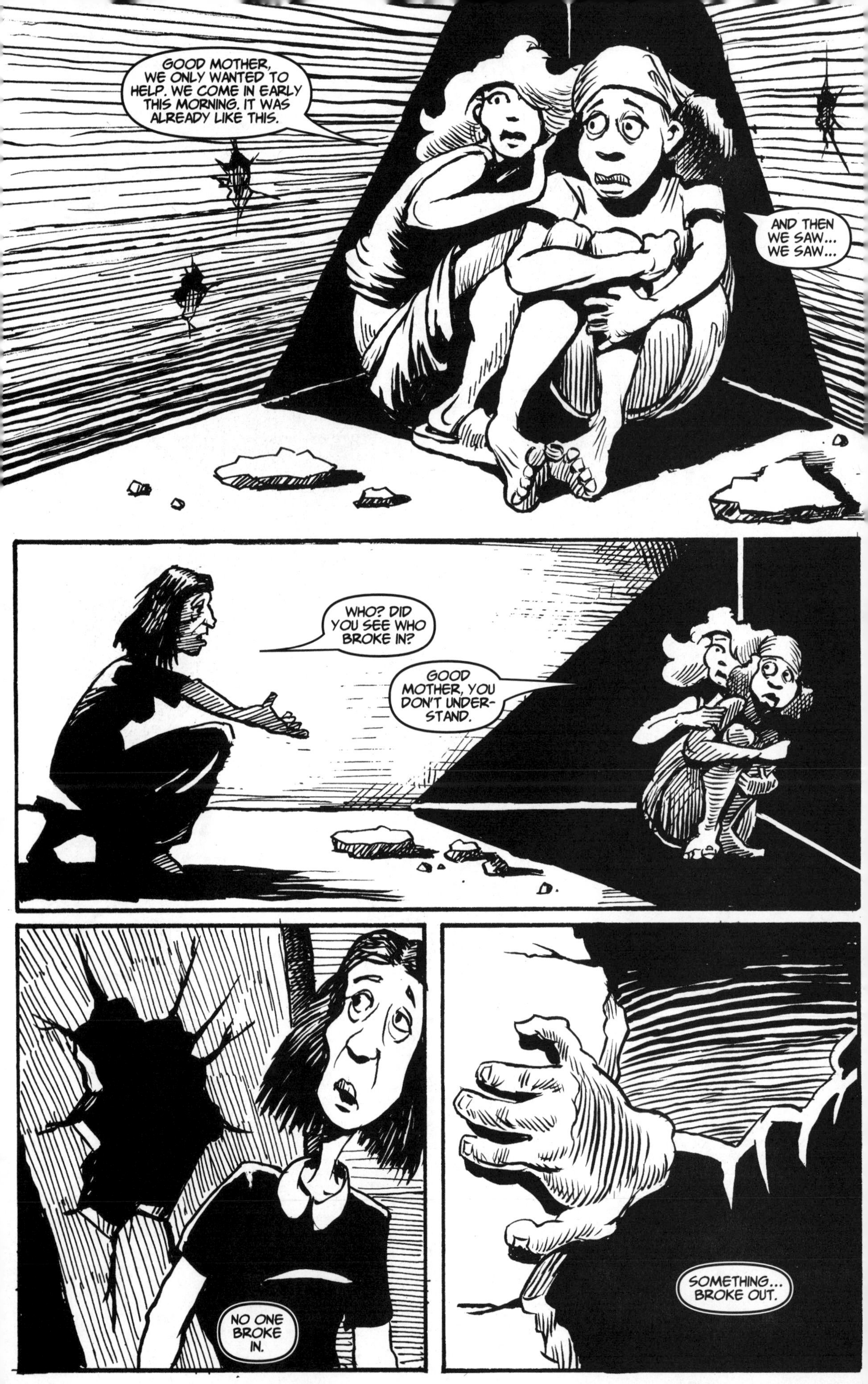
GOOD MOTHER, WE ONLY WANTED TO HELP. WE COME IN EARLY THIS MORNING. IT WAS ALREADY LIKE THIS.
AND THEN WE SAW... WE SAW...
WHO? DID YOU SEE WHO BROKE IN?
GOOD MOTHER, YOU DON'T UNDER-STAND.
NO ONE BROKE IN.
SOMETHING... BROKE OUT.

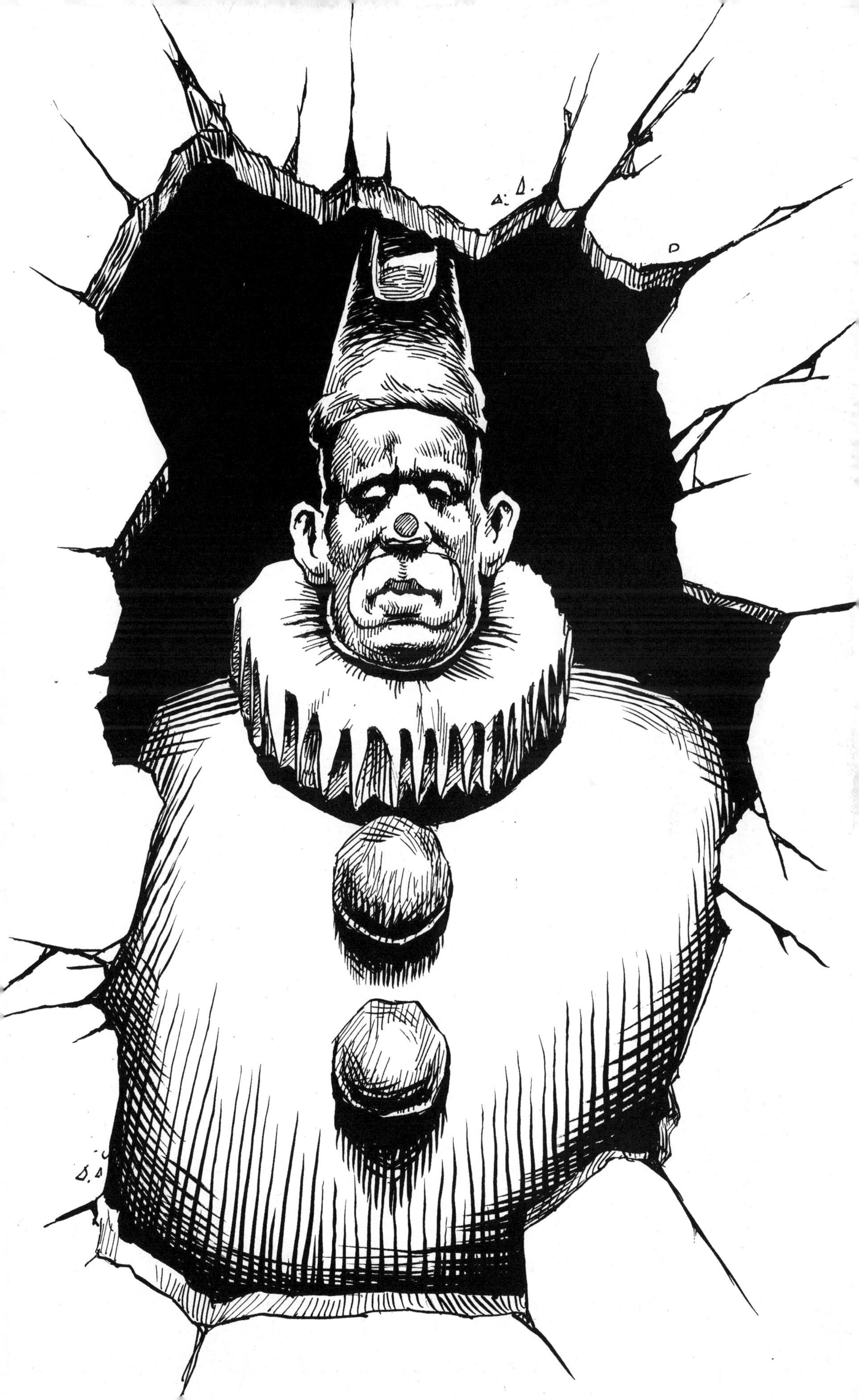

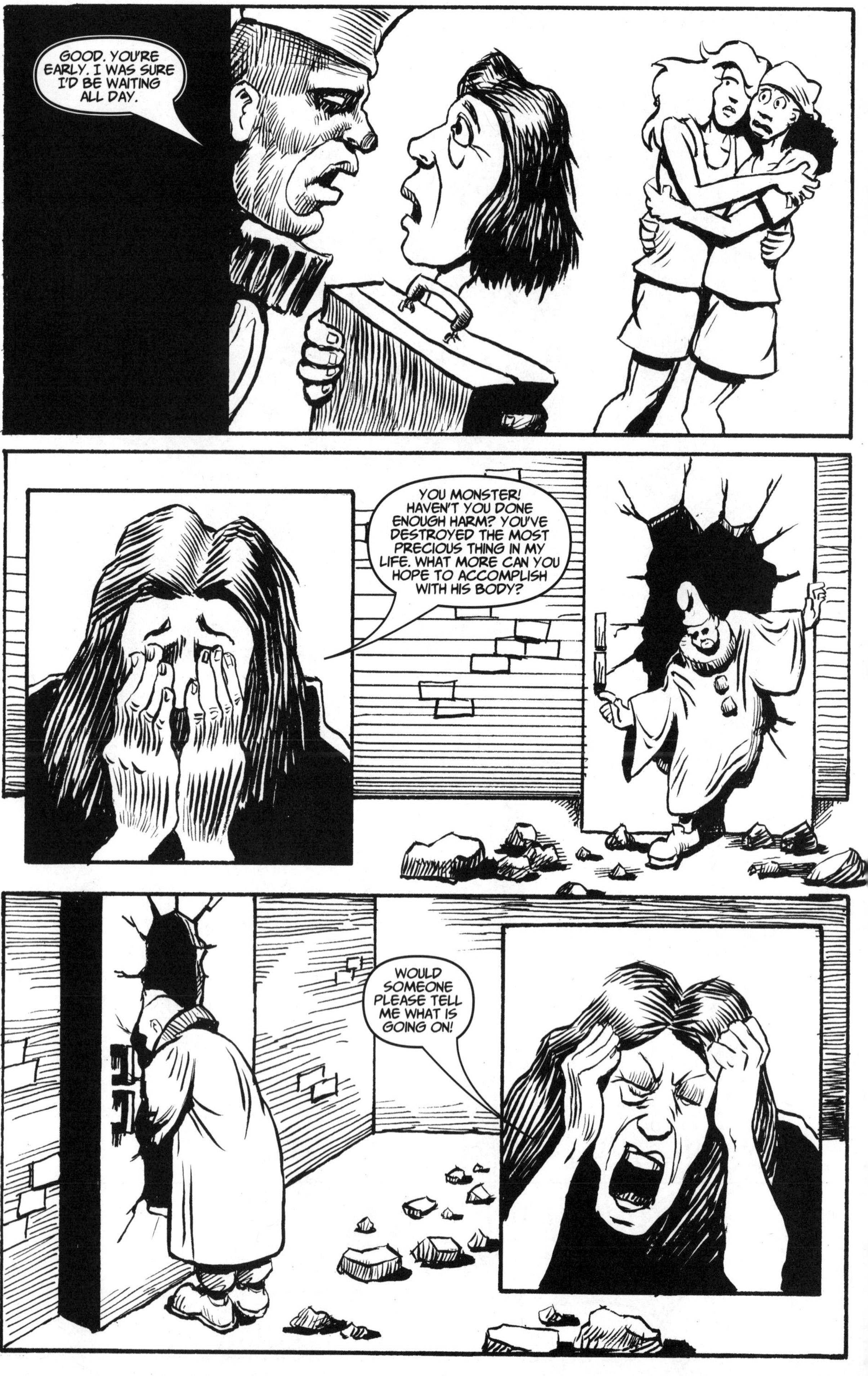
GOOD. YOU'RE EARLY. I WAS SURE I'D BE WAITING ALL DAY.
YOU MONSTER! HAVEN'T YOU DONE ENOUGH HARM? YOU'VE DESTROYED THE MOST PRECIOUS THING IN MY LIFE. WHAT MORE CAN YOU HOPE TO ACCOMPLISH WITH HIS BODY?
WOULD SOMEONE PLEASE TELL ME WHAT IS GOING ON!

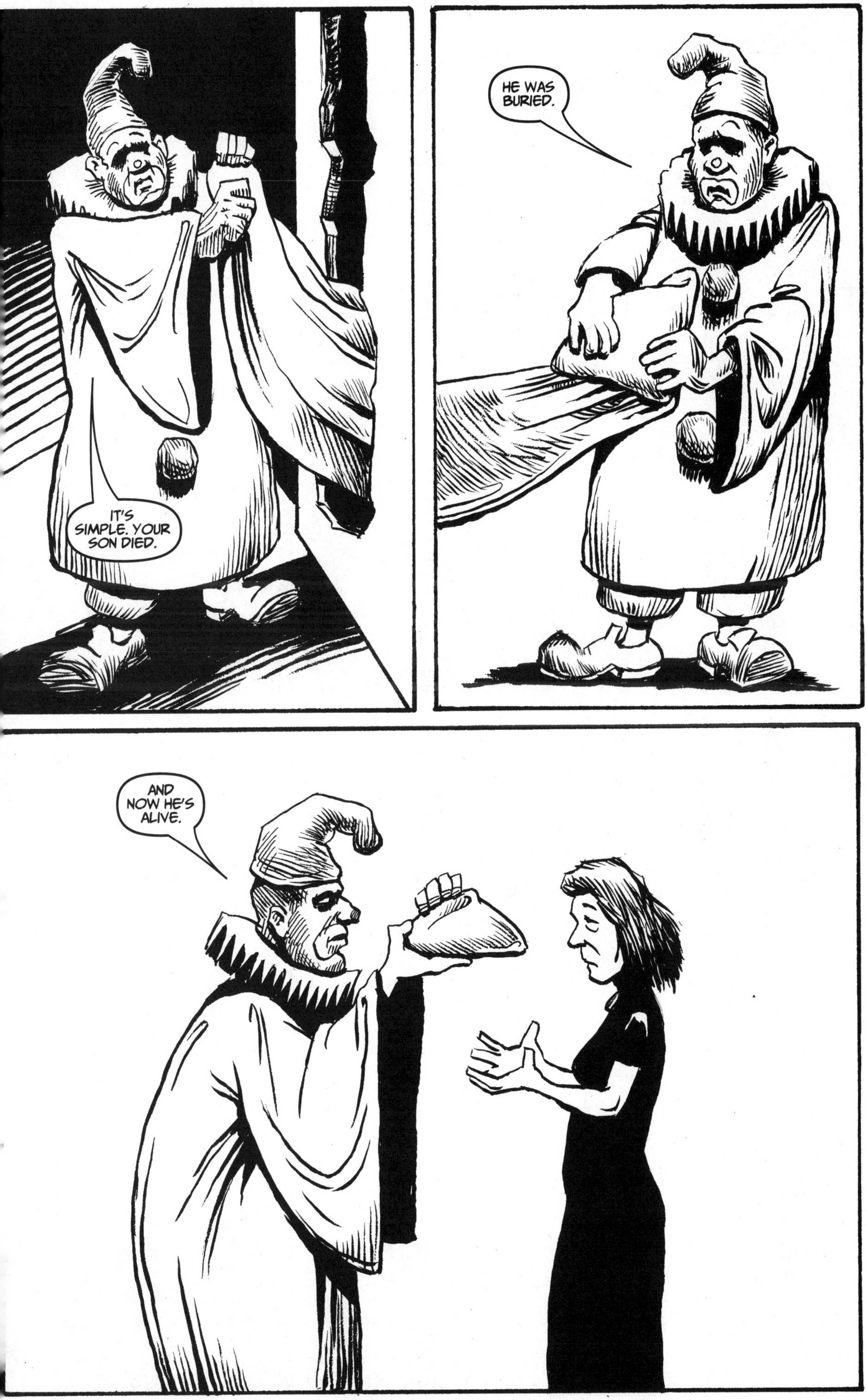
IT'S SIMPLE. YOUR SON DIED.
HE WAS BURIED.
AND NOW HE'S ALIVE.

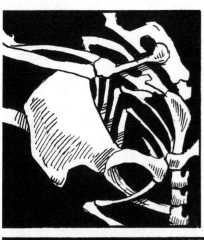

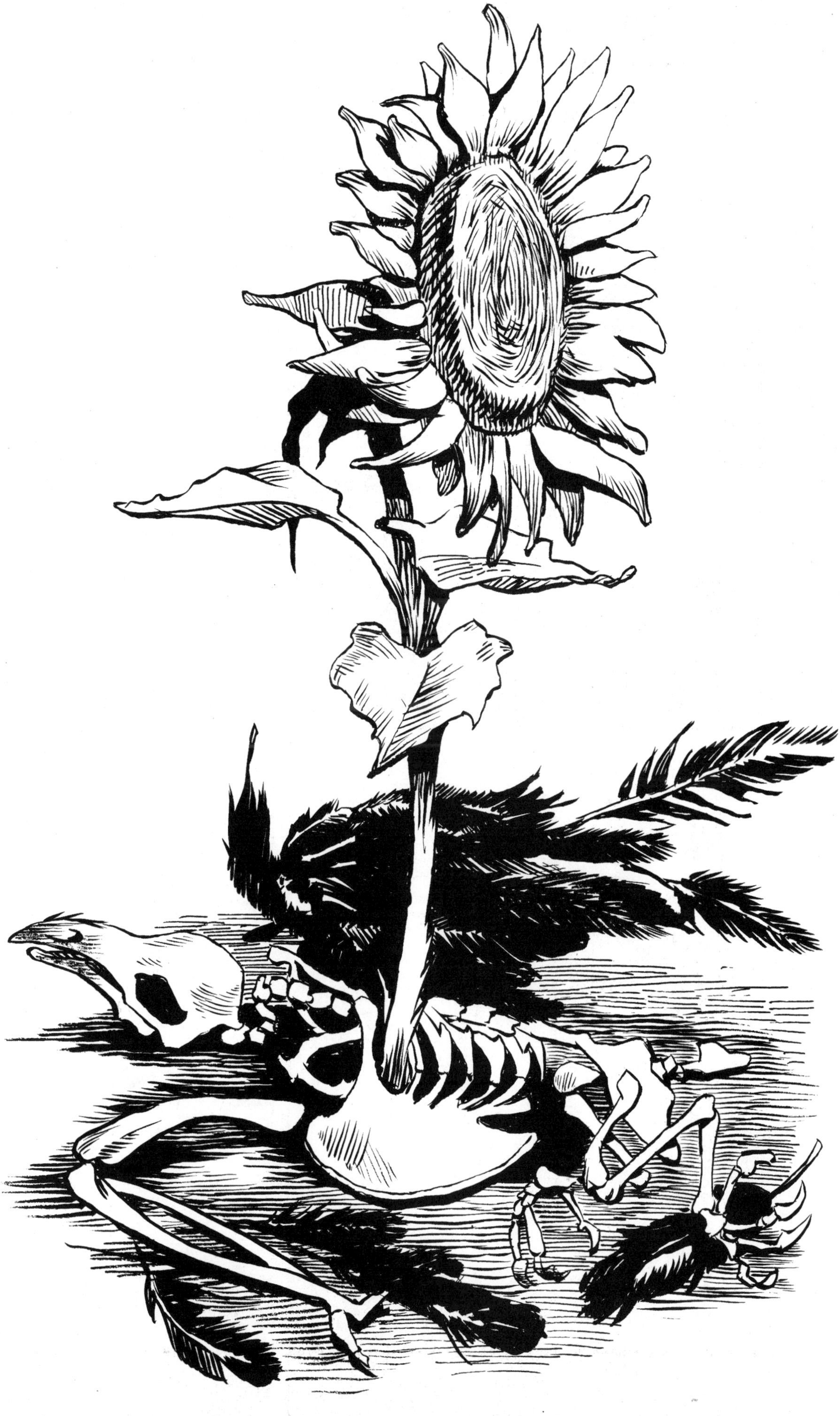